Visual Reflections

OXFORD PSYCHOLOGY SERIES

Editors

Mark D'Esposito   Daniel Schacter
Jon Driver   Anne Treisman
Trevor Robbins   Lawrence Weiskrantz

Visual Reflections

A Perceptual Deficit and
Its Implications

Michael McCloskey

OXFORD
UNIVERSITY PRESS

2009

OXFORD
UNIVERSITY PRESS

Oxford University Press, Inc., publishes works that further
Oxford University's objective of excellence
in research, scholarship, and education.

Oxford New York
Auckland Cape Town Dar es Salaam Hong Kong Karachi
Kuala Lumpur Madrid Melbourne Mexico City Nairobi
New Delhi Shanghai Taipei Toronto

With offices in
Argentina Austria Brazil Chile Czech Republic France Greece
Guatemala Hungary Italy Japan Poland Portugal Singapore
South Korea Switzerland Thailand Turkey Ukraine Vietnam

Published by Oxford University Press, Inc.
198 Madison Avenue, New York, New York 10016
www.oup.com

Library of Congress Cataloging-in-Publication Data

McCloskey, Michael.
Visual reflections : a perceptual deficit and its implications / Michael McCloskey.
p. cm. — (Oxford psychology series ; 47)
Includes bibliographical references and index.
ISBN 978-0-19-516869-3
1. Visual perception. 2. Perception. I. Title.
BF241.M347 2009
152.14—dc22
2008042264

9 8 7 6 5 4 3 2 1

Printed in the United States of America
on acid-free paper

Preface

This book presents an extensive single-case study of a young woman, AH, with a remarkable developmental deficit in visual perception. AH often misperceives the locations and orientations of objects in her visual field, and her errors are highly systematic. In Part I of the book I present the principal empirical findings from testing carried out over a period of more than 3 years. I also consider how AH is able to succeed in academic work and daily life despite her severe perceptual deficit and examine her reading ability in detail. Further, I review other cases that bear some resemblance to AH.

Part II explores the implications of AH's deficit for understanding normal visual perception. I propose hypotheses concerning the representation of location and orientation in high-level vision, making claims about reference frames and the nature of the representations developed within these frames. I also argue that the results from AH challenge existing hypotheses about visual-system organization (e.g., Milner & Goodale, 1995; Ungerleider & Mishkin, 1982) and propose a new conceptualization. Finally, I explore issues concerning visual imagery, visual awareness, and the processes that update visual representations over time.

I hope that the book will interest not only researchers who study perceptual deficits but also those whose work focuses on normal visual perception. Researchers who study developmental dyslexia, developmental dysgraphia, or visuospatial learning disabilities may also find the book to be of interest. Further, most of the chapters should be accessible to advanced undergraduate students, and hence, the book could serve as a supplemental text in courses on perception or cognitive neuropsychology.

This book could not have been written without the help of many people. First and foremost I am extremely grateful to AH for her patience and cheerfulness through countless hours of testing and for her openness in talking about the consequences of her deficit. Working with her and getting to know her has been a privilege. I also thank AH's parents for discussions about her developmental history.

In studying AH's perceptual deficit, I had many collaborators, as reflected in the following alphabetical list of my coauthors on the several journal articles in which some results from the study have previously been reported: Donna Aliminosa, William Bacon, William Badecker, Dana Boatman, Gislin Dagnelie, Barry Gordon, Douglas Johnson, Erica Palmer, Brenda Rapp, Gary Rubin, Janet Sherman, Ronald Tusa, Jussi Valtonen, and Steven Yantis. All of these collaborators made important contributions to the study. However, three deserve special acknowledgment.

Brenda Rapp, my colleague in the Cognitive Science Department at Johns Hopkins, was involved in the study almost from the beginning, and her contributions cannot be overstated. Brenda played a central role in much of the empirical and theoretical work, especially in discovering the effects of visual variables on AH's performance (Chapter 7), in probing AH's reading (Chapters 9 and 10), and in identifying the reference frames implicated in AH's errors (Chapter 13).

Steven Yantis, from the Department of Psychological and Brain Sciences at Johns Hopkins, made critical contributions in exploring and interpreting the effects of visual variables (Chapters 7 and 16) and offered empirical and theoretical advice on many other aspects of the project.

Erica Palmer worked on the study while an undergraduate student at Johns Hopkins. As well as assisting in the development and administration of tasks, she made important conceptual contributions. I am especially grateful for Erica's help with the reading studies (Chapters 9 and10).

Many other colleagues, students, research assistants, and family members contributed to the study in a variety of ways. In particular, I thank Alfonso Caramazza, Howard Egeth, Jill Egeth, Matthew Goldrick, Emma Gregory, Steve Hsaio, Per Jambeck, Kati Keuper, Barbara Landau, Amy Lin, Daniel McCloskey, Sarah McCloskey, Nancy McCloskey, Gabriele Miceli, Anne Murch, Danya Niedzwiedzki, Melissa Oles, Sara Reusing, Scott Sokol, John Whalen, and David Zee. Uyen Le deserves special thanks for her very helpful comments on several of the chapters in this book. Finally, I thank my editor at Oxford University Press, Catharine Carlin, for her advice, encouragement, and patience, and her assistant, Nicholas Liu, for help with the myriad details that required attention in preparing the manuscript for production.

AH gave informed consent for all aspects of the study, and her rights as a research participant were protected. Parts of the study were supported by grants for the National Institutes of Health (NS21047) and the International Association of Learning Disabilities.

Contents

Part I

Introduction and Principal Empirical Findings

1

Introduction

The cognitive mechanisms that allow us to perceive, learn, remember, communicate, and act in the world usually operate so smoothly and effortlessly that we take them for granted. However, when the brain is damaged or fails to develop normally, even the most basic cognitive processes may malfunction. The resulting deficits have unfortunate and sometimes even tragic consequences for the individuals who suffer from them. From a scientific standpoint, however, these deficits have considerable importance, offering unique windows into the structure and functioning of the normal mind. Indeed, cognitive neuropsychological research is founded on the insight that complex mechanisms often reveal their inner workings more clearly when malfunctioning than when operating normally.

Studying abnormalities or malfunctions to shed light on normal structures and processes is a well-established research strategy in the biological sciences. For example, the study of genetic mutations has greatly advanced our understanding of normal genetic mechanisms, research on AIDS and autoimmune disorders has contributed to knowledge of normal immune-system functioning, and studies of pathological conditions such as diabetes and scurvy have played a crucial role in the discovery of many biologically active substances (e.g., insulin, vitamin C) and their physiological functions. More generally, scientists in many disciplines study unusual phenomena as a means of gaining insight into more typical conditions or events. For instance, studies of supernovae have illuminated the processes and products of nuclear fusion in stars, and research on volcanic eruptions has contributed to our understanding of the substances and events in the earth's interior.

Potentially informative abnormalities or unusual phenomena can sometimes be created in the laboratory, as when brain lesions are produced surgically in neuroscience research with laboratory animals or collisions of subatomic particles are engineered in particle accelerators. Often, however, researchers are not able to create the preparations of interest. In such circumstances the study of naturally occurring phenomena—experiments of nature—has proved to be a powerful tool, providing evidence not obtainable through more customary research methods. Studies of supernovae, volcanic eruptions, and human genetic abnormalities are cases in point.

Human cognitive neuropsychology also falls into this category. Obviously, human brain malfunctions cannot be created for purposes of study. Instead, cognitive neuropsychology depends upon natural experiments in which the brain malfunctions as a consequence of injury, disease, or abnormal development.

Like other research with experiments of nature, cognitive neuropsychological research has its disadvantages. Although cognitive deficits can be subjected to rigorous, well-controlled experimental study, the inability to create particular forms of impairment at will is a definite drawback. Balanced against such disadvantages, however, are at least two significant advantages. First, cognitive deficits often reveal in a clear and compelling fashion aspects of normal representation and processing not readily apparent from normal cognitive functioning. Second, cognitive neuropsychological research is inherently opportunistic. The cognitive neuropsychologist typically begins by screening individuals with deficits potentially relevant to issues of interest and then studies in detail those deficits that seem to hold promise for illuminating the issues. This approach looks to nature for clues and then follows the clues wherever they may lead. Relative to research with normal participants—which typically approaches nature with specific predetermined questions—cognitive neuropsychological research therefore offers greater opportunity to be surprised by the unexpected. Indeed, cognitive neuropsychology has a long history of turning up unanticipated phenomena (e.g., blindsight, hemispatial neglect, category-specific deficits, anterograde amnesias) that raise new questions, suggest novel theoretical perspectives, and give rise to productive lines of research.

The AH Study

This book describes an extensive study of an extraordinary deficit in visual perception and explores the implications of this deficit for understanding the structure and functioning of the normal visual system. In the fall of 1991 I was teaching an introductory cognitive science course at Johns Hopkins University. One day late in the semester I gave a lecture on language deficits in brain-damaged patients and what these deficits can reveal about normal language processing. For purposes of illustration, I described one of my own studies involving a patient with a deficit in spelling. After class one of the students came up to me and introduced herself as A_____ H_____. AH said she found the lecture interesting because she had always been a very bad speller. We spoke for a few minutes, and I asked if she might want to try some of the spelling tasks I used in my patient studies. We walked back to my office, and I gave her a seventy-word writing-to-dictation task, saying each word aloud and asking her to write it down. Adults with normal spelling ability make few, if any, errors on this task; AH, however, misspelled nearly half of the words. For example, she wrote *damra* for *drama* and *ferquet* for *frequent*.

Intrigued, I asked if she would allow me to study her spelling. AH agreed, and in December 1991 she began coming to my lab for weekly testing sessions. At first, the testing focused primarily on her spelling ability; but as I began to explore related cognitive functions, I slowly came to realize that AH's impairment extended well beyond spelling. Gradually, the testing revealed a remarkable deficit in visual perception, a deficit that caused AH to misperceive the locations and orientations of visual stimuli. I found, for example, that when she looked at an object positioned to her left, she often quite literally saw it on her right (and vice versa) and that when a stimulus was presented at the top of a computer screen, AH often saw it at the bottom of the screen (and vice versa). In addition, she frequently made left–right and up–down reversals in perceiving the orientations of objects. Furthermore, she was entirely unaware of her perceptual deficit until it was revealed by the laboratory testing. AH had no history of neurological disease or injury, suggesting that the deficit resulted from some unknown abnormality in brain development.

With the help of several colleagues—most importantly Brenda Rapp, my fellow cognitive neuropsychologist in the Cognitive Science Department at Johns Hopkins—I studied AH's deficit extensively over a period of more than 3 years. The testing, which ended only when AH graduated from Hopkins in 1995, generated a large body of data bearing on the nature and consequences of the deficit.

My colleagues and I have published several journal articles reporting results from AH (McCloskey et al., 1995; McCloskey & Rapp, 2000a, 2000b; McCloskey, 2004; McCloskey, Valtonen, & Sherman, 2006). However, these articles are scattered across multiple journals and span more than a decade; furthermore, many important findings from the study have not yet been reported, and many of the implications have not been discussed.

My aim in this book is to present a coherent, integrated narrative that systematically lays out the results from the study and explores the theoretical implications in detail. I hope that the account will also serve more generally to illustrate how cognitive neuropsychological research is carried out and how the study of cognitive impairments can illuminate our understanding of normal cognition.

One point deserves emphasis at the outset: This book is a work of cognitive science, not neuroscience. I will be concerned primarily with mental representations and computations and much less with where or how these representations and computations are implemented in neural tissue. Similarly, I will address the functional architecture of the visual system—that is, the organization of the system into functional subsystems—but will have little to say about the neuroanatomical correlates of the various functional components.

Organization of the Book

The book is organized into two parts. Part I introduces the study of AH and presents the basic empirical evidence concerning her visual deficit. Part II explores the theoretical implications as well as presenting additional data related to these implications.

Part I: Introduction and Principal Empirical Findings

Following the present introductory chapter, Chapters 2–4 report evidence demonstrating that AH has a selective deficit in visual location and orientation perception. Chapter 5 discusses the spelling impairment that first brought AH to my attention, suggesting that this impairment probably resulted from the more fundamental perceptual deficit.

Chapter 6 develops several conclusions about the nature of AH's deficit. In this chapter I also present additional evidence bearing on the conclusions, including evidence that AH's perceptual impairment has been present at least since childhood. Chapter 7 reports dramatic and often counterintuitive effects of visual variables (e.g., exposure duration, flicker) on AH's visual perception and sketches an interpretation that is developed more fully in Part II of the book.

In Chapter 8 I pose a question: How could AH have been unaware of her perceptual deficit until she was studied in my lab? I also suggest a potential answer and present some supporting evidence. Chapters 9 and 10 explore the issue further in the context of AH's reading. In these chapters I describe nonobvious effects of the perceptual deficit on AH's reading performance and her remarkable skill at compensating for these effects.

Chapter 11 concludes Part I by reviewing other reported deficits in processing visual location and orientation information. I highlight a recently reported case (Pflugshaupt et al., 2007) that bears a striking resemblance to that of AH and strengthens the theoretical claims I subsequently advance on the basis of AH's performance.

Part II: Theoretical Issues and Implications

Part II examines several central issues in the study of vision and spatial cognition, bringing the results from AH to bear on these issues. Chapter 12 discusses spatial reference frames, arguing that two questions have routinely been conflated in cognitive and neuroscientific research on frames of reference and further that the dominant research strategy for probing reference frames addresses only one of the issues. Chapter 13 explores both reference-frame issues in light of results from AH, articulating claims about the nature of location representations at the level of the visual system affected by her deficit. One important claim is that locations are represented at this level in the form of coordinates that specify distance and direction of displacement from an origin along reference axes.

Chapters 14 and 15 take up issues concerning object orientation. Chapter 14 presents a coordinate-system theory of orientation representation, and Chapter 15 interprets AH's orientation errors in light of the theory. Chapter 15 also presents results from three other studies conducted recently in my lab, as well as discussing other reports of deficits in processing visual orientation information.

Chapter 16 concerns the functional architecture of the cortical visual system. I argue that AH's performance pattern constitutes evidence against two influential proposals concerning visual subsystems: the Ungerleider-Mishkin (e.g., Ungerleider & Mishkin, 1982) what/where hypothesis and the Milner-Goodale (e.g., Milner & Goodale, 1995) vision-for-perception/vision-for-action hypothesis. I also propose an alternative hypothesis that is consistent not only with AH's performance but also with results cited in support of the prior theoretical proposals.

Chapter 17 presents results from AH that speak to the role of the visual system in mental imagery, and Chapter 18 examines the implications of AH's performance for issues concerning the levels of the visual system that contribute to visual awareness. Chapter 18 also presents results showing that AH's misperceptions of location often remain unchanged when she moves her eyes and offers a speculative interpretation concerning the processes that construct high-level visual location representations. Chapter 19, the concluding chapter, discusses several broader issues raised by the AH study and provides an update on AH's status since the completion of the study.

2

Case History and Initial Findings

In this chapter I provide a brief case history for AH and describe the preliminary results that led to a focus on her processing of visual location and orientation information.

Case History

AH was 18 years old and a freshman at Johns Hopkins University when the study began in December 1991. When testing ended in May 1995, she was 21 years old and had just graduated from Johns Hopkins. She is right-handed and has normal visual acuity (with correction for myopia), normal contrast sensitivity, and full visual fields.

Neurological Status

Interviews with AH and her parents suggested nothing unusual in her medical history. She had never been diagnosed with a neurological disorder; she had never suffered blackouts, seizures, or other symptoms that might suggest neurological problems; and she had no history of diseases or injuries that might have caused brain damage, such as complications during birth, severe blows to the head, or very high fevers. Furthermore, she had no other significant medical conditions, no history of psychiatric disorders, and no past or present problems with drugs or alcohol.

A clinical neurological exam carried out during the study was normal, as was electroencephalography with and without photic stimulation. Structural magnetic resonance imaging also revealed no abnormalities. Notably, all parts of the visual system were well-imaged—including not only the cortical visual areas but also the optic nerves, optic chiasm, optic tracts, lateral geniculate nuclei, and optic radiations—and all appeared normal.

These findings argued strongly against an acquired neurological disorder in which AH's brain was damaged through disease or injury. However, the results left open the possibility of abnormalities in brain development, which often cannot be detected through neurological testing.

Educational History

AH entered kindergarten at the usual age of 5 and progressed at a normal rate, neither repeating nor skipping grades. She graduated from high school at the age of 18 and then entered Johns Hopkins as a regular undergraduate student. Throughout her schooling, she said, her grades had generally been good, As and Bs, with an occasional C.

Nevertheless, AH did describe some difficulties with academic work. Spelling had been a problem at least as early as the third grade and did not seem to improve. In junior high school she had received special spelling lessons, but these had little, if any, beneficial effect.

Math had also consistently been difficult. AH said she understood the concepts but always seemed to make careless errors when working problems. She remembered being tested for a math disability in second or third grade, but as far as she could recall nothing had come of this testing. She still found math difficult, she said, and in college avoided math-related courses whenever possible.

AH described herself as a good reader, stating that she had learned to read early and had been in the most advanced reading group throughout elementary school. She said that she enjoyed reading and had no difficulty completing her reading assignments, even in college courses with heavy reading loads. However, AH also said that she was not very good at sounding out unfamiliar words and that she occasionally failed to recognize familiar words when she encountered them out of context. She also stated that, even for material that was not especially challenging, she sometimes had to read sentences or paragraphs more than once before they made much sense.

Impaired Location and Orientation Processing

Impaired processing of location and orientation information was first observed on several direct copying tasks in which AH copied visual stimuli that remained in view throughout the copying process.

Task 2–1: Rey-Osterrieth Complex Figure

Figure 2-1 presents the Rey-Osterrieth Complex Figure (Rey, 1941; Osterrieth, 1944) and AH's direct copy. The stimulus figure was presented on the top half of a sheet of paper and remained in view while AH drew her copy on the bottom half of the page. She reproduced the shapes of the figure's various components accurately but made numerous errors involving location and orientation of the components.

Asked to reproduce the figure from memory immediately after completing the copy trial, AH produced a drawing very similar to her copy, suggesting that she was not impaired in short-term memory for visual–spatial information.

Task 2–2: Benton Visual Retention Test

AH also made numerous location and orientation errors on the Benton Visual Retention Test (BVRT) (Sivan, 1992), in which visual stimulus figures are

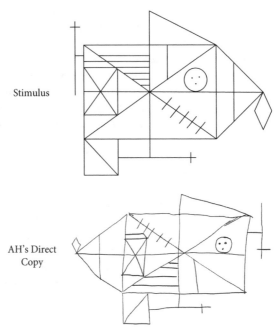

Figure 2–1. The Rey-Osterrieth Complex Figure (Rey, 1941; Osterrieth, 1944) and AH's direct copy. From McCloskey, M., Rapp, B., Yantis, S., Rubin, G., Bacon, W. F., Dagnelie, G., Gordon, B., Aliminosa, D., Boatman, D. F., Badecker, W., Johnson, D. N., Tusa, R. J., & Palmer, E. (1995). A developmental deficit in localizing objects from vision. *Psychological Science, 6,* 112–117. Copyright 1995 by Blackwell Publishing. Reproduced with permission.

reproduced by direct copy or from memory. Each stimulus figure consists of one to three shapes, most of which are simple geometric forms (e.g., circle, square). Under direct-copy conditions, AH reproduced only four of ten figures correctly. Her total error score was 9, indicating that across the six incorrectly copied stimuli, she made nine individual errors in copying figure elements. This level of performance falls into the "grossly defective" range, the lowest of five categories defined on the basis of results from 200 control participants (Sivan, 1992). In another testing session the direct-copy task was repeated with a parallel form of the BVRT, and AH was instructed to go slowly and take special care to copy the figures correctly. She again miscopied six of ten figures, and her total error score was 8 (still well within the grossly defective range).

For both versions of the task, all of AH's copying errors took the form of left–right or up–down mislocations or misorientations of stimulus elements. Examples are presented in Figure 2–2.

In a third test session AH again performed the direct-copy task with ten BVRT figures; then, after completing the copy task, she was asked to compare each of her copies with the corresponding stimulus figure and to score the copy as correct or incorrect. In copying she erred on seven of the ten figures, and as in the earlier sessions all of her errors were left–right or up–down mislocations or misorientations of stimulus elements.

When scoring her responses, she was able to detect only three of the seven errors; the remaining four she accepted as correct. Two of the errors she failed to detect involved misorientation of a stimulus element, and the other two involved gross mislocalizations of elements; examples are presented in Figure 2–3. Whereas the direct-copying errors could conceivably have resulted from impairment either in perceiving the stimulus figures or in producing the drawing responses, AH's impairment in detecting her copying errors suggested a perceptual locus of impairment.

AH's performance in drawing BVRT figures from memory was not substantially worse than her direct-copying performance. On both immediate and 15-second delayed recall of figures presented for 10 seconds each, she was correct on two of ten figures and her total error score was 12. Given that the BVRT recall tasks are more difficult than the direct-copying task for normal individuals (Sivan, 1992), AH's performance (like her immediate recall of the Rey-Osterrieth Complex Figure) suggested that she was not impaired in short-term retention of location and orientation information.

Task 2–3: Simple Nonsense Shapes

Direct-copying errors and difficulty detecting these errors were also observed in a task with stimuli consisting of individual nonsense shapes. Twenty-six simple shapes were presented one at a time on paper, and AH drew her copy in a box to the right of the stimulus. After completing the copy task, she scored each of her copies as correct or incorrect by comparing it to the corresponding stimulus.

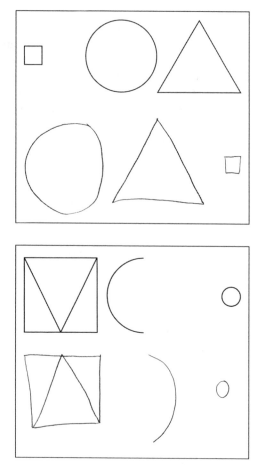

Figure 2–2. Two stimuli from the Benton Visual Retention Test (Sivan, 1992) and AH's direct copies. From *Benton Visual Retention Test* (5th ed.). Copyright 1991 by Harcourt Assessment, Inc. Reproduced with permission. All rights reserved.

In direct copying AH erred on eight of the twenty-six shapes (31%). As illustrated in Figure 2–4, her errors involved left–right or up–down reflection of the entire stimulus shape or one of its components. When scoring her responses, AH detected only four of the eight errors; the remaining four she accepted as correct. Among the errors she failed to detect were the three shown in Figure 2–4.

Task 2–4: Bender-Gestalt Figures

Left–right and up–down reflection errors were also observed when AH was asked to copy the nine Bender-Gestalt figures (Bender, 1938). Figure 2–5

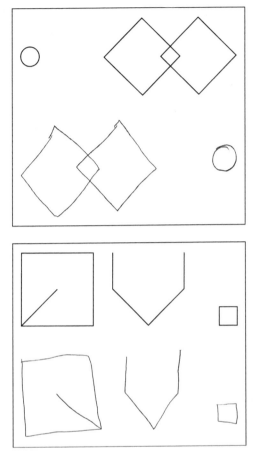

Figure 2–3. Two direct-copy errors that AH failed to detect when asked to score her copying responses on the Benton Visual Retention Test (Sivan, 1992). From *Benton Visual Retention Test* (5th ed.). Copyright 1991 by Harcourt Assessment, Inc. Reproduced with permission. All rights reserved.

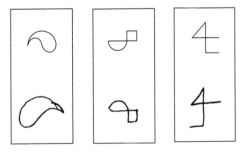

Figure 2–4. Three nonsense shapes and AH's direct-copy errors.

presents her three errors. The first two were left–right reflections of the stimulus figure (Fig. 2–5A, B), and the third involved both a left–right and an up–down reflection of the stimulus (Fig. 2–5C). (Given that a left–right plus an up–down reflection is equivalent to a 180° rotation in the picture plane, the error in Figure 2–5C could also be described as a 180° rotation error. However, I will characterize such errors as reflections rather than rotations because AH's error pattern across a wide range of tasks showed many clear-cut reflection errors but almost no errors that were unequivocally rotations within the picture plane.)

Task 2–5: Line Drawings

AH's direct-copy errors were not limited to abstract stimuli; she also presented with left–right and up–down location and orientation errors in copying line drawings of scenes and objects. Figure 2–6 shows a drawing of a simple scene and AH's direct copy. In making her copy, AH worked carefully, as evidenced by the fact that each line and curve in the stimulus picture also appeared in her copy. Nevertheless, in drawing the house she reversed the left–right positions of the door and window. Figure 2–7 illustrates AH's errors in copying two drawings from the Snodgrass and Vanderwart (1980) set; in both examples she left–right reversed the stimulus picture. However, despite her errors in copying line drawings, AH had no difficulty recognizing the depicted objects. For example, she correctly named the objects in Figure 2–7 as a pitcher and a giraffe, and she accurately described the scene in Figure 2–6 as a house with a fence and two trees.

Tasks 2–6 and 2–7: Numerals and Words

Finally, AH was impaired in direct-copy tasks with numeral and word stimuli. In the numeral task (Task 2–6), the ninety two-digit Arabic numerals (i.e., 10–99) were presented one at a time in random order, and AH copied each numeral while it remained in view. She erred on twelve of the ninety trials (13%), and eleven of the twelve errors involved either transposing digits

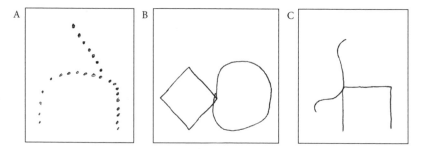

Figure 2–5. AH's direct-copy errors for Bender-Gestalt stimuli (Bender, 1938).

Figure 2–6. Scene stimulus and AH's direct copy.

Figure 2–7. Two line drawings from the Snodgrass and Vanderwart (1980) set, with AH's direct copies. Reproduced with permission of the publisher, Life Science Associates.

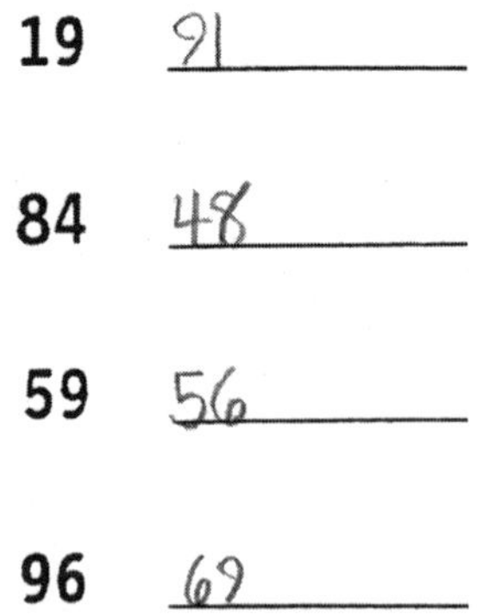

19   91 _____

84   48 _____

59   56 _____

96   69 _____

Figure 2–8. Examples of AH's errors in directly copying of two-digit numerals.

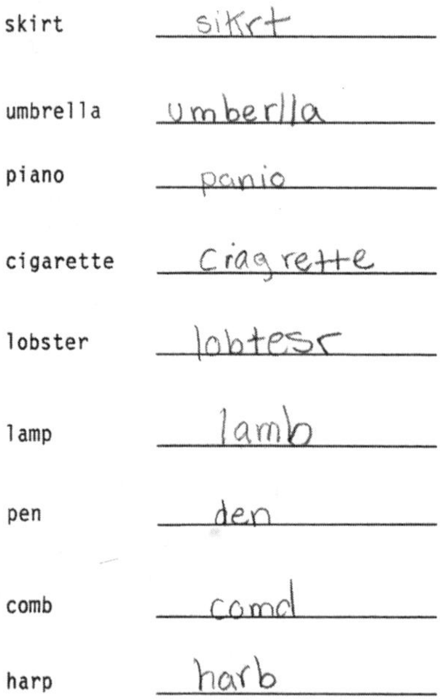

skirt	sikrt
umbrella	umberlla
piano	panio
cigarette	Ciagrette
lobster	lobtesr
lamp	lamb
pen	den
comb	comd
harp	harb

Figure 2–9. Examples of AH's errors in directly copying of words.

(e.g., *76* → *67*) or confusing *9* and *6*, the two digits that differ only in orientation. Figure 2–8 presents several examples.

In Task 2-7 AH copied written words while they remained in view. Stimuli were 144 concrete nouns ranging in length from three to twelve letters (e.g., *truck*).[1] The words were presented on paper in a lowercase sans serif font, and AH wrote her response in lowercase print on a line to the right of each word.

AH miscopied 33% of the words (47/144). Most of her errors involved either missequencing of letters (e.g., *church* → *chruch*, *heart* → *haert*) or confusing letters that differ only in orientation (e.g., *bell* → *dell*, *pig* → *dig*); see Figure 2–9 for additional examples. The word-copying errors appeared to resemble the location and orientation errors AH made in the direct-copy tasks with nonverbal stimuli. The letter-orientation errors were, of course, similar to the orientation errors observed in prior tasks. Further, the letter-sequence errors involved mislocation of stimulus elements (i.e., letters) relative to one another; these errors resembled AH's location errors on the BVRT (see, e.g., the top example in Fig. 2–2).

Conclusions

Across a variety of direct-copy tasks with diverse stimulus materials—simple and complex nonsense shapes, configurations of multiple shapes, line drawings of scenes and objects, and written words—AH was strikingly impaired. Despite the fact that the stimuli remained in view while she produced her copies, she made frequent and blatant errors even for very simple stimuli.

AH's direct-copy errors systematically involved mislocation or misorientation of stimulus objects or their parts. Moreover, the location and orientation errors were not random but instead took the form of left–right or up–down reflections. These results clearly demonstrated that AH suffered from some form of impairment that affected her processing of location and orientation information. Although severe, the deficit was evidently also selective in that it led to highly constrained types of error.

The nature of the impairment—which specific cognitive processes were affected and how these processes were malfunctioning—could not be determined from the direct-copy results alone. AH's difficulty in detecting her copying errors suggested that the deficit might affect the perceptual processes that generate location and orientation representations for visual stimuli; however, more evidence was clearly needed before any firm conclusions could be drawn. The testing described in Chapters 3 and 4 was aimed at obtaining this evidence.

One final result from the initial tests was that AH's performance in drawing visual stimuli from memory was not appreciably worse than her direct-copy performance. This result suggested that her short-term memory for visual–spatial information was largely, if not entirely, intact.

3

Impaired Processing of Visual Location and Orientation Information

The results of the direct-copy tasks suggested a need to probe AH's visual location and orientation processing more thoroughly. Toward this end a broad range of tasks were presented. All of the tasks were nonspeeded and, unless otherwise indicated, AH was not required to maintain fixation during stimulus presentation.

Tests of Visual Location Processing

Task 3–1: Visually Guided Reaching

In this task AH sat with her right hand directly in front of her, resting on the edge of a table (see Fig. 3–1). On each trial she closed her eyes while a 3 cm wooden cube or cylinder was placed on the table. She then opened her eyes, identified the target by saying "cube" or "cylinder," and reached for it with a ballistic movement—that is, without changing direction in mid-movement.

As shown in Figure 3–1, the stimulus locations were arrayed along two semicircular arcs, a close arc 18 cm from the starting position of AH's hand and a distant arc at 36 cm. The five locations on each arc were at angles of 60° left, 30° left, 0°, 30° right, and 60° right (measured from the starting position of AH's hand, with the straight ahead direction defined as 0°). With respect to visual angle, the 30° and 60° close locations were at eccentricities of approximately 8° and 14°, respectively, and the 30° and 60° distant locations had eccentricities of roughly 16° and 26°, respectively. Each location

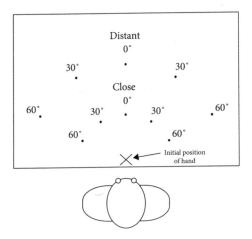

Figure 3–1. Stimulus locations for the visually guided reaching task. Each location was marked only by a small dot; the labels were not shown. Adapted from McCloskey, M., Rapp, B., Yantis, S., Rubin, G., Bacon, W. F., Dagnelie, G., Gordon, B., Aliminosa, D., Boatman, D. F., Badecker, W., Johnson, D. N., Tusa, R. J., & Palmer, E. (1995). A developmental deficit in localizing objects from vision. *Psychological Science, 6,* 112–117. Copyright 1995 by Blackwell Publishing. Used with permission.

was marked by a small dot approximately the size of a period in printed text, to allow the experimenter to see where to place the stimulus objects. Across several testing sessions 120 trials were carried out.

AH was uniformly correct in identifying the object as a cube or cylinder. Furthermore, when the target was directly in front of her (0° locations), she reached accurately on twenty-four of twenty-four trials. However, for targets on her left or right she reached to the wrong side of the table (e.g., right for a target on the left) on fully 66% of the trials (63/96). She reached to the left for 62% of the targets on her right and to the right for 70% of the targets on her left. Virtually all of her errors (59/63, or 94%) involved reaching to the location representing the left/right reflection of the target location across the midline. For example, erroneous responses to stimuli at the distant 60° left location always involved reaching to the distant 60° right location. Figure 3–2 presents a composite video image illustrating this error.

AH's pattern of reaching errors had two interesting features. First, the errors were remarkably selective: AH's erroneous reaching responses were consistently accurate with respect to distance (close vs. distant) and angular displacement (30° vs. 60°); only the direction (left vs. right) was wrong. This finding suggests that at the level(s) of representation giving rise to AH's reaching errors, representations of location are composed of multiple components, each specifying a particular aspect of location, such as direction or distance. Given this assumption, AH's errors could be interpreted by

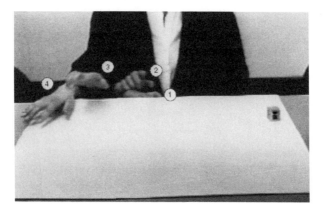

Figure 3–2. Composite video image illustrating a reaching error in which AH reached to the far 60° right position for a target at the far 60° left position. Labels *1–4* indicate successive positions of AH's hand as she reached in the wrong direction. From McCloskey, M., Rapp, B., Yantis, S., Rubin, G., Bacon, W. F., Dagnelie, G., Gordon, B., Aliminosa, D., Boatman, D. F., Badecker, W., Johnson, D. N., Tusa, R. J., & Palmer, E. (1995). A developmental deficit in localizing objects from vision. *Psychological Science, 6,* 112–117. Copyright 1995 by Blackwell Publishing. Reproduced with permission.

assuming that she has a selective deficit in computing the direction component. I will develop this interpretation more fully in Chapter 13.

The second interesting feature of the error pattern was that AH erred on left–right direction more often than if she had simply been guessing. She reached to the wrong side of the table 66% of the time, reliably more often than expected by chance, χ^2 (1, $n = 96$) = 26.04, $p < 0.001$. Below-chance performance was also observed in several other tasks reported later in this chapter and in subsequent chapters. This phenomenon suggests that AH's deficit is not one in which the direction of the target stimulus cannot be computed and a random decision is made at some level of processing. Rather, it appears that AH's reaching errors occurred when some impaired process systematically computed an incorrect direction representation (e.g., right rather than left). This conclusion is consistent with AH's reports of her subjective visual experience. AH denied experiencing confusion or uncertainty about the location of the target object. She stated that on each trial she saw the cube or cylinder at a specific location and reached to that location. Sometimes the perceived location turned out to be correct, and sometimes it turned out to be wrong. These points will also be elaborated in subsequent chapters.

Task 3–2: Touching Screen Locations

Highly selective reaching errors were also evident in a somewhat different task. On each trial an X subtending 1° of visual angle in height and width

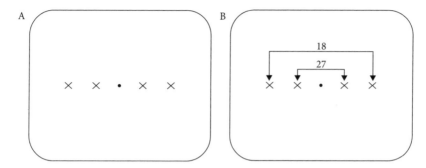

Figure 3–3. (A) The four locations on a computer monitor at which target Xs were presented one at a time in Task 3–2. (B) AH's pattern of localization errors. *Number above each arrow* indicates the number of errors in which a stimulus presented at one of the connected positions was localized to the other position. For example, AH made eighteen errors in which a target presented at the far left position was localized to the far right position or vice versa. From McCloskey, M., & Rapp, B. (2000b). Attention-referenced visual representations: Evidence from impaired visual localization. *Journal of Experimental Psychology: Human Perception and Performance, 26,* 917–933. Copyright 2000 by the American Psychological Association. Reproduced with permission. The use of APA information does not imply endorsement by APA.

was presented for 1 second on a computer monitor at a far left, near left, near right, or far right location (see Fig. 3–3A). Near locations were 4.2° from the central fixation point, and far locations were 9.3° from fixation. Upon stimulus offset AH indicated where the X had appeared by touching the screen. She was instructed to maintain fixation during stimulus presentation, and her eye position was monitored to assess compliance.

AH's performance was severely impaired: on 56% of the trials (45/80) she touched the wrong side of the screen. As illustrated in Figure 3–3B, all of her errors were left–right reflections across the midline (e.g., touching the near right position for a target on the near left). Here again AH's misreaches were accurate with respect to distance but wrong with respect to left–right direction.

Task 3–3: Left–Right and Up–Down Localization

In this task an X was presented on a computer monitor for 250 milliseconds at a location 6.7° left, right, up, or down from a central fixation point (see Fig. 3-4A). AH's task was to indicate the location of the X by moving a mouse (e.g., move left for a stimulus at the left location). Stimuli were presented in random order, with seventy-two trials per location. Three control participants performed the task, with a mean error rate of 0.6%.

In stark contrast, AH erred on 44% of the trials (126/288), with error rates of 57%, 47%, 35%, and 36% at the left, right, up, and down locations, respectively. As shown in Figure 3–4B, her errors were highly systematic: all

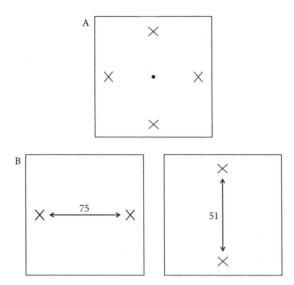

Figure 3–4. (A) The four locations on a computer monitor at which target Xs were presented one at a time in Task 3-3. (B) AH's pattern of localization errors. *Number beside each arrow* indicates the number of errors in which a stimulus presented at one of the connected positions was localized to the other position.

126 mislocalizations were left–right or up–down confusions (e.g., moving the mouse down for a stimulus at the up location). These results demonstrate that AH is impaired in localizing visual stimuli along the up–down as well as the left–right dimension.

Tasks 3–4 and 3–5: Visual Location Naming

AH showed impaired visual localization not only in tasks requiring her to respond by making spatially directed movements but also in tests with verbal responses. In Task 3–4 an X was presented on a computer monitor for 1 second at a location 4.75° left or right from a central fixation point, and AH responded by saying "left" or "right." She erred on twenty-four of the sixty-four trials (38%), with error rates of 34% for left stimuli and 41% for right stimuli. These errors cannot be attributed to an impairment in using the words *left* and *right* because AH's verbal left–right responses were uniformly correct in localization tasks with nonverbal stimuli (see Chapter 4).

In Task 3–5 an X or O was presented on a computer monitor at a far left, near left, near right, or far right location. Near and far locations were 5.5° and 18° from the central fixation point, respectively. On each trial AH identified the stimulus by saying "X" or "O" and the location by saying "near" or "far" and "left" or "right" (e.g., "X far left"). The stimulus remained on the screen until AH had completed her response.

AH identified the stimulus correctly on all thirty-two trials. In naming the location, however, her error rate was 38% (12/32). As in the previous tasks, all of her errors took the form of reflections across the midline; that is, she confused the far left and far right positions and the near left and near right positions but never confused near and far locations on the same or different sides.

Task 3–6: Relative Location

AH also showed impaired performance on tasks requiring localization of multiple visual stimuli relative to one another. In Task 3–6 three, four, or five plastic shapes were placed in a horizontal row in front of AH (e.g., *circle triangle rectangle*). While the stimulus sequence remained in view, AH reproduced it using her own set of shape tokens. Even though she placed her tokens directly below the stimulus shapes, she arranged them in the wrong order on over half of the trials (16/30). For example, she copied the sequence *square rectangle triangle circle* as *square rectangle circle triangle*, placing her triangle token beneath the circle in the stimulus sequence and her circle beneath the triangle stimulus.

Tests of Visual Orientation Processing

Results from several visual orientation tasks demonstrated that AH was impaired in processing not only the location but also the orientation of visual stimuli.

Task 3–7: Judgment of Line Orientation Test

On the Judgment of Line Orientation Test (Benton, Sivan, Hamsher, & Spreen, 1994) the participant is given a key that associates a number with each of eleven lines differing in orientation (see Fig. 3–5A). The key remains in view while test items are presented. Each item consists of two lines, and the task is to report the orientation of the lines by saying the corresponding numbers. AH gave the correct response for only six of the thirty trials, placing her in the "Severely defective" category (which applies to any score less than 17).

The thirty test items collectively included sixty individual lines. Six of these were vertical lines, and AH responded correctly to all of these. However, for lines tilted to the left or right, her error rate was 63% (35/56). Six of the thirty-five errors were near misses, in which she responded with an orientation immediately adjacent to the correct orientation; errors of this sort are also frequently observed in normal individuals. However, the vast majority of AH's errors involved left–right reversal of a line's orientation; errors of this sort are rarely, if ever, made by normal adults. In twenty-three instances AH named the line representing the left–right reflection of a stimulus line. For example, on one test item she responded to a line at orientation 8—tilted 36° to the right of vertical—by saying "4," the label for a line tilted 36° to the left

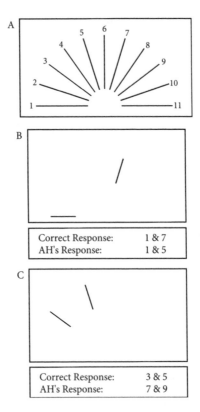

Figure 3–5. Judgment of Line Orientation Test (Benton, Sivan, Hamsher, & Spreen, 1994). (A) Multiple-choice response key. (B) AH error involving left–right reflection of one stimulus line. (C) AH error involving left–right reflection of both stimulus lines. Adapted and reproduced by special permission of the publisher, Psychological Assessment Resources, Inc., 16204 North Florida Avenue, Lutz, Florida 33549, from the Judgment of Line Orientation by Arthur L. Benton, Ph.D., Copyright 1983 by PAR, Inc. Further reproduction is prohibited without permission of PAR, Inc.

of vertical. The remaining six errors apparently involved a left–right reflection combined with a near miss. Figure 3–5B presents two examples of AH's left–right reflection errors. As the examples illustrate, AH sometimes made reflection errors for both of the lines in a stimulus and sometimes reflected only one of the lines while responding correctly to the other.

Task 3–8: Orientation of Arrowheads

In this somewhat simpler task a 1° × 1° arrowhead (> or <) was presented for 2 seconds at the center of a computer screen, and AH moved a mouse left or right to indicate the direction the arrowhead was pointing. Twenty-four left-pointing (<) and twenty-four right-pointing (>) stimuli were presented in random order. Once again, AH's performance was severely impaired (and in fact below chance): Her error rate was 63% (15/24) for both the left- and right-pointing stimuli.

Task 3–9: Picture Orientation

In this task pictures were presented at various left–right and up–down orientations (see Fig. 3–6), and AH answered questions designed to probe her perception of the picture's orientation. Stimuli were twelve pictures from the Snodgrass and Vanderwart (1980) set (e.g., camel, truck, hairbrush). The principal axis of elongation was horizontal in all of the pictures.

For each picture two features were selected, an up–down feature located in the upper or lower half of the picture (e.g., feet for the camel picture) and a left–right feature located on the left or right side (e.g., head).

Across four blocks of trials each picture was presented in four different orientations, representing all combinations of the two possible positions for the up–down feature and the two possible positions for the left–right feature.

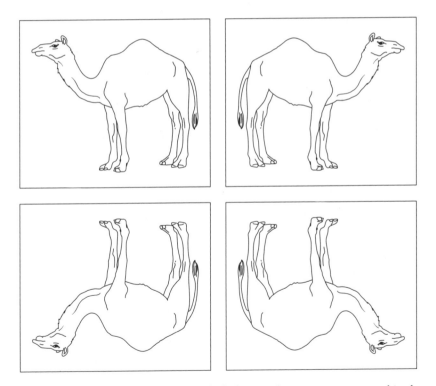

Figure 3–6. The four orientations at which the camel picture was presented in the picture orientation task (Task 3–9). Reproduced with permission of the publisher, Life Science Associates.

For example, as shown in Figure 3–6, the camel picture was presented with feet down and head left; feet down and head right, feet up and head left, and feet up and head right. In each block of trials the twelve pictures were presented once each, with three pictures at each of the four orientations. A different random ordering of the pictures was used in each block.

On each trial AH closed her eyes while a picture was placed in front of her. She then opened her eyes, and (with eyes remaining open) responded verbally to two questions, one concerning the location of the up–down feature in the stimulus picture and the other concerning the location of the left–right feature. For the camel picture, the questions asked whether the feet were up or down in the stimulus picture and whether the head was on the left or right. Instructions made clear that the questions concerned the locations of the features in the pictures as presented and not the positions the features would occupy if the depicted object were at a canonical orientation.

AH answered both questions correctly for only twenty-eight of the forty-eight trials (58%). On eight trials she responded correctly to the up–down question but erred on the left–right question, suggesting misperception of the picture's left–right orientation. For example, when the camel was presented with feet down and head on the left, AH correctly indicated that the feet were down in the picture but erroneously stated that the head was on the right.

On eight other trials AH was correct for the left–right question but wrong for the up–down question, suggesting misperception of the picture's up–down orientation. For instance, when the camel was presented with feet up and head on the right, AH responded correctly that the head was on the right but said that the feet were down. Finally, on four trials AH gave incorrect responses to both questions, suggesting misperception of both left–right and up–down orientation. For example, shown a helicopter with the blades up and the tail on the right, she stated that the blades were down and the tail was on the left.[1]

Task 3–10: Letter Naming

For some letters of the alphabet, inaccurate processing of the letter's orientation could lead to confusion with other letters. More specifically, for eight lowercase letters—b, d, p, q, n, u, m, w—a left–right and/or up–down orientation error could lead to misidentification. For example, b becomes d by left–right reflection, p by up–down reflection, and q by left–right plus up–down reflection. Similarly, lowercase n and u are potentially confusable through up–down reflection, as are m and w. I will refer to these as "orientation-critical" letters.

For the remaining lowercase letters (e.g., e, k, o) left–right and up–down orientation errors leave the letter essentially unchanged (e.g., o) or produce a visual form that would not be confusable with another letter (e.g., ɘ). These "orientation-noncritical" letters would presumably be identifiable despite orientation errors.

In upper case, few letters are orientation-critical. M and W could be confused with one another through up–down orientation errors (even though these letters have slightly different shapes in most fonts). The only other upper-case letter that could be considered orientation-critical is *P*, for which left–right and/or up–down errors could lead to confusion with lowercase *d*, *p*, or *q*.

In Task 3–10 the twenty-six uppercase and twenty-six lowercase letters were presented in random order on a computer monitor in blocks of fifty-two trials. Across two testing sessions twenty-one trial blocks were presented. The lowercase letters *b*, *d*, *p*, and *q* were identical except for orientation, as were *m* and *w* as well as *n* and *u*. In upper case, *M* and *W* were nonidentical in shape but an up–down reflection of either letter would yield a form recognizable as the other letter.

For lowercase letters, AH made naming errors on forty-two of the 546 trials (7.7%). Her error rate was 23% (39/168) for the orientation-critical letters (*b*, *d*, *p*, *q*, *n*, *u*, *m*, *w*) but less than 1% (3/378) for orientation-noncritical letters, $t(20) = 7.37$, $p < 0.001$. All but one of the errors on orientation-critical letters were left–right and/or up–down orientation confusions. For example, across the twenty-one presentations of *d*, AH responded "b" six times, "p" three times, and "q" twice. Similarly, she named *w* as "m" on five trials and *m* as "w" twice.

For uppercase letters, most of which are orientation-noncritical, AH made only twelve errors in 546 trials (2.2%). This error rate was reliably lower than the 7.7% rate for lowercase letters, $t(20) = 5.60$, $p < 0.001$. Nine of the twelve uppercase errors involved the three orientation-critical letters (*M*, *W*, and *P*). AH named *M* as "w" once, *W* as "m" twice, and *P* as "b," "d," or "q" six times.[2]

Considering just those letters that are orientation-critical in lower, but not upper, case (i.e., *b*, *d*, *q*, *n*, *u*), AH made twenty-seven errors on the lowercase forms but no errors on the uppercase forms. This result provides clear evidence that the errors in naming orientation-critical letters arose in processing the visual forms of the letters and not, for example, in retrieving the names of letters that had been identified accurately.

Conclusions

The results reported in this chapter make abundantly clear that AH's impairment in processing visual location and orientation information is not limited to direct-copy tasks. She presented with severely impaired performance across a broad range of tasks that differed widely in the form of the stimuli, the nature of the responses, and other task requirements. As in the direct-copy tasks, her errors were extremely systematic, taking the form of left–right and/or up–down reflections.

The findings presented thus far do not establish, however, whether AH's impairment in processing location and orientation information is a deficit of visual perception, affecting only the processing of visual stimuli, or whether instead she suffers from a more general spatial deficit affecting other forms of stimuli as well (e.g., tactile or auditory stimuli). The tasks discussed in the following chapter were aimed at addressing this issue.

4

Intact Processing of Nonvisual Location and Orientation Information

The findings discussed in the preceding chapter demonstrate that AH makes highly systematic location and orientation errors in a wide variety of tasks with visual stimuli. This chapter presents results showing that, in sharp contrast to her performance with visual stimuli, AH performed normally on location and orientation perception tasks with nonvisual stimuli.

Task 4–1: Auditory Localization

In a series of auditory localization tasks AH sat with eyes closed while a click or sustained tone was presented on her left or right at the 30° and 60° distant locations used in Task 3-1, the visually guided reaching task (see Fig. 3–1). She was 100% correct in indicating the side of the midline from which the sound originated, whether she responded by pointing left or right (80/80), raising her left or right hand (40/40), or saying "left" or "right" (50/50).

AH's normal performance in auditory localization was consistent with an informal observation from the visually guided reaching task. In placing the wooden cube or cylinder on the table at the beginning of a trial, I tried to be quiet; on a few trials, however, the stimulus block made a slight noise as I set it down. On these trials AH, sitting with her eyes closed, said something like, "Oh, I heard you put it down, so I know where it is"; and when I asked her to point to the block, still with eyes closed, she did so accurately. (After the first session of visually guided reaching, I glued a patch of felt to the bottom of each block so I could put them down silently.)

Task 4–2: Kinesthetic Localization

In a kinesthetic localization task a small wooden block was placed at one of the left or right locations from the visually guided reaching task. With eyes closed AH felt around on the table with one hand until she found the block. She then withdrew her hand and, with eyes still closed, reached for the block with her other hand. Her performance was flawless on all sixty trials: After finding the block with one hand, she reached directly to it with the other hand.

Task 4–3: Tactile Localization

AH also showed perfect performance in judging whether a tactile stimulus—a light touch with the eraser end of a pencil—had been presented to the left or right side of her body. She was 100% correct (40/40) in raising her left or right hand to indicate which of her knees had been touched, and she was also perfect (40/40) in saying "left" or "right" to indicate which hand had been touched.

Tasks 4–4 and 4–5: Tactile vs. Visual Localization

In Task 4–4 AH sat with her hands flat on the table in front of her, palms down. In the tactile condition her eyes were closed throughout each trial; the middle finger of her left or right hand was touched, and she indicated which hand had been touched by raising that hand. In the visual condition she closed her eyes while a small wooden cube was placed on the table immediately in front of, but not touching, the middle finger of her left or right hand. She then opened her eyes and raised the hand adjacent to the cube.

In the tactile condition AH raised the correct hand on all forty trials. In the visual condition, however, her accuracy was only 70% (28/40); even though the cube was nearly touching one of her hands and remained in view while she responded, she raised the wrong hand on twelve of the forty trials. The difference between the tactile and visual conditions was highly reliable, $\chi^2 (1, n = 80) = 14.12, p < 0.001$.

In Task 4–5 AH closed her eyes while a stimulus card was placed in front of her. Affixed to the card were two plastic bars, one short (3.1 cm) and the other tall (6.2 cm). The tall bar was to the left of the short bar for half of the trials and to the right for the remaining half. In the tactile condition AH's eyes remained closed while the palm of one hand was placed on the stimulus card. Without moving her hand, she judged the arrangement of the bars and with her other hand pointed left or right to indicate the position of the tall bar relative to the short bar. In the visual condition she looked at the stimulus card and responded by pointing as in the tactile condition. She was 97% correct (39/40) in the tactile condition but only 70% correct (28/40) in the visual condition, χ^2 (1, $n = 80$) = 11.11, $p < 0.001$. In a later testing session with the same stimulus conditions AH responded verbally, saying "left" or "right" to indicate the location of the tall bar relative to the short bar. The results were virtually identical to those obtained with pointing responses: 98% correct (49/50) in the tactile condition and 72% correct (36/50) in the visual condition, χ^2 (1, $n = 80$) = 13.25, $p < 0.001$.

Task 4–6: Tactile vs. Visual Orientation Perception

Tactile and visual orientation perception were compared in a letter-naming task. Stimuli were the eight orientation-critical lowercase letters (*b, d, p, q, n, u, m, w*). In the tactile condition AH closed her eyes and felt a 1 x 1 cm embossed letter with the index finger of her right hand, making a single left-to-right pass across the letter. In the visual condition she viewed letters presented for 1 second on a computer monitor. In both conditions she responded by saying the name of the letter. She was 97% correct (31/32) in the tactile condition but only 62% correct (45/72) in the visual condition, χ^2 (1, $n = 104$) = 11.62, $p < 0.001$. All of her errors in the visual condition were left–right and/or up–down reflections (e.g., *m → w, q → p, p → d*).

Task 4–7: The Arrows Experiment

Taken together, the results of the preceding tasks strongly suggested that AH's performance in processing location and orientation information depended on the form in which stimuli were presented but not on the form of the responses. She had consistently shown impairment in tasks with visual stimuli, regardless of how she was asked to respond; and she had consistently performed normally in tasks with nonvisual stimuli, again regardless of how she responded. These results pointed to a selective deficit in visual perception of location and orientation. The aim of the present experiment was to obtain additional evidence bearing on this conclusion by testing several stimulus and response formats in the context of a single task.

The top panel of Figure 4–1 illustrates the three stimulus formats used in the experiment: picture (visual), pointer (tactile), and words (verbal). On trials with picture stimuli AH viewed a line drawing of an arrow that extended from the center to the edge of a circle. The arrow pointed in one of eight directions: up, down, left, right, up left, up right, down left, or down right.

For trials with pointer stimuli AH felt a wooden pointer that was out of sight inside a box. The pointer was mounted at the center of a cardboard square by a bolt that allowed it to be rotated. On each trial the pointer was set to one of the eight stimulus directions (e.g., down right); AH then reached

Stimulus types

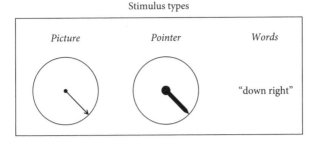

Response types

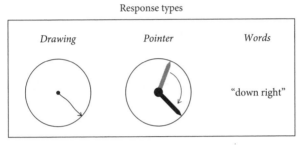

Figure 4–1. Stimulus and response types in the arrows experiment (Task 4–7). From McCloskey, M., Valtonen, J., & Sherman, J. (2006). Representing orientation: A coordinate-system hypothesis, and evidence from developmental deficits. *Cognitive Neuropsychology*, *23*, 680–713. Copyright 2006 Taylor & Francis. Reproduced with permission.

into the box through a small hole and placed her hand flat on the pointer (with fingers pointing in the up direction). The mounting bolt at one end of the pointer and the pointed tip at the other end were sufficiently prominent for her to feel where the pointer began and ended. Finally, on trials with word stimuli the experimenter dictated the stimulus direction (e.g., "down right").

AH's responses also took three forms, as shown in the bottom panel of Figure 4–1: She indicated the stimulus direction either by drawing an arrow, by setting the pointer, or by speaking the appropriate words. On drawing trials AH was given a response sheet showing a circle with a dot at the center and she drew an arrow. For pointer responses the wooden pointer was set to a random position and AH adjusted it to indicate the stimulus direction. As in the case of pointer stimuli, the pointer was out of sight inside a cardboard box. Finally, for word responses AH reported the direction verbally (e.g., "down right").

AH was tested in seven conditions, each involving a particular combination of stimulus and response formats (see Table 4–1). In the picture-to-pointer condition, for example, AH viewed a picture stimulus and then set the pointer to match the direction of the arrow shown in the picture. Twenty-one blocks of trials—three for each of the seven conditions—were

Table 4–1. Conditions in
the Arrows Experiment

Stimulus	Response
Picture	Drawing
Picture	Pointer
Picture	Words
Pointer	Drawing
Pointer	Words
Words	Drawing
Words	Pointer

administered in counterbalanced order. In each trial block the eight stimulus directions were presented once in random order.

The predictions were straightforward: If AH's deficit selectively affected visual perception, she should be impaired in conditions with picture stimuli but normal in conditions with pointer and word stimuli. Further, the type of response should not matter. Regardless of whether she drew an arrow, set the pointer, or said the words describing the arrow's location, AH should perform poorly with picture stimuli and well with pointer and word stimuli.

Results for the picture stimuli were as predicted: AH was severely impaired for all three forms of response. The picture-to-drawing condition was a direct-copying task and, as in other such tasks, AH made many errors, copying only 50% of the pictures (12/24) correctly. Her performance was equally poor in the picture-to-pointer and picture-to-words conditions: 42% (10/24) and 54% (13/24) correct, respectively. In all three conditions her errors were left–right and up–down reflections; some examples are shown in Figure 4–2.

The pointer stimuli—which were tactile rather than visual—yielded near-perfect performance. In the pointer-to-drawing condition, where AH felt the wooden pointer and drew the corresponding arrow, she was 100% correct (24/24); and in the pointer-to-words condition, where she felt the pointer and said its location, she responded correctly on twenty-three of the twenty-four trials (96%). The difference between the picture-stimulus conditions (mean accuracy 49%) and the pointer-stimulus conditions (mean accuracy 98%) was highly reliable, χ^2 (1, $n = 120$) $= 30.12$, $p < 0.001$. The striking contrast between AH's very poor performance with pictures and her excellent performance with the pointer supported the conclusion of a selective visual deficit.

In the conditions with word stimuli a direction (e.g., "down left") was dictated and AH drew the corresponding arrow (words-to-drawing condition) or set the pointer (words-to-pointer condition). For the words-to-pointer condition she performed as expected, setting the pointer correctly for all twenty-four stimuli. However, in the words-to-drawing condition she was correct on only sixteen of twenty-four trials (67%), and her errors were of the same types as in the conditions with picture stimuli. This result was unexpected: If AH suffered from a selective visual deficit, why did she make errors with the nonvisual word stimuli?

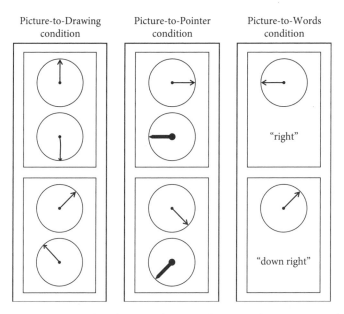

Figure 4–2. Examples of AH's errors from conditions with picture stimuli in the arrows experiment (Task 4–7).

One possible answer was that AH's visual deficit came into play as she looked at the response sheet when making her drawing responses. Perhaps, in other words, her processing of the dictated word stimuli was perfectly normal in the words-to-drawing condition but she sometimes misperceived the spatial layout of the response sheet or the position of her hand and pencil on the sheet, leading her to draw an arrow in the wrong direction.

An obvious problem for this interpretation was AH's perfect performance in the pointer-to-drawing condition, where she felt the pointer and drew the corresponding arrow. If looking at the response sheet caused her to make errors, she should presumably have done poorly in this condition as well as in the words-to-drawing condition. However, the procedures for the words-to-drawing and pointer-to-drawing conditions were subtly different. In the words-to-drawing condition the response sheet was directly in front of AH, where she was almost certain to look at it unless she made a concerted effort not to. In the pointer-to-drawing condition the cardboard box containing the pointer was in front of AH so that she could reach in and feel the pointer. The response sheet was off to her right, and she appeared usually not to look at it while making her drawings. Rather, she first positioned her pencil on the dot marking the center of the circle. Then, she felt the pointer with her left hand and, without looking at the paper, drew her arrow.

Conceivably, then, AH performed poorly in the words-to-drawing condition but well in the pointer-to-drawing condition because she looked at the

Table 4–2. Results of the Arrows Experiment

Stimulus	Response	Number Correct/Total	Percent Correct
Initial test conditions			
Picture	Drawing	12/24	50%
Picture	Pointer	10/24	42%
Picture	Words	13/24	54%
Pointer	Drawing	24/24	100%
Pointer	Words	23/24	96%
Words	Pointer	24/24	100%
Words	Drawing	16/24	67%
Follow-up test conditions			
Words	Drawing (response sheet covered)	24/24	100%
Words	Drawing (look at response sheet)	7/16	44%
Pointer	Drawing (look at response sheet)	5/16	31%
Pointer	Drawing (response sheet covered)	15/16	94%

response sheet in the former condition but not in the latter. This interpretation made two straightforward predictions: First, if AH were prevented from looking at the response sheet in the words-to-drawing condition, her performance should improve to normal; and second, if she were induced to look at the response sheet in the pointer-to-drawing condition her performance should deteriorate.

The first prediction was tested by administering the words-to-drawing condition with the response sheet placed out of sight inside a box. The center of the sheet was marked by the head of a thumbtack so that AH, reaching her hand into the box, could find by touch where to begin drawing her arrow. The results were clear: With the response sheet out of sight, AH was 100% correct (24/24), a level of accuracy reliably higher than the 67% she achieved with the response sheet in view, χ^2 (1, $n = 48$) = 7.35, $p < 0.01$. To ensure that AH had not simply improved with practice at the words-to-drawing task, the task was readministered with the response sheet uncovered, and AH was told to look at the sheet while drawing her arrow. Her performance fell dramatically, to 44% correct (7/16), χ^2 (1, $n = 40$) = 14.34, $p < 0.001$.

The second prediction—that looking at the response sheet would cause AH to err in the pointer-to-drawing condition—was tested by instructing AH to look at the response sheet while drawing her arrow. Again, the results were clear: Whereas her pointer-to-drawing performance was perfect in the initial experiment (where she was apparently not looking at the response sheet), she was only 31% correct (5/16) when instructed to look at the sheet while drawing her arrow. This deterioration in performance was highly reliable, χ^2 $(1, n = 40) = 19.44, p < 0.001$. Finally, the task was repeated with the response sheet out of sight, and AH's performance rebounded to 94% correct (15/16), χ^2 $(1, n = 32) = 10.80, p < 0.01$.

Taken together, the words-to-drawing and pointer-to-drawing tests revealed a consistent pattern: When AH did not look at the response sheet, she was virtually perfect in both conditions, but when instructed to look at the sheet while making her responses, she was severely impaired (44% and 31% correct in the words-to-drawing and pointer-to-drawing conditions, respectively). Her slightly better words-to-drawing performance in the initial experiment—67% correct—may indicate that, in the absence of specific instructions to look at the response sheet, she did not always do so. These results support the hypothesis that AH has a selective visual deficit and demonstrate that the deficit affects her performance not only in tasks with visual stimuli but also in tasks where spatial vision may play a role in generating responses.

Table 4–2 summarizes the results for the entire arrows experiment. The pattern is clear: In conditions requiring visual perception—of either a picture stimulus or a drawing response sheet—AH was severely impaired, with errors taking the form of left–right or up–down reflections. However, in conditions that did not implicate visual perception, her performance was excellent.

Conclusions

The findings reported in this chapter demonstrate that whereas AH is severely impaired in perceiving the location and orientation of visual stimuli, she is intact in processing nonvisual location and orientation information. This pattern of results points clearly to a selective deficit in visual perception.

A second conclusion, which emerged from the arrows experiment, is that AH's visual deficit affects her performance not only in tasks with visual stimuli but also in tasks where spatial vision may play a role in production of responses, such as tasks with drawing responses.

The impact of the deficit on response production may have contributed to AH's poor performance in some of the tasks discussed in the preceding chapters—for example, the direct-copying tasks reported in Chapter 2. However, the effects of the deficit are clearly not limited to response production, as evidenced by AH's impaired performance on tasks in which the stimuli were visual but the responses did not involve vision, such as the visual location-naming tasks described in Chapter 3 (see Tasks 3–4 and 3–5) and the picture-to-words condition in the arrows experiment.

5

Spelling and the Visual Deficit

The hypothesis of a selective deficit in visual perception of location and orientation accounts for AH's impaired performance on the visual location and orientation tasks discussed in Chapters 2 and 3 and her normal performance on the nonvisual tasks reported in Chapter 4. However, the visual-deficit hypothesis does not offer an obvious interpretation for the problem that first brought AH to my attention: her extremely poor spelling. As discussed in Chapter 1, AH showed severely impaired performance on spelling tasks in which a word was dictated and she wrote the word or spelled it aloud. Because the stimuli in these tasks were auditory, it is not immediately apparent how AH's visual deficit could explain her poor performance.

One possibility is that AH's impaired spelling is caused not by her visual deficit but instead by some additional deficit. However, as we shall see, AH's spelling errors resemble the errors observed in visual location and orientation tasks, suggesting that the same deficit may be responsible for her impairment in both visual perception and spelling tasks. Another possible interpretation is suggested by the finding from the arrows experiment (Task 4–7) that looking at the response sheet caused AH to make errors even when the stimulus was nonvisual: Perhaps AH makes spelling errors because her visual deficit leads to confusion when she looks at her written responses while producing them. However, this interpretation cannot account for the finding that AH's spelling was equally impaired in oral and written spelling to dictation. In the oral spelling task, AH spelled words aloud; no written responses (or any other visual stimuli) were involved.

The interpretation I propose for AH's spelling impairment emerges from the observation that processing of visual location and orientation information, although relatively unimportant for performing a spelling task, is of central importance in *learning to spell*. The interpretation can best be explained in the context of assumptions concerning the types of knowledge implicated in spelling. Most theorists assume that spelling involves two forms of learned representation: lexical–orthographic representations and sublexical representations of sound–spelling correspondences (see Tainturier & Rapp, 2001, for a recent overview of this theoretical perspective and relevant evidence). Lexical–orthographic representations specify the spellings of entire words— that is, the identities of the letters and the order in which they occur (e.g., c-o-m-b for the word *comb*). In contrast sublexical sound–spelling correspondence representations describe systematic relationships between sound and spelling units smaller than whole words (e.g., the phoneme /k/ is usually spelled with the letter *c* or the letter *k* but may also be realized in certain contexts as *ck*, *ch*, or *cc*).

In the case of words for which a lexical–orthographic representation has been learned, spelling involves retrieval of this representation. For example, most adults would presumably spell the word *comb* by retrieving the stored representation c-o-m-b. However, if the spelling of a word has not been learned, the sublexical sound–spelling correspondence representations can be used to generate a plausible spelling from the sound of the word. For example, an individual who had not learned to spell the word *arcane* might generate a spelling such as *arcain* through application of sublexical knowledge. As this example illustrates, sublexical representations alone are not sufficient for consistently accurate spelling. At least for languages in which spellings are not entirely predictable from the sounds of words, lexical–orthographic representations are needed.

Visual perception almost certainly plays a crucial role in learning of lexical–orthographic representations; these representations are presumably acquired primarily through repeated visual encounters with the written form of a word. Therefore, assuming that AH's deficit in processing visual location and orientation information dates from birth or early childhood, the deficit may have impaired her ability to acquire lexical–orthographic representations. Errors in perceiving the relative locations of letters could have caused confusion about the ordering of letters (see Task 3–6 for evidence that AH frequently misperceives relative location in a sequence of visual forms), and errors in perceiving letter orientation (see Task 3–10) could have led to confusion about letter identities, at least for words with orientation-critical letters (e.g., *b*, *d*, *p*, *q*).

According to this interpretation, AH's visual system provided extremely noisy input to the processes responsible for acquisition of lexical–orthographic representations (much as if a normal individual were exposed only to texts replete with spelling errors). For example, when AH looked at the written word *comb*, her visual system may sometimes have represented the letter sequence accurately as *c-o-m-b*; however, on other occasions she may have misperceived the word as *c-o-m-d*, *c-o-m-p*, *c-o-b-m*, or so forth. As a consequence, AH may have failed to acquire a lexical–orthographic representation for *comb*, or she may have developed a representation that was indeterminate with respect to some aspects of the spelling (e.g., a representation specifying only that the word begins with *c* and includes *o*, *m*, and either *b* or *d*). Conceivably, she could even have developed a representation specifying a particular incorrect spelling (e.g., *c-o-m-d*) or multiple representations specifying mutually inconsistent spellings (e.g., *c-o-m-b*, *c-o-m-p*, and *c-o-b-m*).

Acquisition of sublexical sound–spelling correspondence representations could also have been affected by AH's visual deficit. Sound–spelling correspondences are presumably acquired by explicitly or implicitly relating the spoken forms of words to their written forms; hence, errors in perceiving the identity or ordering of letters in the written forms could lead to difficulties in acquiring these sublexical spelling representations.

Note that this interpretation for AH's spelling deficit differs in one significant respect from the interpretations I have offered for her impaired performance on visual location and orientation tasks. In the case of the visual tasks, I have argued that AH's perceptual deficit leads her to misperceive the stimuli presented in the tasks themselves; however, with respect to spelling I am suggesting that AH shows poor performance in spelling tasks not because of misperceptions occurring at the time her spelling is tested but rather because of prior misperceptions that occurred as she was learning to spell. Although speculative, this interpretation garners some support from the results of the spelling tasks administered to AH.

Tasks 5–1 through 5–4: Spelling

In Task 5–1 (written spelling to dictation) and Task 5–2 (oral spelling to dictation) words were dictated one at a time. On each trial AH repeated the word to ensure that she had heard it correctly and then wrote it (Task 5–1) or spelled it aloud (Task 5–2). The stimuli were 326 words from the Johns Hopkins Dysgraphia Battery (Goodman & Caramazza, 1985), a set of tasks designed for assessing spelling disorders in individuals who have suffered brain damage. Normal spellers write the words with very high accuracy: Mean performance among fourteen control participants tested by Goodman and Caramazza (1985) was 98% correct, with a range of 93%–100%.

In Task 5–3 (written spelling of picture names) and Task 5–4 (oral spelling of picture names) pictures of concrete objects (e.g., crown, refrigerator) were presented one at a time, and AH wrote the name of the depicted object (Task 5–3) or spelled it aloud (Task 5–4). Four hundred seventy-five pictures were presented for written spelling and fifty-one for oral spelling.

Spelling Accuracy

In all of the tasks AH's spelling was very poor. She was 66% correct in written spelling to dictation (216/326) and 63% correct in oral spelling (206/326). Given that normal spellers perform these tasks with accuracies above 90%, AH's performance indicates a very significant spelling impairment. Results from the tasks with picture stimuli point to the same conclusion: In the written picture-naming task AH's spelling accuracy was 68% (322/475), and in oral spelling of picture names she was 63% (32/51) correct.

Word-Frequency Effect

AH's spelling was more accurate for words that occur frequently in the language, such as *street*, than for words that occur less frequently, such as *sleeve*. The stimuli from the spelling-to-dictation tasks included 146 high- and 146 low-frequency words matched in word length. In the writing-to-dictation task AH was 79% correct for the high-frequency words but only 51% correct for the low-frequency stimuli, χ^2 (1, $n = 292$) $= 26.6$, $p < 0.01$. Similarly, in the oral spelling task her accuracy was 77% and 49% for high- and low-frequency words, respectively, χ^2 (1, $n = 292$) $= 23.5$, $p < 0.01$.

The word-frequency effect implies that AH's spelling impairment results at least in part from inadequate lexical–orthographic representations; a deficit affecting only sublexical representations of sound–spelling correspondences should not differentially affect high- and low-frequency words. The frequency effect suggests that the more often AH was exposed to the written form of a word, the more likely she was to succeed in developing an accurate orthographic representation from the noisy inputs provided by her visual system.

Spelling Errors

AH's error pattern was very similar in all of the spelling tasks. Collapsing across tasks, one-third of her errors (132/402) were phonologically plausible misspellings (e.g., *cloak → cloke, camel → camle, beak → beek*), whereas the remaining two-thirds (270/402) were phonologically implausible (e.g., *shirt → shrit, merge → mrege, slide → slibe*).

Phonologically Plausible Errors

The phonologically plausible errors are consistent with a deficit in acquiring lexical–orthographic representations: Errors of this type are assumed to occur when an individual has not learned or cannot access a lexical–orthographic representation and instead generates a spelling by applying knowledge of sublexical sound–spelling correspondences (e.g., Beauvois & Dérouesné, 1981; Goodman & Caramazza, 1986a; Hatfield & Patterson, 1983). Thus, AH may have spelled *beak* as *beek* because she had not learned the correct spelling and relied instead on sublexical knowledge to translate the phoneme sequence /bik/ into the letter sequence *b-e-e-k*. Phonologically plausible errors may also occur when knowledge of sound–spelling correspondences is used to supplement an incomplete lexical–orthographic representation (Rapp, Epstein, & Tainturier, 2002). For example, AH's spelling of *certain* as *sertain* suggests that she had some lexical–orthographic knowledge about the word; had the word been spelled entirely through application of sublexical sound–spelling correspondences, the vowel in the second syllable would probably have been written as *e* or *a* or *i* or *o* (e.g., *serten*) and not as *ai*. However, the initial *s* in AH's response *sertain* suggests that her lexical–orthographic representation did not fully specify the spelling of the word and that she consequently used sublexical knowledge (e.g., /s/ may be written as *s*) to spell parts of the word that were un- or under-specified in the lexical representation.

The phonologically plausible errors point, then, to deficiencies in AH's lexical–orthographic representations. At the same time these errors indicate that AH has at least some knowledge of sound–spelling correspondences. The occurrence of phonologically plausible errors does not, though, demonstrate that her sublexical knowledge is entirely normal. AH also made many phonologically implausible errors, and incomplete or faulty sublexical knowledge could have contributed to some of these errors.

Phonologically Implausible Errors

AH's phonologically implausible errors were especially interesting because many of them resembled the errors observed in visual location and orientation tasks. The phonologically implausible misspellings were analyzed by a computer program that attempted to interpret each error as a letter substitution, deletion, transposition, insertion, or some combination of these error types. (For a description of the program, see McCloskey, Badecker, Goodman-Schulman, & Aliminosa, 1994.) An error was assigned an interpretation if it could be explained by one of the individual error types or by a combination of two individual errors (e.g., *piano* → *pinaio*, interpreted as transposition of *a* and *n* plus an insertion of *i*). Errors attributable to deletions or insertions of any number of letters were also interpreted as such (e.g., *onion* → *oionion*, interpreted as an insertion of *o* and *i*). If an error could not be interpreted in any of these ways, the program classified it as uninterpreted, on grounds that it was too complex for a meaningful interpretation to be assigned. The program generated interpretations for 258 of the 270 errors (96%). Table 5–1 presents the distribution of the interpreted errors across types; the error counts sum to more than 258 because some misspellings included more than one type of error.

Table 5-1. Distribution of AH's Phonologically Implausible Errors Across Error Types

Error Type	Frequency
Transposition	136
Insertion	82
Substitution	44
Deletion	42

Table 5-2. Examples of AH's Letter-Transposition Errors

Stimulus Word	AH's Spelling
snail	snial
often	ofetn
knock	konck
lobster	lobtser
engine	eingne
solve	slove
crawl	cralw
apple	aplpe
skirt	skrit
skirt	sikrt

Letter transpositions, in which AH misordered the letters in a word were by far the most frequent errors (e.g., *knife* → *kinfe, noise* → *nosie*; see Table 5-2 for additional examples). These errors are obviously similar to the ordering errors AH made in copying words and numerals (Tasks 2-6 and 2-7) and in reproducing sequences of shapes (Task 3-6). The letter transpositions may be interpreted by assuming that in learning to spell AH often misperceived the relative locations of letters in visually presented words and thus acquired lexical and perhaps sublexical representations that were indeterminate or incorrect with respect to ordering of letters. For example, the *knife* → *kinfe* error suggests that AH's lexical–orthographic representation for *knife* either is indeterminate with respect to letter ordering or misrepresents the order as *k-i-n-f-e*. This error is unlikely to have resulted from application of incomplete or faulty sublexical knowledge; the phoneme sequence /nayf/ is unlikely to have been translated into *k-i-n-f-e* even through the use of flawed sublexical knowledge, and the presence of the *k* strongly suggests the use of lexical–orthographic knowledge about the letters in the specific word *knife*. However, some other letter transpositions could conceivably reflect faulty sublexical knowledge. For example, AH spelled seventeen words in which the diphthong /ey/ is realized orthographically as *ai* (e.g., *afraid, snail*). For seven of these seventeen words she wrote *ia* instead of *ai* (e.g., *afriad, snial*). These errors could have resulted from incomplete or erroneous lexical–orthographic representations for the specific words; also possible, however, is that AH's misperceptions of letter order led her to acquire the faulty sublexical "knowledge" that /ey/ may be spelled *ia*.

In addition to letter transpositions, AH made many letter insertions, in which she added an extra letter to the correct spelling of a word (e.g., *sauce* → *sacuce*, *owl* → *olwl*; see also Table 5–3). In nearly three-fourths of the insertion errors (60/82) the inserted letter was one that occurred in the correct spelling. For example, in the *sauce* → *sacuce* error, the inserted letter *c* occurs in the correct spelling *sauce*. These errors, like the transposition errors, may stem from AH's impairment in perception of relative location. For example, if AH variously perceived the visually presented word *sauce* as *sacue* and *sauce* while learning to spell, she might have developed a lexical–orthographic representation that was indeterminate with respect to whether a *c* was present between the *a* and *u*, between the *u* and *e*, or at both positions.

AH's phonologically implausible errors were also notable for the high incidence of letter-orientation confusions. AH made forty-four errors in which she substituted one letter for another, and over half of the substitutions (23/44) took the form of orientation confusions, in which the substituted letter differed from the correct letter only in orientation (e.g., *lamp* → *lamb*, *umbrella* → *umprella*; see Table 5–4 for additional examples). These errors are strikingly similar to the orientation errors AH made in direct copying of words (Task 2–7), letter naming (Task 3–10), and other visual orientation tasks (see Tasks 2–1 through 2–5 and 3–7 through 3–9). The letter-orientation errors in spelling are straightforwardly interpretable by assuming that misperceptions of letter orientation led AH to acquire lexical and/or sublexical representations that were incorrect or indeterminate with respect to the identities of orientation-critical letters (e.g., a lexical representation for *lamp* that specified *d* as the last letter or indicated that the last letter might be *b*, *p*, or *d*).

The remaining phonologically implausible errors—insertions of letters not present in the correct spelling (e.g., *angry* → *agnrey*), substitutions not

Table 5–3. Examples of AH's Letter-Insertion Errors

Stimulus Word	AH's Spelling
adopt	adopot
planet	plantet
fluid	fludid
trout	trount
scissors	sicissors
nature	nauture
edit	eidit
iron	irion
bicycle	biclcyle
cloud	clound

Table 5–4. Examples of AH's Letter-Orientation Confusions in Spelling

Stimulus Word	AH's Spelling
broom	droom
zipper	ziqqer
comb	comp
comb	comd
sandwich	sanbwitch
lamb	lamd
debt	dept
harp	harb
rabbit	raddit
method	methob

taking the form of letter-orientation confusions (e.g., *junk* → *gunk*), and letter deletions (e.g., *artichoke* → *articoke*)—are less directly interpretable in terms of AH's visual deficit but nevertheless could have resulted from this deficit. I will not attempt an exhaustive discussion of these errors but instead will consider a few examples. Some of the errors appear to reflect subtle weaknesses in AH's knowledge of sublexical sound–spelling correspondences. For example, errors like *junk* → *gunk*, *urge* → *erg*, and *strange* → *strang* suggest that AH has learned that the /dʒ/ (the "j" sound in *junk*, *urge*, and *strange*) is sometimes written as *g* but has failed to learn that this sound–spelling correspondence holds only in certain orthographic contexts (specifically, when the *g* is followed by *e*, *i*, or *y*, as in *germ*, *giant*, or *gyroscope*). Subtle deficiencies in sublexical knowledge are perhaps not surprising in light of AH's perceptual deficit; the nuances of sound–spelling correspondences may be difficult to learn when letter order and orientation are frequently misperceived. For example, if AH sometimes misperceived *giant* as *gaint*, *germ* as *grem*, and so forth, these misperceptions might well have prevented her from recognizing that *g* can be used to represent /dʒ/ only in certain orthographic contexts.

Other errors may reflect the use of sublexical knowledge in combination with a faulty lexical–orthographic representation. For example, in the error *screwdriver* → *skrewdirver* the phonologically plausible spelling of *screw* as *skrew* probably reflects the application of sublexical knowledge, whereas the phonologically implausible spelling of *driver* as *dirver* may have been mediated by a lexical–orthographic representation that incorrectly specified the ordering of the *r* and *i*.

As a final example, many of AH's letter-deletion errors (e.g., *watch* → *wath*) may—like the letter transpositions and the insertions of letters occurring elsewhere in the correct spelling—have their origin in AH's impaired perception of letter order. For example, if AH variously misperceived *watch* as *wathc*, *wacth*, *wcath*, *wathc*, and so forth while learning to spell, she may have developed a lexical–orthographic representation that included inconsistent information about sequencing of letters. In particular, she may have learned that the initial *w* was followed by *a* but also that the *w* was followed by *c* (as in *wcath*), that the *a* was followed by *c* but also that the *a* was followed by *t* (as in *wathc*), and so forth. This sort of internally inconsistent lexical–orthographic "knowledge" could give rise to various letter-deletion, transposition, or insertion errors, depending upon which specific pieces of learned sequence information predominated in determining the spelling response. Thus, AH's deletion error *watch* → *wath* might have been produced via activation of learned sequence representations specifying that *w* is followed by *a*, *a* is followed by *t*, and *t* is followed by *h*. In contrast, the transposition error *watch* → *wacth* (another of AH's errors) could have resulted from activation of representations indicating that *w* is followed by *a*, *a* is followed by *c*, *c* is followed by *t*, and *t* is followed by *h*. Similarly, the letter-insertion error *watch* → *wactch* could occur via the activation of sequence information specifying that *w* is followed by *a*, *a* is followed by *c*, *c* is followed by *t*, *t* is followed by *c*, and *c* is followed by *h*.

Conclusions

In this chapter I have suggested that AH's severely impaired spelling may be a nonobvious consequence of her perceptual deficit. Visual perception of location and orientation, although not required for performing a spelling task, is crucial for learning to spell: Experience with visually presented words plays a central role in acquisition of lexical–orthographic representations and sublexical sound–spelling correspondences. AH's deficit in visual location and orientation perception may therefore have disrupted her ability to acquire these forms of knowledge as a child and, hence, impaired her ability to spell as an adult.

Although plausible, this interpretation of AH's spelling deficit must be considered tentative. Spelling errors of the sorts made by AH could result from deficits other than impaired visual location and orientation perception, and indeed such errors have been observed in developmental and acquired spelling deficits that were presumably not caused by perceptual disorders. Children who have difficulty learning to spell may produce phonologically plausible and/or phonologically implausible errors (e.g., Finucci, 1985; Frith, 1980; Romani, Ward, & Olson, 1999), and the same is true of adults with acquired spelling deficits (Baxter & Warrington, 1987; Beauvois & Dérouesné, 1981; Caramazza, Miceli, Villa, & Romani, 1987; Caramazza & Miceli, 1990; Goodman & Caramazza, 1986a, 1986b; McCloskey et al., 1994). In some—but by no means all—children with developmental spelling or reading deficits, the errors may include letter-orientation confusions (e.g., Bigsby, 1985; Chapman & Wedell, 1972; Collette, 1979; Cohn & Stricker, 1976; Fischer, Liberman, & Shankweiler, 1978).

Phonologically plausible errors could result from any deficit that impaired the ability to acquire or retrieve lexical–orthographic representations (e.g., Baxter & Warrington, 1987; Beauvois & Dérouesné, 1981; Goodman & Caramazza, 1986a, 1986b), and phonologically implausible errors could also have multiple causes. For example, in adults with acquired spelling deficits, error patterns characterized by letter substitutions, transpositions, insertions, and deletions have typically been attributed to impairment in maintaining orthographic representations in working memory while the individual letter representations are processed to generate written or oral spelling responses (e.g., Caramazza et al., 1987; McCloskey et al., 1994; Miceli, Silveri, & Caramazza, 1985; see also Frith, 1980, and Roeltgen, Sevush, & Heilman, 1983, for discussion of other potential causes for phonologically implausible errors). In the specific case of letter-orientation confusions the causes are far from obvious (e.g., Bigsby, 1985; Cohn & Stricker, 1976; Fischer et al., 1978), but it is probably safe to say that the errors are not always caused by impaired visual location and orientation perception.

Hence, AH's spelling performance does not point unequivocally to her perceptual deficit as the underlying cause of the spelling impairment. Nevertheless, it is noteworthy that her spelling errors—especially the letter transpositions and letter-orientation confusions—are strikingly similar to the errors she makes in visual location and orientation tasks and that these errors can be interpreted by reference to her impaired location and orientation perception.

One obvious question raised by the discussion of AH's spelling deficit concerns her reading. Visual location and orientation perception is even more important for reading than for spelling because visual perception is implicated not only in learning to read but also in the act of reading itself. Therefore, if AH's perceptual deficit led to her spelling impairment, the deficit should presumably also have impaired her reading. Why, then, did AH report having little or no difficulty with reading? In Chapters 9 and 10 I explore this question in considerable detail, showing that AH has very clear reading impairments but that she is also remarkably skilled at compensating for these impairments.

6

The Nature of the Deficit: Initial Conclusions

In this chapter I consolidate the conclusions from the preceding chapters and extend these conclusions on the basis of additional arguments and evidence.

Selective Visual Deficit

The central conclusion emerging from the results reported thus far is that AH's impairment in processing location and orientation information is a selective visual deficit. Across a wide variety of location and orientation tasks with visual stimuli, she presented with severely impaired performance; yet in tasks with nonvisual stimuli her location and orientation processing was intact. These results point specifically to a deficit of visual perception and rule out a more general spatial deficit affecting the processing of all forms of location and orientation information.

The results also rule out a motor deficit affecting the ability to perform spatially directed movements. In the first place, AH's reaching and pointing movements were normal in tasks with nonvisual stimuli; only with visual stimuli did she reach and point in the wrong direction. Also, in tasks with visual stimuli AH showed impairment even when responding verbally rather than through spatially directed movements—for example, in visual location naming (Tasks 3–4 and 3–5), letter naming (Task 3–10), and the Picture-to-Words condition in the arrows experiment (Task 4–7).

The verbal-response results also imply that AH's performance cannot be attributed to any of the various forms of visuomotor impairment that have been posited to account for impaired visually guided reaching in previous studies of brain-damaged patients (e.g., Battaglia-Mayer & Caminiti, 2002; Buxbaum & Coslett, 1997; Mayer et al., 1998; Milner & Goodale, 1995; Rondot, De Recondo, & Dumas, 1977). For example, AH's results cannot be explained in terms of a visual–motor disconnection in which (accurate) visual location and orientation representations fail to make contact with (perhaps otherwise intact) mechanisms for executing movements. If AH suffered only from a visual–motor disconnection, she should have shown intact performance in visual tasks with verbal responses. For the same reason, AH's performance cannot be attributed to other potential forms of visuomotor impairment, such as a deficit in transforming retinocentric location representations into arm-centered representations for use in visual control of reaching.

Taken together, the findings from the various visual and nonvisual tasks point clearly to a selective visual deficit that affects performance across a broad range of visual location and orientation tasks.[1]

Unitary Deficit

The results also suggest that AH's impaired performance across the various tasks reflects a single underlying deficit. This conclusion encompasses two claims. The first is that AH's orientation errors originate from the same visual-system malfunction as her location errors. Empirical motivation for this claim comes from the finding that AH presented with the same systematic and highly unusual error pattern—high rates of left–right and up–down reflection errors—in both location and orientation tasks. The second claim is that the same visual-system malfunction is responsible for AH's impaired performance across tests with widely varying task requirements and forms of response, including copying shapes and words, reaching for objects, moving a mouse to indicate locations of visual stimuli, arranging shape tokens to match stimulus sequences, naming the locations or orientations of visual stimuli (e.g., by saying "left"), and reading aloud letters. Empirical support again takes the form of similarity in error patterns across tasks: AH showed high rates of left–right and up–down location and orientation errors (more precisely, she made whichever of these error types were possible within a given task) regardless of task requirements or form of response. As discussed in Chapter 5, AH's visual location and orientation deficit may also have impaired her ability to learn the spellings of words and, thus, may be responsible for her impaired spelling as an adult. In Chapter 7, I present additional evidence in support of the unitary-deficit interpretation.

High-Level Visual Deficit

An important implication of the discussion in the preceding section is that AH's impairment affects a level of visual processing that provides location and orientation information to a broad and diverse set of perceptual, cognitive, and motor functions (e.g., verbal reporting of location and orientation, visually guided reaching, drawing, reading). This point might lead one to suspect that her deficit affects processing early in the visual system. However, several aspects of AH's performance suggest that her visual location and orientation errors arise not in low-level vision but rather at a higher level or levels of visual processing, subsequent to that at which the visual scene is parsed into objects. This conclusion emerges from two observations concerning AH's location and orientation errors. First, these errors were frequently partial, in the sense of involving only some elements of the stimulus configuration. Second, the partial errors consistently respected object boundaries.

Tasks 6–1 and 6–2: Localizing Two Targets

Partial errors were observed in a variety of tasks. For example, in Task 6–1 two Xs were presented on a computer monitor for 1 second, either on the same side of the screen (e.g., at near and far left locations) or on opposite sides at noncorresponding positions (e.g., near left and far right). AH's task was to say whether the Xs were on the same or different sides of the screen. On six of the sixteen same-side trials (38%) she responded "different" and on three of the sixteen different-side trials (19%) she said "same." These results suggest that AH frequently made a left–right reflection error for one of the Xs but not the other, yielding a different-side representation for a same-side trial or vice versa.

In Task 6–2 AH closed her eyes while a red block and a blue block were placed on a table in front of her. She then opened her eyes and responded to location questions (e.g., *Where is the red one?*) by pointing. On three of the seven trials in which the two blocks were placed at noncorresponding positions on opposite sides of the midline AH localized one of the blocks correctly but committed a left–right reflection error for the other. For example, on a trial with the red block at a far left position and the blue block at a near right location, AH pointed to the far left for the red block and to the near left for the blue block. After the trial was completed, I asked her whether she had seen both blocks at the same time, one next to the other on the same side, and she responded that she had. Like the results from Task 6–1, these findings imply that AH's errors do not always involve left–right and/or up–down reflection of the entire visual scene; some elements of a scene may be reflected while others are not.

Partial location and orientation errors were observed in other tasks as well. For example, on several trials in the Judgment of Line Orientation test (Task 3–7) AH made a left–right reflection error for only one of the two line segments making up the stimulus (see Fig. 3–5). Also, in direct copy of figures from the Benton Visual Retention Test (Task 2–2) she often made location or orientation errors for only some components of the stimulus.

In all of the tasks, AH's partial errors fell without exception into one of two categories: (1) mislocalization of whole objects and (2) misarrangement of the parts of an object, within the boundaries of that object. (The second category encompasses object-orientation errors as well as the occasional more complex error in arrangement of object parts, such as AH's direct copy of the Rey-Osterrieth Complex Figure; see Fig. 2–1.)

AH never made errors that violated the integrity of an object—that is, she never made errors in which a part of an object became separated from that object or errors in which parts of two objects were amalgamated into a single object. For example, in copying the multiobject figures from the Benton Visual Retention Test, AH never committed errors in which she shifted a part (such as a line segment) or spatial region (such as the upper left corner) from one object to another.

Task 6–3: Colored Letters

AH's errors also maintained the integrity of objects in the sense that she never made localization errors in which two visual attributes (e.g., color and shape) from a single object were localized to different spatial positions or errors in which attributes from different objects were localized to the same position. For example, in Task 6–3 colored letters (e.g., red A, blue Y) were presented at four locations on a computer monitor: up left, up right, down left, and down right. On each trial two letters were presented (e.g., red A at the up left location, green Y at the down left position; see Fig. 6–1). AH's task was to describe each letter and its location (e.g., "red A up left, green Y down left"); the stimulus display remained in view until she had completed her response. On

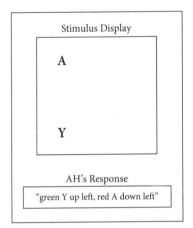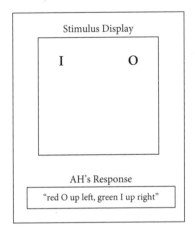

Figure 6–1. Examples of stimulus displays and AH's location exchange errors in Task 6–3. In the trial shown in the left panel the A was red and the Y was green. In the trial shown in the right panel the I was green and O was red. (*See also* COLOR FIG. 6–1 in separate insert.)

11 of 40 trials (28%) AH made left–right or up–down location errors, and in six of these errors the two stimulus letters exchanged locations (see Fig. 6–1 for examples). All of the exchanges involved both color and shape attributes, and hence, the objects in the stimulus display were preserved in AH's response (e.g., stimulus red A and green Y, response red A and green Y; see Fig. 6–1). Location exchanges involving one attribute but not the other (e.g., color but not shape) would have produced illusory conjunction errors (Treisman & Gelade, 1980) in which attributes were miscombined across objects (e.g., stimulus red A and green Y, response green A and red Y), but AH made no such errors. Nor did she make any errors in which a single attribute was copied from one object to another (e.g., stimulus red A and green Y, response green A and green Y).

Even in daily life, with visual stimuli far more complex than those used in the present study, AH's errors apparently respected the integrity of objects. She frequently reported mistakes involving mislocalization of whole objects or misarrangement of parts within an object (e.g., perceiving a purse hanging from a woman's right shoulder as being on her left shoulder, misreading the time on a clock as 10 after rather than 10 before the hour). However, she never described errors in which features or spatial regions were mislocalized or misarranged in ways that cut across object boundaries, such as a left–right mislocalization of a spatial region that was arbitrary with respect to the objects in the scene (e.g., a region including parts of two objects, plus some background).

These observations support the conclusion that AH's deficit affects high-level vision. To explain why her errors maintain the integrity of objects, we must assume that her impairment affects a level (or levels) of representation beyond that at which the visual scene is parsed into objects. In subsequent chapters I present additional evidence that AH's deficit affects high-level vision.

Developmental Deficit

AH's impairment in visual location and orientation processing is evidently not an acquired deficit resulting from brain disease or injury but rather a developmental deficit caused by some aberration in visual system development before birth or in the first few years of life. As previously noted, AH has no history of neurological disease or injury, and a neurological evaluation revealed no abnormalities.

Also, several sources of evidence suggest that AH's deficit has been present since childhood. In interviews both AH and her parents described specific difficulties during her childhood that could have resulted from impaired processing of visual location and orientation information. For example, her mother reported (and AH subsequently confirmed) that as a child she had considerable difficulty setting the table, often putting utensils on the wrong side of the plate. According to her mother, AH also had trouble remembering whether the knife or spoon should be placed closer to the plate and whether the blade of the knife should be turned toward or away from the plate. AH also recalled many other errors that could have resulted from impaired visual location and orientation perception, such as pouring water on the floor when attempting to water plants and putting stamps on the wrong corners of envelopes.

Samples of AH's elementary through secondary schoolwork confirmed her self-reported problems with spelling and math in school and offered indications of difficulty processing location and orientation information. Writing samples from throughout AH's school years showed extremely poor spelling, with errors of the same sorts observed in the present study. Most notably, the schoolwork spelling errors included many phonologically implausible letter transpositions (e.g., *valve → vavle*), insertions of letters present elsewhere in the correct spelling (e.g., *micro → mircro*), and letter-orientation errors (e.g., *work → mork*) (see Fig. 6–2 and Table 6–1 for

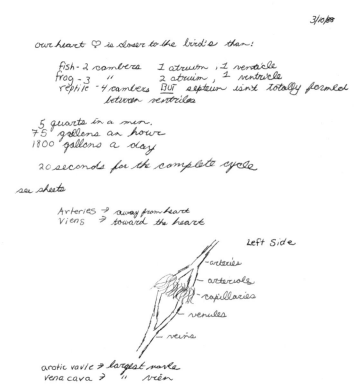

Figure 6–2. A sample of AH's writing at age 15, from a ninth-grade biology class. Note the many phonologically implausible spelling errors, including letter transpositions (e.g., *valve → vavle, vein → vien, aortic → arotic*), insertion of a letter present elsewhere in the correct spelling (*septum → septeum*), and letter deletions (e.g., *chamber → camber, ventricle → ventrile, ventricle → venticle*). (*See also* COLOR FIG. 6–2 in separate insert.)

Table 6-1. Examples of AH's Spelling Errors in Schoolwork Samples from Fifth through Twelfth Grades (Ages 10–18)

Error Type	Stimulus Word	AH's Spelling
Transposition	smoking	somking
	triumph	trumiph
	slim	silm
	erased	earsed
Insertion	micro	mircro
	virus	virsus
	obesity	obesisty
	populations	poplulations
Letter-orientation confusion	work	mork
	antibodies	antipodies
	dad	dab
	my	wy

additional examples). As discussed in Chapter 5, these are the error types that most clearly suggest difficulty in acquiring lexical and sublexical knowledge about the relative location and orientation of letters in the spellings of words. The schoolwork writing samples are therefore consistent with the assumption that AH's deficit in visual location and orientation perception was present in childhood and with the hypothesis that this deficit impaired her learning of spelling.

The schoolwork samples also included several elementary school math papers. In accord with AH's self-report of difficulty with math in school, the papers show frequent errors, some of which may have arisen from errors in perceiving the orientation or ordering of digits. For example, Figure 6–3 shows two errors from an undated homework assignment on division. The first error, $36 \div 6 = 4$, may have resulted from a misperception of the divisor 6 as 9; elsewhere on the homework sheet AH answered $24 \div 6$, $36 \div 9$, and $36 \div 4$ correctly, suggesting that she probably did not mistakenly think that $36 \div 6$ was 4. The second error, $12 \div 3 = 7$, may have resulted from misperception of 12 as 21; AH is unlikely to have thought that $12 \div 3$ was 7, especially given that she answered $12 \div 4$ and $21 \div 7$ correctly.

Errors in various other school papers also suggested difficulty with location and orientation information. For example, multiple errors of location and orientation were evident in a fifth-grade geography assignment that involved decoding of encrypted messages. In deciphering a message created by substituting graphic symbols for letters, AH confused two symbols that were left–right reflections of one another. As illustrated in Figure 6–4A, the symbol for the letter *V* was a circle containing a rightward-pointing arrowhead ($>$), whereas the symbol for *T* was a circle with a leftward-pointing arrowhead ($<$). When AH encountered the symbol for *V*, she first wrote *T*, subsequently

Figure 6–3. Two errors from an undated arithmetic paper, potentially resulting from errors in perceiving the orientation (36 ÷ 6 = 4) and ordering (12 ÷ 3 = 7) of digits. (*See also* COLOR FIG. 6–3 in separate insert.)

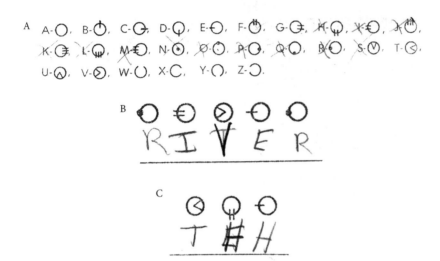

Figure 6–4. (A) The key for a decoding task from a fifth-grade geography assignment. (B) Orientation confusion in which AH initially decoded the symbol for *V* as *T*. The symbols for *V* and *T* differ only in left–right orientation. (C) Error in which AH reversed the positions of H and E in decoding the word the. (*See also* COLOR FIG. 6–4 in separate insert.)

correcting the error by writing the correct letter *V* (see Fig. 6–4B). On the same assignment AH also made several errors in which she wrote a letter not directly under the corresponding symbol but instead under the adjacent symbol. Figure 6–4C presents an example: In decoding the word *the*, AH initially wrote *E* under the symbol for *H* and *H* under the symbol for *E*; she later corrected the first but not the second error. These mistakes, which could have resulted from errors in processing the relative locations of the symbols, appeared similar to AH's mistakes in reproducing sequences of shapes by placing shape tokens directly beneath the stimulus shapes—for example, reproducing *square rectangle triangle circle* as *square rectangle circle triangle* (see Task 3–6).

The most remarkable schoolwork samples, however, were several drawings in the back of a sketchbook from an art class AH took in high school at age 18. During a visit to the National Gallery of Art and the Phillips

Figure 6–5. Renoir's *A Girl with a Watering Can* and AH's sketch. Renoir, Auguste, *A Girl with a Watering Can*, Chester Dale Collection. Image courtesy of the Board of Trustees, National Gallery of Art, Washington, D.C., 1876, oil on canvas. (*See also* COLOR FIG. 6–5 in separate insert.)

Collection in Washington, D.C., she made sketches of five paintings. The detail in the sketches strongly suggested that she had sketched the paintings while standing in front of them, and AH confirmed this conclusion when asked. She also indicated that the sketches had been made not to be turned in as homework but rather for her own use as she tried to select a topic for a term paper. Figures 6–5 through 6–9 present the five sketches along with reproductions of the original paintings.

Comparison of sketches with originals reveals that four of the five sketches contain major errors involving location and/or orientation of objects. Figure 6–5 shows Renoir's *A Girl with a Watering Can* and AH's sketch. Her rendition of the girl is a nearly complete left–right reflection of the figure in the painting. Note in particular that the girl's feet and the spout of the watering can point to the right in the painting but AH drew them pointing left. The tilt of the girl's torso is also reversed.

Figure 6–6 shows Rembrandt's *A Girl with a Broom* and AH's sketch. This sketch appears to be accurate. Figure 6–7 presents Tissot's *Hide and Seek* and AH's sketch. The sketch is not very detailed but clearly left–right reverses the relative positions of the greenhouse and the crawling child: In the painting the greenhouse is on the right and the girl is on the left, but AH's sketch places the greenhouse on the left and the girl on the right.

Figure 6–6. Rembrandt's *A Girl with a Broom* and AH's sketch. Workshop of Rembrandt van Rijn, possibly Fabritius Carel, *A Girl with a Broom,* Andrew W. Mellon Collection. Image courtesy of the Board of Trustees, National Gallery of Art, Washington, D.C., probably begun 1646–1648 and completed 1651, oil on canvas. (*See also* COLOR FIG. 6–6 in separate insert.)

Figure 6–8 shows Rembrandt's *The Mill* and AH's sketch. The painting depicts a cliff with high ground on the left, dropping into water on the right. A mill sits on the high ground in the left half of the painting and a boat with a person rowing is in the lower right-hand corner. AH's sketch left–right reverses the scene, placing the high ground and mill on the right and the boat with rower on the left.

Even more striking is the sketch AH made from Renoir's *Luncheon of the Boating Party* (Fig. 6–9). Her notes on the facing page of the sketchbook indicate that she was having trouble sketching the painting and decided consequently to sketch only the straw hats. As Figure 6–9 illustrates, she made multiple left–right location errors as well as left–right and up–down orientation errors. In particular, the three straw hats on the left side of the painting appear on the right in AH's sketch, and one of these (the hat worn by the woman holding the dog) is clearly left–right reflected in orientation. Further, the orientation of the brim is up–down reversed on the hat in the upper right corner of AH's sketch. Finally, the two hats on the right side of the painting are on the left in AH's sketch, and both are left–right reflected in orientation.

The errors evident in AH's schoolwork are important not only as an indication that her deficit is developmental but also as evidence against the possibility that her performance in the present study represents malingering. The location and orientation errors in work predating the study indicate that AH did not invent her deficit at the time of the study, to gain attention as an interesting research participant. Of course, one might entertain the possibility that AH had been simulating a deficit in visual location

Figure 6–7. Tissot's *Hide and Seek* and AH's sketch. Tissot, James Jacques Joseph, *Hide and Seek*, Chester Dale Fund. Image courtesy of the Board of Trustees, National Gallery of Art, Washington, D.C., ca. 1877, oil on canvas. (*See also* COLOR FIG. 6–7 in separate insert.)

and orientation processing for many years. However, until my review of her schoolwork, AH's location and orientation errors were apparently not recognized as such or at least were not taken to indicate any unusual problem. Her difficulties with spelling and math were viewed by parents and teachers as possibly indicating a learning disability, but the disability was evidently not considered sufficiently severe or unusual to merit serious efforts at evaluation or treatment. An interpretation of malingering would therefore require

Figure 6–8. Rembrandt's *The Mill* and AH's sketch. Rembrandt van Rijn, *The Mill*, Widener Collection. Image courtesy of the Board of Trustees, National Gallery of Art, Washington, D.C., 1645/1648, oil on canvas. (*See also* COLOR FIG. 6–8 in separate insert.)

the assumption that AH began at an early age to simulate a deficit in visual location and orientation perception and persisted for many years despite failing to attract much attention or achieving other benefits. Given the complete absence of evidence that AH suffers from any form of psychiatric disorder,

Figure 6–9. Renoir's *Luncheon of the Boating Party* and AH's sketch. Renoir, Pierre Auguste, *Luncheon of the Boating Party*, 1880–1881, oil on canvas. Acquired 1923. The Phillips Collection, Washington, D.C. (*See also* COLOR FIG. 6–9 in separate insert.)

this interpretation does not seem to merit serious consideration. Another reason for rejecting a malingering interpretation is that a team of researchers in Switzerland (Pflugshaupt et al., 2007) has recently described a brain-damaged patient with a pattern of impairment extremely similar to that of AH. (See Chapter 11 for further discussion of this patient.)

Conclusions

The conclusions from this chapter may be summarized succinctly: AH suffers from a selective developmental deficit in visual location and orientation perception. This deficit, which probably originated prior to AH's birth or in the early years of her life, affects high-level vision and causes distinctive location and orientation errors in a wide range of visual tasks. The deficit may also affect AH's ability to acquire knowledge in circumstances where processing of visual location and/or orientation information is implicated in the learning process (e.g., learning to spell). Subsequent chapters, although focused on different issues, present additional support for these conclusions.

7

Effects of Visual Variables

The findings discussed in the preceding chapters point strongly to the conclusion that AH's location and orientation errors stem from a selective deficit of visual perception. In this chapter I present results showing that AH's visual location and orientation perception are dramatically affected by several visual variables: motion, exposure duration, flicker, contrast, and eccentricity. In addition to buttressing the conclusion that AH's deficit has a visual-system locus, the results have implications for understanding the organization of the normal visual system.

Motion

Whereas AH was severely impaired in localizing stationary visual stimuli, she performed virtually without error in localization of moving stimuli.

Task 7–1: Translational Motion

A 1.8° × 1.2° X or O was displayed on a computer monitor at a far left, near left, near right, or far right location. Near and far locations were 6° and 18° from the central fixation point, respectively. On each trial the stimulus remained in view until AH had completed her response. For half of the trials the stimulus was stationary; for the remaining trials it oscillated up and down over a distance of 6°, at a constant speed of 12°/second. AH identified the stimulus by saying "X" or "O" and touched the screen to indicate its location. For moving stimuli she was instructed to touch the middle of the up–down path of motion.

On both stationary and moving trials AH was perfect at identifying the stimulus as an X or an O. However, her localization performance was dramatically different for stationary and moving stimuli. She reached to the wrong location for 59% of the stationary stimuli (19/32) but only 6% of the moving stimuli (2/32), χ^2 (1, $n = 64$) = 16.22, $p < 0.001$.

As in previous tests, AH's localization errors were highly systematic. In all of the errors she touched the location at the correct distance from the center of the screen but on the wrong side (e.g., near left instead of near right).

Task 7–2: Rotational Motion

A 1.2°-diameter asterisk-like stimulus (three line segments intersecting at their centers at angles of 60°) was presented on a computer monitor at a location 9° up, down, left, or right from a central fixation point. On half of the trials the stimulus was stationary; on the remaining trials it rotated about its center at a rate of 312°/second. AH indicated the location of the stimulus by moving a mouse up, down, left, or right.

For stationary stimuli AH moved the mouse in the wrong direction on 42% of the trials (168/400). For rotating stimuli, however, her error rate was less than 1% (1/400), χ^2 (1, $n = 800$) = 323.13, $p < 0.001$. All of her errors involved moving the mouse in the direction opposite to the correct direction (e.g., down instead of up, right instead of left).

Exposure Duration

Several experiments revealed a strong and surprising effect of exposure duration on AH's processing of visual location and orientation information: Her accuracy was much higher for brief than for long stimulus presentations.

Task 7–3: Location of Disks

A white disk with a diameter of 1.61° and a luminance of 19.4 cd/m² was displayed on the black background of a computer monitor at a location 8.44° left or right of a central fixation point. Exposure duration was varied from 17 to 1000 milliseconds, with seventy-two trials at each of ten durations randomly intermixed within trial blocks. AH responded by pressing a left button for left stimuli and a right button for right stimuli.

As shown in Figure 7–1, her error rate was low for very brief stimuli but rose sharply with increasing exposure duration. Three normal control participants each had error rates less than 3% at each stimulus duration.

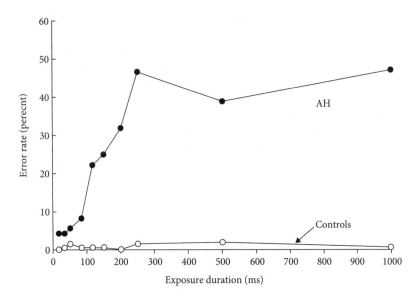

Figure 7–1. Localization-error rate as a function of exposure duration for AH and three normal control participants in Task 7–3. From McCloskey, M., Rapp, B., Yantis, S., Rubin, G., Bacon, W. F., Dagnelie, G., Gordon, B., Aliminosa, D., Boatman, D. F., Badecker, W., Johnson, D. N., Tusa, R. J., & Palmer, E. (1995). A developmental deficit in localizing objects from vision. *Psychological Science, 6,* 112–117. Copyright 1995 by Blackwell Publishing. Reproduced with permission.

Task 7–4: Orientation of Arrowheads

In this task an arrowhead (> or <) was presented at the center of a computer screen, and AH moved a mouse left or right to indicate the direction the arrowhead was pointing. Brief- and long-exposure trials were mixed within blocks. On brief trials the stimulus was presented for 50 milliseconds, whereas on long trials it remained on the screen until AH made her response. A tone was presented 2 seconds after stimulus onset on all trials, and AH was instructed not to respond until she heard the tone. Her error rate was 67% (64/96) for long-exposure stimuli but only 6% (6/96) for stimuli presented briefly, χ^2 (1, $n = 192$) = 73.05, $p < 0.001$.

Task 7–5: Letter Naming

Individual lowercase letters were presented on a computer monitor for 50 milliseconds (brief-exposure trials) or until AH made her response (long-exposure trials). Brief- and long-exposure trials were randomly intermixed within blocks, with each of the twenty-six lowercase letters appearing once per block in the brief-exposure condition and once in the long-exposure condition. AH erred on 13% of the long-exposure trials (20/156), and nineteen of her twenty errors were orientation confusions (e.g., $q \rightarrow$ "b", $n \rightarrow$ "u"). However, for brief-exposure trials her error rate was only 1% (2/156), $t(25) = 2.51, p < 0.05$.

Flicker

AH's visual location and orientation processing were also profoundly affected by flicker: Her accuracy was much higher for flickering stimuli than for stimuli of constant brightness.

Task 7–6: Left–Right Localization

On each trial an X was presented for 1 second on a computer monitor at a location 5.7° to the left or right of a central fixation point. On steady trials the X was displayed continuously; on flicker trials the stimulus was turned on and off at 50-millisecond intervals (i.e., 50 milliseconds on, 50 milliseconds off, 50 milliseconds on, and so forth), causing it to flicker visibly. AH indicated the location of the X by moving a mouse to the left or right or by saying "left" or "right." A high- or low-pitched tone, coincident with stimulus offset, cued her to respond verbally or with the mouse.

For steady stimuli her error rate was 45% with mouse responses (43/96) and 42% with verbal responses (40/96). However, for flickering stimuli she made no errors with either mouse or verbal responses, $\chi^2 (1, n = 192) = 52.86$ (mouse) and 48.03 (verbal), $p < 0.001$.

Task 7–7: Benton Visual Retention Test

Flicker also had a dramatic effect on AH's direct copying of stimulus figures from the Benton Visual Retention Test (BVRT) (Sivan, 1992). In one testing session AH made direct copies of the ten figures on each of two parallel forms of the BVRT. For one form the testing room was illuminated in the usual fashion, with overhead fluorescent lights. For the other form the room lights were turned off and the only illumination came from a strobe light that flashed at a rate of 25 Hz, producing a strong flicker. Normal and strobe lighting conditions alternated in sets of five trials.

Under normal lighting conditions, AH performed very poorly, just as in the previously described direct-copy administrations of the BVRT (see Task 2–2): She copied only three of the ten stimulus figures correctly. However, under strobe light she was 100% correct (10/10). In two later testing sessions AH again performed the BVRT direct-copy task under 25 Hz strobe lighting, and her performance was perfect on both occasions. Collapsing over all administrations of the BVRT direct-copy task, AH copied only 11/30 figures correctly under normal lighting but was correct on 30/30 trials conducted under strobe light, χ^2 (1, $n = 60$) $= 27.80, p < 0.001$.

Tasks 7–8 and 7–9: Letter Naming

In these tasks AH named steady and flickering letters. Steady stimuli were displayed continuously for 1 second, whereas for flicker stimuli the display was turned on and off at 50-millisecond intervals for a 1-second period. Two versions of the experiment were run. In the full-alphabet version (Task 7–8) three blocks of fifty-two trials were presented, with each block including one steady and one flicker presentation of each of the twenty-six lowercase letters. In the orientation-critical version (Task 7–9) only the eight orientation-critical lowercase letters (*b, d, p, q, n, u, m, w*) were tested. Three blocks of forty-eight trials were presented, with each block containing three steady and three flicker presentations of each letter.

In both the full-alphabet and orientation-critical versions, AH's performance was dramatically better for flickering than for steady letters. In the full-alphabet version she erred on 19% of the trials (15/78) in the steady condition but made no errors in the flicker condition, $t(25) = 3.11, p < 0.01$. In the orientation-critical version her error rate was 38% (27/72) in the steady condition but only 1% (1/72) in the flicker condition, $t(8) = 4.48, p < 0.01$. In both versions of the experiment all of AH's errors were orientation confusions for orientation-critical letters.

Contrast

Stimulus contrast also affected AH's processing of visual location and orientation information: Her performance was considerably better for low- than for high-contrast stimuli.

Task 7–10: Left–Right Location

In this task a 1.61° disk was presented for 1 second at a location 8.44° left or right of center on a computer monitor with background luminance of 0.03 cd/m². High-, medium-, and low-contrast stimuli were randomly intermixed within trial blocks. Stimulus luminance was 0.19 cd/m² for low-contrast stimuli, 1.22 cd/m² for medium-contrast stimuli, and 19.4 cd/m² for high-contrast stimuli. AH pressed a left or right button to indicate the side of the screen on which the stimulus appeared.

For high-contrast stimuli, AH was correct on only 30% of the trials (19/64); however, she was 45% correct (29/64) for medium-contrast stimuli and 89% correct (57/64) for low-contrast items, χ^2 (2, $n = 192$) $= 48.93$, $p < 0.001$.

Task 7–11: Left–Right and Up–Down Location

On each trial a high- or low-contrast X was presented for 1 second on a computer monitor at a location 7.5° left, right, up, or down from a central fixation point. AH indicated the location of the X by moving a mouse. Stimulus contrast levels were determined subjectively; high-contrast stimuli were bright but not excessively so, and low-contrast stimuli were much dimmer but still clearly visible. Stimulus luminance was not measured.

For high-contrast stimuli AH was correct on 36% of the trials (23/64), but she was 72% correct (46/64) for low-contrast stimuli, χ^2 (1, n = 128) = 16.63, $p < 0.001$. The effect of contrast was significant for stimuli at the up and down locations (χ^2 [1, n = 64] = 5.40, $p < 0.05$) as well as for stimuli at the left and right locations (χ^2 [1, n = 64] = 9.08, $p < 0.01$).

Task 7–12: Left–Right Orientation

Left- and right-pointing arrowheads ($<$ and $>$) were presented at high and low contrast on a computer monitor and remained on the screen until AH responded by moving a mouse left or right. Contrast levels were the same as in the preceding experiment. AH was 60% correct for high-contrast arrowheads (58/96) and 83% correct for low-contrast stimuli (80/96), χ^2 (1, n = 192) = 11.18, $p < 0.001$.

Stimulus Eccentricity

Finally, AH showed effects of stimulus eccentricity (i.e., the distance of a stimulus from fixation); her localization accuracy increased with eccentricity.

Task 7–13: Eccentricity

In this task an X was presented for 1 second on a computer monitor at a location 3°, 6°, 9°, or 12° to the left or right of a central fixation point. AH indicated whether the X was on the left or right side of the monitor by moving a mouse to the left or right. Her eye position was monitored to ensure that she maintained fixation during stimulus presentation. Five trials were eliminated from analyses due to eye movements.

Figure 7–2 presents AH's percentage of correct responses for each of the four eccentricities, collapsed across corresponding left and right visual field locations. Her left–right localization performance increased monotonically with stimulus eccentricity, $\chi^2(3, n = 571) = 21.9, p < 0.001$, from 33% correct at 3° eccentricity to 60% correct at 12°. The monotonic effect of eccentricity was also observed within each visual field separately, $\chi^2(3, n = 284) = 15.60$, $p < 0.01$ for the left visual field and $\chi^2(3, n = 287) = 8.23, p < 0.05$ for the right visual field.

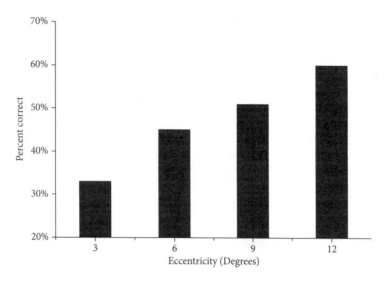

Figure 7–2. AH's percentage of correct responses as a function of stimulus eccentricity in Task 7–13.

Other tasks in which AH maintained fixation during stimulus presentation showed comparable effects of stimulus eccentricity. For example, in Task 3–2, which involved touching a computer monitor to indicate where a stimulus appeared, AH's error rate was higher for near left and right stimulus locations than for far left and right positions (see Fig. 3–3).

Conclusions

Table 7–1 summarizes the effects of the motion, exposure duration, flicker, contrast, and eccentricity experiments. The pattern shown in the table has several significant implications.

Unitary Visual Deficit

First, the observed effects of the visual variables bolster the conclusion that AH's impairment is a selective deficit in visual information processing; if her deficit affected a nonvisual level of representation, one would presumably not expect such effects. Furthermore, the finding that the visual variables have the same—often counterintuitive—effects across tests varying widely in task requirements and forms of response strongly supports the conclusion that a single underlying deficit is responsible for AH's location and orientation errors on all of the tests.

Table 7–1. Effects of Visual Variables on AH's Visual Location and Orientation Perception

	AH's Performance	
Variable	Good	Poor
Motion	Moving	Stationary
Exposure duration	Brief duration	Long duration
Flicker	Flicker	Constant brightness
Contrast	Low contrast	High contrast
Eccentricity	High eccentricity	Low eccentricity

Multiple Visual Subsystems

More importantly, the effects of the visual variables suggest hypotheses about the functional architecture of the normal visual system. The pattern of results described in this chapter may be explained by assuming that the normal cortical visual system includes two subsystems, one of which is intact and one of which is impaired in AH (McCloskey et al., 1995; McCloskey, 2004). More specifically, I assume that the visual system includes *transient* and *sustained* subsystems that are specialized for processing different kinds of stimuli, such that (*a*) the transient subsystem is most sensitive to rapidly changing visual stimuli (e.g., those that are brief, moving, or flickering), whereas the sustained subsystem is most strongly activated by static stimuli of relatively long duration; (*b*) the transient subsystem is sensitive to low-contrast stimuli, whereas the sustained subsystem requires higher levels of contrast; and (*c*) the transient subsystem is more responsive to peripheral than central stimuli, whereas the opposite is true of the sustained subsystem. These proposed distinctions between visual subsystems are neither arbitrary nor ad hoc; related distinctions have previously been drawn on the basis of psychophysical, neuroanatomical, and neurophysiological evidence (for overviews see Breitmeyer & Ganz, 1976; Lennie, 1980; Livingstone, 1990; Livingstone & Hubel, 1987, 1988; Merigan & Maunsell, 1993).

I assume that the transient–sustained distinction applies at least to the level(s) of the cortical visual system giving rise to AH's location and orientation errors and perhaps to other levels as well. In particular, having argued in Chapter 6 that AH's errors arise not in low-level vision but rather in higher-level visual processing, I assume that the transient–sustained distinction applies at least to some aspects of high-level vision. Finally, I assume that both the transient and sustained subsystems process information concerning the location and orientation of visual stimuli.

Given these assumptions, the effects of visual variables may be interpreted by assuming that AH's transient visual subsystem is intact, whereas her sustained subsystem is impaired, often generating incorrect representations of stimulus location and/or orientation. On this account AH's perception of location and orientation is usually accurate when stimulus conditions favor the (intact) transient subsystem, as with brief, moving, flickering, low-contrast, or eccentric stimuli. However, when the (impaired) sustained subsystem is strongly activated—as in the case of static, long-duration, high-contrast, central stimuli—location and orientation errors are likely to occur. In Chapter 16 I develop the transient versus sustained visual subsystems hypothesis in greater detail and discuss the relationship of this hypothesis to other proposals about visual-system organization.

8

A Paradox

The results discussed in the preceding chapters lead to a paradox: On the one hand, data from a broad range of laboratory tasks implied that AH was severely impaired in perceiving the location and orientation of visual stimuli; yet, on the other hand, she was apparently leading a normal life, doing well in school and living independently with no special accommodations. In fact, prior to the present study neither AH nor her parents, friends, or teachers were aware that her visual perception was abnormal. If AH had a severe perceptual deficit, how could she function so well in daily life? And how could she and the people around her be unaware of the deficit?

The selectivity of AH's deficit provides a partial answer to these questions. The testing reported in Chapters 4 and 7 revealed that AH's perception of location and orientation is intact for nonvisual stimuli and for certain forms of visual stimuli, including moving stimuli. When such stimuli are available—as in many everyday circumstances—we might expect AH's performance to be reasonably normal. For example, she probably has no difficulty perceiving the location of a person with whom she is conversing because the auditory stimuli supplied by the person's speech and the moving visual stimuli arising from the person's movements provide a basis for accurate localization.

The selectivity of AH's deficit does not, however, fully resolve the paradox. In many everyday tasks (e.g., reading, picking up stationary objects) the available stimuli are typically limited to forms that, according to the laboratory-task results, she cannot process normally. How, then, can we account for

AH's apparently successful functioning in daily life and for the failure of AH and those around her to recognize her perceptual deficit?

In this chapter I lay out several assumptions that together provide potential answers to these questions, and I motivate these assumptions through observations and evidence concerning AH's performance in both real-world and laboratory tasks. Then, in Chapters 9 and 10, I report an extensive study of AH's reading, showing that the results speak clearly and directly to the proposed assumptions. The points emerging from these chapters not only shed light on issues concerning AH in particular but also have broader implications for understanding, detecting, and diagnosing selective developmental deficits.

Resolving the Paradox

The paradox has two closely related aspects: AH's apparently successful functioning in daily life despite evidence of severely disordered visual perception and the failure of AH and others to become aware of her deficit. In this section I focus largely on the first aspect, although many of the points I develop are also relevant to the second. In a subsequent section I address the second aspect more specifically.

The apparent discrepancy between AH's successful functioning in daily life and the laboratory evidence of a perceptual deficit can, I propose, be resolved on the basis of two assumptions. The first is that, contrary to initial appearances, AH's functioning in everyday life is far from normal. Her deficit, I will argue, causes significant problems in many aspects of her life. The second assumption is that the impact of AH's perceptual deficit is ameliorated in many circumstances by compensatory processes. Some of the compensations are strategies AH applies deliberately, whereas others are processes that apparently operate without her awareness.

The assumption about compensatory processes bears not only on AH's ability to function in daily life but also on the failure of AH and others to recognize her deficit prior to the present study. AH's ability to compensate for some of the difficulties caused by the perceptual deficit may have rendered the deficit less noticeable than it would otherwise have been to AH's parents, teachers, and friends. Successful compensations may also have made the deficit less evident to AH herself, especially when the compensations occurred without her awareness. These assumptions about everyday problems and compensations are motivated by observations and evidence concerning several aspects of AH's daily life.

Visually Guided Reaching

In laboratory testing of visually guided reaching (see Task 3–1), AH made gross errors, frequently reaching to the left for objects on her right and vice versa. However, when first tested in the reaching task, she was surprised and distressed to find herself reaching in the wrong direction and said she was not aware of any previous problems with reaching. Further, when I spoke with AH's parents, they told me they had never noticed that she had difficulty reaching for objects. Why in daily life did AH not make reaching errors like those observed in the lab? Or if she did make reaching errors in everyday circumstances, why were she and others unaware of them?

In the laboratory reaching task AH was instructed to make ballistic reaching movements—that is, she was told to reach in a single motion, without pausing or changing direction. Therefore, once she began reaching in the wrong direction, she had to complete the movement, resulting in a very obvious error. However, reaching movements in daily life need not be ballistic. Conceivably, AH succeeded in everyday reaching by making midcourse adjustments, correcting initially misdirected reaching movements by changing direction in midmovement. In this way, her hand might reach the intended target, albeit by a somewhat circuitous route.

Task 8–1: Nonballistic Reaching

To explore this possibility, I retested AH in the visually guided reaching task, this time telling her simply to reach as she ordinarily would when picking something up. Procedures were otherwise the same as in the earlier testing: AH was seated at a table and closed her eyes while a wooden block was placed on the table at one of ten locations (see Fig. 3–1). She then opened her eyes and reached for the block.

Under the new instructions, AH consistently succeeded in grasping the block. However, for thirty of the forty-four trials in which the block was placed at one of the left or right stimulus locations her hand began moving in the wrong direction, then smoothly changed course and swept back across the table toward the stimulus block. For example, when the block was on her right, her hand frequently began moving left and then swept back to the right. Often during the sweeping movements her fingers were fully extended and spread out in a manner characteristic of brain-damaged patients with deficits in visually guided reaching (e.g., Perenin & Vighetto, 1983).

The sweeping corrective motions—although obvious to someone looking for them and readily apparent on the test-session videotapes—were sufficiently smooth and rapid that AH's reaching did not appear abnormal to casual observation. Watching her perform the task, I realized that I had seen, but ignored, the same sweeping motions many times in earlier testing sessions when she reached for a pencil in order to copy a picture or write a word. AH apparently experienced a similar revelation: Sweeping her hand back and forth, she said, "I just realized I do a lot of this when I'm reaching for things."

The nonballistic reaching results offer a partial solution to the puzzle posed by AH's apparent lack of reaching problems in daily life: Her visually guided reaching *was* abnormal in everyday circumstances, but because she compensated by making midcourse corrections, she succeeded in grasping the target object. Furthermore, because the midcourse adjustments were smooth and rapid, the abnormalities in AH's nonballistic reaching movements were sufficiently subtle to escape notice (by either AH or those around her). This interpretation draws upon both of the assumptions I outlined above: (*1*) AH's functioning in daily life is not entirely normal and (*2*) compensatory processes ameliorate the impact of her deficit.

The sweeping corrective motions do not represent a strategy AH applied deliberately to compensate for errors in perceiving the locations of objects; she was not aware of either the perceptual errors or the compensatory movements. Rather, the midcourse corrections appear to reflect compensatory processes developed and applied without AH's awareness. One interesting question concerns how these processes work. When AH starts reaching in the wrong direction, what leads her to shift direction and sweep her hand toward the correct location? In the nonballistic reaching task AH's midcourse adjustments were usually initiated well before her hand reached the erroneous target location toward which she had begun reaching; hence, the corrections were presumably not invoked by her failure to make contact with the target at the expected location.

One possibility is that the moving visual stimulus provided by her reaching hand helps AH to localize not only the hand but also the stationary objects in the visual field. Some support for this suggestion comes from an informal test in which AH sat at a table with eyes closed while I placed a block to her left or right. She then opened her eyes and reported the block's location by saying "left" or "right." On some trials I swept my hand across the table after she had responded. If she had initially mislocalized the block, she usually corrected herself as soon she saw my moving hand, saying something like, "Oh—no, it's over there" and pointing to the correct location. (If I didn't move my hand across the table, her inaccurate perception usually remained stable over at least 5–10 seconds of viewing the scene. Also, if I swept my hand across the table after AH had given a correct localization response, she didn't change her answer.)

I have no definitive account of why a moving stimulus apparently helps AH localize stationary objects. However, the hypothesis of transient and sustained subsystems introduced in Chapter 7 (see also Chapter 16) suggests a possible interpretation. When the transient visual subsystem—which appears to be intact in AH—is activated by a transient stimulus, transient-subsystem encoding may conceivably be enhanced for other stimuli in the visual field, including sustained stimuli. Suppose, then, that AH's malfunctioning sustained visual subsystem misrepresented a block on her left as being on her right. When she began reaching to the right, the sight of her moving hand would presumably activate her transient visual subsystem. If the transient subsystem consequently generated robust and accurate location representations not only for the moving hand but also for the stationary block, the result would be an inconsistency between the transient and sustained subsystems regarding the block's location. If the conflict were resolved in favor of the transient-subsystem representations, these representations might then provide a basis for the corrective reaching movements and for a rectified perception of the block's position. Task 8-2 provides some support for this interpretation, demonstrating that AH's localization of sustained stimuli is improved by simultaneous presentation of task-irrelevant transient stimuli.

Task 8-2: Localizing Sustained Stimuli in the Presence of Transient Stimuli

In this task a target X was presented on a computer monitor for 250 milliseconds at a location 8.4° left, right, up, or down from a central fixation point. (This exposure duration was presumably long enough to yield robust activation of the sustained subsystem, given that Task 7-3 showed poor localization performance for exposure durations of 250 milliseconds or greater.) AH responded to the location of the X by moving a mouse (e.g., moving right to indicate a stimulus at the right location).

On some trials four task-irrelevant asterisks were also presented, at locations 3.4° left, right, up, and down from fixation (see Fig. 8-1). On trials with asterisks, the asterisks appeared at all four locations and, thus, provided no information about the location of the target X. On sustained-asterisk trials the four asterisks were displayed continuously throughout the 250-millisecond exposure of the target. On transient-asterisk trials the asterisks appeared for 50 millisecond beginning with target onset, then disappeared for 150 milliseconds, and finally appeared again for the final 50 milliseconds of target presentation. On no-asterisk trials the target X was presented in the absence of asterisks.

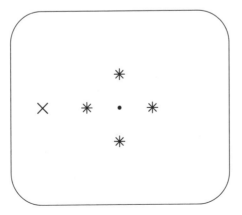

Figure 8-1. Sample trial from Task 8-2, showing a target stimulus at the left location and four task-irrelevant asterisks.

As expected, AH's localization performance on no-asterisk trials was poor: She was only 54% correct (69/128). Presentation of sustained asterisks had little, if any, effect: AH was 63% correct on sustained-asterisk trials (81/128), χ^2 (1, n = 256) = 1.95, p > 0.10. However, her accuracy on transient-asterisk trials was 82% (105/128), significantly higher than for either no-asterisk or sustained-asterisk trials, χ^2 (1, n = 256) = 22.0 and 10.4, respectively, p < 0.01. These findings suggest that transient visual stimuli, by activating the transient visual subsystem, improve AH's localization for concurrent sustained stimuli. The results are therefore consistent with the suggestion that her self-corrections in the nonballistic reaching task resulted from transient-system activation caused by the sight of her moving hand.

Reaching Errors in Daily Life

Once AH's reaching difficulties were revealed in the lab, she began to be aware not only that she frequently made sweeping movements when reaching in everyday life but also that she sometimes made clear-cut errors. In the months following the initial reaching tests, she often came to the lab with stories about reaching mistakes she had recently committed or recollected from past experience. For example, she told me that she kept three piles of sweaters on the top of a wardrobe. She had realized, she said, that when she reached up for a sweater, the one she came down with sometimes wasn't the one she expected. Also, when she reached for a book on the shelf on her desk, she often came away with the wrong one; and when she reached for one of several cereal boxes on a cupboard shelf, she sometimes found she had taken a box other than the one she wanted. She hadn't previously paid much attention to these mistakes, she said, but now she saw them as probable consequences of her deficit. In a later section I will have more to say about AH's failure to recognize the significance of her errors in reaching and other everyday activities prior to the present study.

Telling Time

The impact of AH's perceptual deficit on her daily life was not limited to visually guided reaching. In a series of discussions about her functioning in everyday circumstances, AH reported a variety of other difficulties that probably stemmed from her deficit. In one such discussion she described an error she had made earlier in the day: While walking across the Johns Hopkins campus, she had looked up at the clock tower and was surprised to see that she was 10 minutes late for a 9:00 class. However, when she looked again, she realized that the time on the clock was 10 minutes before the hour, rather than 10 minutes after. Presumably, the initial misreading of the clock resulted from a left–right reflection error in which AH perceived the minute hand at the 10-after rather than the 10-before position.

According to AH, the mistake in reading the campus clock was not an isolated incident; errors like this happened all the time, she said. When she misread the hour hand on a clock or watch, she usually realized her mistake—for example, if she looked at her watch in midmorning and read the time as 2:00, she realized that something was wrong. However, if she misread the minute hand, she sometimes didn't detect the error until later, when she saw that she was early or late for an appointment or event. Occasionally, AH reported, she just couldn't read the time on a clock, even if she looked at it over and over. When this happened, she usually just gave up.

AH stated that her problems with telling time dated from childhood, saying that she had enormous difficulty learning to read clocks and watches. She also recalled that as a child she owned an analogue watch with a downward-pointing triangle at the 12:00 position on the dial. She said that she had enjoyed seeing the watch's minute hand line up with a side of the triangle at 5 minutes before and after the hour, but she always had difficulty knowing whether the hand was at the 5-before or 5-after position.

Tasks 8–3 and 8–4: Oral Naming and Direct Copy of Analogue Clock Times

Results from two tasks confirmed AH's self-report of difficulty with analogue clocks and provided evidence that the difficulty stemmed from her perceptual deficit. Stimuli in both tasks were line drawings of analogue clock faces with hands set to specific times (see Fig. 8–2). Each of the 12 hour positions on the clock face was indicated by a tick mark but not by a number. In the oral naming task AH read aloud the time on the clock, whereas in the direct-copy task she copied the minute and hour hands onto a blank clock face while the stimulus clock remained in view.

AH was severely impaired in both tasks: She was only 58% correct in the oral naming task (14/24) and 50% correct in the direct-copy task (12/24). In both tasks the vast majority of her errors were left–right and/or up–down

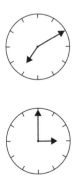

Figure 8–2. Examples of the analogue clock stimuli from Tasks 8–3 and 8–4.

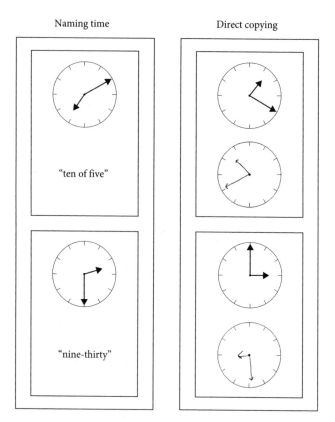

Naming time   Direct copying

"ten of five"

"nine-thirty"

Figure 8–3. Examples of AH's errors in oral naming (Task 8–3) and direct copying (Task 8–4) of analogue clock times.

reflections of one or both hands; Figure 8–3 presents several examples. The oral naming results confirm that AH is impaired in reading analogue clocks. Further, her impaired performance in the direct-copy task and the nature of her errors in both tasks (left–right and up–down reflections) strongly suggest that her clock-reading difficulties stem from her impaired visual location and orientation perception.

Digital Clocks

AH reported that her difficulty telling time was not limited to analogue clocks; digital clocks, she said, also caused her problems because she often seemed to "mix up the numbers." AH's problems with digital clocks probably result from errors in perceiving the orientation and relative location (i.e., ordering) of digits in digital-clock displays. Consistent with this interpretation, AH frequently made digit-orientation and ordering errors in direct copying of Arabic numerals (e.g., 59 → 56, 76 → 67; see Task 2–6).

Compensation

AH compensated for her clock-reading difficulties in a simple and straight-forward manner: She reported that when she wanted to know the time she usually just asked someone. "I don't usually wear a watch anymore," she said. "That way, I can ask people for the time without being embarrassed."

Telephone Numbers

Telephones, AH said, were *very* frustrating. When she looked up a phone number and then tried to dial it, she often made mistakes. "I'm always getting wrong numbers," she told me. "Once I accidentally called Wyoming." AH also reported serious difficulty memorizing phone numbers, including her own. She remembered in particular having trouble learning her new number when she started college at Johns Hopkins. Although everyone makes mistakes with phone numbers occasionally, the problems AH described seemed more severe and more frequent than those experienced by normal individuals. The level of frustration she expressed also suggested an abnormal amount of difficulty.

I had firsthand experience with AH's phone-related problems. At the beginning of the study she gave me her phone number, but when I later tried to call her I discovered that the number was wrong. I consulted the Johns Hopkins student directory and found a different number listed. However, when I called that number, it too turned out to be wrong. I finally obtained the correct number from one of AH's friends. On another occasion a colleague with a phone number similar to mine called to tell me that a student—who turned out to be AH—had left a message for me on his voicemail.

Like her problems with digital clocks, AH's difficulties with phone numbers probably resulted from errors in perceiving the orientations and relative locations of digits. For example, AH's unintended call to Wyoming may have occurred when she looked up the number for one of her friends in northern Virginia (near her family's Maryland home) and misperceived the 703 area code as 307, the code for Wyoming. Impaired perception of digit ordering and orientation could also cause difficulty in learning phone numbers (just as impaired perception of letter ordering and orientation could cause problems in learning to spell, as suggested in Chapter 5).

AH told me she had recently developed a compensatory strategy for keeping the digits in the correct order when she looked at a phone number. She put her two index fingers side-by-side over the number, leaving a space between the fingers just wide enough to show a single digit. By sliding her fingers from left to right over the number she could view the digits one at a time in the proper sequence. She felt that this method helped substantially.

"I Hate Numbers"

AH also described difficulties with numbers in other everyday tasks. She mentioned, for instance, that she often had trouble with price tags when shopping. She had recently bought a blouse with a credit card for what she thought was a price of $46. However, when she examined the receipt after getting home, she realized that the price was actually $64; she had reversed the digits when reading the price tag in the store. The next day she returned the blouse for a refund. Incidents of this sort had happened a number of times, she said.

In fact, AH reported that she had serious problems whenever she encountered numbers. Watching sports on TV, she often misread the scores shown on the screen. When she watched a basketball game, for example, she almost never knew who was winning, and sports scores and statistics in newspapers were similarly difficult.

AH also stated that she was completely unable to read television schedules or movie times in the newspapers and that newspaper or television weather forecasts were very confusing. For example, she might read a high/low temperature report as 65/84 and then realize that these numbers did not make sense. Even if she looked again and saw temperatures that made more sense, such as 68/54, she could not be sure that these numbers were the correct ones.

On one occasion AH and I visited a vending machine while taking a break between tasks during a testing session. The glass-fronted machine displayed snack items (e.g., potato chips) with a number below each (e.g., 21). To obtain the desired item, one had to press the appropriately numbered key on a keypad. AH told me what she wanted and asked me to press the key for her, saying, "I can't work these machines; lots of times I get something different from what I wanted."

According to AH, library call numbers were a nightmare. If she tried to copy down a number from the catalogue, she was likely to get it wrong; and even if she wrote the number accurately, she had trouble finding the book in the stacks because of difficulty reading the numbers on shelves and on the spines of the books. "I always take a friend with me to the library," she said.

Worst of all was math class at school. Despite feeling that she understood the concepts, she made many mistakes when working problems (see, e.g., Fig. 6–3). Her teachers kept telling her that she was making careless errors and admonished her to check her work before turning it in. "I *did* check my work," AH told me rather plaintively, "but it never helped."

"I hate numbers," she added. "I always got stomachaches in math class."

Spelling

I have already discussed AH's spelling impairment at some length and have suggested that the impairment may well be a consequence of her perceptual deficit (see Chapter 5). The point to be made in this chapter is that AH considered her poor spelling to be a significant problem. Her numerous misspellings were embarrassing, she said, and made her appear stupid. The spelling impairment was most often a problem in school but also occasionally affected other aspects of her life. For example, she remembered working one summer at a farm store and being told to make signs showing the names and prices of the various fruits and vegetables. She asked another employee to do the task for her, she said, because her spelling was so bad that she couldn't be confident of writing even simple words like *apple* correctly.

AH attempted to compensate for her spelling difficulties by using a spell checker and sometimes by asking friends to proofread her homework. These measures were somewhat helpful but certainly did not resolve the problem. Neither spell checkers nor friends were available, for example, to help with spelling during in-class exams, and spell checkers do not detect errors in which a word is misspelled as another word. For instance, a spell checker would not have prevented a mistake AH mentioned in one of our discussions: Explaining that she had difficulty spelling the word *angle*, she said, "I once wrote a geometry paper about angels."

Graphs and Diagrams

AH reported great difficulty with graphs and diagrams, especially in school. She stated that she had problems interpreting and drawing graphs in math, science, and economics classes. She also recalled that in her high school physics lab, she often erred in using diagrams to set up experiments. When I asked for examples, she described difficulty with diagrams showing arrangements of pulleys and ropes or ramps facing in particular directions. AH stated that her teachers usually interpreted her mistakes with graphs and diagrams as careless errors and sometimes suggested that to avoid such errors she should work slowly or make her drawings large. These suggestions were not helpful.

Visual Alignment

AH also described problems in everyday situations that required her to perceive the alignment of visual stimuli with one another. She reported having difficulty in stores when the price of a product was on the shelf instead of on the product itself because she had trouble telling which price went with which product. Similarly, at ticket booths in movie theaters she had trouble reading the listings of movies and times posted above the booth. She had difficulty not only in reading the times themselves but also in determining which times went with which movies. Alignment was also a source of difficulty when AH attempted to work multidigit arithmetic problems; she tended to mix up the digits in one column with those in another. During her

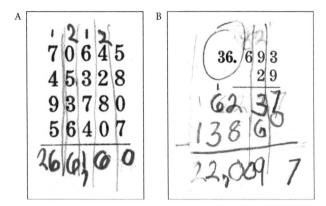

Figure 8–4. Examples from elementary school arithmetic tests in which AH drew lines to separate columns of digits. (A) Addition problem. (B) Multiplication problem. Note the misalignment of the digits in the final answer with the columns above. The correct answer is 20,097.

elementary school years, AH devised (or was taught) the strategy of drawing lines to separate the columns, as illustrated in Figure 8–4. She felt that this strategy was only moderately helpful.

AH's difficulties with visual alignment are readily interpretable in terms of her impaired location perception. For example, misperceiving the locations of products on a shelf and/or the location of price labels on the edge of the shelf would probably lead to errors in matching prices with products. (See Task 3–6 and Fig. 6–4C for errors involving misalignment between the elements of a visual stimulus and the elements of AH's response.)

Getting Dressed

One afternoon AH came into the lab and described a brief confusion that had happened earlier in the day as she was putting on earrings in front of a mirror. She had put on one earring and was looking at herself in the mirror. Seeing the earring on her left ear, she raised the other earring to her right ear but then found that the first earring was there already, rather than on the left as she had thought. Apparently, she had misperceived the location of the earring. Prior to learning of her deficit, she told me, she would have ignored or shrugged off the mistake. Now, however, she was alert to possible perceptual errors, and this one had caught her attention.

AH was inclined to think that similar errors occurred fairly often when she was getting dressed. For example, she remembered incidents in which she put on a shoe and then, while looking at her feet, reached with the other shoe to what she thought was the unshod foot, only to find that the first shoe was already there.

Driving

AH had a driver's license and considered herself an adequate driver. She had been in a few minor accidents, but her driving record was apparently not any worse than that of many other young people. Presumably, AH is able to drive because most visual stimuli critical for driving are moving relative to the driver and AH is able to perceive location and orientation accurately for moving visual stimuli.

AH did, however, report some driving-related problems. For example, she said she had trouble reading street signs with arrows because she was often not confident about which way the arrow was pointing. She mentioned that when she wanted to turn onto a one-way street, she couldn't rely on the one-way sign to tell her whether she was allowed to turn in the desired direction. Instead, she looked down the street to see which way the parked cars were facing. If the headlights of the parked cars were pointed toward her, she knew she couldn't turn in that direction.

Blinking: A General Compensatory Strategy?

During a visit to Johns Hopkins University, Dr. Gabriele Miceli, a neurologist on the faculty of the Università Cattolica in Rome, met AH and spoke with her for several minutes. After the conversation Gabriele remarked that AH blinked her eyes at a higher than normal rate. Having heard about the tasks with flickering stimuli (see Chapter 7), he suggested that AH's high blink rate might be an unconscious adaptation to her perceptual deficit, serving to introduce some flicker into the incoming visual stream. Stated in terms of transient and sustained visual subsystems, blinking could serve to activate AH's intact transient subsystem for stimuli that would otherwise have been processed predominantly by the impaired sustained subsystem.

Examination of videotapes from multiple testing sessions suggested that AH's blink rate might indeed be abnormally high. Regardless of whether she was waiting while I prepared a task, performing the task, or talking with me, she blinked at what appeared to be an unusually high rate and frequently made bursts of several blinks in rapid succession. In order to compare AH's blinking rate with published data on normal rates, I counted blinks from four test sessions during periods in which AH was not performing a task but rather was conversing with me. During these four conversations, which totaled 10.6 minutes, AH blinked on average fifty-nine times per minute, with a range across conversations of fifty-six to sixty-two.[1]

Doughty (2001) reviewed research on normal eye-blink rates, tabulating results from studies conducted over a 75-year period. Combining results across fourteen studies of adults' eye-blink rates during conversation, Doughty arrived at a normal rate of 21.5 ± 5.6 blinks/minute. He concluded that conversational blink rates of about eleven to thirty-three should be considered normal. AH's rate of fifty-nine blinks/minute therefore appears to be far above the normal range (more than six standard deviations above the normal mean). Although definitive conclusions would require comparisons between AH and controls tested under the same conditions, the available evidence strongly suggests that AH blinks her eyes at a higher than normal rate. Another potentially relevant observation is that attempts to use an eye tracker with AH had to be abandoned because she blinked so often that the tracker was unable to maintain a lock on her eye position.

If AH's high blink rate does serve as a compensatory strategy, one might expect her to perform better on visual perception tasks when she blinks than when she does not. Task 8–5 tested this prediction.

Task 8–5: Blinking

An X was presented for 1 second at a left or right location on a computer monitor, and AH responded to the target's location by pressing a left or right key. On each trial a high or low tone was presented, followed 1 second after tone onset by the target X. A high tone signaled AH to blink her eyes continuously, starting as soon as she heard the tone and continuing until after offset of the target stimulus (blink condition); the low tone indicated that AH should refrain from blinking until after target offset (no-blink condition). On half of the trials in each condition the target was displayed steadily, and on the remaining trials the target flickered.

The predictions were straightforward: Flickering stimuli should activate the transient subsystem strongly whether or not AH blinked during stimulus presentation. Accordingly, performance should be good for both the blink and no-blink conditions. For the steady stimuli, however, a blinking effect was expected. In the no-blink condition AH's performance should be poor because the steady, long-duration stimulus should activate predominantly the impaired sustained subsystem, especially in the absence of any blinking. However, in the blink condition performance should be somewhat better because AH's blinking should cause some activation of the intact transient subsystem.

The results were as predicted. Blinking had no effect on AH's localization performance for flickering targets: She was 99% correct in both blink and no-blink conditions. However, for steady targets blinking produced a significant improvement in accuracy: AH was 67% correct (96/144) in the blink condition but only 54% correct (78/144) in the no-blink condition, $\chi^2 (1, n = 288) = 4.70, p < 0.05$. The blinking-related improvement was modest; AH's 67% accuracy for steady stimuli in the blink condition did not approach her 99% accuracy for flickering stimuli. This result is not surprising, given that the blinking rates AH achieved in the task—approximately three or four blinks per second—were much lower than the 20 Hz flicker rate for the flickering stimuli, so probably activated the transient subsystem less strongly.

Caution must be exercised in using the present results as a basis for conclusions about the effects of AH's blinking in daily life, given especially that her blink rate in the laboratory task was higher than her rate under ordinary conditions (apparently about one per second, although with frequent bursts of several per second). Nevertheless, the results of Task 8–5 are certainly consistent with the notion that AH's high blinking rate represents an unconscious strategy for ameliorating her perceptual deficit by increasing activation of her intact transient subsystem.

AH's Functioning in Daily Life: Conclusions

The evidence from AH's self-reports and from the tasks reported in this section supports the assumptions I offered to resolve the apparent discrepancy between the laboratory evidence of a severe perceptual deficit and AH's evidently successful functioning in daily life. First, AH's perceptual deficit does cause problems in many aspects of her daily life, including telling time, using the phone, shopping, and writing. Second, the impact of the deficit is reduced to some extent by an array of compensatory processes, some of which are deliberate (e.g., the strategy for viewing phone numbers one digit at a time) and some of which operate without AH's awareness (e.g., blinking, midcourse corrections in visually guided reaching). In the next section I address the failure of AH and others to identify her perceptual deficit prior to the present study.

Failure to Recognize the Deficit

Many of the points discussed in the preceding section bear on the question of why AH and those around her failed to recognize her perceptual deficit. Because AH's deficit is selective and because she compensates successfully for some of the problems caused by the deficit, she can function at least adequately in most everyday situations. In these situations her deficit would perhaps not be readily apparent. However, given that she does experience significant difficulty in some daily pursuits, the question remains as to why neither she nor her parents, friends, or teachers recognized that her visual perception was abnormal.

The answer, I suggest, is twofold. First, AH, her parents, and her teachers did recognize that she had significant problems in a variety of domains, although they failed to identify the underlying cause of the problems. AH's self-reports indicate that prior to the present study she was well aware of her difficulties with spelling and math. More generally, AH reported feeling throughout her secondary school years that her grades, although adequate, were not as high as they should be given her ability and effort. She stated in particular that although she thought she was as smart as her friends and worked at least as hard, she never seemed to do as well as they did, especially in math and science classes. This sense of underachievement had long been a source of puzzlement and distress to AH. Clearly, then, AH was aware of difficulties in school and elsewhere, although she did not identify impaired visual perception as the source of the problems. (Learning about her perceptual deficit came as a relief to AH, allowing her to make sense of her difficulties in school and elsewhere and to attribute these difficulties to a cause other than lack of intelligence or effort.)

Discussions with AH's parents revealed that they too were aware she had a surprising degree of difficulty with spelling, math, telling time, and some other tasks (e.g., setting the table; see Chapter 6). Like AH, however, they did not identify the cause of the problems. Finally, at least some of AH's teachers recognized that she had more difficulty with some aspects of schoolwork than would be expected given her obviously high intelligence. According to AH and her parents, she was referred for testing in elementary school as a consequence of difficulties with math and received special help with her spelling. Further, in a telephone conversation one of AH's high school teachers told me, "We knew [AH] had a learning disability, and we tried to work around it." Apparently, however, none of AH's teachers suspected an impairment of visual perception.

That AH, her parents, and her teachers failed to pinpoint the cause of her difficulties cannot be considered surprising. AH's most noticeable difficulties (e.g., problems with spelling, math, and telling time) do not immediately suggest a deficit of visual location and orientation perception; such difficulties are more plausibly attributed to a commonplace learning disability than to an exotic perceptual deficit. (Indeed, I tested AH's spelling for many months before coming to suspect a perceptual impairment.) Similarly, errors such as pouring water on the floor when attempting to water a plant or putting stamps on the wrong corners of envelopes could readily be (and were) attributed to carelessness or absent-mindedness.

The fact that AH's perceptual deficit is developmental rather than acquired may also be relevant for understanding why it was not identified—especially by AH herself—prior to the present study. Had AH grown to adulthood with normal visual perception and then acquired her deficit as a consequence of brain damage, she would probably have recognized her misperceptions of location and orientation as abnormal, given that such errors would not have occurred in her premorbid perceptual experience. However, because AH's deficit is developmental, she had no baseline of normal perception to contrast with her abnormal perceptual experiences. Accordingly, AH probably took her perceptual errors for granted, simply accepting these errors and their consequences (e.g., occasionally grasping the wrong sweater or book when reaching) as a normal part of life. If she thought about the errors at all, she probably assumed that everyone made them. Only when she learned about her perceptual deficit through the testing in the present study did she begin to notice perceptual errors in daily life and interpret these errors as effects of the deficit.

These observations suggest more generally that selective developmental deficits in perception or cognition may often go unrecognized even by those who suffer from them. Once a deficit is diagnosed, its symptoms may appear obvious in hindsight; but prior to diagnosis even seemingly blatant signs may be ignored or misinterpreted. Lest this contention appear implausible, I offer three relevant, albeit informal, observations.

First, when a child is diagnosed as dyslexic, it is not uncommon for one or both parents to realize for the first time that they are also dyslexic, their reading difficulties having previously been either unrecognized or attributed to other causes, such as laziness or lack of intelligence.

The second observation comes from my own experience with a congenital color-vision defect. Although I am not entirely colorblind, my color perception is substantially impaired relative to that of individuals with normal color vision. For example, I have difficulty discriminating black from brown shoes, I have trouble telling whether fruits are ripe, I usually cannot perceive the colors of thin lines in graphs, and so on. Nevertheless, I was unaware of my color deficiency until I was in high school, when the abnormality was detected by an ophthalmologist. Before this time I had not only ignored the sorts of symptoms described above but even dismissed my failure at color-vision tests I encountered in books on vision. More than once I had looked at reproductions of Ishihara plates, the circles of colored dots within which individuals with normal color vision can see numerals. When I failed to see the numerals, I did not, as one might expect, conclude that anything was wrong with my color vision. Rather, I assumed that the figures in the book were poor reproductions of the actual test stimuli.

Once my color deficiency was diagnosed, however, I realized why I had difficulty with shoes, fruit, and graphs (as well as tests of color vision). I realized why red objects (e.g., holly berries on a bush, a red bird in a tree) seemed to pop out for other people but not for me, and I realized why I didn't appreciate the beauty of fall foliage.

In retrospect, my failure to recognize the color deficiency seemed difficult to understand. To be sure, I had no experience of normal color vision with which to compare my deficient perceptions. However, I had many opportunities to realize that my color vision differed from that of other people, yet I failed to do so.

My third observation comes from Kay Redfield Jamison's book *An Unquiet Mind*, which describes her battle with serious manic–depressive illness. Although Jamison had suffered from the disorder since childhood, she failed to recognize her condition even when studying psychiatric diagnosis in medical school:

> Despite the fact that we were being taught how to make clinical diagnoses, I still did not make any connection in my own mind between the problems I had experienced and what was described as manic–depressive illness in the textbooks.... I blithely went on

with my clinical training and never put my mood swings into any medical context whatsoever. When I look back on it, my denial and ignorance seem virtually incomprehensible. (Jamison, 1995, pp. 58–59)

Given these observations, AH's failure to identify her perceptual deficit is perhaps not as surprising as it may at first appear.

Conclusions

This chapter posed a paradox: Results from a broad range of perceptual tests demonstrated that AH was severely impaired in visual location and orientation perception, yet she appeared to function normally in everyday life. Furthermore, neither AH nor those around her were aware of her deficit prior to the present study. In attempting to resolve the paradox, I developed several points. First, AH is intact in extracting location and orientation information from certain forms of stimuli (e.g., moving visual stimuli), allowing her to succeed in many everyday tasks. Second, AH's performance in daily life is not, in fact, normal: Her self-reports and the results from laboratory tasks indicate that she encounters difficulty in a variety of circumstances. Third, compensatory processes help to reduce the impact of the deficit. These points, supported by AH's self-reports and data from several tasks, indicate that AH's performance in daily life can be reconciled with the laboratory evidence of a serious perceptual deficit.

With respect to the failure of AH and others to recognize her deficit, I argued that AH, her parents, and her teachers were aware that she experienced difficulty in several cognitive domains (e.g., spelling, numbers, telling time). Although no one identified faulty visual perception as the underlying cause, this failure is unsurprising given that AH's most noticeable difficulties do not immediately suggest a perceptual impairment. Finally, I suggested that AH's own failure to recognize the abnormality of her visual perception may be related to the fact that the deficit is developmental rather than acquired. More generally, individuals may often be unaware of deficits that have been present from birth or early in life, appreciating the significance of the symptoms only after the deficit is formally diagnosed. This point has obvious relevance for efforts to identify and diagnose developmental deficits.

In the next two chapters I address the paradox introduced in the present chapter and the proposed resolution in the context of AH's reading.

9

Does AH's Deficit Affect Her Reading?

The paradox discussed in the preceding chapter arises forcefully in the context of AH's reading. AH claimed to be an excellent reader, stating that she had no difficulty learning to read, that she enjoyed reading, and that she had no difficulty completing her college reading assignments. Further, her academic achievements appeared to bear out these claims. How, though, could she read normally despite a severe deficit in visual location and orientation perception? Or, if her reading was impaired, why were she and others not aware of the impairment?

In this chapter and the next I describe a detailed study of AH's reading, carried out in collaboration with Brenda Rapp (McCloskey & Rapp, 2000a). In the present chapter I first show that, contrary to appearances, AH's reading is far from normal: When tested with appropriately chosen tasks, she shows clear and dramatic impairment. Next, I present strong evidence that AH's impaired reading performance is caused by her deficit in visual location and orientation perception. Then, in the following chapter, I consider how AH is apparently able to read successfully in daily life and why she and others were unaware of her reading difficulties. I argue that the answers lie in sophisticated compensatory processes developed and applied without AH's awareness.

General Procedures

Brenda Rapp and I tested AH's reading in a variety of tasks with stimuli ranging from single words to paragraphs. All tasks were nonspeeded; that is,

AH was under no pressure to respond quickly. Except where otherwise indicated, the stimulus on each trial remained in view until AH completed her response. In some tasks the stimuli were presented on paper, printed in Times Roman, Century Schoolbook, or Courier font ranging in size from 12 to 24 points. (These variations had no discernible effect on AH's performance.) In other tasks the stimuli were presented on a computer monitor in a sans serif font, as white characters on a dark background. Unless otherwise indicated, stimuli were presented in lowercase characters and centered on the page or computer monitor. AH viewed the computer displays in a lighted room from a distance of approximately 40 cm. At this distance each character subtended approximately 0.5° of visual angle horizontally and between 0.5° and 1° vertically.

For some of the tasks presented to AH normal control participants were also tested. These participants were undergraduate students at Johns Hopkins University, matched to AH in age and educational level.

Impaired Reading Performance

In a preliminary exploration of AH's reading we asked her to read aloud individual words and sequences of unrelated words.

Task 9–1: Reading Aloud Individual Words

Stimuli were the names of 144 concrete objects selected from the Snodgrass and Vanderwart (1980) pictures (e.g., *sun, envelope, crown, refrigerator*). AH was 100% correct (144/144) in naming the pictures orally, demonstrating that she was familiar with the stimulus words and able to produce them in spoken form.

The words, which varied in length from three to twelve letters, were presented on paper one at a time in random order, and AH read each word aloud. The stimulus list was presented three times, once in each of three testing sessions. Four control participants each read the words aloud once; these participants collectively made one error in 576 trials (0.2%).

AH, however, erred on fifty-three of 432 trials (12%) across the three presentations of the list. The fifty-three errors were distributed over thirty-nine of the 144 stimulus words: twenty-eight words were misread once, eight were misread twice, and three elicited errors on all three presentations. On some trials AH hesitated noticeably before producing a response. However, most responses, both correct and erroneous, were made without hesitation and AH usually seemed unaware of her errors.

Table 9–1 presents examples of AH's erroneous responses. As the examples illustrate, AH's errors were not restricted to low-frequency words such as *anchor*; she also misread short, high-frequency words such as *dog, pen,*

Table 9-1. Examples of AH's Errors in Reading Words Aloud

Stimulus	Response
dog	bog
pen	den
lamp	lamb
snail	nails
chain	cabin
hand	band
nose	noise
church	cherish
apple	appeal

and *hand*. All of the erroneous response words were visually similar to the corresponding stimulus words.

Impaired performance in reading words aloud could conceivably arise from a deficit affecting any of the cognitive processes required by the task. For example, errors could occur in constructing visual or orthographic representations of a stimulus word, recognizing the word by matching the stimulus representation to a stored lexical–orthographic representation of a familiar word, retrieving semantic information about the word, or accessing the phonological representation needed to generate a spoken response.

Task 9–2: Reading and Defining Words

In an effort to narrow the range of possibilities, we asked AH to define words as she read them aloud. The question of interest was whether definitions for words read incorrectly would correspond to the stimulus or instead to the erroneous response. For example, if AH read *dog* as "bog," would she define the former or the latter? A definition corresponding to the stimulus *dog* would suggest that AH matched the stimulus word to the correct lexical representation and accessed the appropriate semantic information but erred in some subsequent process (e.g., retrieving the phonological form of the word). In contrast, a definition appropriate to the response word *bog* would indicate that processing had gone awry prior to accessing the word's meaning, perhaps in constructing a visual or orthographic representation of the visual stimulus or in matching the stimulus representation to the stored representation of a familiar word.

Stimuli were the 144-word list used in the previous word-reading task and a list of ninety-two common nouns varying in length from three to eight letters. In one presentation of each list AH read the word aloud and then gave a brief definition. In a second presentation of the ninety-two-word list AH first gave the definition and then read the word aloud.

Table 9-2. Examples of AH's errors in reading and defining words

Stimulus	Reading Response	Definition
dog	bog	Murky swamp
bone	done	When an activity is completed
pig	dig	To make a hole in the earth
star	tars	When someone puts tar on something
rib	rip	To tear
sun	nuns	Catholic women who have given certain vows
skirt	skit	Very short play, usually without props or costumes
dust	dusk	Time of day just after the sun sets

The results demonstrated clearly that AH's word-reading errors arose prior to accessing the meaning of the word. Collapsing across lists, AH made reading errors on seventy-five of the 328 trials (23%), and in all cases her definition matched her erroneous reading response. For example, she read *bread* as "beard" and gave the definition "man's facial hair." (See Table 9-2 for additional examples.) Twenty-one of the reading errors with corresponding incorrect definitions occurred in the define-then-read presentation of the ninety-two-word list, ruling out the possibility that errors in defining words occurred only because AH was confused by hearing her incorrect reading response.

As one would expect, AH's definitions also matched her reading responses for words she read accurately: She gave an adequate definition for 251 of the 253 words she read correctly (99%).

Task 9-3: Reading Aloud Word Sequences

In this experiment AH read aloud sequences of four unrelated words (e.g., *peacock comet napkin dolphin*) presented in a horizontal row on a computer monitor. Twenty sequences were created from eighty nouns of five to seven letters. Words with salient visually similar neighbors were avoided in order to minimize AH's difficulty with individual words. Words were assigned randomly to sequences and to positions within sequences. Two blocks of twenty trials were presented, with each word sequence appearing once in each block.

On two-thirds of the trials (27/40) AH read the words out of sequence (e.g., *peacock comet napkin dolphin* → "peacock napkin comet dolphin"). All but one of the errors involved transposition of adjacent words. In addition to the ordering errors, AH misread thirteen of the 160 individual words (e.g., *recipe* → "receipt"). On most trials AH read the word sequence fluently and seemed unaware that she was making errors.

Reading and the Visual Deficit

AH's errors in reading words and word sequences seemed likely to have resulted from her deficit in visual location and orientation perception. Many of her word-reading errors took the form of letter-orientation confusions (e.g., *rib* → "rip," *bone* → "done," *pig* → "dig") or letter-sequence confusions (e.g., *snail* → "nails," *bread* → "beard").[1] These errors may be interpreted by assuming that AH sometimes misperceived the orientation or relative location (i.e., ordering) of the letters in the stimulus words. Also, AH's stored lexical–orthographic representations may be deficient, as a consequence of perceptual errors occurring from the time she began learning to read. For example, AH's lexical representations for *rib* and/or *rip* may fail to specify unambiguously whether the last letter is *b* or *p*, and her representations for *bread* and/or *beard* may be indeterminate with respect to the ordering of the letters. Such deficiencies in lexical–orthographic representations could contribute to letter-orientation or letter-sequence errors in reading.[2]

Finally, the word-sequence errors observed in Task 9–3 (e.g., *bakery juice airline galaxy* → "bakery juice galaxy airline") suggest that AH often misperceives the relative locations of words in a sequence, leading to misrepresentations of word order. AH's impaired visual location and orientation perception may, then, affect her reading in several ways.

Although the data from the word- and word sequence–reading tasks are suggestive, they do not constitute definitive evidence that AH's visual localization deficit was the cause of her impaired performance on the tasks. For example, we cannot rule out the possibility that errors such as *rib* → "rip" occurred for reasons other than misperception of letter orientation. To explore more systematically the relationship between AH's localization deficit and her reading, we carried out a number of experiments in which she read aloud words and word sequences. The rationale for these experiments was straightforward: If AH's reading errors were caused by her perceptual deficit, then her reading performance should show effects of visual variables (e.g., exposure duration) comparable to the effects observed in tasks with nonverbal visual stimuli (see Chapter 7). We tested AH's reading performance with brief and flickering stimuli, predicting that these manipulations would improve her ability to perceive the orientation and ordering of letters within words and the ordering of words in word sequences. (Brief exposures and flicker were not expected, however, to resolve any deficiencies that might be present in AH's stored lexical–orthographic representations.) In one experiment we also manipulated letter case (i.e., upper vs. lower case), predicting that AH's error pattern would reflect differences in visual form between some uppercase letters and their lowercase counterparts (e.g., misperception of letter orientation could lead to confusion of *b* with *d* but not of *B* with *D*).

The report on these experiments is organized as follows:

Reading Single Words
Task 9–4   Upper vs. lower case
Task 9–5   Brief vs. long exposure duration
Task 9–6   Steady vs. flickering displays
Reading Word Sequences
Task 9–7   Brief vs. long exposure duration
Task 9–8   Steady vs. flickering displays

Reading Aloud Single Words

Task 9–4: Reading Aloud Upper- and Lowercase Words

In this task AH was presented with words for which letter-orientation or letter-sequence errors could lead to confusion with another word. For example, the orientation-critical word *duck* could be confused with *buck* or *puck* if the orientation of the *b* were misrepresented, and the sequence-critical word *saw* could be confused with *was* if the ordering of letters were misrepresented.

Words were presented in both upper and lower case. For most words we expected case to have little or no effect on AH's performance. However, because some letters are orientation-critical only in lower case, some stimulus words were orientation-critical in lower, but not upper, case. For example, lowercase *duck* is orientation-critical but uppercase *DUCK* is not. Whereas the *d* in *duck* might be confused with *b* or *p*, the *D* in *DUCK* should not be confused with any other letter even if its orientation is misperceived. Hence, we expected words that were orientation-critical only in lower case to elicit letter-orientation errors with lower-, but not upper-, case presentation, leading to higher error rates for the lowercase forms.

Method

Stimuli were eighty words ranging in length from three to twelve letters. Forty of the words were orientation-critical in lower case. Of these, ten were also orientation-critical in upper case (e.g., *WAIL*) and thirty were not (e.g., *DUCK*). Twenty words (e.g., *saw*) were sequence-critical (in both upper and lower case), and the remaining twenty words were fillers (e.g., *curve*). The eighty words were randomly divided into two sets of forty—sets A and B—with the constraint that half of the words of each type were assigned to each set.

Words were presented in random order on a computer monitor and remained in view until AH responded. Four blocks of eighty trials were presented over two testing sessions. In blocks 1 and 4 the set A words were in lower case and the set B words were in upper case; in blocks 2 and 3 the assignment of word sets to upper and lower case was reversed.

Results and Discussion

For lowercase stimuli AH's error rate was 27% (43/160). Letter-orientation errors (e.g., *bill* → "pill," *dean* → "bean," *wink* → "mink") occurred on twenty-five of the eighty orientation-critical trials (31%), and one error on a sequence-critical word (*pets* → "debts") apparently involved an orientation confusion. Letter-sequence confusions (e.g., *saw* → "was," *spot* → "pots") were observed on eight of the forty sequence-critical trials (20%) as well as on one of the orientation-critical trials (*lips* → "lisp"). AH also made eight additional visually similar word errors on lowercase stimuli (e.g., *thorough* → "through").

For uppercase stimuli AH's error rate was 15% (24/160), reliably lower than the 27% rate for lowercase stimuli, $t(79) = 2.61$, $p < 0.05$. Letter-orientation errors (e.g., *MADE* → "wade") occurred on four of the twenty orientation-critical trials (20%), and letter-sequence errors (e.g., *BOARD* → "broad," *SILVER* → "sliver") were observed for seven of the forty sequence-critical trials (18%). AH also made thirteen additional errors (e.g., *PETS* → "pits"), one of which (*FRIEND* → "fired") may have resulted in part from a letter-sequence confusion.

For the words that were orientation-critical in lower, but not upper, case, AH's error rate was 35% (21/60) with lowercase presentation but only 8% (5/60) with uppercase presentation, $t(29) = 3.40$, $p < 0.01$. Seventeen of the twenty-one lowercase errors (81%) were letter-orientation confusions. These findings argue strongly that at least some of AH's word-reading errors arose in processing the visual forms of letters and specifically that some of the errors resulted from misrepresentations of letter orientation. More generally, the results for the orientation-critical items, in conjunction with the finding that AH made a substantial number of letter-sequence errors (e.g., *saw* → "was"), support the assumption that AH's impairment in reading words aloud is due at least in part to her deficit in visual location and orientation perception.

Task 9–5: Exposure Duration

In this experiment AH read aloud lowercase words presented for either 90 milliseconds (brief-exposure condition) or 1000 milliseconds (long-exposure condition).

Method

Stimulus lists were constructed from seventy-two word pairs: forty-eight orientation-critical pairs (e.g., *mall* and *wall*) and twenty-four sequence-critical pairs (e.g., *arid* and *raid*). Individual words ranged in length from three to seven letters.

Two blocks of randomly intermixed brief- and long-exposure trials were presented. In the first block one word from each pair was presented in the brief-exposure condition and the other word was presented in the long-exposure condition; in the second block the assignment of words to exposure conditions was reversed. Procedures were otherwise the same as in Task 9–4.

Results and Discussion

AH's word reading showed the same effect of exposure duration observed with nonverbal visual stimuli: Her error rate was 24% (34/144) in the long-exposure condition but only 9% (13/144) in the brief-exposure condition, $\chi^2(1, n = 288) = 11.21, p < 0.001$.

In the long-exposure condition AH made twenty-one letter-orientation errors (e.g., *bell* → "dell," *mind* → "wind"), eight letter-sequence errors (e.g., *arm* → "ram," *raid* → "arid"), and five other visually similar word errors (e.g., *cub* → "club"). In the brief-exposure condition five of AH's thirteen errors were letter-orientation confusions and four were letter-sequence confusions. On three of the remaining four error trials she indicated that the stimulus presentation had been too brief for her to identify the word.

The finding of improved reading performance with brief exposures supports the hypothesis that AH's word-reading errors under normal reading conditions occur at least in part because her perceptual deficit causes her to misperceive the orientation and ordering of letters when she looks at a word.

Task 9–6: Flicker

In this experiment AH read aloud individual words presented either continuously (steady condition) or flickering (flicker condition). Stimuli and procedures were the same as in Task 9–5, except that the flicker condition replaced the brief-exposure condition. In both conditions the stimulus words were presented for 1000 milliseconds. The flickering displays were created by turning the stimulus on and off at 50-millisecond intervals throughout the display interval.

Results and Discussion

The effects of flicker were even more dramatic than those of exposure duration: AH's error rate was 23% in the steady condition (33/144) but only 1% (1/144) in the flicker condition, $\chi^2(1, n = 288) = 34.15, p < 0.001$. In the steady condition she made twenty-six letter-orientation errors (e.g., *wound* → "mound"), two letter-sequence errors (e.g., *alter* → "later"), and five other errors. The single error in the flicker condition was a letter-orientation confusion.

Taken together, the effects of case, exposure duration, and flicker provide strong evidence that AH's word-reading impairment stems from her visual localization deficit.

Reading Aloud Word Sequences

These experiments explored the effects of exposure duration and flicker on AH's performance in reading aloud sequences of unrelated words. We predicted that brief exposures and flicker would improve her ability to produce the words in the correct order.

Task 9–7: Exposure Duration

In this experiment AH read aloud two-word sequences presented in brief- (90 milliseconds) or long- (1500 milliseconds) exposure conditions.

Method

The seventy-two stimulus sequences (e.g., *ant hat*) were generated by taking all possible pairs of nine three-letter words (*ant, egg, fox, hat, key, log, rim, set, van*). (We used short words and short sequences to ensure that the entire stimulus could be perceived in a brief exposure.)

Three blocks of 144 trials were presented. In each block the seventy-two word pairs occurred once in the brief-exposure condition and once in the long-exposure condition. Pairs were presented in random order, with brief- and long-exposure trials intermixed. On each trial the stimulus words were arrayed horizontally, with two character spaces between words.

Results and Discussion

In the long-exposure condition AH made word-sequence errors (*fox ant → ant fox*) on fifty-five of the 216 trials (25%). In the brief-exposure condition, however, she made only one sequence error (0.5%), t (71) = 9.87, $p < 0.001$.

In addition to the word-sequence confusions AH made five other errors. In four of these (two in each condition) AH replaced one of the words with another word from the nine-word pool (e.g., *key ant →* "log ant"). In the fifth error, occurring in the brief-exposure condition, AH reported that she had not seen the stimulus sequence.

Task 9–8: Flicker

In this experiment AH read aloud five-word sequences presented in steady and flicker conditions.

Method

Two hundred nouns of four to seven letters were used to construct forty random sequences of five words (e.g., *earth paint puzzle chemical muscle*).

An effort was made to avoid orientation- and sequence-critical words. Words were assigned randomly to sequences and to positions within sequences.

Two blocks of forty trials were presented, with flicker and steady trials randomly intermixed within blocks. In the first block twenty sequences were presented in the steady condition, and the remaining twenty were presented in the flicker condition; in the second block the assignment of sequences to conditions was reversed. On each trial the stimulus sequence remained in view until AH completed her response.

Results and Discussion

In the steady condition AH made word-sequence errors (e.g., *figure soccer circle knife cactus* → "figure circle knife soccer cactus") on fully thirty-three of the forty trials (84%). In the flicker condition, however, she made only one word-sequence error (3%), $\chi^2(1, n = 80) = 52.4, p < 0.001$.

Tasks 9–7 and 9–8 demonstrate that AH's word-sequence reading shows the same effects of exposure duration and flicker observed in visual location and orientation tasks with nonverbal stimuli. These results argue strongly that her word-sequence errors, like her letter-naming and word-reading errors, arise from her visual localization deficit.

Conclusions

Although AH's academic achievements and self-report suggested normal reading comprehension, Tasks 9–1 through 9–3 showed her to be profoundly impaired in reading aloud isolated words and sequences of unrelated words. The nature of her errors suggested that her perceptual deficit might be responsible. In particular, AH might frequently misperceive the orientation and ordering of letters and the ordering of words, leading to letter-orientation confusions (e.g., *box* → "pox"), letter-sequence confusions (e.g., *snail* → "nails"), and word-sequence confusions (e.g., *shore lemon picnic fabric* → "lemon shore picnic fabric").

To test this interpretation, we carried out five additional experiments in which AH read aloud letters, words, and word sequences. Task 9–4 showed that when accurate perception of letter orientation was critical for identifying an isolated word presented in lower case (e.g., *duck*) but not in upper case (e.g., *DUCK*), AH's performance was much worse for the lowercase form. Experiments 9–5 and 9–6 showed further that two visual variables—exposure duration and flicker—had the same effects in single-word reading as in tasks with nonverbal visual stimuli. In particular, AH's performance in reading words aloud was dramatically better for brief than for long exposures and for flickering than for continuous displays. Tasks 9–7 and 9–8 demonstrated that brief exposure or flicker virtually eliminated AH's word-ordering errors in the word-sequence reading task. These results provide compelling evidence that AH's deficit in perceiving the location and orientation of visual stimuli affects her processing of words and word sequences in reading tasks: When AH looks at a word under ordinary presentation conditions (i.e., long exposures with steady illumination), she frequently misperceives the orientation and ordering of letters; and when she looks at word sequences, she frequently misperceives word order.

One question left unanswered by the present experiments is whether AH's word-reading errors result entirely from misperception of the stimulus words or whether deficiencies in stored lexical–orthographic representations also play a role. Her low error rates in reading single words under brief exposure (9%) and especially flicker conditions (1%) may seem to suggest that her stored lexical representations are adequate to support good performance when stimulus words are accurately perceived. However, the stimuli in these tasks were not chosen with the aim of probing AH's stored orthographic representations. For example, most were highly regular (e.g., *beep*, *rob*); that is, the pronunciation was entirely predictable from the spelling. Regular words, if accurately perceived, can be read aloud correctly by sublexical orthography-to-phonology conversion processes (i.e., by sounding the words out) without reference to lexical representations. Hence, good performance on regular words does not necessarily imply normal lexical–orthographic representations.[3]

Despite the fact that questions about AH's lexical–orthographic representations remain unanswered, the results presented in this chapter provide the first piece of a resolution to the paradox posed by AH's apparently normal reading: AH's reading is not normal, and the abnormalities are directly attributable to her perceptual deficit. The findings presented in the next chapter provide the remaining pieces of the puzzle.

10

How Does AH Succeed at Reading?

The evidence presented in Chapter 9 demonstrates that AH's visual localization deficit dramatically affects her reading, at least for individual words
and sequences of unrelated words. How, then, can she achieve apparently
normal reading comprehension in her daily life and academic endeavors?
And how could she, her parents, and her teachers have been unaware of her
reading problems? In this chapter I show that the answers to these questions
lie in sophisticated compensatory processes developed and applied without
AH's awareness.

Knowledge-Based Constraints in Reading

In comprehending words, sentences, or text, normal readers rely not only on
the visual information extracted from the stimulus itself but also on knowledge
of the regularities present at many levels in written language (e.g., Foss, 1982;
Morris, 1994; Morris & Folk, 1998; O'Seagdha, 1989, 1997; Potter, Moryadas,
Abrams, & Noel, 1993; Potter, Stiefbold, & Moryadas, 1998; Rayner, Pacht, &
Duffy, 1994; Sharkey & Sharkey, 1992; Tabossi, 1988; West & Stanovich, 1986;
Williams, 1988; Wright & Garrett, 1984). Consider the following sequence of
words from a hypothetical sentence: *the horse's hoo_*. Knowledge of English
orthography suggests that the missing letter is very unlikely to be a vowel,
although it could be any of a number of consonants. Syntactic knowledge
indicates that the incomplete word may be a noun, adjective, or adverb;
lexical–orthographic knowledge suggests more specifically that the word

may be *hoot, hoof,* or *hoop*; and general world knowledge suggests that *hoof* is the most likely candidate. These and other sorts of knowledge may facilitate comprehension by imposing (typically probabilistic) constraints on the interpretation of information from the stimulus itself. I will refer to these constraints as "knowledge-based constraints."

Several points of clarification may be in order here. First, I do not intend to suggest that the use of knowledge-based constraints—either by normal readers or by AH—is a conscious problem-solving process or even that the knowledge exploited is necessarily available to awareness. Second, although I draw a distinction between knowledge-based constraints and stimulus information, applying knowledge-based constraints in interpreting some stimulus element (e.g., a word or phrase) often involves the use of information about other elements of the stimulus (e.g., neighboring words or phrases). Third, I use the term *knowledge-based constraints* rather than the seemingly more straightforward *contextual constraints* because some constraints that could conceivably be brought to bear are not contextual in the usual sense of the term (e.g., constraints based on knowledge of simple letter or word frequencies).

In the normal reader application of knowledge-based constraints may occasionally lead to misrepresentation of stimulus elements that are improbable in context, as when one fails to detect misspellings or syntactic anomalies in proofreading. However, stimulus information is usually weighted heavily enough that accurate internal representations are generated even for low-probability stimuli (e.g., *the horse's hoop*).

For AH, I suggest, the situation is somewhat different. Because of her visual localization deficit, the stimulus representations generated by her visual system are unreliable: The orientations of letters, ordering of letters, and ordering of words are frequently misrepresented (and presumably have been since the time of her first exposure to written language). The situation AH faces in reading may therefore be similar to that of a hypothetical normal individual who, from his or her first encounter with written language, was exposed only to error-ridden material such as the following:

> *Stupents exhibiting disruptive pehavior be may evlauated learning fro disaqiliites.*

Under these circumstances, AH's reading processes may have developed in such a way as to place less than normal weight on visual stimulus information and greater than normal weight on knowledge-based constraints. More specifically, I propose that AH's reading mechanisms in essence assume that the material being processed is well-formed and meaningful (even when the representations provided by the visual system indicate otherwise) and further that these mechanisms skillfully exploit constraints at multiple levels (e.g., orthographic, syntactic, semantic) to arrive at a coherent interpretation that is as consistent as possible with the stimulus information. On this account the visual stimulus representations are treated as informative but potentially unreliable clues.

When strong knowledge-based constraints can be brought to bear—as is typically the case with meaningful sentences and text—AH's reading processes may usually be able to recover from the errors introduced by her visual system. (Consider, for example, that the distorted sentence in the above example may be "decoded" without too much effort, yielding *Students exhibiting disruptive behavior may be evaluated for learning disabilities.*) However, when the knowledge-based constraints are weaker—as for words presented out of context or word sequences lacking syntactic structure or semantic coherence—AH's reading processes may be unable to overcome her visual system's errors.

I have no specific proposal to offer about how AH's reading processes combine stimulus information and knowledge-based constraints in arriving at an interpretation. Nevertheless, the knowledge-based constraints hypothesis provides at least a general account of both AH's apparently normal reading comprehension under high-constraint conditions and her severely impaired performance when the constraints are few and weak. The hypothesis also makes some interesting predictions, which Brenda Rapp and I tested in several experiments (McCloskey & Rapp, 2000a). However, before reporting these experiments, I discuss AH's errors in reading individual words, suggesting that the knowledge-based constraints hypothesis may explain some aspects of the error pattern that do not follow obviously from her visual localization deficit.

AH's Word-Reading Errors

Collapsing over the various tasks in which AH read individual lowercase words under ordinary conditions (i.e., long exposures of nonflickering stimuli), she made a total of 238 errors. Ninety-five of these errors (40%) were pure letter-orientation confusions (e.g., *dear* → "bear") and twenty-two (9%) were pure letter-sequence confusions (e.g., *mar* → "ram"). One hundred eight of the errors (45%) were other types of visually similar word errors: letter deletions (e.g., *finger* → "finer"), letter insertions (e.g., *nose* → "noise"), and letter substitutions (e.g., *ship* → "snip"). The remaining thirty-two errors (13%) appeared to involve two or more of the above error types (e.g., *sled* → "sleep," *shoulder* → "shudder").

The letter-orientation and letter-sequence confusions may be interpreted by assuming that an orientation or sequence error introduced by AH's visual system resulted in a stimulus representation corresponding not to the stimulus word (e.g., *bone*) but instead to a different word (e.g., *done*). However, some aspects of the error pattern cannot be interpreted so straightforwardly. Most notable among these is the finding that all of AH's erroneous responses were words. Clearly, we cannot assume that the errors introduced by her visual system always, or even usually, transformed the stimulus word into another word; presumably, the visual-system errors often resulted in a representation not corresponding exactly to any word (e.g., *finegr* for the stimulus *finger*, *slep* for *sled*, *rbother* for *brother*). Why, then, did AH never produce nonword responses or report that a stimulus was a nonpronounceable letter string?

The knowledge-based constraint hypothesis suggests a possible answer: AH's word-recognition process implicitly assumes that any letter string encountered in reading is a familiar word and selects as a match for the stimulus word the most strongly activated entry in the orthographic lexicon, even when this entry does not fully match the stimulus representation. By accepting imperfect matches, the word-recognition process would probably often succeed in correctly identifying a stimulus word even if the representation generated by the visual system contained letter-orientation or letter-sequence errors. However, in some instances, the erroneous representation of a stimulus word might most closely match the lexical entry for a different word, leading to an error.

This interpretation accounts for the finding that all of AH's errors were words and may also explain why approximately half of the errors were visually similar word errors other than letter-orientation and letter-sequence confusions (e.g., *finger* → "finer," *sled* → "sleep"). If, for example, a letter-sequence error in the visual processing of *finger* resulted in the stimulus representation *finegr*, the word-recognition process might match this representation with the lexical entry for *finer* rather than the entry for *finger*; similarly, the stimulus representation *slep* might activate the lexical entry for *sleep* more strongly than the entry for *sled*.[1]

The interpretation also makes a prediction about AH's performance on lexical decision tests, in which letter strings (e.g., *solve*, *plesty*) must be classified as words or nonwords. If her word-recognition processes are biased toward accepting letter strings as words—even when these strings do not perfectly match entries in the orthographic lexicon—then she should show a particular pattern of impairment in lexical decision. For word stimuli (e.g., *crime*), AH should perform well, categorizing these stimuli as words with high accuracy. Even if her perceptual deficit introduced letter-orientation or letter-sequence errors, the stimulus representation should usually match a lexical entry well enough to be accepted as a word. However, for nonword stimuli (e.g., *crame*) AH should perform poorly, frequently classifying these letter strings as words. Even if a nonword stimulus (e.g., *fanal*) were not likely to be transformed into a word by a letter-orientation or letter-sequence error, AH's word-recognition processes—biased toward accepting imperfect matches to lexical entries—should frequently "recognize" it as a word. She might show less bias toward accepting imperfect matches in a lexical decision test, where her task is specifically to discriminate between words and nonwords, than in ordinary reading, where she can assume that almost all of the letter strings are words. However, unless she could completely eliminate the habitual bias toward accepting imperfect matches between perceived letter strings and stored lexical entries, she should show higher than normal error rates for nonword stimuli.

Task 10–1: Lexical Decision

This prediction was tested in a yes–no lexical decision task in which letter strings were presented one at a time and AH classified each as a word or a nonword.

Method

Stimuli were 240 matched pairs of letter strings, each consisting of a word (e.g., *CACTUS*) and a pronounceable nonword created by substituting a single letter in the word with a different letter (e.g., *CAFTUS*). No special effort was made to create nonwords that would be confusable with words via letter-orientation or letter-sequence confusions (e.g., by substituting *W* for *M*). Further, letter strings were presented in upper case to minimize letter-orientation confusions.

The 480 stimuli were divided into two sets, each consisting of 120 word and 120 nonword stimuli. The word (e.g., CACTUS) and nonword (e.g., CAFTUS) from each matched pair were assigned to different sets. One of the 240-item sets was presented in each of two testing sessions. Ordering of the stimuli within each set was random.

Results

The results showed the predicted pattern. AH was 99% correct (237/240) for the word stimuli. However, for the nonwords she was only 52% correct (125/240), categorizing nearly half of these stimuli as words. She erroneously classified as words not only nonword stimuli that could have been transformed into words by letter-orientation or sequence errors (e.g., *MEAVE, HUST*) but also nonwords that her perceptual deficit was unlikely to make into words (e.g., *CAFTUS, FANAL*).

Collapsing the results over word and nonword stimuli makes clear that AH was, as predicted, strongly biased toward accepting written letter strings as words. Overall she categorized 73% of the stimuli (352/480) as words, even though only half were actually words. However, at least in the context of lexical decision, the bias was not total: AH classified 27% of the stimuli as nonwords.

Another point emerging from the results is that AH does have some ability to distinguish words from nonwords: She was much more likely to accept word stimuli than nonword stimuli as words, placing 99% of the word stimuli, but only 48% of the nonword stimuli, in the "word" category. This result makes perfect sense. As long as AH does not accept every letter string as a word, she should be more likely to accept words than nonwords because word stimuli should usually match stored lexical entries more closely than do nonword stimuli. Word stimuli may sometimes match lexical entries imperfectly due to letter-orientation or letter-sequence errors introduced by AH's perceptual deficit. However, nonword stimuli not only are subject to these perceptual errors but also mismatch lexical entries in some other way. For example, the nonwords in the present experiment (e.g., *FANAL*) mismatched lexical entries due to the letter substitutions that produced the nonwords from words, over and above any errors introduced by AH's perceptual deficit.[2]

Whereas the lexical decision experiment addressed AH's general bias to accept letter strings as words, the following experiments were aimed more specifically at testing the hypothesis that AH's reading processes automatically repair the sorts of errors introduced by her perceptual deficit.

Task 10–2: Reading Paragraphs

In this experiment AH read aloud brief paragraphs adapted from various works of fiction and nonfiction. Paragraphs in the normal condition were syntactically correct and semantically coherent. However, for paragraphs in the sequence-altered condition several syntactic errors were introduced by transposing adjacent words, as in the following example:

> The policeman always sat on his horse halfway up the first block
> from subway the station. For as many mornings as he remember
> could Arthur had always and stopped given the horse three sugar
> cubes. The horse had learned to him recognize and always pawed
> at the curb and stretched out his eagerly neck at Arthur's approach.
> It was the nicest in thing Arthur's day.

AH's task was to read each paragraph as it was written. The principal prediction was that she would frequently restore the transposed words to a syntactically acceptable order when reading the sequence-altered paragraphs (e.g., *he remember could* → "he could remember"). The basis for this prediction is straightforward: Unless AH's reading processes can somehow distinguish a word-sequence error actually present in a text from a word-sequence error introduced by her visual system, the former as well as the latter should frequently be repaired.

Method

Stimuli were ten normal and ten sequence-altered paragraphs, each printed on a separate page. The two sets of paragraphs were matched in number of words and number of sentences. Individual paragraphs ranged in length from sixty-one to ninety-four words and included four to eight sentences. In each of the ten sequence-altered paragraphs six pairs of adjacent words were transposed to create syntactically unacceptable word sequences. In all sixty transpositions the two transposed words were in the same sentence, and in fifty-eight of the transpositions the two words appeared on the same line in the printed paragraph.

The ten normal paragraphs were presented first, followed by the ten sequence-altered paragraphs. (This presentation order was adopted to exclude the possibility that reading of normal paragraphs would be influenced by recognition that some paragraphs had errors.) AH was instructed to read each paragraph aloud as it was written; no mention was made of errors in the texts. Five control participants were also tested.

Results and Discussion

Considering first the normal paragraphs, control participants read these paragraphs at a mean rate of 219 words/minute (wpm), with rates for individual participants ranging from 196 to 232 wpm. The control participants made an average of 11.8 reading errors across the ten paragraphs; for individual participants the number of errors ranged from one to twenty-three. The errors included word omissions, word insertions, and misreadings of individual words; in the vast majority of cases the errors did not significantly alter the meaning of the text.

AH's reading speed for the normal paragraphs—227 wpm—fell within the control range. However, she made forty-seven reading errors, four times the control participants' mean and over twice the control participants' maximum. AH's errors included nine word omissions (e.g., *he had played with them and had come to know* → "he had played with them and come to know"), nine word insertions (e.g., *as if* → "just as if"), and eleven misreadings of individual words (e.g., *sleeping* → "sleepy"). These types of errors occurred at roughly three times the control-participant rate.

However, the most striking difference between AH's errors and those of the controls involved word-sequence confusions. AH made eighteen errors of this type, most involving words whose order was not tightly constrained by context (e.g., *speed and determination* → "determination and speed," *fine, yellowed marble* → "yellowed, fine marble," *large and dark and cool* → "dark, cool, and large"). Control participants, in contrast, averaged 1.8 word-sequence errors, and none of these participants made more than four. AH's errors, like those of the control participants, in most cases did not substantially alter the meaning of the text. Therefore, her comprehension may well have been good despite her higher than normal error rate.

Nevertheless, AH's ability to read material verbatim is clearly not normal, even for connected text. This finding meshes well with the knowledge-based constraint hypothesis. In the case of coherent paragraphs, the available constraints may usually be sufficient to allow a reasonably accurate interpretation—in particular, an interpretation that preserves the meaning—to be generated from distorted visual representations. However, a fully accurate verbatim reconstruction may not always be possible (as in the case of underdetermined word orders like *large and dark and cool*).

Turning now to the sequence-altered paragraphs, control participants read these paragraphs at an average speed of 175 wpm, 44 wpm slower than their mean rate of 219 wpm for the normal paragraphs, $t(4) = 14.83$, $p < 0.001$. Reading rates for individual participants ranged from 160 to 191 wpm.

AH also slowed her reading on the altered paragraphs but not as much as the control participants: Her reading rate for sequence-altered paragraphs was 205 wpm, only 22 wpm slower than her rate for the normal paragraphs.

Control participants read the critical pairs of transposed words (e.g., *him recognize* in *The horse had learned to him recognize*) with a mean accuracy of 72%; that is, on average they read 43.2 of the sixty pairs as written, in the anomalous order. Accuracy for individual participants ranged from 57% to 88%. For 24% of the critical pairs, control participants restored the transposed words to their "proper" order (e.g., *people were who frightened* → "people who were frightened"); I will refer to such errors as "sequence-repair errors." On the remaining 4% of the pairs the controls made some other type of error.

Individual control participants' rates of repair errors ranged from 8% (5/60) to 37% (22/60). In thirty-one of the seventy-one total sequence-repair errors, the participant realized the error immediately and reread the sequence accurately. The mean rate of uncorrected sequence-repair errors was 14% (8.2/60), with individual participants' rates ranging from 0% to 25%.

These results indicate that the control participants exploited knowledge-based constraints in reading the paragraphs, sometimes to the point of failing to read the material verbatim. Although the participants eventually detected 86% of the word transpositions, they initially read one-fourth of the transposed pairs in an order that, while highly probable, was not the actual order in the text; and for 14% of the transposed pairs the controls produced the words in the most probable order without realizing that the actual order was different.

AH's performance on the critical word pairs is presented in Table 10-1, along with the control-participant means. Remarkably, AH read only three of the sixty transposed word pairs (5%) accurately. For fifty-one of the sixty pairs (85%) she made a sequence-repair error, and for the remaining six pairs (10%) she made some other type of error. In forty-two of the fifty-one sequence-repair errors AH simply restored the transposed words to their "proper" order (e.g., *favorite their foods* → "their favorite foods"); in the other nine repair errors she revised the text more extensively. For example, she read *This is why so children many who live in towns are naughty* (with transposed words *children* and *many*) as "That is why children who live in many towns

Table 10-1. Performance of AH and Control Participants on Critical Word Transpositions in Task 10-2

Participants	Response Distribution on Critical Word Transpositions		
	Accurate	Sequence-Repair Error	Other Error
AH	5%	85%	10%
Controls	72%	24%	4%

are so naughty." Whereas the control participants noticed and corrected nearly half of their sequence-repair errors, AH made no such corrections.

AH was remarkably fluent as she repaired the word transpositions; for only eight of the fifty-one sequence-repair errors was there any noticeable hesitation or stumbling over words. When asked at the end of the experiment whether she had noticed anything unusual about any of the paragraphs, AH said that she had not. In contrast, all five control participants were very much aware of the word transpositions.

The results of this experiment strongly support the hypothesis that AH's reading processes, operating under the implicit assumption that the material being read is well-formed and coherent, apply knowledge-based constraints to repair errors introduced by her visual system. The results further suggest that the reading processes have little or no ability to distinguish errors actually present in a text from errors produced by the visual system and therefore repair the former as well as the latter.

After completion of the reading studies, I discussed the results with AH. When I described the sequence-repair errors, she recalled an incident she had not previously understood. In one of her high school English classes the students sometimes read aloud from Shakespeare's plays. AH said that she had enjoyed reading the part of Juliet, except that the teacher kept admonishing her to "stop correcting Shakespeare's word order."

Task 10–3: Sentence-Acceptability Judgments

In Task 10–2 AH was not informed that the stimulus paragraphs contained errors. However, in Task 10–3 sentences were presented with the explicit instruction that some contained clear grammatical errors. AH was told to read each sentence aloud exactly as it was written and then to indicate whether the sentence was grammatically acceptable. If AH's reading processes operate without her awareness or control to correct errors of the sorts introduced by her visual system, we would expect her to have difficulty detecting such errors even when explicitly instructed to do so.

Three types of sentences were presented. *Acceptable* sentences were syntactically acceptable and semantically coherent (e.g., *The boys were swimming across the lake*). *Unacceptable-sequence* sentences were syntactically unacceptable due to transposition of two adjacent words or morphemes in an otherwise acceptable sentence (e.g., *My parents are doing they all can to help me*). *Unacceptable-other* sentences were syntactically unacceptable for other reasons (e.g., *My brother learned to dress herself by the age of three*). Additional examples of each sentence type are presented in Table 10–2.

We expected AH to perform well on the acceptable sentences because errors introduced by her visual system should usually be repaired by her reading processes. For the unacceptable-sequence sentences we expected AH's reading processes to repair many of the word-sequence errors without her awareness or control, leading her to judge many of the sentences

Table 10–2. Examples of the Sentence Types from Task 10–3

Sentence Type	Examples
Acceptable	You think the man's story is true, don't you?
	We ate so many cookies we thought we'd burst.
	They questioned the constitutionality of the law.
Unacceptable–sequence	My town has the mansion finest in this state.
	The children doing were well in their classes.
	The dog was when gone we arrived at home.
Unacceptable–other	We ran into several friend at the pool this weekend.
	We did a great job given the circumstances, don't we?
	After the fight, the dog had much wounds to lick.

grammatically acceptable. For the unacceptable-other sentences our expectations were less clear; because the errors in these sentences were not of the sorts frequently introduced by AH's visual system, we were uncertain to what extent her reading processes would effect repairs.

Method

Stimuli were twenty syntactically and semantically acceptable sentences and thirty-seven syntactically unacceptable sentences ranging in length from six to thirteen words. The sixteen unacceptable-sequence sentences were created by transposing two adjacent words (fourteen sentences) or bound morphemes (two sentences) of an initially grammatical sentence (e.g., *The dog was when gone we arrived at home* or *I was surprised by his father's boynessish*). The twenty-one unacceptable-other sentences were generated by introducing other types of syntactic errors, such as violations of number or gender agreement or inappropriate use of prepositions (e.g., *We ran into several friend at the pool this weekend* or *I found the book and gave it at him*).

Sentences were presented one at a time on paper. AH first read the sentence aloud and then indicated whether it was acceptable. Instructions stressed that the sentences were to be read exactly as they were written and that the errors were not subtle flaws such as using *who* instead of *whom*. Five control participants were also tested.

Results and Discussion

For the acceptable and unacceptable-other sentences the control participants were 99% correct at both reading and judging acceptability. For each of these sentence types, one of the control participants made a single error. On the unacceptable-sequence sentences control-participant performance ranged from 94% to 100% correct, with a mean of 96%. Two of the control participants made no errors on the unacceptable-sequence sentences; the other three controls each made one error in which they repaired the ungrammatical word order in reading a sentence and then judged the sentence acceptable.

AH's performance on the acceptable sentences was comparable to that of the control participants. She made only one minor reading error (*It's a beautiful day, isn't it?* → "It's a beautiful day today, isn't it?"), and she judged all of the sentences acceptable.

For the unacceptable-sequence sentences, however, AH made correct reading responses and acceptability judgments for only three of the sixteen sentences (19%). For the remaining thirteen items (81%) she repaired the ungrammatical word or morpheme order when reading the sentence aloud (e.g., *My parents are doing they all can to help me* → "My parents are doing all they can to help me") and then judged the sentence acceptable. In most instances AH's reading was fluent and she appeared unaware that she had altered the ordering of words or morphemes. These results provide additional evidence that AH's reading processes operate to repair anomalies in stimulus representations and that the repairs occur outside of AH's awareness.

On the unacceptable-other sentences AH's performance was better, although far below the perfect performance of the control participants. For thirteen of the twenty-one items in this condition (62%) she read the sentence accurately and judged it unacceptable. For the other eight sentences (38%) she repaired the syntactic error in her reading response (e.g., *My brother learned to dress herself by the age of three* → "My brother learned to dress himself by the age of three") and judged the sentence acceptable.

The difference in rate of repair errors between unacceptable-sequence sentences (81%) and unacceptable-other sentences (38%) suggests that AH's reading processes may in some sense be tuned to the types of errors her visual system frequently introduces. In particular, her reading processes may be highly skilled at repairing word-sequence errors, with the result that she rarely became aware of these errors when reading the unacceptable-sequence sentences. In contrast, the reading mechanisms may be much less adept at repairing infrequently encountered errors such as those in the unacceptable-other sentences, with the consequence that these errors were more likely to come to her attention.

Task 10–4: Detecting and Correcting Errors

The preceding tasks focused primarily on AH's detection and repair of word-sequence errors in written sentences. Task 10–3 showed that she was largely unable to detect these errors, and Tasks 10–2 and 10–3 demonstrated that she tended to correct the errors spontaneously. One aim of the present task was to explore AH's detection and repair of the other types of errors likely to be introduced by her perceptual deficit. Accordingly, the errors introduced into the stimulus sentences included not only word-sequence errors but also letter-orientation errors (e.g., *b* in place of *d* or *n* for *u*) and letter-sequence errors (e.g., *folwer* for *flower*).

Another aim of the present task was to explore the limits of AH's skill in repairing the errors her perceptual deficit introduced as she read and the limits of her apparent lack of awareness of the errors and her repair processes. Whereas the sentences in the previous experiments contained only one or (in Task 10–2) at most two word-sequence errors, sentences in the present experiment included at least three errors, and some had many more.

AH was presented with four sentence types that varied in number of errors: *no-error* sentences were error-free; *low-error* sentences each contained three errors; *moderate-error* sentences had six errors each, and *high-error* sentences contained between eight and twenty-two errors, with a mean of 13.7 errors per sentence. Several examples of each sentence type are presented in Table 10–3. As the examples illustrate, erroneous sentences included the three types of errors likely to be caused by AH's visual localization deficit: word-sequence errors, letter-sequence errors (misorderings of letters within words), and letter-orientation errors. For instance, the first low-error sentence shown in the table includes one word-sequence error (*life longer* in place of *longer life*), one letter-sequence error (*toher* instead of *other*), and one letter-orientation error (*sqan* in place of *span*).

Table 10–3. Examples of the Sentence Types from Task 10–4

Sentence Type	Examples
No error	Doctors, physical trainers, and athletes agree that stair climbing is one of the best forms of aerobic exercise.
	An innovative approach to defense was the key to the team's success.
	Soliciting private funds is often more effective than going to federal agencies.
Low error	The wealthiest segment of society has a life longer sqan than toher groups.
	Institutes of higher learning will to have adjust to bemographic chagnes.
	The interviewer was impressed the wiht applicant's education, exqerience, and references.
Moderate error	The young boy took hte quppy long on afteruoon walks, often stopping to fetch paly.
	The most scenic away to across travel the coutnry py is dus.
	The agency uses comquter models and to simluations prebict the effects of human itneraction the with bay.
High error	The computer lab is otfeu durign bnsy the week lats of calsess any in given esmseter.
	The slow rate redroduction of fish some maeks exitnction radib bosisdiltiy a.
	Every student has the ot dotential maek to contridutions the drocess leraning.

Method

Forty sentences—ten of each type—were presented one at a time on paper in random order, and AH read each sentence aloud as quickly as she could. Because we wanted to see how skilled she was at repairing errors on the fly, we asked her not to read the erroneous parts as they were written but instead to correct the mistakes as she read. For example, the correct reading response for the first moderate-error sentence in the table was "The young boy took the puppy on long afternoon walks, often stopping to play fetch."

We also asked AH to indicate, after reading a sentence, whether it was correct as written or whether instead it contained errors. Instructions emphasized that the judgment about whether the sentence contained errors pertained to the written stimulus sentence and not to the repaired version she produced as a reading response.

Results and Discussion

AH read the no-error sentences with reasonable accuracy. Her only notable mistake was reading *Doctors, physical trainers, and athletes* as "Doctors, athletes, and physical trainers." For all ten of the no-error trials, she correctly reported that the sentence contained no errors.

On the sentences with errors, however, AH's performance was remarkable. She read most of the low-error sentences and many of the moderate-error sentences smoothly and rapidly, repairing the errors without apparent effort. For example, given *The agency uses comquter models and to simluations prebict the effects of human itneraction the with bay,* she immediately said "The agency uses computer models and simulations to predict the effects of human interaction with the bay." For some of the moderate-error sentences she stumbled occasionally but still repaired the errors with only an occasional minor mistake.

More often than not, she was unaware that the low- and moderate-error sentences contained mistakes. For seven of the ten low- and eight of the ten moderate-error sentences AH failed to notice anything wrong, even though the low-error sentences each had three errors and the moderate-error sentences had six errors each. She even failed to detect errors in three of the high-error sentences. Among the sentences she accepted as error-free were all of the low-, moderate-, and high-error examples in Table 10–4.

Only for high-error sentences did AH have obvious difficulty repairing errors, and only for these sentences was she usually aware of the errors. In reading the high-error sentences she was generally slow and hesitant, but for nine of ten she eventually produced a response that was nearly or entirely correct. For example, she read *Ont laeuing pebroom the wipnow, hse see conld baentiful the grapen folwer* as "Looking out the bedroom window, she could see the beautiful flower garden." Her only mistake was saying "looking" rather than "leaning."

Table 10-4. Percentage of Low-, Moderate-, and High-Error
Sentences Accepted by AH as Error-Free in Task 10-4

Sentence Type	Percent Judged Error-Free
Low-error	70%
Moderate-error	80%
High-error	30%

Table 10-4 summarizes AH performance in detecting the presence of errors in low-, moderate-, and high-error sentences.

In the next task we used sentences without errors to test another prediction of the knowledge-based constraint hypothesis.

Task 10-5: Reading and Comprehending Sentences

According to the knowledge-based constraint hypothesis, AH's reading comprehension is good for meaningful material because her reading processes can usually exploit constraints at multiple levels (e.g., orthographic, syntactic, semantic) to repair errors introduced by her visual system. This account predicts that AH should show impaired comprehension when the available constraints are insufficient for identifying or repairing visual-system errors that alter the meaning of the stimulus material.

Consider the following sentence: *The Smiths moved from Pittsburgh to Philadelphia.* Syntactic and semantic constraints would probably be sufficient for repairing word-sequence errors involving some parts of the sentence (e.g., *The moved Smiths from . . .*). However, in the absence of additional context, the available constraints would be inadequate for identifying or repairing at least some sequence errors involving the words *Pittsburgh* and *Philadelphia*. For example, if these words were transposed by AH's visual system (yielding *from Philadelphia to Pittsburgh*), knowledge-based constraints would presumably provide no grounds for determining that an error had occurred and the sentence would be misinterpreted. For other possible sequence errors (e.g., *from Philadelphia Pittsburgh to*) the available constraints might be consistent with more than one repair (e.g., *from Pittsburgh to Philadelphia* or *from Philadelphia to Pittsburgh*), again creating the possibility of a comprehension error.

Method

Thirty-eight sentences were constructed such that (*a*) the ordering of two critical words could not be predicted from knowledge-based constraints and (*b*) the actual order of the words was crucial for determining the meaning of the sentence. The critical words were separated by one word in thirty-four sentences, by a bound morpheme in three sentences (e.g., *My husband's mother is in town for the game*), and by a comma in one sentence (*According to Ed, Bill is coming at 4:00 p.m.*). For each sentence, a question was constructed to probe comprehension of the critical word sequence (e.g., *Where is their new home?* for *The Smiths moved from Pittsburgh to Philadelphia*).

The sentences were presented one at a time on a computer monitor in random order. After AH read the sentence aloud, it was replaced on the monitor by a comprehension question, and AH gave a spoken response to the question. Five control participants were also tested.

Results and Discussion

The control participants made no errors in reading critical word sequences. AH, however, transposed the critical words in nine of the thirty-eight sentences (24%). For example, she read *The Smiths moved from Pittsburgh to Philadelphia* as "The Smiths moved from Philadelphia to Pittsburgh" and *My husband's mother is in town for the game* as "My mother's husband is in town for the game." Table 10–5 presents additional examples of AH's errors.

On the comprehension questions the controls ranged in accuracy from 87% to 100%, with a mean of 95%. AH, however, was correct on only 68% of the questions (26/38). For twenty-five of the twenty-nine trials in which she read the critical words in the correct order (86%), she answered the comprehension question correctly. However, for eight of the nine sentences in which she transposed the critical words her answer to the question was consistent with the erroneous reading response and therefore incorrect. For example, after reading *At the party Mary gave John a birthday present* as "At the party John gave Mary a birthday present," she responded "Mary" to the question *Whose birthday was it?* These results confirm the prediction that AH's comprehension would be impaired when knowledge-based constraints were too weak to remedy errors her visual system was likely to introduce.

In addition to transpositions of critical words, AH made ten other errors in reading the sentences. Most of these were misreadings of individual words

Table 10–5. Examples of AH's Reading Errors on Critical Word Sequences in Task 10–5

Stimulus Sentence	AH's Reading Response
The display changed from blue to pink.	The display changed from *pink* to *blue*.
The final score was Pirates 6, Dodgers 5.	The final score was Pirates *5*, Dodgers *6*.
They preferred strawberries to raspberries.	They preferred *raspberries* to *strawberries*.
At the party Mary gave John a birthday present.	At the party *John* gave *Mary* a birthday present.

(e.g., *Bert* → "Bret"), although two were word-sequence confusions involving noncritical words (e.g., *The toy car* → "The car toy").

Task 10–6: Flicker

If the word-sequence errors observed in Task 10–5 resulted from AH's visual localization deficit, then flickering presentation of sentences should reduce the error rate. To test this prediction, we presented sentences similar to those from Task 10–5 in steady and flicker conditions.

Method

Stimuli were 120 sentences in which the ordering of two or more critical words was not predictable from knowledge-based constraints (e.g., *Lucy said Betty was an extraordinary person*). Two blocks of 120 trials were presented, with steady and flicker trials randomly intermixed within blocks. In the first block half of the sentences were presented in the steady condition and the other half were presented in the flicker condition; in the second block the assignment of sentences to conditions was reversed.

Results and Discussion

Flicker dramatically affected AH's reading performance. The rate of critical word transpositions was 28% (33/120) in the steady condition but only 2% (2/120) in the flicker condition, $\chi^2(1, n = 240) = 32.1, p < 0.001$. This result provides strong evidence that the word-sequence errors observed in the absence of flicker stemmed from AH's visual localization deficit and, hence, that the deficit is implicated in her reading of meaningful material.

Conclusions

In Chapter 9 I presented evidence that AH's perceptual deficit dramatically affects her ability to read words and word sequences. The aim of the present chapter was to consider whether this conclusion could be reconciled with AH's seemingly normal reading comprehension in her academic pursuits and daily life. I proposed that AH's reading processes rely heavily on knowledge of regularities at multiple levels in written language to constrain interpretation of the potentially inaccurate stimulus representations generated by her visual system. When the available constraints are strong, as in reading connected text, AH's reading processes may usually be able to "repair" the visual-system errors, resulting in good comprehension. However, when the constraints are weak, as with isolated words or sequences of unrelated words, recovery from visual errors may often not be possible. The use of knowledge-based constraints is not, I argued, a conscious problem-solving process but rather proceeds without AH's awareness or control.

The knowledge-based constraints hypothesis was tested in several experiments. The lexical decision results from Task 10–1 demonstrated that AH's word-recognition processes are strongly biased toward accepting letter strings as words, suggesting that these processes are tuned to compensate for visual-system errors by accepting imperfect matches between stimulus representations and entries in the orthographic lexicon. Tasks 10–2, 10–3, and 10–4 demonstrated that when AH read paragraphs or sentences containing errors of the sorts frequently introduced by her visual system, she spontaneously repaired the errors (e.g., *from subway the station* → "from the subway station"). Further, she was usually unaware of the errors and rarely could detect and report them even when explicitly instructed to do so, unless the stimulus was replete with errors. These tasks provided evidence that AH relies heavily on knowledge-based constraints in reading. Task 10–5 demonstrated that reliance on knowledge-based constraints was in fact necessary for her to achieve adequate comprehension of meaningful material: AH's reading comprehension was impaired for meaningful sentences in which the ordering of two critical words could not be determined from the available constraints (e.g., *Mary* and *John* in *At the party Mary gave John a birthday present*). Finally, Task 10–6 showed that AH's reading errors on sentences of this sort were virtually eliminated with flickering sentence displays, indicating that these errors, like her errors with letters, words, and word sequences, arose from her visual localization deficit.

The results from these tasks not only help to explain AH's excellent reading performance in most everyday circumstances but also shed light on the occasional hints of reading difficulty. For example, in an interview at the beginning of the study AH stated that she occasionally failed to recognize familiar words when she encountered them out of context (see Chapter 2). Also, in reviewing AH's academic records I found a standardized test report from tenth grade. A graph of vocabulary scores in this report showed AH at the top of the scale on a "Synonyms in Context" subtest but at the lower end of the scale on "Synonyms in Isolation." These data fit nicely with the interpretation that AH relies heavily on knowledge-based constraints in reading.

Implications for the Study of Developmental Cognitive Deficits

The present study provides a strong demonstration that the theoretical and methodological tools of cognitive science can shed light on underlying cognitive dysfunctions in developmental cognitive impairments. The results I have reported not only allowed AH's reading performance to be characterized in some detail but also, and more importantly, linked this performance convincingly to a specific deficit of visual perception.

What are the implications of the results for understanding developmental dyslexia? I certainly do not suggest that impaired visual localization is the underlying deficit in all or even many cases of developmental reading disability. However, the results from AH do demonstrate that a developmental reading deficit can arise from causes other than those posited by most current theories of developmental dyslexia. The most widely accepted theory (e.g., Bradley & Bryant, 1978, 1983, 1985; Liberman, 1982; Shankweiler & Liberman, 1972) assumes that developmental dyslexia is caused by a phonological deficit; and the principal alternative account (e.g., Galaburda & Livingstone, 1993; Lovegrove, 1993) attributes dyslexia to a dysfunction of the magnocellular (M) visual pathway, which appears to be intact in AH. (The M pathway is thought to be specialized for processing transient and low-contrast stimuli, just the types of stimuli for which AH's location and orientation perception is most accurate.)

Reading is a complex process requiring a multitude of perceptual and cognitive mechanisms, and reading impairments could presumably arise from deficits affecting any of these mechanisms. Indeed, the literature on developmental reading disorders suggests considerable variation in the underlying cognitive dysfunctions (e.g., Ellis, 1985; Martin, 1995). Given these points, the search for a single cause of developmental dyslexia, which characterizes most research in the area, is unlikely to prove fruitful. Furthermore, the probable heterogeneity of the dyslexia category undercuts the rationale for the group-study approach adopted in most developmental dyslexia research. This approach, in which results are averaged over groups of participants classified as dyslexic, rests on the assumption that the groups (and indeed the population from which they were sampled) are homogeneous at the level of underlying dysfunction.

An alternative approach involves single-case analyses of underlying deficits in many individuals with developmental reading disabilities. This approach, exemplified by the present study (see also Broom & Doctor, 1995; Castles & Coltheart, 1993; Rayner, Murphy, Henderson & Pollatsek, 1989; Snowling & Hume, 1989; Temple & Marshall, 1983), should provide a basis for characterizing the extent and nature of variation among dyslexics in underlying deficits and may also contribute to resolving the apparent contradictions among many of the reported results that are based on group averages.

Achieving an understanding of the potentially diverse underlying dysfunctions is of central importance in developing effective diagnosis and treatment methods for developmental dyslexia (or any other form of developmental cognitive impairment). For example, during her elementary school years AH endured several efforts to remediate her severe spelling impairment (which may stem, like her reading impairments, from her visual localization deficit; see Chapter 5). The remediation programs consisted primarily of exercises such as copying words repeatedly or looking up words in a dictionary. Given that these exercises required accurate perception of written words, it is unsurprising that AH derived no apparent benefit. Had attempts been made to address her difficulties in reading letters or isolated words, these attempts would surely also have been misdirected. Certainly, no one would have suggested that AH read under a strobe light.

Implications for Research on Normal Cognition

The results also have implications for issues in the study of normal cognition. The effects of flicker and exposure duration on AH's reading provide new evidence concerning the distinction between sustained and transient visual subsystems I drew on the basis of the findings described in Chapter 7. First, the present results suggest that reading mechanisms have access to information from both the sustained and transient subsystems. AH's impaired performance with long-duration, continuous presentations of words and word sequences implies that reading processes receive input from the (impaired) sustained subsystem, whereas her dramatically better performance with brief or flickering displays indicates that the reading processes also receive information from the (intact) transient subsystem.

The present findings also speak to the functions served by the sustained and transient subsystems. I have argued from AH's performance with non-verbal visual stimuli that both subsystems compute the location of visual stimuli. The results from the word-sequence reading task provide additional support for this conclusion. AH's high rate of word-sequence errors with long-duration continuous displays implicates the sustained subsystem in computing the relative locations of words in a string, and her virtually error-free performance with brief or flickering displays implies that the transient subsystem also computes relative location. Similarly, the conclusion that both transient and sustained subsystems process orientation information is supported by the findings of frequent letter-orientation errors in the word-reading tasks with long, continuous exposures and reduced rates of orientation errors in tasks with brief or flickering displays.

Finally, the results from our paragraph- and sentence-reading experiments (including the control participants' performance on the sequence-altered paragraphs) add to the available evidence that knowledge-based constraints play a significant role in reading. AH's performance in these experiments as well as her good reading comprehension in daily life suggest that these constraints are often quite powerful in meaningful material. Just how powerful the constraints can be, even for sentences in isolation, was illustrated by Task 10–4, in which AH usually succeeded in repairing sentences with multiple errors, such as *Every student has the ot dotential maek to contridutions the drocess leraning.*

Although impressive, AH's ability to repair errors can with practice be approximated by normal individuals. Our own experience, and informal experimentation with colleagues, indicates that sentences with multiple errors are quite difficult at first but become much easier after some practice. (Normal individuals continue, however, to be aware that the sentences are full of errors.) These observations suggest that rather minimal stimulus information may often suffice in reading of meaningful material and that the use of knowledge-based constraints to minimize stimulus processing may be a significant component of reading skill.

11

Related Cases

The preceding chapters provide a detailed description of AH's deficit in visual location and orientation perception. In the present chapter I discuss related patterns of impairment reported in other studies. The neurological and neuropsychological literatures on visual location and orientation deficits extend back as far as the late nineteenth and early twentieth centuries (e.g., Best, 1917; Beyer, 1895; Bálint, 1909; Holmes, 1918; Yealland, 1916; Smith & Holmes, 1916). As we shall see, many of the reported cases are bizarre and fascinating, and some exhibit points of similarity to AH. Nevertheless, no case closely resembling AH had been described at the time my colleagues and I published our initial reports (McCloskey et al., 1995; McCloskey & Rapp, 2000a, 2000b; McCloskey, 2004). However, in 2007 a team of researchers in Switzerland presented the case of a brain-damaged patient whose performance pattern is remarkably similar to that of AH (Pflugshaupt et al., 2007). I begin by discussing this new case and then turn to previously reported cases that bear some, although lesser, resemblance to AH.

Patient PR

PR is a 33-year-old woman who suffered septic shock[1] and coma as a result of pneumococcal pneumonia (Pflugshaupt et al., 2007). Magnetic resonance imaging and electroencephalography (EEG) carried out after she recovered were normal. However, a positron emission tomographic scan showed hypometabolism in frontal, temporal, and occipital areas of both hemispheres, presumably due to hypoxia during the episode of septic shock. Visual testing revealed that PR's visual fields were full—that is, she had no blind areas within her field of vision.

Visual Location and Orientation Perception

In visual location and orientation tasks PR made left–right reflection errors very similar to those of AH. She left–right reflected the orientations of objects in direct copying, as illustrated in Figure 11-1. (Compare AH's direct copies in Fig. 2–7.) Furthermore, in visually guided reaching tasks, PR reached toward the left–right reflection of the target location. She began reaching in the wrong direction and then corrected herself, just as AH did in the nonballistic reaching task (Task 8–1).

Impaired visual localization was also evident in a saccadic eye movement task. When PR attempted to shift her eyes to a visual target presented at various locations to the left or right of fixation, her saccades were almost always in the wrong direction. More specifically, she saccaded to the left–right reflection of the target location, usually with a slight undershoot. In Chapter 18 I show that AH also made left–right reflections in saccade tasks.

Reading and Writing

PR's reading and writing were severely affected. Pflugshaupt and colleagues (2007, p. 2080) note that when she came to their outpatient clinic for evaluation after recovery from septic shock, the letter of admission included a

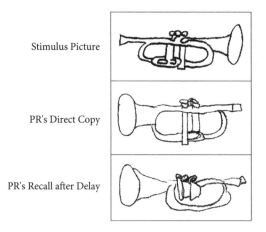

Stimulus Picture

PR's Direct Copy

PR's Recall after Delay

Figure 11–1. Example of PR's (Pflugshaupt et al., 2007) direct copy of a picture and her recall of the picture after a delay. Reprinted from Pflugshaupt, T., Nyffeler, T., von Wartburg, R., Wurtz, P., Lüthi, M., Hubl, D., Gutbrod, K., Juengling, F. D., Hess, C. W., & Müri, R. M. (2007). When left becomes right and vice versa: Mirrored vision after cerebral hypoxia. *Neuropsychologia, 45,* 2078–2091. With permission from Elsevier.

PR's Writing Prior
to Coma

Writing after Recovery

Mirror Reflection of
Post-Recovery Writing

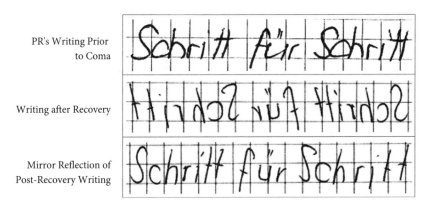

Figure 11–2. Example of PR's (Pflugshaupt et al., 2007) mirror writing. Reprinted from Pflugshaupt, T., Nyffeler, T., von Wartburg, R., Wurtz, P., Lüthi, M., Hubl, D., Gutbrod, K., Juengling, F. D., Hess, C. W., & Müri, R. M. (2007). When left becomes right and vice versa: Mirrored vision after cerebral hypoxia. *Neuropsychologia, 45,* 2078–2091. With permission from Elsevier.

rather unusual description of her reading problems: Although she was still not able to read normal script, her son had discovered that PR could fluently read the very same text when it was held against a mirror.

Consistent with this description, laboratory testing revealed that PR read mirror-reflected sentences much more quickly and accurately than normal sentences. When attempting to read normal text, she scanned each word letter-by-letter from right to left. In writing PR moved her hand from right to left across the page, producing mirror-reversed output (see Fig. 11–2).[2]

Effects of Visual Variables

Perhaps most remarkably, the effects of exposure duration, motion, flicker, and eccentricity reported for AH in Chapter 7 were also observed for PR. A beneficial effect of motion was noticed by PR herself:

> PR told us that in everyday situations, motion helps her to correctly localise objects. For instance, she was able to easily identify the position of a fly in space as long as the insect was moving, but failed to orient toward flies whenever they lingered motionless on a surface. (Pflugshaupt et al., 2007, p. 2086)

Also, whereas PR reached and pointed in the wrong direction in tasks with stationary objects, she reached accurately for falling objects. Finally, effects of motion were observed in an eye movement task. On each trial a visual target appeared to the left or right of fixation and then began moving, either immediately or after a 1-second delay. In the delayed-movement condition

PR consistently saccaded in the wrong direction during the period when the target was stationary and then shifted her eyes to the correct location shortly after the target started to move. Further, in the immediate-movement condition her initial saccade was usually in the correct direction.

Effects of exposure duration were assessed in a picture orientation task. On each trial, a picture showing a side view of an animal was presented and PR pressed a left or right button to indicate the direction in which the animal was facing. She was nearly 100% correct for the shortest exposure durations (50 and 150 milliseconds) but virtually never correct for longer exposures (200–2000 milliseconds). This pattern of results is very similar to that observed for AH (see Fig. 7–1), except that PR shows more severe impairment than AH at the longer durations.

The same task was used to evaluate effects of flicker. Pictures were presented for 1000 milliseconds, with illumination that was either steady or flickered at 10 Hz. PR was 100% correct for flickering pictures but 0% correct for the steady stimuli. Flicker apparently also affected PR's ability to read: "during a rock concert in a bar under flickering lighting conditions, PR realised that she could easily read normal script" (Pflugshaupt et al., 2007, p. 2087). The parallels to AH are again obvious.

Pflugshaupt and colleagues (2007) did not report results concerning effects of stimulus eccentricity in their article on PR. However, in a personal communication Pflugshaupt mentioned that in testing with highly eccentric visual stimuli PR's vision appeared normal—she did not commit left–right reflection errors (Pflugshaupt, personal communication, August 28, 2007).

Comparison with AH

PR's pattern of performance is strikingly similar to that of AH. Both AH and PR showed impairment across a broad range of visual location and orientation tasks, including visually guided reaching, direct copying, orientation judgment, and reading tasks. Furthermore, both individuals made systematic left–right reflection errors in both location and orientation tasks. Finally, AH and PR both exhibited the same effects of motion, exposure duration, flicker, and eccentricity, including the counterintuitive effect of higher accuracy for brief than for long exposures.

These commonalities strongly suggest that PR suffers from a visual-system deficit closely related to that of AH. In particular, the results reported by Pflugshaupt and colleagues (2007) indicate that PR, like AH, is impaired at a level of visual processing that provides location and orientation information to a broad range of perceptual, cognitive, and motor functions. Further, the effects of visual variables suggest that for PR, as for AH, the deficit selectively affects a visual subsystem specialized for processing sustained stimuli (i.e., stationary, long-duration, steady stimuli), with a subsystem attuned to transient visual stimuli remaining intact. (See Chapter 16 for more detailed discussion of transient and sustained subsystems.) Finally, PR's reflection errors suggest that her impairment, like that of AH, leads to systematic misrepresentation of the location and orientation of visual stimuli along the horizontal (left–right) dimension. (See Chapters 13–15 for a more specific interpretation of reflection errors.)

PR's performance was not entirely identical to that of AH. First, whereas AH committed both left–right and up–down reflection errors, PR made only left–right reflections. This difference suggests that whereas AH's deficit affects the representation of location and orientation along both horizontal and vertical dimensions, in PR only the horizontal dimension is affected. Second, in visual location and orientation tasks with sustained stimuli PR's accuracy was at or near 0%, whereas AH more typically scored somewhere in the range of 30%–70% correct. Apparently, PR's sustained visual subsystem always or nearly always reverses left and right in computing the location and orientation of visual stimuli, whereas AH's sustained subsystem misrepresents location and orientation only some of the time.

Third, PR's reading impairments were somewhat different from those exhibited by AH. PR's reading was far better with mirror-reversed than with normal text, and she showed grossly abnormal eye movements when attempting to read normal text. In contrast, AH read mirror-reversed text adequately but somewhat more slowly than normal text; and although AH's eye movements during reading were not studied extensively, a single session of eye movement recording with a scanning laser ophthalmoscope indicated that her fixation pattern during reading was at least reasonably normal. These reading differences between the two cases may stem in part from the greater severity of PR's deficit. Perhaps even more significant is that AH's deficit has been present at least since childhood, whereas PR's visual perception was presumably normal until she suffered brain damage in adulthood. As discussed in Chapter 10, AH has developed compensatory skills that allow her to read reasonably well despite her perceptual deficit. Because her deficit was presumably present from the time she began learning to read, she has had many years to develop these skills. PR, however, has had much less time to compensate. Furthermore, in the case of PR the reading processes that receive input from the impaired visual processing mechanisms presumably experienced an abrupt change in the quality of the information received from the visual system. Adapting to such a change may well be much more difficult than compensating for inputs that have always been noisy or inaccurate.

Implications

Notwithstanding the differences between AH and PR, the extensive and striking similarities clearly indicate that the two individuals have closely related deficits. This conclusion has important implications. In the following chapters I will use the findings from AH as a basis for inferences about the normal visual system, arguing that her performance sheds light on issues concerning visual location and orientation representations, frames of reference, and the functional architecture of the visual system.

In most cognitive neuropsychological research, inferences about normal cognition are drawn from adult acquired deficits, in which an initially normal and fully developed brain suffers damage. AH's deficit, however, is developmental rather than acquired, and the use of developmental deficits as a basis for conclusions about normal cognition has been called into question (see, e.g., the target article and commentaries in Thomas & Karmiloff-Smith, 2002). The principal argument is as follows: In developmental deficits neural development may have followed a far from normal course, producing not a basically normal brain with specific malfunctions but instead a brain that differs in its fundamental structure and functioning from the normal brain. Because the brains of individuals with developmental deficits may be fundamentally different from the brains of normal individuals, conclusions about normal cognition cannot properly be drawn from developmental deficits.

In Chapter 19 I suggest that this argument is too strong for several reasons. However, the point to be made here is that the close resemblance between AH and PR (a case of adult acquired impairment) strongly suggests that AH's pattern of impairment reflects a basically normal brain with a selective malfunction, rather than a fundamentally abnormal brain. If AH's brain had followed a grossly abnormal course of development, we would not expect to find a close resemblance between her deficit and that of an individual whose brain was presumably normal before suffering damage in adulthood. Consequently, the Pflugshaupt et al. (2007) report on patient PR provides grounds for increased confidence in conclusions about the normal visual system drawn from AH's performance.

The report on PR should also put to rest any concern that AH might be malingering. To maintain a malingering interpretation one would have to assume that AH happened by coincidence to simulate in exquisite detail a form of impairment that could in fact result from brain damage but had not yet been reported. This assumption obviously strains credulity well beyond the breaking point.

Previous Reports of Impaired Visual Localization

No other case in the neurological or neuropsychological literature resembles AH as closely as patient PR (Pflugshaupt et al., 2007). Nevertheless, many other patients show some similarities to AH. In this section I discuss patients exhibiting impaired visual localization, and in the next section I explore deficits in processing visual orientation information.

Holmes, Bálint, and Optic Ataxia

In a series of articles published during and shortly after World War I, Gordon Holmes described eight patients with severe visuospatial deficits resulting from head wounds received in the war (Holmes, 1918, 1919; Holmes &

Horrax, 1919; Smith & Holmes, 1916). All of the patients had bilateral pari-etal damage, and in some cases the lesions extended to other brain areas as well. The patients presented with a variety of impairments, prominent among which was inaccuracy in reaching (or pointing) to visual stimuli. The patients either reached seemingly at random or reached to the vicinity, but not the exact location, of the visual target. For example, Holmes (1918) described the performance of one patient (Private M.) as follows:

> When a pencil was held up in front of him he would often project his arm in a totally wrong direction, as though by chance rather than by deliberate decision, or more frequently he would bring his hand to one or other side of it, above or below it, or he would attempt to seize the pencil before he had reached it, or after his hand had passed it. When he failed to touch the object at once he continued groping for it until his hand or arm came in contact with it, in a manner more or less like a man searching for a small object in the dark. (Holmes, 1918, p. 452)

A second patient (Sergeant K.) exhibited similar difficulties:

> the most striking symptom in this case, too, was the patient's inability to localize correctly in space objects which he could see and recognize perfectly well. When, for instance, he was asked to touch a piece of paper attached to the end of a metal rod, he rarely reached it directly, but brought his hand to one or other side of it, or above it or below, and continued to grope till his hand came in contact with it. (Holmes, 1918, p. 458)

All of Holmes' patients had visual field defects (areas of blindness or reduced acuity). However, Holmes argued that field defects could not account for the patients' reaching errors because the errors occurred even when stimuli were presented in intact regions of the visual field, under conditions in which the patient reported seeing and recognizing the stimuli.

Holmes also argued that the reaching errors could not be attributed to simple motor deficits (i.e., deficits in controlling the movement of the arm or hand) because reaching movements were accurate in response to nonvi-sual stimuli. In particular, the patients could reach accurately to the loca-tion of a sound or to a body part that was touched (Holmes, 1919). (These results also imply that the patients' deficits affected visual representations and not multi- or amodal levels of spatial representation.) Impaired reaching of the sort observed in Holmes' patients is usually referred to as *optic ataxia*. This term, introduced by Bálint (1909), applies to inaccurate visually guided reaching when the inaccuracy cannot be attributed to visual-field defects or motor deficits.[3]

Many other cases resembling those described by Holmes have been reported under various rubrics, including *visual disorientation, Bálint's syn-drome*, and *Bálint-Holmes syndrome* (e.g., Allison, Hurwitz, White, & Wilmot,

1969; Baylis & Baylis, 2001; Best, 1917; Brain, 1941; Godwin-Austen, 1965; Cole, Schutta, & Warrington, 1962; Friedman-Hill, Robertson, & Treisman, 1995; Karnath & Ferber, 2003; Kase, Troncoso, Court, Tapia, & Mohr, 1977; Kim & Robertson, 2001; Michel, Jeannerod, & Devic, 1965; Phan, Schendel, Recanzone, & Robertson, 2000; Ratcliff & Davies-Jones, 1972; Riddoch, 1935; Robertson, Treisman, Friedman-Hill, & Grabowecky, 1997; Ross Russell & Bharucha, 1984; Warrington, 1986; Yealland, 1916; for overviews, see De Renzi, 1996; Milner & Goodale, 1995; Rizzo & Vecera, 2002).

The interpretation of these cases has been a matter of some controversy. Holmes (1918, 1919) concluded that his patients misreached because they were unable to determine the locations of objects from vision. In this interpretation the patients' impaired reaching was just one symptom of a comprehensive visual localization deficit—that is, a deficit affecting visual processes common to all tasks requiring localization of visual stimuli. Researchers reporting similar cases have often followed Holmes' lead, attributing the observed performance to generalized impairment of visual localization (e.g., Brain, 1941; Godwin-Austen, 1965; Cole et al., 1962; Riddoch, 1935; Robertson et al., 1997).

However, a number of theorists have argued that optic ataxia, the principal evidence of deficient visual localization in Holmes' cases (and the similar cases reported subsequently), arises not from a generalized impairment of visual localization but rather from a more specific visuomotor impairment—that is, from a deficit selectively affecting the visual guidance of action (e.g., Battaglia-Mayer & Caminiti, 2002; Buxbaum & Coslett, 1997; Damasio & Benton, 1979; Harvey & Milner, 1995; Mayer et al., 1998; Milner & Goodale, 1995; Perenin & Vighetto, 1983, 1988; Pisella et al., 2000; Rondot et al., 1977; Rossetti, Pisella, & Vighetto, 2003). Visuomotor interpretations typically attribute optic ataxia to a disconnection between visual and motor areas of the brain or to deficits in carrying out spatial transformations required specifically for visually guided action (e.g., transformations of retinocentric location representations into arm-centered representations needed for control of reaching).

For some patients exhibiting optic ataxia the data clearly favor a visuomotor interpretation. For example, the patient described in Bálint's classic report (Bálint, 1909; see also Bálint, 1909/1995; Harvey & Milner, 1995) showed impaired visually guided reaching only with his right hand; with his left hand he reached accurately. Differences in reaching performance between left and right hands have also been reported in a number of other cases (e.g., Berti, Papagno, & Vallar, 1986; Buxbaum & Coslett, 1997; Levine, Kaufman, & Mohr, 1978; Perenin & Vighetto, 1983; Rondot et al., 1977). For these cases the impaired–visual perception account can be ruled out and a visuomotor interpretation is highly plausible. (Differences between hands could result from disconnections affecting only some of the linkages between visual and motor areas or from disruption of spatial transformations within a single cerebral hemisphere.) Some researchers (e.g., Perenin & Vighetto, 1983, 1988;

Piccirilli et al., 1983) have also presented other evidence for intact visual localization perception in optic ataxic patients (although this evidence is typically less compelling than the evidence concerning differences between hands).

Evidence that optic ataxia sometimes results from visuomotor deficits does not, however, demonstrate that this symptom always reflects visuomotor impairment. Optic ataxia, like any other symptom of physical or mental dysfunction, might well occur for different reasons in different cases—the inaccurate reaching might be caused, in some instances, by a specific visuomotor deficit and, in other instances, by a more generalized deficit in visual localization. Indeed, for some cases the evidence strongly suggests a comprehensive visual localization deficit. The clearest example is that of patient RM, a 56-year-old man with bilateral parieto-occipital damage who has been the subject of numerous studies (e.g., Baylis & Baylis, 2001; Friedman-Hill et al., 1995; Kim & Robertson, 2001; Phan et al., 2000; Robertson et al., 1997). In addition to optic ataxia, RM exhibited impairment in many visual localization tasks that did not require visually guided movements, including verbal description of the location of a stimulus in a 3 × 3 array (Baylis & Baylis, 2001); stating whether an X presented on a computer screen was to the left of, to the right of, or at a central screen location; and stating whether an X was above, below, or at the central position (Friedman-Hill et al., 1995; Robertson et al., 1997). RM was also impaired in saying whether an X and O presented sequentially were at the same or different locations (Robertson et al., 1997) and in detecting when a stimulus light changed location (Phan et al., 2000).

Comparison with AH

The brain-damaged patients reported under the rubrics *disturbance of visual orientation, visual disorientation, Bálint's syndrome, Bálint-Holmes syndrome,* and *optic ataxia* showed impaired performance in visually guided reaching and also, in some cases, other visual localization tasks. Nevertheless, none of these patients closely resembles AH. The patients whose reaching errors resulted from visuomotor deficits (e.g., Bálint, 1909) are obviously different from AH because AH's deficit is a comprehensive impairment of visual localization and not a visuomotor impairment. (See Chapter 6 for further discussion.) Furthermore, all of the patients—both those with visuomotor deficits (e.g., Bálint, 1909) and those with comprehensive visual localization deficits (e.g., Robertson et al., 1997)—clearly differ from AH with respect to the nature of their errors. In visually guided reaching and other visual localization tasks, AH showed systematic patterns of left–right and up–down reflection errors. In contrast, none of the patients discussed in this section exhibited systematic reflection errors. Rather, the patients' errors took the form of largely random responses or, more commonly, responses directed to locations in the vicinity of, but not precisely at, the target locations.

With respect to the other phenomena observed for AH (e.g., orientation errors, effects of visual variables such as flicker), the published reports on the brain-damaged patients contain little relevant information. Orientation errors are mentioned in a few cases (e.g., Perenin & Vighetto, 1988, see case 3), but no report describes any effects of visual variables similar to those shown by AH.

Visual Allesthesia

Visual allesthesia is an umbrella term covering a heterogeneous collection of deficits that vary substantially in their symptomatology and almost certainly in their underlying causes. The common denominator is that the patient reports seeing visual stimuli at locations other than their actual locations (Ardila, Botero, & Gomez, 1987; Bender, Wortis, & Cramer, 1948; Beyer, 1895; Critchley, 1949, 1951; Eretto, Schoen, Krohel, & Pechette, 1982; Grossi et al., 2005; Halligan, Marshall, & Wade, 1992; Herrmann & Pötzl, 1928; Jacobs, 1980; Joanette & Brouchon, 1984; Kasten & Poggel, 2006; Nakajima, Yasue, Kaito, Kamikubo, & Sakai, 1991). For example, Jacobs (1980) presented the case of a 24-year-old woman with right parieto-occipital damage. The patient reported brief episodes in which an object in her right visual field suddenly appeared in her left field as well—that is, she saw the object not only at the correct location on the right but also at an erroneous location on her left. (Jacobs did not report whether the erroneous left-field location was systematically related to the actual right-field location.)

The illusory left-field percepts were *palinoptic*, persisting after the actual object was no longer in view:

> She experienced diplopia (illusory object on the left, real object on the right) as long as the real object remained in view. The diplopia disappeared as soon as she turned her gaze away from the real object, but the illusory object persisted in view off to her left as a palinoptic image for up to 15 minutes. The palinoptic image seemed to be smaller than the real one, and it oscillated vertically; otherwise it was an exact replica of the original. It disappeared abruptly, and then vision again appeared to be normal. (Jacobs, 1980, p. 1059)

The allesthetic left-field percepts seemed sufficiently real that the patient was sometimes unaware they were illusory. For example, Jacobs reported an incident in which the patient became confused over the location of a sidewalk:

> she did not know which sidewalk to walk along—the real one to her right or the illusory one to her left. When she looked to the left, the real sidewalk was no longer in view, but the illusory one persisted and she attempted to walk along it so that she veered to the left across a lawn and into the street. (Jacobs, 1980, p. 1060)

The patient's visual allesthesia was almost certainly related to seizures arising in her damaged brain region. The allesthetic episodes were accompanied by behavioral symptoms of seizure (e.g., lack of responsiveness and twitching). Also, abnormalities indicative of seizure disorder were evident in EEGs obtained during the 5-month period in which the patient experienced allesthesia. Furthermore, anticonvulsive medication eliminated the seizure symptoms and the allesthetic incidents. Upon withdrawal of the medication, the patient again began experiencing episodes of allesthesia, but the episodes stopped when the medication was reintroduced.

Comparison with AH

The number of reported visual allesthesia cases is small, and most of the reported cases were not studied systematically. In fact, most of the published reports provide no behavioral data beyond the patients' retrospective accounts of brief allesthetic episodes. Nevertheless, almost all of the reported cases clearly differed from AH, usually in multiple respects. For nearly every patient, mislocalizations occurred in only one direction (e.g., from the right side to the left side but not vice versa). Also, in many cases the patient reported seeing visual stimuli at both correct and incorrect locations (e.g., Ardila et al., 1987; Jacobs, 1980; Grossi et al., 2005; Kasten & Poggel, 2006; Nakajima et al., 1991) and the erroneous percept was often palinoptic (e.g., Jacobs, 1980; Eretto et al., 1982; Nakajima et al., 1991). Further, for most cases the misperceived locations were not left–right or up–down reflections of the correct locations (e.g., Critchley, 1949, case 7; Joanette & Brouchon, 1984; Kasten & Poggel, 2006), or the relationship between correct and incorrect locations was not reported (e.g., Ardila et al., 1987; Bender et al., 1948; Beyer, 1895; Jacobs, 1980). Finally, in many cases the phenomenon was apparently related to visual-field defects (e.g., Beyer, 1895; Kasten & Poggel, 2006; Nakajima et al., 1991) or seizures (e.g., Jacobs, 1980; Eretto et al., 1982).

Only one of the reported visual allesthesia patients appears to have experienced location misperceptions resembling those of AH. Critchley (1951, case 4) presented the case of LH, a 58-year-old man with bilateral parietooccipital lesions. In a lengthy account of the patient's many deficits Critchley provided a brief description of visual allesthesia:

> Optical alloaesthesia constituted yet another of the visuopsychic
> rarities. A stimulus-object exposed to one side of the mid-line was
> at times perceived, but incorrectly located to a corresponding point
> in the opposite half-field. This phenomenon took place either from
> right to left or left to right. (Critchley, 1951, p. 279)

However, the extent to which left–right reflections occurred systematically in visual location perception is unclear because other results reported by Critchley suggest that the patient made visual localization errors that were not left–right reflections. Further complicating matters is the fact that LH suffered from a variety of other visual impairments, including an inconsistent right visual-field defect, difficulty fixating visual stimuli, impaired motion perception, palinopsia, visual agnosia, and *simultanagnosia* (inability to combine parts of an object or scene into a coherent integrated percept).

Regardless of what significance we attach to the reported left–right reflections, LH apparently did not make up–down reflection errors in visual localization tasks and, therefore, differed from AH in this respect. LH and AH cannot be compared with regard to visual perception of orientation because Critchley (1951) did not discuss LH's performance on orientation perception tasks. Not surprisingly, Critchley also reported no information about effects of visual variables such as exposure duration or flicker. Hence, LH exhibits both similarities to and differences from AH, but the full extent of the similarities and differences cannot be determined from the information available.

Previous Reports of Impaired Visual Orientation Processing

In addition to cases of impaired visual localization, the neurological and neuropsychological literatures include reports of impaired visual orientation processing.

Impaired Processing of Object Orientation

Many published reports have described brain-damaged patients with impairments in perceiving, retaining, or using visual information about the orientation of objects (e.g., Best, 1917; Caterini, Della Salla, Spinnler, Stangalino, & Turnbull, 2002; Cooper & Humphreys, 2000; Davidoff & Warrington, 1999, 2001; Goodale, Milner, Jakobson, & Carey, 1991; Goodale et al., 1994; Harris, Harris, & Caine, 2001; Karnath, Ferber, & Bülthoff, 2000; Karnath & Ferber, 2003; Lambon-Ralph, Jarvis, & Ellis, 1997; Perenin & Vighetto, 1983, 1988; Priftis, Rusconi, Umiltà, & Zorzi, 2003; Riddoch & Humphreys, 1988; Riddoch et al., 2004; Solms, Kaplan-Solms, Saling, & Miller, 1988; Solms, Turnbull, Kaplan-Solms, & Miller, 1998; Turnbull, 1997; Turnbull, Beschin, & Della Salla, 1997; Turnbull, Della Salla, & Beschin, 2002; Turnbull, Laws, & McCarthy, 1995; Turnbull & McCarthy, 1996a, 1996b; Warrington & Davidoff, 2000). However, the patients described in these reports do not appear highly similar to AH. None of the studies reports reflection errors in visual localization tasks, and none reports any effects of visual variables comparable to those observed for AH. Furthermore, in most studies the evidence suggests that the patient's impairment was not a comprehensive deficit of orientation perception that affected performance across a broad range of stimulus and task types but rather a postperceptual deficit with more limited scope. Finally, in many cases the patients' errors did not specifically involve left–right or up–down orientation reflections.

Nevertheless, results from a few patients suggest perceptual-level deficits selectively affecting the ability to distinguish stimuli differing only by left–right reflection (e.g., Turnbull & McCarthy, 1996a; Riddoch & Humphreys, 1988). For example, Turnbull and McCarthy (1996a) described patient RJ, a 61-year-old man with bilateral parietal damage. RJ exhibited an interesting pattern of performance in a series of odd-one-out tasks. On each trial three pictures were presented, and RJ's task was to say which picture was different from the other two (see Fig. 11–3 for examples). RJ had no difficulty recognizing the stimulus pictures, as indicated by his ability to name them. Further, he was 100% correct (50/50) in identifying the odd-one-out when the discrepant picture differed from the other two in some visual detail

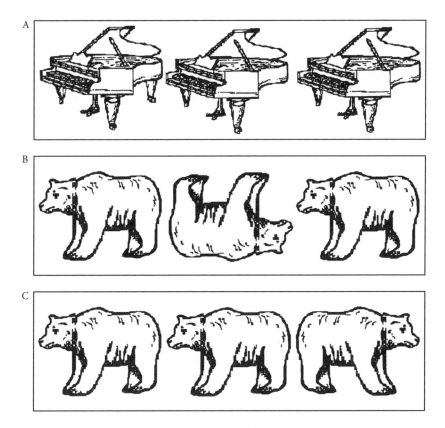

Figure 11–3. Examples of stimuli from odd-one-out task presented to patient RJ. (A) Stimulus from task in which discrepant picture differed from others by a visual detail. (B) Stimulus in which discrepant picture differed from others by 180° rotation. (C) Stimulus in which discrepant picture differed by left–right reflection. Reprinted from Turnbull, O. H., & McCarthy, R. (1996a). Failure to discriminate between mirror-image objects: A case of viewpoint-independent object recognition? *Neurocase*, 2, 63–72, with permission from Taylor & Francis, Ltd., http://www.informaworld.com.

(e.g., the presence or absence of a leg on a grand piano; see Fig. 11–3A). He was also perfect (50/50) when the odd stimulus differed from the others by a 180° rotation (Fig. 11–3B). However, when the odd-one-out differed from the other stimuli by a left–right reflection (Fig. 11–3C), RJ's performance fell to below 50% correct, regardless of whether the three pictures were arranged horizontally (21/50) or vertically (22/50). Control participants performed this task without error. RJ was also severely impaired when shown a single picture (e.g., a bear facing left) and asked to indicate which way it was facing (by pointing to a left or right arrow).

Finally, RJ stated that left–right mirror images looked the same to him. For example, Turnbull and McCarthy (1996a) reported that RJ had great difficulty understanding the instructions for a mental rotation task that required him to distinguish a shape from its left–right reflection. Describing their attempts to explain the task, the authors stated the following:

> Line drawings of the standard and mirror-image items were shown to him, and he was asked to note that they were mirror-images. Despite repeated attempts to explain the nature of the task, RJ denied that there was any difference between these mirror-image items. In a further attempt to show their difference, a pair of the items, printed on paper, was held up to the light and superimposed. When the pair were identical, RJ agreed that they could be superimposed exactly. He also agreed that exact superimposition was not possible for the mirror-images. However, he remained convinced that, when he compared the items when they were not superimposed, they appeared to be the same, saying: "I know from what you did that they should be different…but when I look at one, then the other, they look just the same to me." (Turnbull & McCarthy, 1996a, p. 64)

Similarly, in the odd-one-out task involving left–right reflections, RJ commented, "it seems like I can see them all together, but they all look the same…I know they're different but which is which…?" (Turnbull & McCarthy, 1996a, p. 66).

The results from RJ strongly suggest a perceptual deficit in representing the left–right orientation of visual stimuli; apparently, RJ's perceptual representations of visual stimuli often failed to distinguish orientations differing only by left–right reflection. We cannot, however, be entirely certain that the deficit affected only left–right orientation. RJ's excellent performance in the odd-one-out task with 180° rotations demonstrates that he could represent some aspects of object orientation. This result also suggests more specifically that RJ could probably distinguish orientations differing by up–down reflection because 180° rotation is equivalent to left–right plus up–down reflection. Given that RJ was impaired in representing left–right orientation, he would probably have performed poorly with 180° rotations if he were also impaired in representing up–down orientation. However, testing with pictures that differed only by up–down reflection would have provided stronger evidence on this point. Also, RJ was not tested with stimuli differing by rotations less than 180°; hence, we do not know whether he would have had difficulty discriminating smaller rotational differences. Therefore, although the data suggest a selective deficit in representing left–right orientation, this conclusion must be stated with some caution.

Comparison with AH

I have already noted that most brain-damaged patients showing impaired performance in visual orientation tasks differ from AH in many respects. Even for RJ (Turnbull & McCarthy, 1996a), the orientation-impaired patient perhaps most similar to AH, the resemblance does not appear to be close. First, whereas AH made both left–right and up–down reflection errors in orientation tasks, RJ's impairment probably affected only left–right orientation. Also, whereas AH made left–right and up–down reflection errors in location as well as orientation tasks, RJ apparently did not suffer from any comparable impairment of visual localization. For example, Turnbull and McCarthy (1996a) reported that RJ could point accurately to specific parts of stimulus pictures (e.g., the handlebars of a motorcycle).

Inverted Vision

Inverted vision is a rare and remarkable phenomenon in which the entire visual world briefly appears to be upside down. Over a period of 200 years roughly thirty cases of this phenomenon—also referred to as *reversal of vision metamorphopsia* and sometimes categorized as visual allesthesia—have been reported. Solms and colleagues (1988) reviewed twenty-one cases, as well as reporting a case of their own (see also Charles et al., 1992; River, Ben Hur, & Steiner, 1998; Ropper, 1983; Steiner, Shahin, & Melamed, 1987; Unfug, 1978). The Solms et al. patient, WB, was a 12-year-old boy hospitalized with severe frontal headache and nausea. Computed tomography revealed bilateral frontal-lobe abscesses, and these were drained successfully. On a follow-up visit to the hospital several months after being discharged, WB described, apparently with some reluctance, episodes of inverted vision:

> When we next saw W.B. . . . he recounted the following experience
> in response to a direct question about his vision: One morning,
> a few days after he had been discharged from hospital, he was
> sitting at home at the kitchen table going over some school-work
> he had missed while he was away. He got up to make himself a
> cup of tea, and, when he returned to the table, he suddenly gained
> the impression that everything he had written in his exercise
> book was upside-down. Alarmed by this, he turned his glance
> away from the book, only to discover that the kitchen stove was
> also upside-down. He then realized, to his dismay, that the entire
> kitchen was inverted; the floor was at the top and the ceiling at the

bottom. He stood up and walked—a little unsteadily—towards
the kitchen door, which now appeared to hang from the ceiling.
(Only the external visual scene seemed to be inverted; the patient
himself did not feel any changes in his body position.) When he
reached the door and looked outside, he saw that the whole world
was upside-down, with the sky at the bottom and the landscape
at the top. He sat down on the doorstep and stared disbelievingly
at this scene for a few minutes. Sitting there, a wave of nausea
overcame him. He closed his eyes and rubbed them with his
hands. When he re-opened them his vision had re-orientated itself.
This entire episode lasted for approximately four minutes....On
the morning of the next day the phenomenon re-appeared. The
patient was playing in the garden at the time. His attention was
suddenly drawn to a tree which seemed to be moving. As he looked
at the tree it rotated slowly, in a clockwise direction, until it was
completely upside-down. The patient then briefly closed his eyes,
and the inverted vision immediately disappeared. When asked
to describe the illusion in more detail, he reported that the tree
did not rotate in isolation; the entire external visual scene turned
through 180° in the coronal plane....During the ensuing months
episodes like this recurred "a few more times," but the patient
refused further discussion on the matter. This was the first time
that he had described the experience to anyone, and he clearly did
not enjoy talking about it. (Solms et al., 1988, p. 503)

Ropper (1983) reported a similar episode experienced by a 71-year-old
woman suffering from a cerebellar lesion as well as ischemia (reduced
blood flow) affecting the brainstem and posterior portions of the cerebral
hemispheres:

That evening she awakened and immediately saw everything
upside down, the room seeming to turn exactly 180° for
5 minutes.... The light normally above her bed seemed to be
shining up from the floor. Furniture appeared on the ceiling with
usual interrelationships preserved. Most striking to her was a
tumbler on her night table which stood upside down without water
spilling. (Ropper, 1983, p. 148)

River and colleagues (1998) described a patient who made inaccurate reaching
movements during an episode of inverted vision. The patient, a 79-year-old
man whose symptoms were attributed to ischemia affecting the brainstem,
cerebellum, and posterior cerebral hemispheres, was described as follows:

He saw people walking on their heads, and the floor next to his bed
appeared to be over his head. To the patient's embarrassment, he
made the wrong hand movements when he tried to cover himself
with the blanket or to pick up a cup of tea.... When presented with

an object in his right upper visual field, he directed his hands to his lower left hemispace. (River et al., 1998, pp. 1363–1364)

The reported cases of inverted vision differ from one another in various respects; nevertheless, as Solms et al. (1988) pointed out, many commonalities are apparent across cases. The episodes were usually brief (lasting a few seconds to a few minutes) and had a sudden onset and resolution. Also, at the onset of episodes many patients experienced a rotation of the visual world from upright through intermediate orientations to inverted, rather than simply seeing the world upright at one moment and inverted the next. Further, the episodes were usually accompanied by nausea, vomiting, dizziness, or a general feeling of malaise.

Inverted vision has usually been attributed to temporary disruption of signals from the vestibular system at the level of the brainstem or impaired processing of these signals in the cerebellum or posterior cerebral cortex. The vestibular system, an inner-ear structure that includes the semicircular canals and otolith organs, provides information important for balance and sense of spatial position, including information about the orientation of the head relative to gravity. Accordingly, it is argued, disruption or impaired processing of vestibular information could lead to misrepresentation of one's orientation relative to the visual world. This interpretation has not been developed in great detail; for example, as Heilman and Nadeau (1998) pointed out, no explanation is offered for why the visual world, instead of the patient him- or herself, is perceived as upside-down. Nevertheless, the interpretation gains some plausibility from the frequent association of inverted vision with brainstem, cerebellar, or posterior cerebral dysfunction and from some aspects of the inverted-vision phenomenology. Especially suggestive of a relationship to the vestibular system is the finding that many inverted-vision patients reported seeing the visual world rotate from upright through intermediate orientations to an inverted state. (Vestibular-system disease or damage often produces vertigo, a sensation that oneself—*subjective vertigo*— or the visual world—*objective vertigo*—is rotating or swaying.) The nausea and dizziness almost always associated with inverted vision are also consistent with impaired processing of vestibular information.

What significance attaches to the fact that the world is perceived to be completely upside-down, rather than tilted to some random extent? One possibility is that interruption or impaired processing of certain vestibular signals leads systematically to perception of the world as upside-down (in which case the phenomenon might have important implications for understanding the nature of the relevant signals and how these signals are used to establish the perceiver's orientation with respect to the visual world). On the other hand, inverted vision may simply be the most extreme form of a more general symptom in which the visual world is perceived as tilted to some extent. In addition to patients experiencing fully inverted vision, patients describing lesser tilting of the visual world have been reported (e.g., Girkin, Perry, & Miller, 1999; Ropper, 1983; River et al., 1998; Solms et al., 1988). Cases of fully inverted vision may well be more common in the literature than cases involving less extreme tilting. However, even if a tabulation of cases revealed this pattern, a reporting bias could conceivably be responsible: A patient who claims to experience upside-down vision may be deemed more interesting and more significant than a patient who describes episodes in which the world appears tilted to some lesser extent.

Comparison with AH

The inverted-vision phenomenon, although superficially reminiscent of AH's up–down location and orientation errors, is obviously quite different. Most notably, the entire visual world is perceived as upside-down in cases of inverted vision. AH, in contrast, never reported, and in fact emphatically denied, experiencing anything of the sort. Even when questioned during or after tasks that elicited frequent up–down errors, AH stated that she had never felt either herself or the world to be upside down (or otherwise tilted). Also, whereas many inverted-vision patients experienced rotation of the visual world, AH stated that she never saw objects moving or rotating between correct and incorrect locations or orientations. Furthermore, AH did not report dizziness, nausea, vertigo, or other symptoms of dysfunction related to the vestibular system, either in association with her up–down errors or at other times, nor did a neurological exam reveal any such symptoms.

Conclusions

The present chapter explored the resemblance between AH and other cases in the neurological and neuropsychological literatures. The conclusions can be stated succinctly: Many previously reported cases resemble AH to some extent, but clear differences are apparent in almost every instance. However, PR, the brain-damaged patient described by Pflugshaupt and colleagues (2007), appears strikingly similar to AH. Both AH and PR were impaired in location and orientation perception, both made systematic left–right reflection errors, and both showed the same dramatic effects of exposure duration, motion, flicker, and eccentricity (although only AH made up–down reflection errors). The commonalities between the two cases strongly suggest that the underlying deficits are very similar and provide a basis for increased confidence in conclusions about the normal visual system drawn from AH's (or PR's) performance.

In surveying the literature on impaired processing of visual location and orientation information, I have focused largely on the extent to which the reported cases resemble AH. However, independent of their similarity to AH, these cases may have implications for understanding normal visual representations and processes. Hence, I will return to some of the cases in subsequent chapters, when I explore theoretical issues concerning representation of location and orientation information in the normal visual system.

Part II

Theoretical Issues and Implications

12

Spatial Representations and Frames of Reference: Theoretical Foundations

Spatial locations and orientations can be specified only in relation to a reference system of some sort—that is, within a frame of reference. For example, I cannot communicate the location of a pencil on my desk by saying that the pencil is 15 cm forward, unless I also say in relation to what (e.g., 15 cm forward from the center of the desk surface, with *forward* defined as the direction of a vector in the horizontal plane pointing from my body toward the center of the desk). Similarly, I cannot specify the pencil's orientation simply as –24°; again, I must say in relation to what (e.g., –24° relative to the front–back axis of the desk, with clockwise defined as the positive direction). The importance of reference frames in spatial representation is reflected in the central role played by the reference-frame concept in research on virtually every facet of spatial cognition, including object recognition (e.g., Marr, 1982), spatial vision (e.g., Andersen & Mountcastle, 1983; Andersen, 1989; Pouget, Fisher, & Sejnowski, 1993), spatial language (e.g., Levelt, 1996; Levinson, 1996; Tversky, 1996), attention (e.g., Farah, Brunn, Wong, Wallace, & Carpenter, 1990; Nicoletti & Umiltà, 1989, 1994; Tipper, Weaver, Jerreat, & Burak, 1994; Tipper & Behrmann, 1996; Umiltà & Nicoletti, 1992; Umiltà, Castiello, Fontana, & Vestri, 1995), action and motor control (e.g., Andersen, Snyder, Bradley, & Xing, 1997; Flanders, Helms Tillery, & Soechting, 1992; Goodale & Haffenden, 1998; Graziano, Yap, & Gross, 1994; Soechting & Flanders, 1989, 1992), and navigation (e.g., O'Keefe & Nadel, 1978; Taube, Muller, & Ranck, 1990; Tipper et al., 1994; Wehner, Michel, & Antonsen, 1996). A large body of literature on these and other topics documents efforts to identify the frames of reference used by the brain in representing spatial information.

In the present chapter I discuss the frame-of-reference concept, arguing that this concept has been the subject of considerable confusion in cognitive and neuroscientific research on spatial representation. In particular, I argue that two distinct questions about frames of reference in the brain have been massively conflated and that the dominant empirical method for probing reference frames speaks to only one of these questions. Finally, I suggest that both questions can be addressed empirically. With this discussion as a foundation, I argue in Chapters 13–15 that results from AH speak to both of the reference-frame questions in the context of location and orientation representation in the visual system.

Two Frame-of-Reference Questions

Imagine a simple perceptual task involving an observer seated at a computer monitor, with eyes focused on a fixation cross (see Fig. 12–1). Suppose that on each trial a black square is displayed on the screen. The observer's visual system will represent, among other things, the location of the square, and different levels of the visual system may use different reference frames to represent this location. For any of these reference frames, we can ask at least two questions about the representation of location within the frame:

1. In relation to what are locations defined?
2. In what form are locations represented?

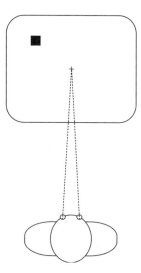

Figure 12–1. An observer viewing a square displayed on a computer screen. For convenience, the schematic shows a top view of the observer and a frontal view of the screen. *Dashed lines* indicate that the observer is fixating the cross displayed at the center of the screen.

I will refer to first question as the "definition" question and to the second as the "format" question. These questions can be asked about representation of orientation as well as location. However, in the present chapter (and Chapter 13) I will focus on location representations; representation of orientation is considered in Chapters 14 and 15.

The Definition Question

The definition question has to do with what gives a location its identity (or, in the terminology of Brewer & Pears [1993] with the basis for *individuating* locations). Answering the definition question tells us on what basis a reference frame defines locations to be the same as or different from one another within and across situations. For reference frames in the visual system, locations could conceivably be defined by their relation to the retina, their relation to the head, their relation to objects in the visual environment, and so forth. In a retina-based frame of reference, what gives a location its identity is its relation to the retina. For example, Figure 12–2 shows three trials from the hypothetical perceptual task. In trials 1 and 2 the square stands in the same relation to the retina and, thus, has the same retina-based location. Therefore, within a retina-based frame of reference, the square would have the same location representation on both trials. However, in trial 3 the square is in a different location relative to the retina and, thus, would have a different location representation in a retina-based frame of reference. In contrast, given a screen-based or head-based frame of reference, the square's location and location representation would be the same on trial 1 and trial 3, with trial 2 having a different location (and location representation).[1]

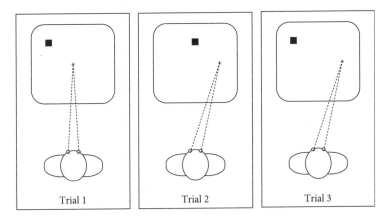

Figure 12–2. Three trials in a hypothetical perceptual task in which stimulus location and fixation location are varied. In trials 1 and 2 the stimulus is at different screen locations but the same location relative to fixation. In trials 1 and 3 the screen location is the same but the location relative to fixation is different.

The Format Question

The format question concerns the form in which locations are represented. This question may best be clarified by considering not internal representations in the brain but rather external representations on paper. Suppose that I decide to write down the location of the stimulus square on each trial in the hypothetical perceptual task. Suppose further that I adopt a screen-based definition of location and therefore decide to record screen-based locations. I still have another decision to make: In what form should I write the screen-based locations? I could simply assign a label to each location, writing A for trial 1, B for trial 2, and A for trial 3. These labels would indicate that the square was in the same (screen-based) location on trials 1 and 3 but in a different location on trial 2. Gallistel (1990) calls this form of representation a "nominal representation" because each location is simply labeled (i.e., named). In daily life we use nominal location representations when, for example, we refer to a city by name (e.g., London, Rome, New York).

I could also write the stimulus locations in the form of coordinates. Consider, for example, a Cartesian coordinate system defined by horizontal and vertical axes through the center of the screen, with distances measured in centimeters. In this coordinate system I could represent the square's screen-based location on trials 1–3 as (–10, +10), (0, +10), and (–10, +10), respectively. Latitude and longitude representations for locations of cities (e.g., 39° N, 77° W) provide another example of coordinate-system representations.

Note that decisions about the form of the representation (the format question) are distinct from decisions about the basis for defining locations (the definition question). For example, had I decided to record retina-based rather than screen-based locations, I could still have chosen a nominal or coordinate form of representation.

Coordinate and nominal representations illustrate a fundamental distinction between what I will call "compositional" and "noncompositional" location representations. *Compositional representations* are composed of multiple components, each of which specifies a different aspect of the to-be-represented location. For example, Cartesian coordinate representations consist of separate horizontal and vertical components that specify the displacement from the origin along the horizontal and vertical reference axes, respectively. Further, each of these components can be decomposed into separate direction (+ or –) and distance (e.g., 10) subcomponents. Thus, the representation (–10, +10) indicates a location displaced from the origin 10 units horizontally in the negative direction and 10 units vertically in the positive direction. Similarly, latitude-longitude representations consist of separate components specifying angular displacement from the equator (latitude) and angular displacement from the Greenwich meridian (longitude), with each component further decomposable into direction (e.g., north, west) and magnitude (e.g., 39°, 77°) subcomponents. In contrast, a *noncompositional representation* (e.g., a nominal representation such as A or London) does not

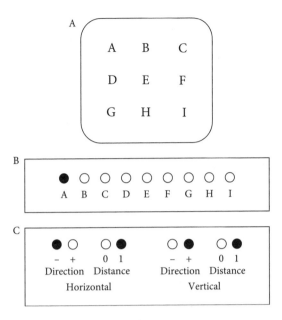

Figure 12–3. (A) Nine locations on a computer screen. (B) A noncompositional location representation. (C) A compositional location representation.

separately specify different aspects of a location; rather, the representation designates the location as a whole. A noncompositional representation may have multiple parts—for example, the written word *London* has six letters—but the different parts do not stand for different aspects of the represented location.

The distinction between compositional and noncompositional forms of representation may also be illustrated by considering potential location representations in a connectionist network. Suppose that we want to represent the nine screen-based locations labeled A through I in Figure 12–3A. We could assign a unit (or set of units) to each location, as illustrated in Figure 12–3B, and represent a location by activating the corresponding unit (or set). The figure shows a representation of location A created by activating the unit assigned to represent that location. This representational scheme is noncompositional: Whether we assign a single unit or a set of units to each location, the location is represented as a whole; parts of the representation do not correspond to aspects of the location.

We could also implement a Cartesian coordinate representation in which units (or sets of units) are assigned to represent direction and distance along horizontal and vertical reference axes passing through the center of the screen. In this form of representation, illustrated in Figure 12–3C, location A could be represented by activating the units corresponding to a negative direction and a distance of 1 along the horizontal axis and a positive direction and distance of 1 along the vertical axis (assuming for convenience that the distance between screen locations is defined as 1). (See Zipser & Andersen [1988] for simulations incorporating similar nominal and coordinate representations.)

Although the compositional representation in Figure 12–3C is distributed and the noncompositional representation in Figure 12–3B is local, the distinction between compositional and noncompositional representations should not be confused with the distinction between distributed and local representations. A distributed representation is noncompositional as long as parts of the representation do not correspond to aspects of the to-be-represented locations. For example, Figure 12–4 illustrates a distributed representational scheme in which each location is represented by an arbitrary pattern of activation across a set of units. These representations are noncompositional because no systematic correspondence exists between individual units or subsets of units and aspects of the locations (e.g., horizontal or vertical displacement from the center of the screen). In contrast, the distributed representations in Figure 12–3C are compositional because parts of the representation correspond to aspects of the to-be-represented locations.

I have discussed the representational format question and the distinction between compositional and noncompositional location representations in terms of external representations—that is, representations outside the head. However, the format question and the compositional/noncompositional distinction also apply to location representations in the brain. In

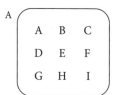

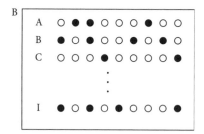

Figure 12–4. (A) The nine screen locations. (B) Distributed but noncompositional location representations, illustrating the point that the distinction between compositional and noncompositional representations is different from that between distributed and local representations.

attempting to characterize the frames of reference used by the brain in representing location, we may ask not only how locations are defined but also in what form locations are represented. For example, regardless of whether we are engaged in symbolic, connectionist, or neural theorizing, we may ask not only whether the representations under consideration are retina-based, head-based, or environment-based but also whether the representations are compositional or noncompositional.

A final point deserving emphasis is that the definition and format questions are separate. Hence, answering one of the questions does not necessarily answer the other. For instance, results implying that certain location representations are retina-based may have nothing to say about whether the representations are compositional or noncompositional. In the following section I show that the strategy adopted in most reference-frame research speaks to the definition question and has nothing to say about the format question.

The Canonical Research Strategy

The overwhelming majority of studies aimed at characterizing the reference frames underlying perceptual, cognitive, or motor functions apply some variant of a single research strategy. In this strategy participants are presented with stimuli that have the same location in some reference frames but different locations in other frames, and the resulting location representations are probed. Consider, for example, the hypothetical trials in Figure 12–2. In a retina-based frame of reference the stimulus square has the same location on trials 1 and 2 but a different location on trial 3. However, in a head-based or screen-based reference frame, the square's location is the same on trials 1 and 3 but different on trial 2. Now, suppose we have a method for determining whether the observer's location representation at some level of the visual system is the same or different across trials. We could then make inferences about the frame of reference at that level by testing observers with trials 1–3 (or, to be more realistic, with multiple instances of each trial type). Results indicating that the location representation was the same on trials 1 and 2 but different on trial 3 would be consistent with a retina-based frame of reference. On the other hand, data showing that the representation was the same on trials 1 and 3 but different on trial 2 would suggest a head- or screen-based frame of reference or some other reference frame that happened to coincide with these frames (e.g., a frame based on the trunk of the observer's body). Given this latter result, we might conduct further tests to distinguish among head-based, screen-based, and other reference frames. For instance, a screen-based reference frame could be distinguished from head-based, trunk-based, and other body-based frames by shifting the observer's head and body out of alignment with the center of the screen on some trials, as illustrated in Figure 12–5.

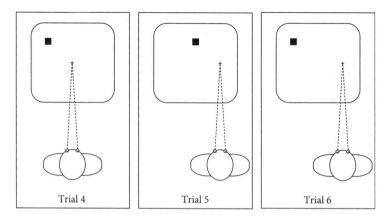

Figure 12–5. Three hypothetical trials illustrating a method for distinguishing screen-based from head-, trunk-, or other body-based frames of reference. In trials 4 and 5 the stimulus has the same location in head- and other body-based reference frames but different locations in a screen-based frame. In trials 4 and 6 the screen-based location is the same but the head- and other body-based locations are different.

The research strategy I have described is an excellent method for addressing the definitional reference-frame question: In relation to what are locations defined? However, the strategy fails to address the format question: In what form are locations represented? As a consequence, most reference-frame studies bear on the definition question but have nothing to say about the format question. This point is not readily apparent from the cognitive and neuroscientific literature on reference frames because the two questions are virtually never distinguished and because the language used for discussing reference frames conflates definition and format issues. In the next section I describe two studies to illustrate how the strategy for identifying reference frames has been implemented, how the results have been interpreted, and what conclusions can legitimately be drawn.

Two Reference-Frame Studies

The studies I discuss in this section—a neurophysiological study by Graziano et al. (1994) and a behavioral study by Cave et al. (1994)—were not selected as especially egregious examples of failure to distinguish between the definitional and format reference-frame questions. On the contrary, the studies were chosen because they exemplify standard practice in reference-frame research. Many other studies would have served equally well as examples, and my intent is not to single out the Graziano et al. (1994) and Cave et al. (1994) studies for criticism.

Frames of Reference in Macaque Ventral Intraparietal Cortex

Graziano et al. (1994) recorded from neurons in the ventral premotor cortex of macaque monkeys, with the aim of identifying the reference frame(s) used in this brain area to represent the locations of visual stimuli. Most of the studied neurons were bimodal, responding to both visual and tactile stimuli.

Single-cell recording was carried out while the monkey, with head immobilized, fixated one of three positions (labeled LF, CF, and RF in Fig. 12–6). For each fixation location visual stimuli were presented in four different locations (A–D in the figure) and the neuron's responses were recorded. The question of interest was how the neuron's receptive field (i.e., the region of visual space to which the neuron responded when appropriate stimuli were presented) would vary as the fixation and stimulus locations were manipulated. Suppose that when the monkey is fixating the center of the screen (i.e., location CF) the neuron's receptive field is restricted to location C such that the neuron responds to stimuli presented at C but not to stimuli at other locations (see Fig. 12–7A). Suppose now that the fixation point is shifted rightward to location RF while the monkey's head and body remain in their original positions. If the neuron is involved in representing retina-based locations of stimuli, its receptive field should shift to a new location on the screen when the point of fixation is changed. In particular, the neuron should no longer respond to stimuli at location C but instead to stimuli at D (see Fig. 12–7B). On the other hand, if the neuron is implicated in representing location in some body-based or environment-based frame of reference, its receptive field should not change when the fixation point is moved. The neuron should continue responding only to stimuli at location C, regardless of where the eyes are fixated (Fig. 12–7C).

For most of the studied neurons, Graziano et al. (1994) found that the receptive field remained at the same location in space (i.e., the same location relative to the monkey's body and the visual environment) regardless of where the monkey's eyes were fixated. This result suggests that most ventral premotor neurons are involved in representing location not in a retina-based frame of reference but rather in some body- or environment-based frame(s).

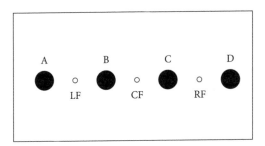

Figure 12–6. The four stimulus locations (A, B, C, D) and three fixation locations (LF, CF, RF) in the Graziano et al. (1994) study.

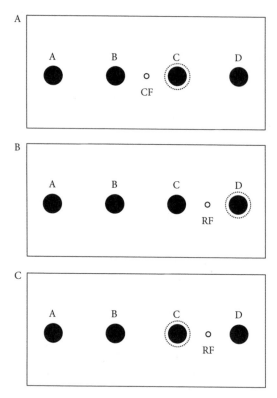

Figure 12–7. (A) Schematic illustrating the receptive field of a neuron at location D when the monkey's eyes are fixed on location CF. *Dotted circle* depicts the receptive field. (B) Expected result when fixation is shifted to the right, if the neuron is implicated in representing retina-based location: The receptive field moves with the eyes. (C) Expected result if the neuron is involved in representing non-retina-based location: The receptive field remains fixed while the eyes move.

For bimodal visual–tactile neurons with tactile receptive fields on the arm, Graziano et al. (1994) also recorded responses to visual stimuli while varying the position of the arm. In most cases they found that the visual receptive field shifted with the arm. For example, a neuron that responded to visual stimuli at location D when the arm was positioned to the monkey's right responded instead to location C when the monkey's arm was shifted leftward (see Fig. 12–8). This finding suggests that many visual premotor neurons may play a role in representing location in an arm-based frame of reference.

The Graziano et al. (1994) results clearly speak to the definitional reference-frame question: In relation to what are locations defined? However, the results have little to say about the format question: In what form are locations represented? For example, we cannot infer from the Graziano et al. findings whether the location representations in the ventral premotor cortex are compositional or noncompositional.

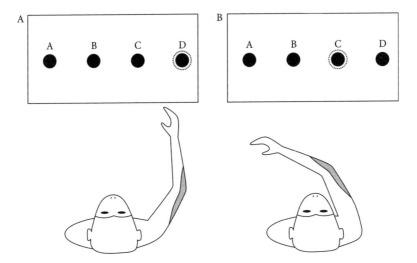

Figure 12–8. Variation in neuron's responses as a function of the monkey's arm position, suggesting arm-based location representations. *Dotted circle* indicates stimulus location eliciting strongest neural response. (A) With the arm positioned to the monkey's right, the neuron responds most strongly to stimuli at location D. (B) When the monkey's arm shifted leftward, the strongest response is for stimuli at location C.

Nevertheless, Graziano et al. (1994), like many other researchers, described their methods and results in the language of coordinate systems. For example, they posed the following question about the receptive fields of ventral premotor neurons: "Are the RFs [receptive fields] of these cells retinocentric, or are they expressed in a coordinate system attached to the head, trunk, or some other part of the body?" (p. 1054). Further, they summarized their answer to the question by stating, "These visual receptive fields were found to move when the arm moved but not when the eye moved; that is, they are in arm-centered, not retinocentric, coordinates" (p. 1054). This use of coordinate-system terminology reflects a failure to distinguish the two reference-frame questions: Whereas the Graziano et al. results speak to the definition question, claims about coordinate systems have to do with the format question. Note especially that in the second quotation Graziano et al. cite a result that bears only on the definition question (receptive fields moved with the arm) in support of what appears to be a format claim (coordinate representations).

Graziano et al. (1994) may not have intended to posit location representations in coordinate format. The rather vague concept of a reference frame that pervades research on spatial representation does not distinguish between the basis for defining locations (e.g., retina, head) and the form in which locations are represented (e.g., nominal, coordinate-system). It perhaps for this reason that in most discussions of reference frames, coordinate-system vocabulary is apparently not intended to have any special significance; for example, *retinocentric coordinate system* and *retinocentric frame of reference* are apparently considered synonymous. Therefore, Graziano et al.'s statements about coordinates and coordinate systems probably should not be regarded as specific claims about the format of location representations; and the same is true of most other reference-frame discussions couched in coordinate-system terms (e.g., Andersen et al., 1997; Arguin & Bub, 1993; Behrmann & Moscovitch, 1994; Chatterjee, 1994; Colby & Goldberg, 1999; Driver & Halligan, 1991; Farah et al., 1990; Karnath, Schenkel, & Fischer, 1991; Làdavas, 1987; Tipper & Behrmann, 1996).

Casual use of coordinate-system language can, however, lead to confusion. When results speak only to the definition question, stating conclusions in terms of coordinates and coordinate systems may create the misleading impression that the data also bear on the form of spatial representations. Haphazard use of coordinate-system terminology also obscures the difference between statements that carry no intended implications about representational format and assertions that are put forth as explicit claims about internal coordinate-system representations (e.g., Lacquaniti, Guigon, Bianchi, Ferraina, & Caminiti, 1995; McCloskey & Rapp, 2000b; Soechting & Flanders, 1989).

Representation of Location in Mental Images

Conflation of definition and format questions is not limited to neurophysiological studies but is also rampant in behavioral research. For example, Cave et al. (1994) conducted a series of mental rotation experiments to explore the representation of location in mental images. On each trial one of three characters (R, J, or 4) was presented at one of several rotation angles (e.g., 45° clockwise from upright) and the participant pressed a button as quickly as possible to indicate whether the stimulus was normal (e.g., R) or mirror-reversed (e.g., Я). In the first experiment participants saw a cue and then, after a brief delay, the target stimulus was presented. In the "shape cue" condition participants were cued with the target character (R, J, 4) at the target rotation angle, as shown in Figure 12–9A. Hence, the cue provided accurate information about the shape and rotation angle of the target. However, the cue did not indicate whether the target stimulus would be normal or mirror-reversed because the normal version of the character was always used as the cue. In the "no shape cue" condition, the cue was an arrow indicating the rotation angle but not the shape of the target stimulus (see Fig. 12–9B). The results showed that performance was facilitated by the shape cue: Responses were faster and less affected by rotation angle in the shape cue condition than in the no shape cue condition. Cave et al. interpreted this result by assuming that the shape cue reduced the need for mental rotation. According to this interpretation, participants in the shape cue condition performed the task primarily by generating a mental image of the cued character at the cued rotation angle

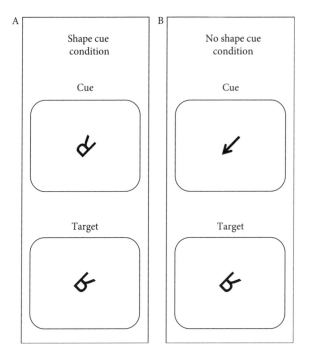

Figure 12–9. Examples of cue and target stimuli in the shape cue and no shape cue conditions in experiment 1 of the Cave et al. (1994) study.

and then comparing this image with a representation of the target stimulus. Given this strategy, no mental rotation of the target is required. However, in the no shape cue condition the cue failed to provide information about the shape of the upcoming target stimulus, so participants could not generate an image for comparison with the target. As a consequence, they were forced to perform the task by mentally rotating the target stimulus to upright.

In a second experiment Cave et al. (1994) found that shape cues produced greater facilitation when presented at the same location as the subsequent target stimulus (see Fig. 12–10A) than when the cue and target were at different locations (Fig. 12–10B). Cave et al. took this finding as evidence that participants' mental images of the cue represented the cued character's location as well as its shape and orientation. They argued that when the cue and target were presented at the same location the mental representation of the cue could simply be compared to the target representation, whereas when the cue and target were at different locations cue and target representations could not be compared until the location of the cue character within the mental image had been adjusted to match the location of the target.

Cave et al.'s (1994) third experiment asked within what frame of reference participants' mental images represented the location of the cue. On some trials, the fixation point was moved after cue offset but before target onset

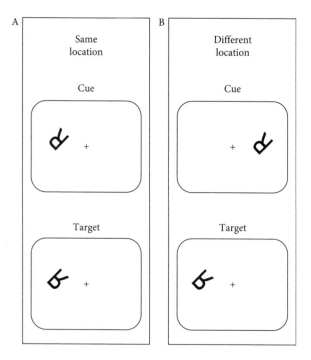

Figure 12–10. Examples of same-location and different-location trials in experiment 2 of the Cave et al. (1994) study.

and participants shifted their eyes to the new fixation location. In this way, Cave et al. sought to dissociate retina-based and non-retina-based frames of reference (which they referred to as "retinotopic" and "spatiotopic" frames, respectively). Consider the trials illustrated in Figure 12–11. In the "same spatiotopic–different retinotopic" trial in Figure 12–11A, the fixation point is on the left side of the screen and the cue is presented at a central screen location. The fixation point then shifts to the right side of the screen, and the target stimulus is subsequently presented at the central location. On this trial the cue and target have the same location in many non-retina-based reference frames (e.g., screen-based, head-based, trunk-based). However, the cue and target differ in retina-based location: The cue is presented to the right of fixation, whereas the target appears to the left of fixation.

Now consider the "same retinotopic–different spatiotopic" trial in Figure 12–11B. The fixation point is on the left side of the screen, and the cue is presented 5.5° to the left of fixation. Fixation then shifts to the right side of the screen (5.5° right of center), and the target stimulus is subsequently presented at the central screen location. On this trial the cue and target have the same retina-based location (i.e., 5.5° left of fixation) but different locations in screen-based, head-based, trunk-based, and other frames of reference.

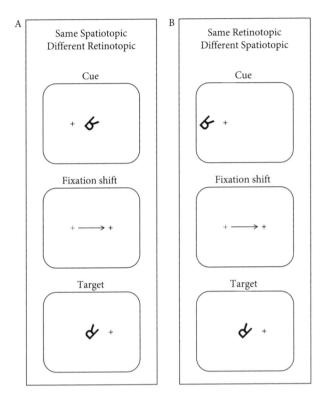

Figure 12–11. Examples of same spatiotopic–different retinotopic and same retinotopic–different spatiotopic trials in experiment 3 of the Cave et al. (1994) study.

Cave et al. (1994) reasoned that if participants' mental images represented cue location in a retina-based frame of reference, then shape cues should produce greater facilitation on same retinotopic–different spatiotopic trials than on same spatiotopic–different retinotopic trials (because the former would function as same-location trials and the latter as different-location trials). In contrast, if the mental images implicated a non-retina-based reference frame, facilitation should be greater for same spatiotopic–different retinotopic trials than for same retinotopic–different spatiotopic trials. (An implicit assumption underlying these predictions is that targets are represented in the reference frame of the cue for purposes of cue–target comparison.) The results showed greater facilitation for the same retinotopic–different spatiotopic trials, leading Cave et al. to conclude that participants' mental images represented location in a retina-based frame of reference.

Like the neurophysiological evidence reported by Graziano et al. (1994), Cave et al.'s (1994) behavioral data speak to the definitional reference-frame question (In relation to what are locations defined?) and have nothing to say about the format question (In what form are locations represented?). However, also like Graziano et al., Cave et al. couched their questions and conclusions in coordinate-system terms (e.g., "retinotopic coordinates," "spatiotopic location coordinates," "coordinate transform"). As I have already noted, this conflation of definition and format questions can lead only to confusion about the implications of results and the substance of theoretical claims.

Addressing the Format Question

I have argued that most frame-of-reference studies, including those described in the preceding section, have little to say about the format question: In what form are locations represented? This contention might lead one to wonder what kinds of evidence could be brought to bear on the question or even whether any conceivable evidence would be germane. To illustrate that the format question is accessible to empirical inquiry, I briefly describe a study that yielded evidence suggesting coordinate-system representations in the brain.

Lacquaniti et al. (1995) recorded from spatially tuned neurons in macaque area 5 (superior parietal lobule) while the monkey reached to targets in three-dimensional space. They reported that the activity of most neurons was related not to the target location taken as a whole but rather to the target's position on a single spatial dimension. Some neurons responded according to the target's horizontal position (i.e., left–right position), independent of its vertical position (high vs. low) or depth (near vs. far). Other neurons responded selectively to vertical position, and still others responded to depth. For example, one neuron that responded selectively to horizontal position showed a monotonic increase in firing rate from the rightmost to the leftmost of six horizontal target positions; however, for any given horizontal position the neuron's rate of firing was the same regardless of the target's position on the vertical or depth dimensions. Lacquaniti et al. interpreted these findings as evidence that the superior parietal lobule represents location in the form of three spatial coordinates, with different sets of neurons representing each coordinate. More specifically, they suggested that the neurally represented coordinates corresponded to azimuth, elevation, and distance within a spherical coordinate system (though their results are equally consistent with a Cartesian coordinate representation defined by horizontal, vertical, and depth axes). Other single-cell recording studies have also reported neurons that respond selectively to variation along a single spatial dimension (see, e.g., Duhamel, Bremmer, BenHamed, & Graf, 1997).

In Chapter 13 I present behavioral evidence from AH bearing on both frame-of-reference questions.

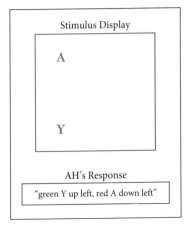

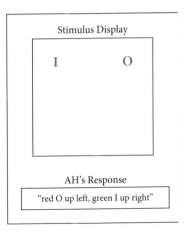

Stimulus Display

A

Y

AH's Response

"green Y up left, red A down left"

Stimulus Display

I   O

AH's Response

"red O up left, green I up right"

Color Figure 6–1. Examples of stimulus displays and AH's location exchange errors in Task 6–3.

3/10/88

our heart ♡ is closer to the bird's than:

fish - 2 cambers   1 atruum , 1 venticle
frog - 3   "   2 atruim , 1 ventricle
reptile - 4 cambers BUT septeum isn't totally formed
         between ventriles

5 quarts in a min.
75 gallons an hour
1800 gallons a day

20 seconds for the complete cycle

see sheets

Arteries → away from heart
Viens → toward the heart

                                    Left Side

                                  — arteries
                                  — arteriole
                                  — capillaries
                                  — venules

                              — veins

arotic vavle → largest narle
Vena cava → "   vien

Color Figure 6–2. A sample of AH's writing at age 15, from a ninth-grade biology class. Note the many phonologically implausible spelling errors, including letter transpositions (e.g., *valve → vavle, vein → vien, aortic → arotic*), insertion of a letter present elsewhere in the correct spelling (*septum → septeum*), and letter deletions (e.g., *chamber → camber, ventricle → ventrile, ventricle → venticle*).

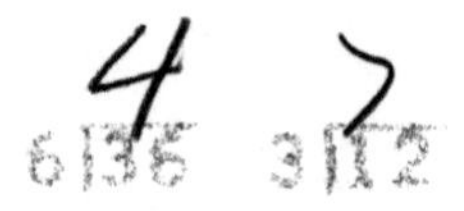

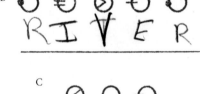

Color Figure 6–3. Two errors from an undated arithmetic paper, potentially result-ing from errors in perceiving the orientation (36 ÷ 6 = 4) and ordering (12 ÷ 3 = 7) of digits.

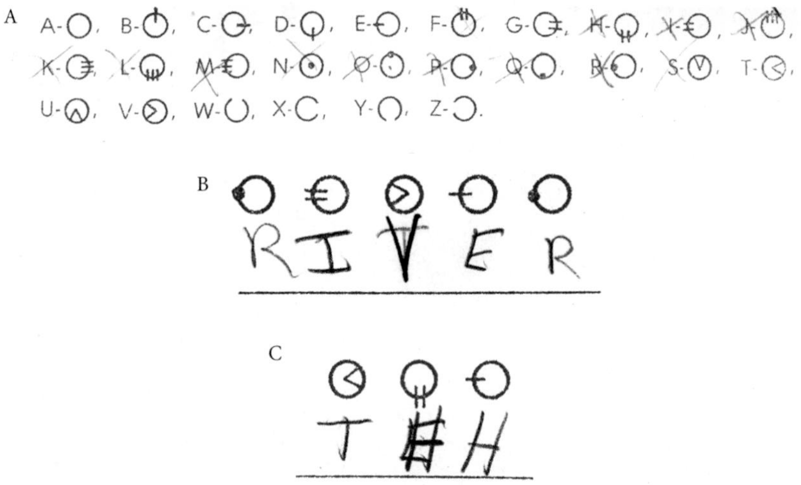

A   A-○, B-⊕, C-⊖, D-Ⓠ, E-⊖, F-⊕, G-⊖, H-Ⓠ, ⊖, ⊕,

K-⊖, L-Ⓠ, M-⊖, N-⊙, ○-⊙, P-⊖, Q-○, B-⊖, S-Ⓥ, T-⊘,

U-Ⓐ, V-⊘, W-○, X-C, Y-○, Z-○.

B   ○ ⊖ ⊘ ⊖ ○
    R I V E R

C   ⊘ Ⓠ ⊖
         T # H

Color Figure 6–4. (A) The key for a decoding task from a fifth-grade geography assignment. (B) Orientation confusion in which AH initially decoded the symbol for *V* as *T*. The symbols for *V* and *T* differ only in left–right orientation. (C) Error in which AH reversed the positions of H and E in decoding the word the.

Color Figure 6–5. Renoir's *A Girl with a Watering Can* and AH's sketch. Renoir, Auguste, *A Girl with a Watering Can*, Chester Dale Collection. Image courtesy of the Board of Trustees, National Gallery of Art, Washington, D.C., 1876, oil on canvas.

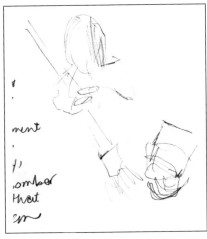

Color Figure 6–6. Rembrandt's *A Girl with a Broom* and AH's sketch. Workshop of Rembrandt van Rijn, possibly Fabritius Carel, *A Girl with a Broom*, Andrew W. Mellon Collection. Image courtesy of the Board of Trustees, National Gallery of Art, Washington, D.C., probably begun 1646–1648 and completed 1651, oil on canvas.

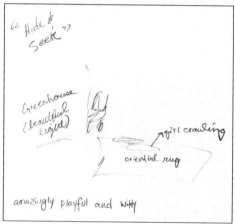

Color Figure 6–7. Tissot's *Hide and Seek* and AH's sketch. Tissot, James Jacques Joseph, *Hide and Seek*, Chester Dale Fund. Image courtesy of the Board of Trustees, National Gallery of Art, Washington, D.C., ca. 1877, oil on canvas.

Color Figure 6–8. Rembrandt's *The Mill* and AH's sketch. Rembrandt van Rijn, *The Mill*, Widener Collection. Image courtesy of the Board of Trustees, National Gallery of Art, Washington, D.C., 1645/1648, oil on canvas.

Color Figure 6–9. Renoir's *Luncheon of the Boating Party* and AH's sketch. Renoir, Pierre Auguste, *Luncheon of the Boating Party*, 1880–1881, oil on canvas. Acquired 1923. The Phillips Collection, Washington, D.C.

Color Figure 15–17. Examples of stimuli from the Gregory and McCloskey (2007) orientation study with normal adults.

Color Figure 15–18. The sixteen orientations at which stimuli were presented.

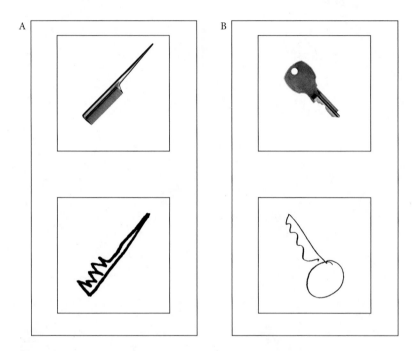

Color Figure 15–19. Two examples of object-axis reflection errors made by normal adult participants.

13

Location Representations and Frames of Reference: Evidence from AH

In Chapter 12 I distinguished definition and format questions concerning the representation of location in a frame of reference:

1. In relation to what are locations defined?
2. In what form are locations represented?

Whereas the vast majority of research on frames of reference has focused on the definition question, AH's perceptual deficit offers the opportunity to address both definition and format questions as they apply to the level(s) of representation giving rise to her localization errors. I begin with the format question and then consider the definitional question.

Coordinate-System Representations in the Visual System

The results presented in Part I (see especially Chapter 3) demonstrate that AH's location and orientation errors are highly systematic, taking the form of left–right and up–down reflections. For example, in the visually guided reaching task (Task 3–1, see Fig. 3–1) virtually all of her errors involved reaching to the location representing the left-right reflection of the target location across the midline. Accordingly, erroneous responses to stimuli at the 60° distant left location always involved reaching to the 60° distant right location, and errors for stimuli at the 30° close right location involved reaching to the 30° close left location.

AH's left–right and up–down reflection errors provide evidence for compositional location representations in the normal visual system (McCloskey et al., 1995). More specifically, her error pattern suggests that at the level(s) of the visual system where her errors arise, locations are represented in a spatial coordinate system defined by a reference point that serves as the origin and orthogonal axes through that point.

According to this coordinate-system hypothesis, an object's location is represented by specifying its distance and direction of displacement from the origin along each reference axis. For example, given a visual display involving a fixation point and a target stimulus (Fig. 13–1A), a coordinate system might be defined by horizontal and vertical axes through the fixation point (Fig. 13–1B). Assuming for convenience that polarity is assigned to the axes such that right and up are the positive directions and left and down are negative, the location of the target might be represented as follows (with distance in arbitrary units):

> Displacement from Origin on Horizontal Axis
> Direction   −
> Distance   50
> Displacement from Origin on Vertical Axis
> Direction   +
> Distance   20

The crucial assumptions of this hypothesis are (1) that location is represented with respect to orthogonal reference axes, (2) that the horizontal and vertical components of the location are represented separately, and (3) that for each of these components distance and direction of displacement along the reference axis are represented separately. Given these assumptions, AH's location errors may be interpreted by positing a selective visual deficit in which distance along reference axes is represented accurately but direction of displacement is frequently misrepresented. Misrepresenting a target's direction of displacement along a reference axis should lead to a localization error taking the form of a reflection across the orthogonal reference axis. For example, if direction of displacement along the horizontal axis were mistakenly specified as "+" for the X, the result would be a reflection across the vertical axis (see Fig. 13–1C). Similarly, if direction of displacement along the vertical axis were specified as "−," a reflection across the horizontal axis would result (Fig. 13–1D).[1]

As discussed in Chapter 12, cognitive scientists and neuroscientists often refer to hypothesized spatial representations with terms like *coordinates, coordinate system,* and *coordinate frame*; but in most instances the intended meaning is rather nonspecific—the terms are apparently not intended to imply that locations are represented as distances or angular displacements from reference points along reference axes (e.g., Arguin & Bub, 1993; Farah et al., 1990; Graziano et al., 1994). However, some researchers have posited explicit coordinate-system representations on the basis of behavioral

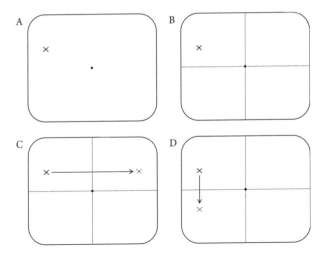

Figure 13–1. (A) A fixation point and an X displayed on a computer monitor. (B) Horizontal and vertical reference axes through the fixation point. (C) Localization error that would result from specifying + rather than – as the direction of displacement along the horizontal reference axis. (D) Localization error that would result from specifying – rather than + as the direction of displacement along the vertical reference axis. From McCloskey, M., & Rapp, B. (2000b). Attention-referenced visual representations: Evidence from impaired visual localization. *Journal of Experimental Psychology: Human Perception and Performance, 26,* 917–933. Copyright 2000 by the American Psychological Association. Reproduced with permission. The use of APA information does not imply endorsement by APA.

or neurophysiological evidence (e.g., Lacquaniti et al., 1995; O'Keefe & Nadel, 1978; O'Keefe, 1993; Soechting & Flanders, 1989, 1992). For example, Soechting and Flanders (1989, 1992) assessed people's accuracy in pointing to visually specified targets under several conditions and argued from the results that targeted arm movements require a transformation from an extrinsic coordinate system that represents target location in terms of azimuth, elevation, and radial distance from the shoulder to an intrinsic coordinate system specifying location in terms of yaw and elevation of the upper arm and forearm. AH's error pattern converges with the results of these previous studies to support the conclusion that the brain implements coordinate-system representations at some levels of spatial representation.

Like AH, patient PR (Pflugshaupt et al., 2007) exhibited reflection errors in visual localization tasks (see Chapter 11). As in the case of AH, PR's location reflections may be attributed to misrepresentations of displacement direction in coordinate-system representations, although for PR the misrepresentations are apparently limited to the horizontal axis (given that PR made left–right but not up–down reflections). Some of the other localization impairments discussed in Chapter 11 may also conceivably have resulted from deficits in creating or processing coordinate-system location representations.

For example, impaired representation of displacement direction along reference axes may have been implicated in some of the cases I described under the heading of Visual Allesthesia (e.g., Critchley, 1951, case 4). However, as I noted in reviewing the allesthesia cases, most were not studied in sufficient detail to permit clear conclusions. Impairment in representing distance along reference axes could perhaps underlie the near-miss errors made by some brain-damaged patients in reaching or other visual localization tasks (e.g., Holmes, 1918). If representations of distance along reference axes were noisy (either within the visual system or at some other level of spatial representation implicated in performing a task), the expected result would be responses directed to locations in the vicinity of, but not precisely at, the target locations. Again, however, no firm conclusions can be drawn because near-miss errors could also arise from spatial representations not in the form of coordinates.

Defining a Spatial Coordinate System

Having discussed the representational format question, I now turn to the definitional question: In relation to what are locations defined? This question is actually somewhat more complex than I implied in the preceding chapter, at least in the case of coordinate-system representations. A spatial coordinate system is characterized by several basic parameters, including (in the case of a Cartesian system) the location of the origin, the orientation and polarity of the reference axes, and the metric for scaling distances along the axes (e.g., Driver & Halligan, 1991; Logan, 1995). The definitional reference-frame question arises for each of these parameters, and the answer need not be the same for all parameters. For example, the origin of a coordinate system might be defined to coincide with the center of a visual display, whereas the orientation of the vertical axis might be defined by the direction of the gravitational force.

Given the assumptions of the coordinate-system hypothesis, AH's localization deficit can be used as a tool for probing certain parameters of the coordinate system(s) underlying her errors. More specifically, AH's error patterns permit inferences concerning the position of the origin and the orientation of the reference axes.

Consider, for example, the pattern of errors shown in Figure 13–2, in which an X was presented at one of the four positions shown and AH touched the screen to indicate where the X had appeared (see Task 3–2 in Chapter 3). Her pattern of left–right reflections implies a reference axis coinciding with a vertical line bisecting the display screen. An axis with a different orientation or a different horizontal position (e.g., somewhere to the right of the screen's center) could not account for the error pattern. We can therefore conclude that in the coordinate system giving rise to the errors one of the reference axes has a vertical orientation. Further, given that the vertical reference axis

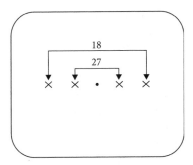

Figure 13–2. AH's pattern of localization errors for Task 3–2, in which a target stimulus was presented at one of four positions. Number above each arrow indicates the number of errors in which a stimulus presented at one of the connected positions was localized to the other position. For example, AH made eighteen errors in which a target presented at the far left position was localized to the far right position or vice versa. From McCloskey, M., & Rapp, B. (2000). Attention-referenced visual representations: Evidence from impaired visual localization. *Journal of Experimental Psychology: Human Perception and Performance, 26,* 917–933. Copyright 2000 by the American Psychological Association. Reproduced with permission. The use of APA information does not imply endorsement by APA.

by definition passes through the coordinate system's origin, the origin must lie somewhere along that axis. Put differently, the error pattern constrains the origin to a particular position along the horizontal dimension but does not specify its vertical position. (The vertical position of the origin can, however, be ascertained from AH's up–down errors; see Task 13–3.)

Whereas inferences about the position of the origin and the orientation of reference axes can be drawn rather straightforwardly from AH's errors, the bases for defining these parameters are more difficult to identify. In the task illustrated in Figure 13–2 AH faced the center of the display screen with head and body upright, looking at (and presumably attending to) the central fixation point. Under these circumstances, AH's retinal, head, and body midlines, the side borders of the display screen, and the direction of the gravitational force all had the same orientation (i.e., vertical). As a consequence, any of these potential sources of orientation information could have been used to define the orientation of the vertical reference axis revealed by AH's errors.

The basis for defining the origin of the coordinate system is similarly unclear. Given AH's error pattern, one possible location for the origin is the center of the display screen. An origin at this location could have been defined on the basis of the point of fixation, the dot that served as a fixation stimulus, AH's focus of attention, or the geometry of the screen itself. Although these potential bases for defining an origin were confounded in the task under discussion, they are conceptually distinct and potentially separable. For example, a dot on the display screen could be used to define a coordinate system origin, even if the dot did not coincide with the point of fixation. Similarly, the point fixated by the eyes could presumably define an origin, even if no visual stimulus were present at that point.

AH's head or body midline could conceivably also have played a role in defining the coordinate-system origin. Projected onto the plane of the display, both of these midlines coincided with a line bisecting the display screen. As a consequence, either midline could have been used to define the horizontal component of the origin's position. For instance, the head midline might have been used to define both the horizontal position of the origin and the orientation of the vertical reference axis. Some additional basis for defining the origin's position along the vertical dimension would then have been required.[2]

In this section I describe a study aimed at teasing apart the various potential bases for defining the origin of the coordinate system(s) underlying AH's localization deficit (McCloskey & Rapp, 2000b). The results from four tasks demonstrate that AH's errors vary systematically according to where her attention is focused, independently of how her eyes, head, or body are positioned or what potential reference stimuli are present in the visual field. From these findings I conclude that some level(s) of the normal visual system constructs *attention-centered* spatial representations, in which the focus of attention defines the origin of a spatial coordinate system.[3] By motivating this specific conclusion, the results also support the more general hypothesis that some of the brain's spatial representations take the form of coordinate systems in which locations are represented as displacements from an origin along reference axes.

Task 13–1

In this task an X was presented on a computer screen at a left, center, or right target location (L, C, and R in Fig. 13–3, respectively). Upon stimulus offset, AH touched the screen to indicate where the X had appeared. In the fixate right condition she was seated to the left of the screen's center, with her head and body facing a left intermediate position (LI in Fig. 13–3) between the left and center target locations. During each trial in this condition her eyes were fixated on a dot displayed at a right intermediate position (RI). In the fixate left condition AH was seated with head and body facing the right intermediate position and she fixated on the left intermediate position.

This experimental design dissociates several potential bases for defining the origin of a spatial coordinate system.[4] Because AH fixated on one screen location while her head and body faced another, the point of fixation and the to-be-fixated dot were separated horizontally from the head and body midlines. Further, all of these potential determinants of origin position were separated horizontally from the center of the display screen. As a consequence, AH's error pattern should vary according to how the origin is defined in the coordinate system(s) giving rise to the errors.

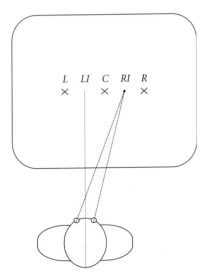

Figure 13–3. Screen locations for Task 13–1 (L, C, and R are left, center, and right target locations, respectively; LI and RI are left and right intermediate locations, respectively). Also shown is AH's position in the fixate right condition. *Dotted line* from the LI location indicates that AH's head and body midlines were aligned with this location; *dashed lines* from the RI location indicate that her eyes were fixated on this location. For convenience, the schematic shows a top view of AH and a frontal view of the screen. From McCloskey, M., & Rapp, B. (2000). Attention-referenced visual representations: Evidence from impaired visual localization. *Journal of Experimental Psychology: Human Perception and Performance, 26,* 917–933. Copyright 2000 by the American Psychological Association. Reproduced with permission.The use of APA information does not imply endorsement by APA.

If the origin were defined by the point of fixation or the to-be-fixated dot, then the vertical reference axis would pass through the fixated intermediate location (i.e., the left intermediate position in the fixate left condition and the right intermediate position in the fixate right condition). In this case AH's errors should take the form of reflections across the fixated location, as illustrated in Figure 13–4A for a target stimulus presented at the center target position in the fixate right condition. In contrast, if the head or body midline served to define the horizontal position of the origin, then the vertical reference axis would pass through the intermediate position AH's head and body were facing (i.e., the right intermediate position in the fixate left condition and the left intermediate position in the fixate right condition). Her errors should then take the form of reflections across this location (see Fig. 13–4B). If instead the origin were defined to coincide with the center of the display screen, AH's errors should be reflections across this central location (Fig. 13–4C). Finally, consider the possibility of an origin defined by AH's focus of attention. This possibility is suggested by the work of Nicoletti

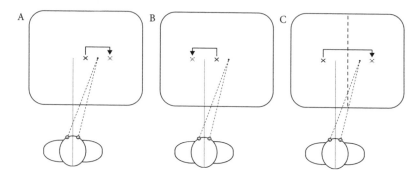

Figure 13–4. (A) Localization error expected in the fixate right condition for impairment involving a spatial coordinate system with vertical axis defined by the retinal midline, the fixation dot, or the focus of attention. (B) Localization error expected for coordinate system with vertical axis defined by head or body midline. (C) Localization error expected for coordinate system with vertical axis defined by center of screen. (*Vertical dashed line shows* vertical axis through the center of the screen.) From McCloskey, M., & Rapp, B. (2000). Attention-referenced visual representations: Evidence from impaired visual localization. *Journal of Experimental Psychology: Human Perception and Performance, 26,* 917–933. Copyright 2000 by the American Psychological Association. Reproduced with permission. The use of APA information does not imply endorsement by APA.

and Umiltà (1989, 1994) in which left–right stimulus–response compatibility effects were apparently determined by the position of the stimulus relative to the focus of attention and not its position relative to other potential reference points such as the fixation point or the center of the display screen.

    If the origin were defined by the focus of attention at the relevant level(s) of AH's visual system, her errors should take the form of reflections across the attended location. In the present task AH was not given any instructions about where to direct her attention; presumably, she simply attended to the location her eyes were fixating. Therefore, the expected errors for an origin defined by the focus of attention are the same as those for an origin defined by the point of fixation or the fixation dot: reflections across the fixated intermediate location (see Fig. 13–4A).

    Other potential determinants of the origin's position could also be considered (e.g., visual objects or features beyond the borders of the display screen, AH's right shoulder, and so forth). However, origins defined on grounds such as these would lead to mislocalizations of target stimuli to positions beyond the screen borders or at least would not yield reflections across the center, fixated intermediate, or nonfixated intermediate screen locations. Therefore, to the extent that AH's errors fall into one or more of these types, it seems reasonable to limit consideration to the potential origin determinants detailed in the preceding discussion.

Method

The target stimulus was a 0.95° × 0.95° white X presented for 1000 milliseconds on a black background. The fixation dot was a 0.14°-diameter white circle. The center target position was at the horizontal and vertical center of the screen, and the left and right target locations were displaced 8.4° horizontally from the center. The left and right intermediate locations were 4.2° from the center of the screen.

Four blocks of thirty-six trials—two fixate right blocks and two fixate left blocks—were presented in an ABBA design. In each block twelve stimuli were presented at each of the three target locations. Ordering of stimuli within blocks was random.

AH was tested in a lighted room at a distance of 41 cm from a computer monitor. She was seated with head and body straight ahead, facing the left (fixate right) or right (fixate left) intermediate position. A chin and forehead rest stabilized her head. A video camera beside the computer monitor was focused on her eyes and recorded eye position during the localization task. The videotape was subsequently reviewed by a judge who was blind to the stimulus and response on each trial, and all trials with detectable eye movements were excluded from analyses. (Pretesting revealed that eye movements as small as 0.84°—the smallest movements included in the pretest—were reliably detectable.)

Each trial began with the presentation of a flashing fixation dot at the right intermediate location (fixate right blocks) or the left intermediate location (fixate left blocks). After 500 milliseconds, the fixation dot became steady, and 1200 milliseconds later the target X was presented. The target and the fixation dot were displayed together for 1000 milliseconds, after which the screen went blank. A tone coincident with display offset signaled that a response could be made. AH responded by touching the screen with the eraser end of a pencil held in her right hand. (This procedure was used in preference to touching the screen with a finger, to avoid leaving marks on the screen.)

AH's responses were scored from the videotape. In this task, and the subsequent tasks reported in this chapter, the responses fell into clear clusters around specific screen locations. (The sole exceptions were one response from the present task and one response from Task 13–3 that fell between two clusters.) The scatter of responses around locations was comparable to that observed in pilot testing with normal participants. Also, AH's incorrect responses to a location (e.g., touching the right target position in response to a stimulus presented elsewhere) showed no more scatter than the correct responses to that location (e.g., touching the right target position in response to a target at that position). Therefore, I report responses classified according to the cluster into which they fell. For example, responses to the right target position are those falling within the cluster around that position.

Results

Eleven of the 144 trials (six from the fixate right condition and five from the fixate left condition) were excluded from analyses because of eye movements during stimulus presentation. On the remaining 133 trials AH made fifty-four errors in localizing the target stimulus. She erred on twenty-six of the sixty-six trials (39%) in the fixate right condition, and twenty-eight of the sixty-seven trials (42%) in the fixate left condition.

The localization errors showed a very clear pattern: fifty-three of the fifty-four errors (98%) were reflections across the fixated position. None of the errors was a reflection across the point AH's head and body were facing or a reflection across the center of the screen (see Fig. 13–5).

In the fixate right condition the point of fixation was halfway between the center and right target locations, and AH made sixteen errors in which she confused these two locations (Fig. 13–5A). In ten of the errors a stimulus presented at the center target position was reflected across fixation to the right position, and in the other six errors a stimulus at the right location was reflected to the center position. AH also made nine errors in which a stimulus presented at the left target position was localized to a far right position corresponding to the reflection of the stimulus location across the fixated position. These errors are particularly striking in that no stimulus was ever presented at the far right location. In the one remaining error a stimulus presented at the center position was localized to a position between the right and far right locations.

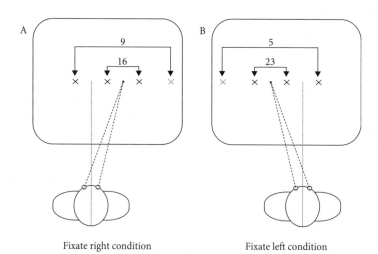

Fixate right condition   Fixate left condition

Figure 13–5. Localization errors involving reflection across the point of fixation in Task 13–1. From McCloskey, M., & Rapp, B. (2000). Attention-referenced visual representations: Evidence from impaired visual localization. *Journal of Experimental Psychology: Human Perception and Performance, 26*, 917–933. Copyright 2000 by the American Psychological Association. Reproduced with permission. The use of APA information does not imply endorsement by APA.

In the fixate left condition the center and left target locations were on opposite sides of fixation, and AH made twenty-three errors in which she confused these two locations (Fig. 13–5B). Eleven of the errors were reflections from the left to the center location, and twelve were center-to-left reflections. AH also made five errors in which a stimulus presented at the right target position was reflected across fixation to a far left position.

These results exhibit a straightforward pattern. AH made no errors taking the form of reflections across the location her head and body were facing, indicating that in the coordinate system(s) giving rise to the errors the horizontal position of the origin was not determined by the head or body midline. Further, no reflections across the center of the display screen were observed, implying that the origin was not defined by the center of the screen. Virtually all of the observed errors (53/54) were reflections across the fixated location. This error pattern conforms to that predicted for a coordinate system in which the origin was determined by the point fixated by the eyes, the fixation dot, or the focus of attention. The next two tasks were designed to tease apart these possibilities.

Task 13–2

This task dissociated the focus of attention from the point of eye fixation and the fixation dot. On each trial a target X was presented at one of four locations, as shown in Figure 13–6. AH was tested in two conditions—attend left and attend right—presented in separate blocks of trials. In both conditions she sat facing the center of the screen and maintained fixation on a central fixation dot. In the attend left condition she attended to a left intermediate position located between the near left and far left target locations; in the attend right condition she attended to a right intermediate position located between the near right and far right target locations. In both attention conditions the left and right intermediate positions were marked with small boxes.

AH was instructed that her primary task was to monitor the box at the specified intermediate position (right in the attend right condition, left in the attend left condition) for dots displayed briefly within the box. The dots, ranging in number from zero to three, were presented one at a time for 200 milliseconds each, centered in the box, and at unpredictable times before and/or during presentation of the target X. Upon stimulus offset, AH first reported the number of dots and then touched the screen to indicate where the X had appeared.

This procedure separates the focus of attention (i.e., the left or right intermediate position) from the point of eye fixation and the location of the fixation dot (i.e., the center position). If the origin is determined by the point of fixation or by the fixation dot at the relevant level(s) of representation, then regardless of where AH's attention is focused her errors should be

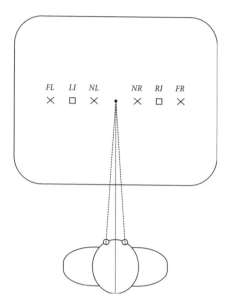

Figure 13–6. Screen locations for Task 13–2. Shown are the four target locations (indicated by Xs), the central fixation point, and the boxes marking the left and right intermediate locations. From McCloskey, M., & Rapp, B. (2000). Attention-referenced visual representations: Evidence from impaired visual localization. *Journal of Experimental Psychology: Human Perception and Performance, 26,* 917–933. Copyright 2000 by the American Psychological Association. Reproduced with permission. The use of APA information does not imply endorsement by APA.

reflections across the point of fixation. Specifically, in both the attend left and attend right conditions AH should confuse the far left position with the far right position and the near left position with the near right position.

In contrast, if the origin is determined by the focus of attention, AH's errors should be reflections across the attended location. In the attend left condition the attended location (the left intermediate position) is midway between the near left and far left target positions and AH should therefore confuse these two positions (e.g., stimulus at far left position, response to near left position). Similarly, in the attend right condition she should confuse the near right and far right positions (e.g., stimulus near right, response far right).

An origin could also be defined on the basis of the boxes displayed at the intermediate screen locations or the dots presented at the attended intermediate location on some trials. Rather than describing here the predicted error patterns for these various features of the visual environment, I postpone the discussion until after presenting the data, focusing then on environmental features that could have played a role in producing the observed error pattern.

Method

The near and far target positions were 3.37° and 10.11°, respectively, from the central fixation point. The intermediate position on each side was 6.74° from fixation, equidistant from the near and far target locations. The boxes marking the intermediate positions subtended 1° vertically and horizontally. The to-be-counted dots, which were presented within the attended box, were unfilled circles with a diameter of 0.14°.

AH was presented with four blocks of forty-eight trials, two in the attend left condition and two in the attend right condition. Each block included twelve presentations of the target X at each of the four locations. For each target location, the number of to-be-counted dots was zero on half of the trials and one, two, or three on the remaining half. Ordering of trials within blocks was random.

AH was seated facing the center of the screen, with her head in a chin and forehead rest. Instructions at the beginning of each block of trials specified the location to which attention should be directed. Each trial began with presentation of a flashing fixation point at the center of the screen and boxes (which did not flash) at the left and right intermediate positions. After 500 milliseconds the fixation point became steady, and 1200 milliseconds later the target X was presented. The target was displayed with the fixation point and boxes for 1000 milliseconds, after which the screen went blank. On trials with to-be-counted dots, each dot was displayed for 200 milliseconds, with at least 200 milliseconds between successive dots, at randomly chosen times during the interval beginning 300 milliseconds before presentation of the target X and ending with display offset. AH responded by first reporting the number of dots and then touching the location where the target X appeared. Eye movements were monitored as in Task 13–1.

Results

Ten of the 192 trials (three in the attend right and seven in the attend left condition) were excluded from analyses because of eye movements during stimulus presentation. Considering the remaining trials, AH made localization errors for twenty-four of the ninety-three target stimuli in the attend right condition (26%) and twenty-four of the eighty-nine stimuli in the attend left condition (27%). In counting the dots presented at the attended location she was 84% correct (78/93) in the attend right condition and 83% correct (74/89) in the attend left condition.

Examination of the localization errors revealed both reflections across the attended location and reflections across the point of fixation. For convenience I will refer to these error types as "attention-related" and "fixation-related" reflections, respectively, intending these terms as theoretically neutral labels. I consider first the attention-related errors and then the fixation-related errors.

Attention-Related Errors In the attend right condition the attended location was between the near right and far right target locations, and AH made fourteen errors in which she confused these two locations (see Fig. 13–7A). In eight of these errors a stimulus at the near right position was reflected across the attended location to the far right position, and in the other six errors a stimulus at the far right position was reflected to the near right. These errors did not stem from a general tendency to confuse near and far locations as AH made no errors confusing the near left and far left locations, which flanked the nonattended left intermediate location.

In the attend left condition AH's attention was focused between the near left and far left locations, and she made fourteen near left–far left confusions (nine far-to-near and five near-to-far errors; see Fig. 13–7B). No confusions between the near and far right locations were observed.

Combining the results from the two conditions, AH made twenty-eight errors involving reflection across the attended intermediate location but no errors involving reflection across the nonattended intermediate location ($p < 0.001$ by sign test). This pattern is evident even if we consider only the trials on which no dots were presented at the attended location. For no-dot trials the stimuli were physically identical across the attend left and attend right conditions; only the focus of attention varied. On these trials AH made twelve errors involving reflection across the attended intermediate location and no errors involving reflection across the unattended intermediate location ($p < 0.001$ by sign test).[5]

Because AH's eyes fixated the central screen position while her attention was focused on the left or right intermediate position, the attention-related

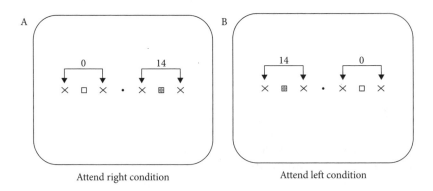

Attend right condition   Attend left condition

Figure 13–7. Localization errors involving reflection across the attended location in Task 13–2. *Gray dot* indicates the attended location. From McCloskey, M., & Rapp, B. (2000). Attention-referenced visual representations: Evidence from impaired visual localization. *Journal of Experimental Psychology: Human Perception and Performance, 26*, 917–933. Copyright 2000 by the American Psychological Association. Reproduced with permission. The use of APA information does not imply endorsement by APA.

errors cannot be attributed to a spatial coordinate system in which the origin was defined by the point of fixation or the fixation dot. Instead, the errors suggest that AH's deficit implicates an attention-centered coordinate system, in which the origin was determined by the focus of attention.

However, a potential alternative interpretation is that reflections around the attended location occurred not because attention was focused there but rather because visual stimuli presented at this location were used to define a coordinate-system origin. Considering first the to-be-counted dots presented on some trials at the attended location, "attention-related" errors could conceivably arise from a coordinate system with an origin defined on the basis of the dots. However, this interpretation could be applied only to trials in which to-be-counted dots were presented; it cannot account for the attention-related errors observed on no-dot trials.

The box displayed at the attended location might also have played a role in defining an origin. Because the box was present on every trial, a coordinate system with origin defined by the box could potentially account for attention-related errors on no-dot trials as well as on trials with dots. However, the attention-related errors cannot be interpreted simply by assuming that the origin was defined on the basis of the box, without regard to where attention was focused. On every trial identical boxes were displayed at the attended and nonattended intermediate locations. Therefore, if attention played no role in defining an origin, the origin should have been determined as often by the nonattended box as by the attended box and errors involving reflection across the nonattended location should have been as frequent as reflections across the attended location. The data, however, show twenty-eight reflections across the attended intermediate location and no reflections across the nonattended intermediate location.

The observed error pattern can be interpreted in terms of an origin defined by the attended box only by assuming that in the relevant spatial coordinate system(s) the origin was determined jointly by attention and by objects or features in the visual scene. Suppose in particular that attention serves the function of selecting visual stimuli to be used in defining an origin (and perhaps other coordinate-system parameters). In the present task the attended box, but not the nonattended box, might be selected as a basis for defining an origin, leading to reflections across the attended, but not the nonattended, location.

The attention-related errors are consistent, then, with two potential interpretations, both of which assume that attention plays a prominent role in defining the spatial coordinate system(s) underlying AH's localization errors. On one account the focus of attention per se provides the basis for defining the origin, without regard to whatever visual stimuli (if any) are present at the attended location. On the other account attention serves to pick out visual objects or features, which are then used to define an origin. In a subsequent task (Task 13–4) I attempt to tease apart these alternatives, asking whether the focus of attention can define the origin of a coordinate system even when no visual stimuli are present at the attended location.

Fixation-Related Errors In addition to attention-related errors, AH made twenty errors involving reflection across the central fixation point. In the attend right condition she made seven errors confusing the far left and far right locations and three errors confusing the near left and near right positions. In the attend left condition she made four far left–far right confusions and six near left–near right confusions. (These counts remain unchanged if we consider only trials for which AH was correct in counting the dots presented at the attended location.)

The fixation-related errors may indicate that AH's deficit implicates not only a spatial coordinate system in which attention plays a defining role but also a coordinate system with an origin determined by the point of fixation or the fixation dot. However, another possibility is that the fixation-related errors, like the attention-related errors, arose from an attention-centered coordinate system. Suppose that on some trials AH failed to attend to the designated intermediate location but instead kept her attention focused on the fixation point. For trials on which attention remained at fixation, an attentional interpretation could assume either that the focus of attention per se served as the basis for defining an origin or that attention selected the fixation dot as the visual stimulus to be used in defining the origin. In either case, errors occurring in the resulting coordinate system would take the form of reflections across the point of fixation.

Some support for the attentional interpretation comes from the finding that all twenty of the fixation-related errors occurred on trials in which no dots were presented at the attended location. If the dots played some role in drawing AH's attention to the to-be-attended location (acting as "exogenous" cues; see, e.g., Posner, 1980), then failures to shift attention from the fixation point would presumably have been more likely on no-dot trials than on trials with dots. Regardless of how we interpret the fixation-related errors, however, the attention-related errors provide strong evidence for a spatial coordinate system in which attention plays a defining role.

Task 13–3

I have interpreted the attention-related errors observed in Task 13–2 as evidence of a spatial coordinate system in which the origin is defined by the focus of attention per se or by a visual stimulus picked out by attention (in this case the box presented at the attended location). On this interpretation the origin of the coordinate system coincides with the attended location. However, because Task 13–2 tested only left–right localization, the observed attention-related errors speak to the position of the origin only along the horizontal dimension; the errors do not specify the vertical position of the origin. As a consequence, the pattern of attention-related errors could be interpreted in terms of a coordinate system with an origin located anywhere along a vertical line passing through the attended location. In Task 13–3 I used AH's impaired up–down localization to ask whether the origin of the coordinate system(s) giving rise to attention-related errors coincides vertically as well as horizontally with the attended location.

Method

Procedures were virtually identical to those of Task 13-2, except that stimulus locations were arrayed vertically rather than horizontally (see Fig. 13-8). On each trial a target X was presented at a far up, near up, near down, or far down location. AH sat facing the center of the screen and maintained fixation on a central fixation dot. In the attend up condition she attended to an up intermediate position, and in the attend down condition she attended to a down intermediate position. In both attention conditions the up and down intermediate positions were marked with boxes and to-be-counted dots were presented in the box at the attended location. The near and far target positions were 2.12° and 6.36°, respectively, from the central fixation point. The intermediate positions were 4.24° from fixation, equidistant from the near and far target locations. (The vertical spacing between locations—2.12°—was somewhat smaller than the horizontal spacing in Task 13-2—3.37°—because preliminary testing indicated that shifting attention a substantial distance from fixation was more difficult for vertical than for horizontal displacements.) AH was presented with six blocks of forty-eight trials, three in the attend up condition and three in the attend down condition.

Results

Twenty-one of the 288 trials (eleven in the attend up and ten in the attend down condition) were excluded from analyses because of eye movements during stimulus presentation. Considering the remaining trials, AH made localization errors for twelve of the 133 target stimuli in the attend up condition (9%) and fourteen of the 134 stimuli in the attend down condition (10%).

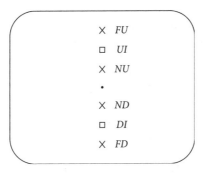

Figure 13–8. Screen locations for Task 13-3. Shown are the four target locations (indicated by Xs), the central fixation point, and the boxes marking the up and down intermediate locations.

Consistent with findings from previous tasks with AH (see, e.g., Task 3–3) the error rates for up–down localization were lower than those observed in Task 13–2 for left–right localization. (Nevertheless, AH's up–down localization performance is clearly impaired; error rates for pilot participants were less than 1%.) In counting the dots presented at the attended location, AH was 79% correct (105/133) in the attend up condition and 87% correct (117/134) in the attend down condition.

The pattern of localization errors was very similar to that of Task 13–2. In the attend up condition AH made nine attention-related errors in which she confused the near up and far up target positions (see Fig. 13–9A). In the attend down condition she made ten attention-related errors, confusing the near and far down locations (Fig. 13–9B). In contrast, she made no errors in either condition involving confusion of near and far locations on the nonattended side. Collapsing across conditions, AH made nineteen errors involving reflection across the attended intermediate location and no errors involving reflection across the nonattended intermediate location ($p < 0.001$ by sign test). Considering only the trials on which no dots were presented at the attended location, AH made seven errors involving reflection across the attended intermediate location and no errors involving reflection across the unattended intermediate location ($p < 0.01$ by sign test). For these no-dot trials the stimuli were physically identical across the attend up and attend down conditions.[6]

By the logic I have used in interpreting AH's left–right localization errors, the up–down attention-related errors imply a horizontal reference axis passing through the attended location and, hence, an origin lying somewhere along that axis. The error pattern therefore indicates that the origin's position along the vertical dimension is the same as that of the attended location. Taken together with the results of Task 13–2, this finding supports the conclusion that in the coordinate system(s) giving rise to attention-related errors the origin coincides (both vertically and horizontally) with the attended location.

In addition to the attention-related reflections, AH made six errors involving reflection across the central fixation point. In the attend up condition she made three errors confusing the far up and far down locations; in the attend down condition she made two far up/far down confusions and one near up/near down confusion. As in Task 13–2 the fixation-related errors may have arisen from a coordinate system in which the origin was defined by the point of fixation or the fixation dot. On the other hand, these errors may have originated within an attention-centered coordinate system, on trials in which AH failed to shift her attention away from the fixation point. Once again, all of the fixation-related errors occurred on no-dot trials, providing some support for the attentional interpretation.

Finally, AH made a single error that did not fall into any of the response clusters centered on target locations: In the attend down condition, a target presented at the near up location was localized to a position between the near

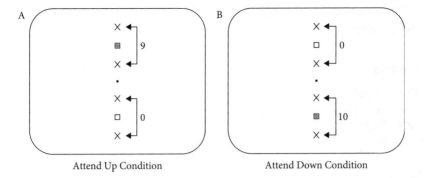

Figure 13–9. Localization errors involving reflection across the attended location in Task 13–3. *Gray dot* indicates the attended location. From McCloskey, M., & Rapp, B. (2000). Attention-referenced visual representations: Evidence from impaired visual localization. *Journal of Experimental Psychology: Human Perception and Performance, 26,* 917–933. Copyright 2000 by the American Psychological Association. Reproduced with permission. The use of APA information does not imply endorsement by APA.

up and far up response clusters, at approximately the up intermediate location. This response was counted as an error but was not sorted into any of the error categories discussed above.

Task 13–4

Tasks 13–2 and 13–3 provide evidence that attention is involved in defining the origin of the spatial coordinate system(s) implicated in AH's deficit. However, because a box was displayed at the attended (and nonattended) intermediate locations in these tasks, the results do not establish whether the focus of attention per se can serve as the basis for defining an origin or whether instead attention acts to pick out a visual object or feature which is then used to define an origin. The aim of Task 13–4 was to distinguish between these alternatives.

This left–right localization task was a straightforward replication of Task 13–2, with the exception that no box was displayed at either the attended or nonattended intermediate location. As in Task 13–2, to-be-counted dots were presented at the attended location on half of the trials and no dots were presented on the remaining half of the trials.

The trials of particular interest were the no-dot trials. For these trials no visual stimulus was presented at the attended location; rather, the location was blank throughout the trial. As a consequence, reflections across the attended location on the no-dot trials could not be attributed to a coordinate system in which the origin is anchored to visual stimuli at the attended location. If, then, we observe attention-related reflections on no-dot trials, this result would indicate that the origin can be defined by the focus of attention per se, independent of objects or features in the visual scene.

Method

Stimuli and procedures were identical to those of Task 13–2, except that no boxes were presented at the intermediate locations and AH was instructed to attend to the appropriate (unmarked) region on the screen. Ten blocks of forty-eight trials were presented, five in each of the two attention conditions.

Results

Thirty of the 480 trials (fifteen in each of the attention conditions) were excluded from analyses because of eye movements. Considering the remaining trials, AH made localization errors for 19% of the target stimuli in both the attend right condition and the attend left condition (43/225 in each condition). In counting the dots at the attended location her accuracy was 90% (203/225) in the attend right condition and 89% (201/225) in the attend left condition.

As in Tasks 13–2 and 13–3, AH's localization errors were strongly influenced by where her attention was focused (see Fig. 13–10). In the attend right condition she made twenty-one errors in which she confused the near right and far right target positions. In contrast, she made only one near left–far left confusion. In the attend left condition AH made twenty-six confusions of the near and far left locations and no confusions of near and far right locations. Collapsing across conditions, AH made forty-seven errors involving reflection across the attended intermediate location but only one error involving reflection across the nonattended intermediate location ($p < 0.001$ by sign test).[7]

Of particular importance are the trials in which no dots were presented at the attended location. On the no-dot trials AH made eleven errors involving reflection across the attended intermediate location but only one error involving reflection across the unattended intermediate location ($p < 0.01$ by sign test). The attention-related reflections cannot be attributed to a coordinate system with an origin anchored to some visual object or feature because no visual stimuli appeared at the attended location on no-dot trials. The occurrence of attention-related errors on these trials therefore supports the hypothesis that the origin of an attention-centered coordinate system can be defined by the focus of attention per se and need not be anchored to visual objects or features.

In addition to attention-related errors, AH made thirty-eight errors involving reflection across the central fixation point. In the attend right condition she made nine errors confusing the far left and far right locations and twelve errors confusing the near left and near right positions. In the attend left condition she made six far left/far right confusions and eleven near

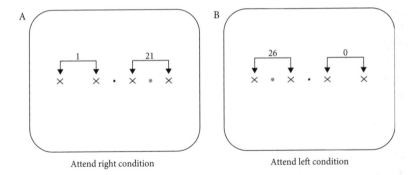

Figure 13–10. Localization errors involving reflection across the attended location in Task 13–4. *Gray dot* indicates the attended location.

left/near right confusions. As in the previous tasks, all of the fixation-related errors occurred on no-dot trials, suggesting yet again that these errors may have originated from an attention-centered coordinate system on trials in which AH failed to shift her attention away from the fixation point.

Implications and Conclusions

The results from Tasks 13–1 through 13–4 speak to the basis for defining locations at the level of the visual system from which AH's localization errors arise. In Task 13–1 AH's head and body faced one location on a display screen, while she fixated—and presumably attended to—a different location. Virtually all of her errors took the form of left–right reflections across the location she was fixating and attending to; none of the errors was a reflection across the location her head and body were facing or a reflection across the center of the screen. These results indicated that in the spatial coordinate system(s) giving rise to AH's errors the origin was not defined (in whole or in part) by the head midline, the body midline, or the center of the display screen. The data suggested instead that the origin was determined by the point AH's eyes were fixating, the dot that served as a fixation stimulus, or the focus of attention. In Task 13–2 AH fixated one location while attending to another, dissociating the focus of attention from the point of fixation and the fixation dot. She made many errors involving left–right reflection across the attended location, suggesting that her deficit implicates an attention-centered coordinate system in which the origin is defined either by the focus of attention per se or by a visual stimulus on which attention is focused. In Task 13–3 AH showed a systematic pattern of attention-related errors in up–down localization, demonstrating that attention is involved in defining the vertical as well as the horizontal position of the origin at the level(s) of representation implicated in her deficit. Finally, in Task 13–4 AH made attention-related reflection errors even when no visual stimuli were presented at the attended location, indicating that in the coordinate system(s) giving rise to her errors the origin can be defined by the focus of attention per se, without regard to objects or features in the visual environment. More generally, these findings support the hypothesis that at least some spatial representations in the visual system take the form of coordinate systems in which locations of objects are represented as displacements from an origin along reference axes.

The results of the present experiments also have implications for conclusions about the level(s) of the visual system at which AH's errors arise. Given the evidence that visual stimuli are represented in retina-based frames of reference at least through the V1/V2/V3 complex (see, e.g., Livingstone & Hubel, 1988; Sereno et al., 1995; Tootell et al., 1995; Zeki, 1993), the attention-based representations revealed by the present experiments are presumably to be found in some later visual area(s). (Neurons in early cortical visual areas may show increased spontaneous activity and enhanced responses to stimuli when the focus of attention includes the neuron's receptive field [see, e.g., Kastner, Pinsk, De Weerd, Desimone, & Ungerleider, 1999; Luck, Chelazzi, Hillyard, & Desimone, 1997; Motter, 1993]. However, these forms of attentional modulation do not appear sufficient to implement spatial representations in which location is represented in terms of distance and direction of displacement from the focus of attention.) Consequently, AH's attention-related reflection errors presumably did not arise at some early retina-based level(s) of the visual system but rather at a subsequent level (or levels). Hence, the results of the attention experiments support the conclusion, drawn on other grounds in Chapter 6, that AH's deficit affects high-level vision.

Whether all of AH's errors arise within an attention-centered coordinate system is not entirely certain. At the least, however, it may safely be said that the present results provide no clear evidence of errors originating at any other level of representation. Task 13–1 created conditions conducive for observing errors arising from head-, body-, and environment-centered frames of reference; but AH made no such errors. In Tasks 13–2 through 13–4, which separated the to-be-attended location from the point of eye fixation, AH committed some errors involving reflection across the point of fixation. However, these errors could be interpreted straightforwardly as attention-centered reflections, given the assumption that AH sometimes failed to shift her attention away from the fixation point: On trials in which AH's attention remained at fixation, attention-centered errors would take the form of reflections across the point of fixation. This interpretation is especially plausible in light of the finding that all of the fixation-related reflections occurred on no-dot trials. When dots were presented at the to-be-attended location, AH's attention was presumably drawn to that location; however, on no-dot trials she may sometimes have had difficulty shifting her attention away from fixation. Note that the association between fixation-related errors and no-dot trials was clearly not coincidental. Across Tasks 13–2 through 13–4, AH made sixty-four fixation-related errors, and these errors occurred without exception on no-dot trials. Given that dots were presented on half of the trials in each task, the probability of all sixty-four fixation-related errors occurring by chance on no-dot trials is vanishingly small (i.e., 1 in 2^{64}).

Given these considerations, the most plausible conclusion appears to be that AH's errors arise solely within an attention-centered frame of reference. As the preceding discussion suggests, however, this conclusion must be considered tentative.

Additional Evidence for Attention-Based Representations

In addition to the results from AH, two other sets of findings provide some evidence for attention-based spatial representations.

Attention and the Simon Effect

One form of evidence involves a stimulus–response compatibility phenomenon referred to as the "Simon effect" (see Lu & Proctor, 1995, for a comprehensive review). In a typical Simon effect study participants press a left or right response key based on some nonspatial attribute of a stimulus presented on the left or right (e.g., red square → left key, green square → right key). Although the location of the stimulus is task-irrelevant, a spatial compatibility effect is usually observed: Left-key responses are faster for left-side than right-side stimuli, and right-key responses are faster for right- than left-side stimuli (e.g., Craft & Simon, 1970; Hedge & Marsh, 1975; Umiltà & Liotti, 1987). This result is usually interpreted by assuming that the location of the stimulus, although irrelevant, is nevertheless encoded, leading to Stroop-like interference if the stimulus and response are on opposite sides.

Nicoletti and Umiltà (1989, 1994) have reported Simon effect experiments in which the compatibility of a stimulus with a left- or right-key response was apparently determined by the position of the stimulus relative to the focus of attention and not its position relative to other potential reference points (e.g., the head or body midline, the fixation point). Nicoletti and Umiltà (1989, 1994; Umiltà & Nicoletti, 1992; see also Stoffer, 1991; Stoffer & Yakin, 1994) interpret this finding as evidence that stimulus location is coded with respect to the point where attention is focused.

Hommel (1993) has criticized this interpretation, arguing that the Nicoletti and Umiltà results may reflect spatial representations defined on the basis of objects in the visual environment: "stimuli may not have been coded in relation to the focus of spatial attention, but in relation to a certain reference object that also happened to be the object to which spatial attention was currently directed" (p. 209). Hommel is apparently referring to the fact that in Nicoletti and Umiltà's experiments the to-be-attended location was marked by a black square or digit. In Nicoletti and Umiltà's (1989) experiment 5 the marker stimulus was present throughout each trial; in the three other experiments showing attention-related Simon effects—experiments 3 and 4 in Nicoletti and Umiltà

(1989) and experiment 1 in Nicoletti and Umiltà (1994)—the marker appeared at the beginning of each trial and terminated 500 milliseconds before presentation of the target stimulus. Conceivably, the marker stimulus could have been used as a basis for defining the origin of a spatial coordinate system, and the location of the target stimulus could then have been represented within that system. If we assume that the defined coordinate system could be maintained at least briefly following the offset of the marker stimulus, this interpretation would apply to all four of the Nicoletti and Umiltà experiments.

Accordingly, the Nicoletti and Umiltà (1989, 1994) findings should probably not be taken as evidence that the focus of attention per se can define the origin of a coordinate system. However, the results do support the weaker claim that attention either plays a direct role in defining an origin or contributes indirectly by picking out a visual object or feature which is then used to ground the origin. In particular, attention must presumably be invoked to explain why the stimulus marking the to-be-attended location, as opposed to one of the many other visual stimuli present in the Nicoletti and Umiltà (1989, 1994) displays, was chosen as a basis for defining the origin. This is especially true for Nicoletti and Umiltà's (1989) experiment 5, in which five digits were present on each trial, with only one of these marking the to-be-attended location.

The attention-related representations revealed by the Nicoletti and Umiltà (1989, 1994) experiments are not necessarily visual representations; more abstract spatial representations, or perhaps even response-related representations, could conceivably underlie the reported effects. Hence, Nicoletti and Umiltà's findings suggest that attention is implicated in defining some forms of spatial representation but do not argue specifically that attention per se provides a basis for defining coordinate-system representations in the visual system.

Single-Cell Recording

A different form of evidence for attention-based representations has been reported by Connor, Gallant, Preddie, and Van Essen (1996, 1997), who recorded from single cells in macaque area V4. For each cell, rectangular bars were presented in the cell's retinal receptive field while the monkey attended (without making eye movements) to one of four circles displayed at the corners of an imaginary square surrounding the receptive field. For over 80% of the recorded cells, firing rate in response to the bar stimuli varied systematically as a function of where attention was focused. For example, Connor et al. (1996) illustrate the behavior of a cell that responded more strongly to a stimulus in its receptive field when the receptive field was above or to the right of the point where attention was focused than when the receptive field was below or to the left of the attended location.

Although strong conclusions would be premature, these V4 cells appear to code jointly for retinal location and attention-based location. Consider a neuronal population that includes cells corresponding to each possible combination of retinal receptive field location and preferred direction relative to the focus of attention. The pattern of activity across the population could be thought of as cross-classifying a stimulus according to its retinal location and its attention-based location. Although this form of representation is not purely attention-based, the retinal and attention-based location information are potentially separable: Retinal location can be recovered by considering the pattern of activity only in relation to the cells' retinal receptive fields, and attention-based location is recoverable by considering the activity pattern only with respect to the cells' preferred directions relative to the focus of attention.

I do not offer the Connor et al. (1996, 1997) results as evidence that the attention-based representations underlying AH's errors are implemented by cells in V4. For one thing, attention-based representations could be computed within more than one visual subsystem. Also, because a visual stimulus was present at the attended location throughout each trial in the Connor et al. study, the findings do not provide evidence that the focus of attention per se can serve as a basis for defining a spatial reference frame. Finally, it is not clear that the spatial representations probed by Connor et al. are coordinate-system representations, in which location is represented in terms of distance and direction from reference axes. Hence, I view the Connor et al. findings simply as enhancing the plausibility of the hypothesis that attention-based representations are among those used by the visual system in representing location.

Constructing Attention-Centered Coordinate Systems

In proposing that attention defines the origin of spatial coordinate systems at some level(s) of the visual system, I have thus far had nothing to say about how the focus of attention could be used to define an origin. This is an important issue, especially given that theories of attention often assume that spatial representations provide the basis for directing attention to locations or objects (e.g., Posner & Cohen, 1984; Treisman & Gelade, 1980; van der Heijden, 1992; see Logan, 1995, for a general discussion). If spatial representations are needed to direct attention, how can attention be used to define spatial representations?

Although I cannot offer a detailed theory concerning the construction of attention-centered coordinate systems, I can provide a rough sketch of how the process might work. I assume that the starting point is a pre-existing spatial representation of the visual stimuli to be placed within the attention-centered framework. This prior representation, which I call the "parent representation," could take a variety of forms; for example, it need not be retina-based, and it need not be a coordinate-system representation. However, for purposes of illustration I will assume a parent representation in the form of a coordinate system with horizontal and vertical reference axes running through an origin defined by the point of fixation. Figure 13–11A depicts a representation of this sort for a fixation dot and a far left target stimulus presented in the attend left condition of Task 13–4. The fixation point, which coincides with the origin of the coordinate system, has coordinates (0,0). The target stimulus has coordinates (–90,0), corresponding to a displacement along the horizontal axis of 90 units in the negative direction and no displacement along the vertical axis.

Creating an attention-centered coordinate system is a matter of defining the system's parameters (e.g., position of origin, orientation of axes) with respect to the parent framework. Accordingly, as a prerequisite for defining the origin of the attention-centered system, attention must be directed to, and within, the parent representation. I assume that attention can be directed to a point or region in this representation and that the process of directing attention involves representing the location of the attentional focus within the parent representation. Figure 13–11B illustrates the result of this process: The attentional focus, indicated by the gray dot, has been assigned fixation-centered coordinates (–60,0). Representing the location of the attentional focus may be important for allocating processing resources to the attended region. However, for the present purposes, the important point is that once the focus of attention is represented within the parent representation, the

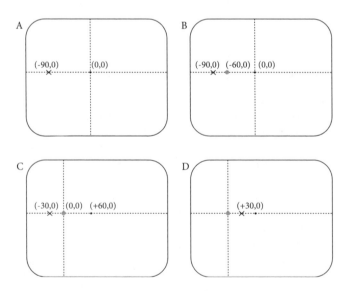

Figure 13–11. (A) Retina-based parent representation for a target stimulus and fixation dot. (B) Parent representation with the focus of attention marked (indicated by the *dotted circle*). (C) Accurate attention-centered representation. (D) Inaccurate attention-centered representation resulting from an error in representing direction of displacement along the horizontal axis.

origin of an attention-centered coordinate system may be defined simply as the represented location.[8]

The other parameters of the attention-centered system (e.g., orientation of axes) would also be defined within, or in relation to, the parent representation. For instance, to define a vertical axis orientation on the basis of gravity, the orientation of the gravitational force would have to be related to the retina-based parent representation in some way (e.g., through vestibular information about the orientation of the head with respect to gravity taken together with information about the orientation of the retina relative to the head).

Defining the parameters of the attention-centered coordinate system with respect to the parent system provides the basis for transforming the parent's representations of location into attention-centered coordinates. For example, assuming for simplicity that the axes of the attention-centered system were defined to have the same orientation and polarity as those of the parent system, the attention-centered representation in Figure 13–11C could be constructed from the parent representation in Figure 13–11B. By virtue of its role as the origin of the attention-centered system, the attentional focus has coordinates (0,0). The coordinates for the target stimulus are (–30,0), and the location of the fixation point is represented as (+60,0).[9]

This sketch, although speculative and incomplete, suffices to show that the notion of an attention-centered coordinate system is not inconsistent with current theories of attention. My assumptions allow for both a role of spatial representations in directing attention and a role of attention in constructing spatial representations: The parent representation provides a basis for directing attention to locations or objects, and the focus of attention defined within the parent representation then provides a basis for constructing attention-centered coordinate systems.

In light of the preceding discussion I can now suggest an interpretation for AH's visual localization errors that is somewhat more specific than the account presented earlier in this chapter. In particular, I suggest that AH's localization errors occur when processes that construct attention-centered location representations from lower-level representations err in specifying direction of displacement along reference axes in the attention-centered coordinate system. For example, Figure 13–11D illustrates an error in which the target's direction of displacement along the horizontal axis of the attention-centered frame is misrepresented as positive rather than negative, resulting in a horizontal reflection across the focus of attention.

Functions of Attention-Based Representations

One important question for subsequent research is, what functions might attention-based representations serve in visual–spatial processing? Nicoletti and Umiltà (1994; Umiltà & Nicoletti, 1992; see also Stoffer & Yakin, 1994) suggest that these representations may be used in programming shifts of attention, pointing out that a representation specifying the distance and direction of an object from the current focus of attention gives the distance and direction over which attention must be shifted to reach that object. Although this hypothesis may have merit, attention-based representations could not be the only basis for directing attention to an object or location; as we have seen, attention must be directed within a prior representation in order to construct an attention-based representation in the first place.

The attention-related reaching errors made by AH in the present tasks suggest that attention-based representations play a role in reaching to visually specified targets. Theories of motor programming usually take as given that reaching is mediated by some form of body-based representation (e.g., a representation referenced to the shoulder; see, e.g., Soechting & Flanders, 1989, 1992). However, the present results raise the possibility that at least some reaching movements are planned within an attention-based coordinate system. An alternative possibility is that attention-based representations are computed as an intermediate step in the process of transforming initial retina-based representations of target location into the body-based representations needed for reaching. However, this interpretation stands in contrast to the conventional assumption that retinal representations are transformed to head-based representations and thence to body-based representations, without involvement of attention-based representations. Thus, AH's reaching errors pose interesting challenges to our understanding of motor programming and visual–spatial representation.

AH makes left–right and up–down reflection errors not only in reaching but also in many other circumstances (e.g., copying drawings, responding verbally to the location of a visual stimulus). This observation suggests the hypothesis—admittedly speculative—that attention-based representations are implicated in a broad range of visual–spatial functions. Determining what specific functions implicate attention-based representations and what specific roles these representations play are important goals for future research.

Finally, I note that, almost without exception, studies aimed at identifying the reference frame(s) underlying particular aspects of normal or impaired spatial processing (e.g., object recognition, planning of movements, mental rotation, hemispatial neglect) have not considered the possibility that object location or orientation might be represented in an attention-based coordinate system. To mention just one example, in the mental rotation study described in Chapter 12, Cave et al. (1994) interpreted their findings as evidence for retina-based location representations in mental images. However, attention-based representations, which Cave et al. did not consider, are equally consistent with the data. Given the possibility that attention-based representations may be broadly implicated in visual–spatial processing, I suggest that researchers take account of this possibility when designing experiments to dissociate reference frames.

14

Orientation Representations and Frames of Reference: The COR Hypothesis

Representing the orientation of objects in the visual field is important for a variety of reasons. For example, perceiving the direction in which predators or potential prey are facing is a life-or-death matter for many creatures, and a person reaching out to grasp an object must apprehend how that object is oriented in order to position her hand appropriately. Even in circumstances not involving direct interaction with objects, information about orientation may be crucial for interpreting a visual scene. The significance of a scene may, for instance, be quite different depending upon whether two people in the scene are facing toward or away from one another. Orientation is also important in processing visual symbols, such as arrows on street signs or letters of the alphabet (e.g., *b, d, n, u*).

Despite the importance of orientation information, little attention has been directed toward questions concerning how the orientation of objects is represented in the visual system (or elsewhere in the brain). Neurophysiological research has identified cells in primary visual cortex that are sensitive to the orientation of edges (e.g., Hubel & Wiesel, 1968). However, encoding the orientation of an entire object presumably implicates higher-order representations at more central levels of the visual system, and the available neurophysiological evidence does not speak to the nature of such representations.

A substantial body of behavioral research explores orientation processing in normal and impaired children and adults as well as in nonhuman species. In addition to clarifying the concept of orientation (Howard & Templeton, 1966; Howard, 1982), this research documents a variety of interesting phenomena, including difficulties in processing oblique orientations (for reviews, see Appelle, 1972; Rudel, 1982) and problems in mirror-image discrimination (for reviews, see Corballis & Beale, 1976; Bornstein, 1982; see also Davidoff & Warrington, 2001; Harris et al., 2001; Turnbull, 1997; Turnbull et al., 1995, 1997, 2002; Turnbull & McCarthy, 1996a). In the context of these phenomena, some general suggestions about representation of orientation have been offered. For example, several researchers have suggested that difficulties in discriminating left–right mirror images (e.g., *b* and *d*, → and ←) are a consequence of *reduction coding*, in which the internal representation of a stimulus (somehow) fails to represent the difference between the two mirror-image orientations, or *duplication coding*, in which representations of both orientations are generated regardless of the actual orientation of the stimulus (see, e.g., Corballis & Beale, 1976, 1984; Deregowski, McGeorge, & Wynn, 2000; Noble, 1968; Orton, 1937). However, these suggestions say nothing about how an object's orientation is represented.

Progress in understanding normal and impaired processing of object orientation requires the formulation of specific hypotheses concerning the nature of orientation representations. My aim in this chapter is to present one such hypothesis. The hypothesis builds upon the assumptions of the coordinate-system hypothesis of location representation discussed in the preceding chapter.

Representing Orientation

Extension of the coordinate-system location-representation hypothesis to encompass orientation is not entirely trivial. Orientation representations are somewhat more complex than location representations because representations of orientation involve (I will suggest) not a single reference frame but rather relationships between reference frames. Furthermore, in representing the relationship of one reference frame to another multiple parameters must be specified. For most of these parameters various alternative forms of representation can be envisioned, and in some cases I had no firm basis for choosing one form over another. I have nevertheless opted to make a specific, albeit somewhat arbitrary, choice in these cases, believing that an erroneous but specific hypothesis is preferable to a vague proposal that does not allow clear predictions or interpretations. (In several such cases, I mention potential variants of, or alternatives to, my assumptions.) Hence, the hypothesis should be viewed as a preliminary proposal. A number of researchers have previously discussed orientation in terms of relationships between reference frames (e.g., Davidoff & Warrington, 2001; Harris et al., 2001; Howard, 1982; Ittelson, Mowafy, & Magid, 1991; Priftis et al., 2003; Riddoch & Humphreys, 1988; Turnbull & McCarthy, 1996a) but have not developed the notion into specific hypotheses about the nature of orientation representations in the brain.

In the following sections I first lay out the assumptions of the coordinate-system hypothesis of orientation representation and then discuss the various forms of orientation errors that could arise in constructing or using the posited representations. For convenience of expression, I refer to the proposal as the COR (Coordinate-system Orientation Representation) hypothesis.

Relating Object-Based and External Frames of Reference

I assume that at some level(s) of representation—in the visual system and perhaps in other perceptual, cognitive, or motor systems—the orientation of an object is represented as a relationship between an object-based frame of reference and a second frame of reference external to the object. For the sake of simplicity, I will consider only two-dimensional objects and reference frames; the hypothesis I develop could, however, be extended straightforwardly to three dimensions.

Consider the simple stimulus in Figure 14–1A, which has a particular orientation relative to the external frame of reference indicated by the dashed lines. The external frame (in this example or in any instance of orientation representation) could be defined by the axes of the observer's body or on some nonegocentric basis (e.g., the direction of the gravitational force, the walls of a room). For the present purposes, I simply assume an external coordinate system with orthogonal axes (which I will refer to as "vertical" and "horizontal"), without considering how the axes were defined. I further assume that each axis has a polarity, with one end designated positive (+) and the other negative (–). Finally, I assume that the external reference frame

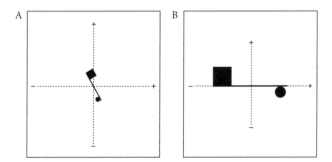

Figure 14–1. (A) Stimulus object in an external reference frame defined by horizontal and vertical axes. (B) Object-based representation, with principal axis defined by the object's major axis of elongation and secondary axis perpendicular to the principal axis. From McCloskey, M., Valtonen, J., & Sherman, J. (2006). Representing orientation: A coordinate-system hypothesis, and evidence from developmental deficits. *Cognitive Neuropsychology, 23,* 680–713. Copyright 2006 Taylor & Francis. Reproduced with permission.

need not be centered on the object; the centering in the figure is merely for illustrative convenience.

Figure 14–1B depicts an object-based representation of the stimulus object. I assume that the representation specifies the arrangement of object parts within a coordinate system defined by the object's principal axis of elongation and a secondary axis orthogonal to the principal axis. The representation might look something like the following:

    BAR
        LOCATION (0,0)
        TILT (0°)
    CIRCLE
        LOCATION (+20, −5)
    SQUARE
        LOCATION (−20, +10)
        TILT (0°)

The TILT component indicates how the part is tilted with respect to the principal object axis, and LOCATION (x, y) is shorthand for representations of displacement distance and direction along the principal and secondary axes. For example, LOCATION (+20, −5) indicates that the circle is displaced from the origin twenty units in the positive direction along the principal axis and five units in the negative direction along the secondary axis.

The representation as described is highly incomplete—for example, it says nothing about the sizes of the parts—and none of the details are intended as serious proposals about the form of object-based representations. My intent is merely to illustrate the general assumption that the object-based representation specifies how the parts of the object are arranged within an object-based coordinate system. Note that the object-based representation is *orientation-invariant*—that is, the representation carries no information about how the object or any of its parts is tilted or otherwise arranged relative to any external reference frame. For example, even though the bar is tilted relative to the axes of the external reference frame (as shown in Figure 14-1A), the object-based representation specifies a 0° tilt because the bar is aligned with the principal axis of the object-based frame; the bar's tilt relative to the external axes is simply not addressed. (Hence, in any illustration of an object-based representation, such as that in Figure 14–1B, the depicted orientation is arbitrary. Any other orientation could have been used, as long as the relationships between axes and object parts were maintained.)[1]

Given an object-based representation, the object's orientation relative to an external reference frame may be represented by specifying the relationship between the object-based frame and the external frame. I assume that the orientation representation specifies (*1*) a correspondence between object axes and external axes, (*2*) the tilt of the object axes relative to the external axes, and (*3*) the relationship between the polarity of the object axes and the polarity of the external axes. I consider each of these components in turn.

Axis Correspondence

This representational component specifies which object axes will be represented in relation to which external axes. In the case of a two-dimensional representation, two object-to-external axis mappings are possible. First, as illustrated in Figure 14–2A, the object's principal axis may be placed in correspondence with (i.e., represented in relation to) the external vertical axis, with the object's secondary axis mapped onto the external horizontal axis. I abbreviate this axis-to-axis mapping as PVSH (principal-vertical/secondary-horizontal). The other possible axis mapping is, of course, principal-horizontal/secondary-vertical (PHSV). I assume, then, that orientation representations include an axis correspondence component with two possible values (PVSH and PHSV).[2]

Establishing an object-to-external axis correspondence is necessary because the remaining components of the representation depend upon this correspondence. For example, given the stimulus in Figure 14–2A, the representation of the object's tilt depends on whether the object's principal axis is represented in relation to the external vertical axis (in which case the tilt is 30° counterclockwise) or in relation to the external horizontal axis (in which case the tilt is 60° clockwise).

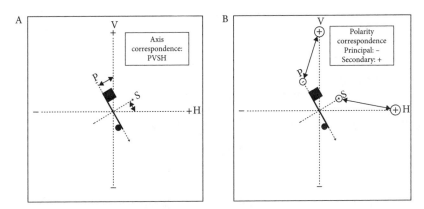

Figure 14–2. (A) Establishing axis correspondences. The principal axis of the object-based reference frame is mapped onto the vertical axis of the external frame, and the secondary object axis is mapped onto the horizontal external axis. (B) Establishing polarity correspondences. The negative pole of the object's principal axis is mapped onto the positive pole of the corresponding (vertical) external axis (negative polarity correspondence), and the positive pole of the object's secondary axis is mapped onto the positive pole of the corresponding (horizontal) external axis (positive polarity correspondence). V, vertical axis; H, horizontal axis; P, principal axis; S, secondary axis. From McCloskey, M., Valtonen, J., & Sherman, J. (2006). Representing orientation: A coordinate-system hypothesis, and evidence from developmental deficits. *Cognitive Neuropsychology, 23,* 680–713. Copyright 2006 Taylor & Francis. Reproduced with permission.

For the moment I assume that orientation representations may adopt either of the two possible axis mappings (PVSH or PHSV) for any stimulus object. One might speculate, however, that an object axis is more likely to be placed in correspondence with an external axis the smaller the angular difference between the axes. For the stimulus in Figure 14–2A, the PVSH mapping might therefore be more likely than the reverse mapping. Hence, for this stimulus the axis correspondence component may take a form something like the following:

AXIS CORRESPONDENCE: PVSH

Other possibilities can be envisioned. For example, an object axis may *always* be placed in correspondence with the external axis at the smallest angular distance. Alternatively, the axis correspondence could conceivably be constant (e.g., PVSH) in all orientation representations.

Polarity Correspondence

I assume that orientation representations specify not only which object axes correspond to which external axes but also how the polarity of each object axis is related to the polarity of the corresponding external axis. In the present example, the principal object axis is aligned with its negative pole toward the positive pole of the corresponding external axis (i.e., the vertical axis, assuming a PVSH axis correspondence), as illustrated in Figure 14–2B. I will refer to this negative-to-positive polarity correspondence as a "negative polarity mapping." In contrast, the secondary axis has a positive polarity relation to its corresponding (horizontal) external axis: The positive pole of the secondary object axis maps onto the positive pole of the external horizontal axis. For this stimulus the polarity-correspondence component of the orientation representation might look something like the following:

POLARITY CORRESPONDENCE
PRINCIPAL: –
SECONDARY: +

The polarity-correspondence component is critical for representing how the features of an object are positioned relative to the external reference frame. For example, the difference between Figure 14–6A and Figure 14–6B is one of polarity correspondence between the object's secondary axis and the external horizontal axis. I will develop this point more fully in discussing forms of orientation error.

Tilt

Finally, I assume that orientation representations specify the tilt of the object axes relative to their corresponding external axes. For a two-dimensional representation, once the tilt is specified for one object–external axis pair, a representation of tilt for the other axis pair would be entirely redundant—for example, if the object's principal axis is tilted 70° clockwise from the external vertical axis, the secondary axis must be tilted 70° clockwise from the horizontal axis. For the sake of simplicity, I therefore assume that tilt is represented only for the object's principal axis.[3]

I assume that tilt is represented by specifying the direction and magnitude of the angular displacement between the object's principal axis and the corresponding external axis. For example, in Figures 14–1 and 14–2 the principal object axis is tilted 30° counterclockwise from the external vertical axis. Arbitrarily designating clockwise as the positive direction and counterclockwise as negative, tilt could therefore be represented as follows:

TILT
    DIRECTION: –
    MAGNITUDE: 30°

An important feature of the posited tilt representations is that direction and magnitude of tilt are represented separately, just as displacement direction and distance are represented separately in the location representations I discussed in Chapter 13. I assume that the direction and magnitude representations are based upon the smaller of the two angles between the object's principal axis and the corresponding external axis. For example, I assume that for the stimulus in Figure 14–1 the tilt would be represented as –30° and not as +330°.

Several alternative forms of tilt representation could be considered. For example, one might assume that, as in a typical polar coordinate system, angles are always defined in a standard direction (e.g., clockwise) and, thus, can be specified solely in terms of magnitude, with no separate representation of direction. In such a scheme the angle in Figure 14–1 might be represented not as –30° but rather as 150°. I will argue, however, that positing separate direction and magnitude components provides a basis for interpreting certain forms of orientation error.

Substantive Assumptions

Bringing together the various representational components I have discussed, the orientation of the stimulus in Figure 14–1 might be represented as follows:

    AXIS CORRESPONDENCE: PVSH
    POLARITY CORRESPONDENCE
        PRINCIPAL: –
        SECONDARY: +
    TILT
        DIRECTION: –
        MAGNITUDE: 30°

The details of the notation are largely irrelevant and should not be taken too literally. The substantive assumptions are as follows:

1. Mental representations of object orientation specify the relationship between an object-based (orientation-invariant) frame of reference and a frame of reference external to the object.
2. Orientation representations are compositional, consisting of several independent components.
3. One component specifies which object axes map onto which external axes.
4. A second component specifies, for each object axis, how the poles of that axis map onto the poles of the corresponding external axis.
5. A third component specifies the tilt of the object reference frame relative to the external frame.
6. The tilt component separately represents direction and magnitude of tilt.

Note that these assumptions speak to both of the reference-frame questions discussed in Chapter 12. With respect to the definitional question (In relation to what are locations—and orientations—defined?), I have assumed that orientation representations implicate object-based as well as external frames of reference, although I have had (and will have) little to say about specific external frames. Further, I have assumed that representing orientation amounts to specifying relationships between object and external reference frames. With respect to the format question (In what form are locations and orientations represented?), I have assumed that object-based and external reference frames are in coordinate-system form, and I have also offered specific assumptions about the form in which relationships between reference frames are represented.

Relating External Reference Frames to One Another

Once a representation relating an object-based frame of reference to an external frame has been generated from a stimulus, this orientation representation may be used for a variety of purposes—for example, reaching for an object, describing the object's orientation verbally, or drawing the object. Using an orientation representation to perform a task will often (perhaps even always) involve relating the original external reference frame to a different external frame appropriate for the task. Consider, for example, an individual who views a stimulus object presented on a sheet of paper and then draws the object on another sheet, either by copying or from memory (see Fig. 14–3). Assume that the orientation representation generated from the stimulus encodes the relationship between an object-based frame of reference and an external frame defined by the stimulus sheet—that is, a frame centered on the sheet, with vertical and horizontal axes aligned with the sheet's edges. To produce a correctly oriented drawing, the individual must relate the external

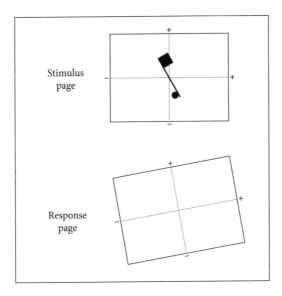

Figure 14–3. Direct-copy task in which the figure presented on the stimulus sheet is to be copied onto the response sheet. Axes of the stimulus external reference frame are shown on the stimulus sheet, and axes of the response external frame are shown on the response sheet. In performing the copying task the stimulus external frame must be mapped onto the response external frame. From McCloskey, M., Valtonen, J., & Sherman, J. (2006). Representing orientation: A coordinate-system hypothesis, and evidence from developmental deficits. *Cognitive Neuropsychology, 23*, 680–713. Copyright 2006 Taylor & Francis. Reproduced with permission.

frame defined by the stimulus sheet to an external frame defined by the response sheet. In other words, the individual must represent the orientation of the stimulus external frame relative to the response external frame. Because the orientation of the stimulus object was initially represented relative to the stimulus external frame, relating this frame to the response external frame provides the link needed to orient the stimulus object relative to the response frame.

Representing the orientation of one external frame relative to another is, I assume, no different from representing the orientation of an object-based frame relative to an external frame: Axis correspondences, axis polarity correspondences, and tilt must be specified. In the present example the vertical and horizontal stimulus frame axes correspond to vertical and horizontal response frame axes, respectively, and both axis polarity correspondences are positive (i.e., the positive pole of each stimulus axis maps onto the positive pole of the corresponding response axis). The response axes are, however, slightly tilted relative to the stimulus axes.

Processing of spatial information (including orientation) may often involve a progression through many different frames of reference; hence, several reference frames may conceivably intervene between an object-based frame and the frame most directly involved in producing a response. I offer no specific assumptions about the processing that occurs in such circumstances. For instance, the representations linking each pair of reference frames may be used to generate a representation that directly relates the object-based representation to the response frame of reference. Alternatively, the response may be generated from the chain of linked reference frames, without constructing a representation that directly places the object-based frame in relation to the response frame.

Orientation Errors

The assumptions of the COR hypothesis lead to clear predictions about potential types of orientation error and the underlying causes of the various error types. The hypothesis suggests that in any task that requires the processing of object orientation, orientation errors could arise from failures in the construction, retention, or use of either (a) orientation representations that relate an object-based representation to an external reference frame or (b) orientation representations that relate one external frame to another. Consider once again an individual (normal or impaired) who copies or draws from memory the stimulus in Figure 14–1. The processes that construct an orientation representation from the stimulus might fail to represent, or misrepresent, one or more components—for instance, the magnitude of the tilt between object and external axes might remain unspecified or might be misrepresented as 45°. Even if the orientation representation were initially complete and accurate, information could also be lost (or perhaps even altered) as the representation was held in memory, or misprocessed in some way when the representation was used to perform a task. The same points apply to representations that link one external reference frame to another.

In discussing types of orientation error I will not attempt to distinguish among errors arising in the construction, retention, and use of a representation; as far as I am able to see, failures at each of these points will generally produce the same types of error. Rather, I will focus my discussion on how error types should vary according to the particular representational component that is affected (e.g., tilt magnitude) and according to whether the orientation representation relates an object-based frame to an external frame or two external frames to one another. For convenience, I will discuss errors largely in the context of constructing representations, with the understanding that the same forms of error are expected from failures at other points in processing.

I further limit my discussion by focusing on the tilt and polarity-correspondence components of orientation representations because these are the components potentially relevant for understanding AH's orientation errors as well as the errors observed in two additional developmental cases I discuss in the following chapter. Certain forms of orientation error could conceivably arise from impairments affecting axis correspondence representations, but consideration of these error types is beyond the scope of the present discussion.

Tilt Errors

I begin with tilt errors because these are perhaps the most straightforward. The posited tilt representations have two elements: a direction element and a magnitude element. Failures affecting either element should produce orientation errors. I discuss tilt errors in the context of representing the relationship between an object-based reference frame and an external frame. Analogous errors could arise for representations relating one external frame to another.

Tilt-Direction Errors

In relating an object-based frame to an external frame, misrepresenting the direction of tilt should lead to errors in which the object is tilted the correct amount but in the wrong direction relative to the external axes. For example, given the stimulus in Figure 14–4A, representing the tilt direction as + rather than – would yield the error shown in Figure 14–4B. Note that this error is not a mirror reflection of the object across the external vertical axis—the object is tilted in the wrong direction but not mirror-reflected. (See Fig. 14–6D for the mirror reflection.)

Note also, however, that a tilt-direction error cannot be distinguished from a mirror reflection across an external axis for stimuli that are bilaterally symmetric. Consider, for example, the arrow in Figure 14–5A. The error in Figure 14–5B could result either from misrepresentation of tilt direction or from representation or processing failure that led to a reflection of the entire figure across an external vertical axis. (Later, I discuss how such reflections might occur.) This observation is one instance of a general point that will arise repeatedly: The stimuli used in most orientation tasks (including most

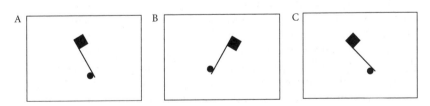

Figure 14–4. (A) Stimulus object. (B) Tilt-direction error. (C) Tilt-magnitude error. From McCloskey, M., Valtonen, J., & Sherman, J. (2006). Representing orientation: A coordinate-system hypothesis, and evidence from developmental deficits. *Cognitive Neuropsychology, 23,* 680–713. Copyright 2006 Taylor & Francis. Reproduced with permission.

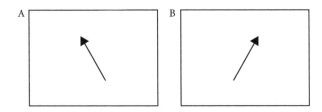

Figure 14–5. (A) Stimulus arrow. (B) Tilt direction error or reflection error. From McCloskey, M., Valtonen, J., & Sherman, J. (2006). Representing orientation: A coordinate-system hypothesis, and evidence from developmental deficits. *Cognitive Neuropsychology, 23,* 680–713. Copyright 2006 Taylor & Francis. Reproduced with permission.

of the tasks presented to AH) are inadequate to distinguish among at least some forms of orientation error.

Tilt-Magnitude Errors

Errors in representing tilt magnitude could take at least two forms. First, random error may be introduced into the representation or processing of tilt magnitude, due to noise or other limitations in perceptual, memory, motoric, or other processes. For example, a 30° tilt magnitude might be misrepresented or misproduced as 20° or 45° (see Fig. 14–4C).

In tasks requiring participants to reproduce the orientation of stimuli (e.g., by copying or drawing from memory) this form of representational or processing imprecision should lead to a response pattern in which response orientations are clustered around the corresponding correct orientations, with a degree of scatter determined by the extent of random error. In normal adults the imprecision may be rather small, whereas in young children or individuals with tilt-magnitude deficits the imprecision may be much larger (see, e.g., Goodale et al., 1991; Dilks, Reiss, Landau, & Hoffman, 2004).

Tilt-magnitude errors could also perhaps result from crude encoding of, memory for, or use of tilt-magnitude information. For example, an orientation representation might specify tilt magnitude only with the precision afforded by a small number of crude tilt categories based on "standard" tilts, such as *roughly 0°, roughly 45°, roughly 90°,* and so forth. The 30° tilt magnitude in our example might thus be represented as *roughly 45°* or perhaps *slightly less than 45°.* Crude representation of tilt magnitude should lead to errors in which response orientations are systematically displaced from the correct orientations toward or to the nearest standard orientation. This type of error pattern has been observed in tasks requiring normal participants to reproduce orientations from memory. For example, Barbara Tversky (1981) asked participants to place a cutout map of South America in the appropriate orientation on a page on which the compass directions were indicated. The long axis of the continent is tilted about 15° relative to the north–south axis, but three-fourths of the participants positioned the cutout with the axis closer to a north–south orientation. Similar effects were obtained in tasks with artificial maps: Orientations of geographical features were recalled as being closer to north–south or east–west than they actually were.

Polarity-Correspondence Errors

Polarity-correspondence misrepresentations should lead to mirror reflection of the stimulus figure. According to the COR hypothesis, two major forms of reflection could occur—reflections across an object axis and reflections across an external axis—with the form of error depending upon what frames of reference are implicated in the error.

Polarity-correspondence errors in representations relating an object-based reference frame to an external frame should result in reflection across an object axis. Consider once again our illustrative object (reproduced in Fig. 14-6A). If the polarity correspondence between the object's secondary axis and the external horizontal axis were misrepresented as negative (negative secondary axis pole corresponding to positive horizontal axis pole), the result would be a reflection across the object's principal axis, as shown in Figure 14-6B. Similarly, misrepresenting the polarity relation between the object's principal axis and the external vertical axis would lead to a reflection across the object's secondary axis, as illustrated in Figure 14-6C.

In contrast, polarity-correspondence errors in representations relating the stimulus external frame of reference to another external frame should produce a subtly different form of error: reflection across an axis of the stimulus external frame. For example, given the stimulus in Figure 14-6A, misrepresenting the polarity correspondence between stimulus and response frame horizontal axes (e.g., in a copying task) would lead to a (left–right) reflection across the vertical axis of the external stimulus frame (see Fig. 14-6D). If the polarity correspondence were misrepresented for the external vertical axes, a reflection across the external stimulus frame's horizontal axis would occur (Fig. 14-6E).

Note that the incorrect orientation resulting from a polarity correspondence error is different from that produced by a tilt direction error. In a tilt-direction error the stimulus is tilted in the wrong direction but is not reflected across any axis (e.g., Fig. 14-4B). In polarity-correspondence errors, however, the stimulus is reflected across either an object axis or an external axis. Compare, for example, Figures 14-4B (tilt-direction error), 14-6B (polarity-correspondence error in relating an object-based frame to an external frame), and 14-6D (polarity-correspondence error in relating the stimulus external frame to another external frame).

Here again, however, we encounter the point that many stimulus types are inadequate for distinguishing among certain forms of orientation error. I have already noted that for bilaterally symmetric stimuli (e.g., the arrow in Fig. 14-5) tilt-direction errors cannot be distinguished from reflections

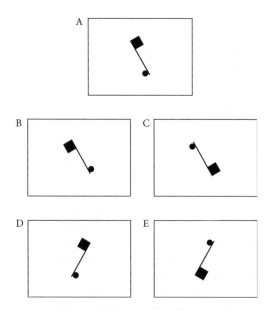

Figure 14–6. (A) Stimulus object. (B) Reflection across the object's principal axis, resulting from misrepresentation of the polarity correspondence between the secondary axis and an external horizontal axis. (C) Reflection across the object's secondary axis, resulting from misrepresentation of the polarity correspondence between the principal axis and an external vertical axis. (D) Reflection across an external vertical axis, resulting from misrepresentation of the polarity correspondence between the horizontal axes of two external reference frames. (E) Reflection across an external horizontal axis, resulting from misrepresentation of the polarity correspondence between the vertical axes of two external reference frames. From McCloskey, M., Valtonen, J., & Sherman, J. (2006). Representing orientation: A coordinate-system hypothesis, and evidence from developmental deficits. *Cognitive Neuropsychology, 23,* 680–713. Copyright 2006 Taylor & Francis. Reproduced with permission.

across an external stimulus axis (which I have now attributed to polarity-correspondence errors in relating the external stimulus frame to another external frame). Bilaterally symmetric stimuli also have the shortcoming that some difficulties in processing polarity-correspondence information simply cannot be detected. For an arrow, which is symmetric about its principal axis, polarity-correspondence errors in relating the secondary axis to an external axis are undetectable—reflecting the arrow across its principal axis (the result of a polarity-correspondence error for the secondary axis) would not produce a detectable change. (For objects that are symmetric across both object axes, such as a simple line, neither principal- nor secondary-axis polarity-correspondence errors can be detected.)

A different ambiguity arises for stimuli in which the object axes are aligned with (i.e., parallel to) the axes of the external reference frame, as in Figure 14–7A. Specifically, polarity-correspondence errors in the mapping between

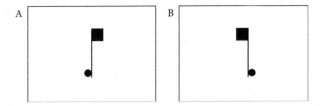

Figure 14–7. (A) Vertically oriented stimulus object. (B) Reflection error. This error could have been caused by misrepresentation of polarity correspondence either in relating an object-based representation to a stimulus external frame or in relating one external frame to another. From McCloskey, M., Valtonen, J., & Sherman, J. (2006). Representing orientation: A coordinate-system hypothesis, and evidence from developmental deficits. *Cognitive Neuropsychology, 23,* 680–713. Copyright 2006 Taylor & Francis. Reproduced with permission.

object-based and external stimulus frames (which lead to reflections across object axes) cannot be distinguished from polarity-correspondence errors in relating the external stimulus frame to another external frame (which lead to reflections across external stimulus axes). Thus, the reflection in Figure 14–7B could be caused by either form of polarity-correspondence error.

An Alternative Formulation?

The orientation representations I have posited may seem unnecessarily complex. I assume that an object's shape is represented within an object-based frame of reference and that orientation is represented in terms of a complex relationship between the object-based frame and an external reference frame (which in turn may be mapped onto other external frames). Perhaps, though, the proposal could be simplified. Perhaps in particular we could dispense with the object-based representations by assuming that an object's parts are represented directly within the external stimulus frame, without an object-based reference frame as an intermediary.

Adopting this direct-representation approach, the object in our example might be represented by specifying the location and tilt of each part (line, square, circle) in the external reference frame. The representation might look something like the following:

BAR
    LOCATION (+20,+20)
    TILT (–30°)
CIRCLE
    LOCATION (+25,+15)
SQUARE
    LOCATION (+15,+30)
    TILT (–30°)

This representation, which is no more complex than the object-based representations I have posited, carries all the information necessary to determine not only the object's shape but also its orientation relative to the external stimulus frame. Hence, if we were to assume this sort of direct representation of object parts in the external frame, we could dispense with the added complexity of orientation representations that relate object-based frames to external stimulus frames. Why, then, have I opted for the more complex hypothesis?

Three points may be made in response to this question. First, many researchers have argued on theoretical and empirical grounds that the visual system constructs some form(s) of object-based representation for purposes of object recognition (e.g., Marr, 1982). If object-recognition processes generate representations that describe an object's shape independently of external reference frames, it seems plausible to suppose that these representations could provide a basis for representing the object's orientation. Second, even if we were to dispense with representations that relate object-based to external stimulus frames, we would still need to posit the same type of representation for purposes of relating other reference frames to one another (in the processing of orientation information and in many other forms of spatial processing). The direct-representation hypothesis does not therefore eliminate a type of representation but serves only to deny that one particular frame-to-frame relationship is implicated in processing orientation information. Given that many reference frames may well intervene between stimulus and response in most orientation tasks, the direct-representation hypothesis seems neither strongly motivated nor particularly effective in reducing complexity.

However, the strongest reason for preferring the object-based representation version to the direct-representation alternative is that the latter has difficulty accounting for certain forms of orientation error. Specifically, the direct-representation position cannot readily account for reflections across an object axis, such as those shown in Figures 14–6B and C. (Note that stimuli in which the object axes are tilted with respect to the external axes are required to distinguish these errors from reflections across external axes.) According to my proposal, reflections across object axes result from polarity-correspondence errors in relating object axes to external stimulus axes. Representations in which individual object parts are represented directly with respect to the external stimulus frame predict that such errors should not occur. As we shall see, however, both AH and normal adults clearly make such errors.

Conclusions

In this chapter I presented a coordinate-system hypothesis of orientation representation (COR). The following chapter discusses AH's orientation errors and shows that these errors are interpretable within the COR framework. However, before turning to data and interpretations, I offer a few brief comments about the current status and future development of the COR hypothesis.

The COR hypothesis is at an early stage of development in several respects. As I noted when introducing the hypothesis, many of the assumptions are tentative and plausible variants can be envisioned. Also, in formulating the hypothesis I have focused largely on reflection errors. Hence, an important goal for subsequent theoretical work is to evaluate and refine the hypothesis by considering other types of errors observed in studies of orientation. For example, in copying visual stimuli young children often have difficulty with diagonal lines, tending to align them with external vertical and horizontal axes (e.g., copying a × shape as a +; see, e.g., Olson, 1970; Tada & Stiles, 1996). Perhaps this phenomenon can be understood in terms of difficulty in relating an object-based frame of reference (with axes aligned with the diagonal lines in the stimulus) to an external reference frame with vertical and horizontal axes.

Even in its current preliminary state, however, the COR hypothesis has significant value. The hypothesis provides something that has been lacking in cognitive research on orientation: a conceptual framework for thinking about how the orientation of objects might be represented. Also, the hypothesis calls attention to nonobvious differences among forms of orientation error (e.g., tilt-direction errors, reflections across object axes, reflections across external axes) and suggests underlying causes for each error type. Most notably, the hypothesis provides specific interpretations for the various forms of mirror-reflection error. These striking errors have been observed in many previous studies, but distinctions among types of reflection error have not been defined, nor have specific interpretations been offered. The COR hypothesis also allows us to recognize the characteristics a stimulus must have for distinguishing among potential underlying causes of orientation error. To tease apart the various potential error types I have described, a stimulus object must be asymmetric across both primary and secondary axes and must be presented with object axes tilted relative to external axes.

Finally, the hypothesis suggests directions for research. Patterns of orientation errors should be explored systematically with tilted, asymmetric stimuli in studies that aim to identify the functional loci at which errors arise and the reference frames affected. Pursuing this agenda in studies of normal and impaired children and adults should add significantly to our understanding of how orientation is represented in the human brain.

15

Orientation Representations:
Empirical Evidence

In this chapter I first discuss AH's performance on orientation perception tasks in light of the COR hypothesis, arguing that the hypothesis can
account for her errors. I also describe three additional orientation studies
my colleagues and I have recently carried out, again arguing that the COR
hypothesis can explain the results. I conclude that the findings from all of the
studies support the fundamental COR assumptions about representation of
orientation.

AH's Orientation Errors

As discussed in earlier chapters, AH made orientation errors in a variety
of tasks with visual stimuli. These errors, like her localization errors, took
the form of left–right and up–down reflections. Figures 15–1 through 15–3
present examples of AH's orientation-reflection errors in direct copying of
nonsense figures (Task 2–2), line drawings (Task 2–5), and words (Task 2–7).
Comparable errors were observed in tasks that involved discriminating
between left- and right-facing arrowheads ($<$ vs. $>$, Task 3–8), judging the
orientation of line drawings (Task 3–9), naming letters (Task 3–10), and reading words aloud (see Chapters 9 and 10). For instance, in naming lowercase
letters and reading words aloud, AH frequently confused *b*, *d*, *p*, and *q*, as
well as committing *n–u* and *m–w* errors (e.g., reading *bill* as "pill" and *wink*
as "mink"). Finally, when arrow stimuli were presented visually (Task 4–7),
AH made left–right and up–down orientation errors regardless of whether

she copied the arrow, set a pointer to indicate its orientation, or named the orientation aloud (see Fig. 15–4).

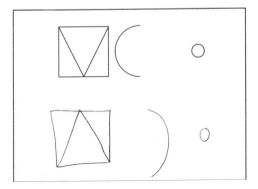

Figure 15–1. AH's direct copy of a stimulus from the Benton Visual Retention Test (Sivan, 1992). *Benton Visual Retention Test* (5th ed.). Copyright 1991 by Harcourt Assessment, Inc. Reproduced with permission. All rights reserved.

Figure 15–2. AH's direct copies of two line drawings (Snodgrass & Vanderwart, 1980). Reproduced with permission of the publisher, Life Science Associates.

Figure 15–3. Examples of AH's letter-orientation errors in direct copy of words.

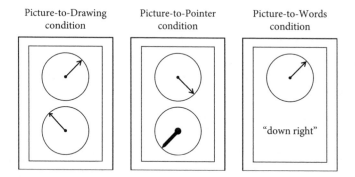

Figure 15–4. Examples of AH's reflection errors in the arrows experiment. Each panel shows a visual stimulus at the top and AH's drawing, pointer-setting, or verbal response at the *bottom*. Adapted from McCloskey, M., Valtonen, J., & Sherman, J. (2006). Representing orientation: A coordinate-system hypothesis, and evidence from developmental deficits. *Cognitive Neuropsychology, 23,* 680–713. Copyright 2006 Taylor & Francis. Used with permission.

Interpreting AH's Errors

AH's orientation errors are readily interpretable within the COR framework. However, given the characteristics of the stimuli presented to AH, each error admits of two different interpretations. For most stimuli (e.g., the pitcher in Fig. 15–2) the object-based axes were aligned with (i.e., parallel to) external vertical and horizontal axes. For these nontilted stimuli AH's orientation reflections may be interpreted as polarity-correspondence errors in relating the axes of one reference frame to those of another. Consider, for example, the left–right reflection of the pitcher. Assume for convenience that the principal axis of the object-based reference frame corresponds to the top–bottom axis of the pitcher, with the secondary axis corresponding to the orthogonal spout–handle axis (see Fig. 15–5A).[1]

In relating the pitcher's object-based frame to an external frame (e.g., a frame defined by the page on which the figure was printed), axis

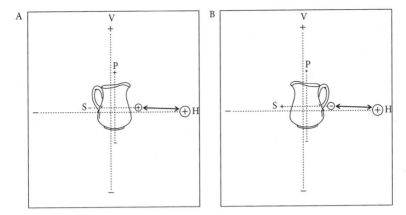

Figure 15–5. (A) Schematic depiction of orientation representation for the pitcher stimulus drawing in Figure 15–2, showing accurate representation of polarity correspondence between the secondary object axis and the external horizontal axis. Not all components of the orientation representation are shown. (B) Misrepresentation of the pitcher's orientation resulting from erroneous representation of polarity correspondence. Pitcher drawing from Snodgrass & Vanderwart (1980). Used with permission of the publisher, Life Science Associates.

correspondences would presumably be established between the object principal axis and the external vertical axis and between the object secondary axis and the external horizontal axis (axis correspondence = principal-vertical/secondary-horizontal [PVSH]). Given these axis correspondences, AH's left–right reflection in copying the pitcher could have resulted from a misrepresentation of polarity correspondence in relating the secondary object axis to the external horizontal axis. Assuming that the spout end of the secondary object axis is the positive end and similarly that the right end of the external horizontal axis is positive, a positive polarity correspondence should be established—in other words, the positive pole of the pitcher's secondary axis should be placed in correspondence with the positive pole of the external horizontal axis, as shown in Figure 15–5A. A representation specifying a negative axis polarity (i.e., negative pole of secondary axis mapped onto positive pole of horizontal axis) would indicate mistakenly that the pitcher was oriented with the spout to the left and the handle to the right (see Fig. 15–5B). Therefore, the expected result of the misrepresentation would be the reflection error shown in Figure 15–2. On this interpretation the error is a reflection across the principal (top–bottom) object axis.

However, reflection errors for nontilted stimulus objects could also result from polarity-correspondence errors in relating one external reference frame to another; whenever object axes are aligned with external horizontal and vertical axes, polarity-correspondence errors in relating object to external reference frames cannot be distinguished from polarity-correspondence errors in relating one external frame to another. For example, the left–right reflection of the pitcher could have occurred in the process of relating a reference frame defined by the stimulus page to a frame defined by the page on which the copy was to be made. If the horizontal-axis polarity correspondence were represented as negative rather than positive, a left–right reflection would be the result. On this interpretation the error is a reflection across an external reference axis. To summarize, the reflection errors for nontilted stimuli point clearly to misrepresentation of polarity correspondence. However, we cannot determine whether the errors arose in relating object frames to external frames, in relating external frames to one another, or both.

In the arrows task (Task 4–7) some of the arrow stimuli were tilted 45° (see Fig. 15–4); for these stimuli, the object axes (i.e., the arrow's axes) were not aligned with external horizontal and vertical axes. Nevertheless, ambiguity arises in interpreting AH's errors in the task because the arrows were bilaterally symmetric. Her left–right and up–down reflections for the tilted arrow stimuli could have resulted from misrepresentation of tilt direction in relating an object-based frame to the external stimulus frame. For example, the up right to up left copying error shown in Figure 15–4 could have resulted from misrepresenting the tilt of the arrow's principal axis relative to the vertical external axis as –45° (negative tilt direction) rather than +45° (positive tilt direction). However, the errors for tilted arrows could also have resulted from polarity-correspondence errors in relating external reference frames to one another. On this latter interpretation, the up right to up left error in Figure 15–4 resulted from misrepresenting the polarity mapping between two external horizontal axes as negative rather than positive.[2]

Fortunately, AH was tested in one direct-copying task that allowed unambiguous interpretation of errors.

Task 15–1: Direct Copy with Tilted Asymmetric Figures

In this task AH copied simple stimulus figures that were asymmetric across both primary and secondary axes and tilted relative to external reference

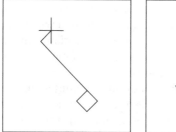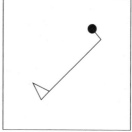

Figure 15–6. Examples of two tilted asymmetric stimuli from Task 15–1.

axes. As illustrated in Figure 15–6, each stimulus consisted of a straight line with an additional feature at one or both ends. Three blocks of twenty-four stimuli were presented. On sixteen of the twenty-four trials in each block the principal object axis was tilted 45° from vertical (eight clockwise, eight counterclockwise). Each block also included four horizontally oriented and four vertically oriented stimuli.

Most of AH's errors involved left–right or up–down reflection of the entire stimulus figure. However, she also made some errors in which she misoriented a feature within a stimulus object. I first discuss the whole-figure reflections and then consider the within-object errors.

Whole-Figure Reflections

AH's errors for vertical and horizontal stimuli were similar to those observed in previous tasks. Collapsing across the vertical and horizontal orientations, AH made seven left–right and two up–down reflections of the entire stimulus figure.

Results for the tilted stimuli were more interesting. AH made seven errors in which she reflected the stimulus object across its principal axis; an example is presented in Figure 15–7A. She also made one error in which the stimulus was reflected across its secondary axis (see Fig. 15–7B). These errors indicate impairment in representing polarity correspondence between object-based

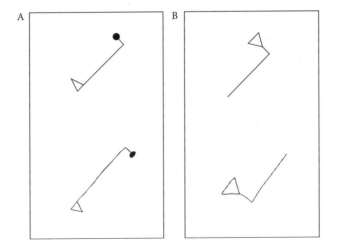

Figure 15–7. AH's direct copies of two tilted asymmetric figures. (A) Reflection across the principal object axis. (B) Reflection across the secondary object axis. From McCloskey, M., Valtonen, J., & Sherman, J. (2006). Representing orientation: A coordinate-system hypothesis, and evidence from developmental deficits. *Cognitive Neuropsychology, 23,* 680–713. Copyright 2006 Taylor & Francis. Reproduced with permission.

and external reference frames. The reflections across the principal axis may be attributed to misrepresentation of polarity correspondence between the secondary object axis and an external axis. Assume, for example, that for the stimulus in Figure 15–7A the principal object axis was placed in correspondence with the vertical external axis (i.e., axis correspondence = PVSH). Misrepresenting the polarity correspondence between the secondary object axis and the external horizontal axis would produce the error made by AH. For instance, if the feature-laden side of the secondary axis were designated positive, the secondary-to-horizontal polarity correspondence should be negative, indicating that the feature-rich side of the secondary axis should be related to the left side of the horizontal axis (see Fig. 15–8A). Misrepresenting the correspondence as positive would yield the observed error, as illustrated in Figure 15–8B. By the same logic, the error in which AH reflected the stimulus object about its secondary axis may be attributed to misrepresentation of the polarity correspondence between the principal object axis and the relevant external axis.

In addition to the reflections across object axes, AH made one error in which she left–right reflected the stimulus across a vertical external axis. This response, shown in Figure 15–9A, is interpretable as a polarity-correspondence error in relating the horizontal axes of two external reference frames. For example, AH may have misrepresented the polarity correspondence between the horizontal axes of stimulus and response external frames as negative rather than positive. Unlike reflection errors for bilaterally symmetric stimuli, the error cannot be interpreted as a tilt-direction error;

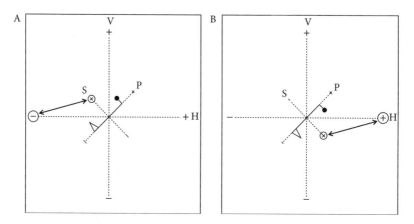

Figure 15–8. (A) Schematic depiction of orientation representation for the tilted asymmetric figure in Figure 15–7A, showing accurate representation of polarity correspondence between the secondary object axis and the external horizontal axis. Not all components of the orientation representation are shown. (B) Misrepresentation of the figure's orientation resulting from erroneous representation of polarity correspondence.

misrepresenting tilt direction (relative to the external vertical axis) would have produced the hypothetical error illustrated in Figure 15–9B. (No actual tilt-direction errors were observed.)

AH also made four errors in which her response was 180° rotated relative to the stimulus. Even in the context of tilted asymmetric stimuli, such responses are ambiguous. I will not develop this point at length but simply assert that 180° rotations could result from misrepresentation of polarity correspondence for both axis pairs either in relating an object frame to an external frame or in relating one external frame to another.

To summarize, the results for the tilted asymmetric stimuli clearly demonstrate that AH is impaired in representing polarity correspondences between object and external axes, especially in relating a secondary object axis to an external axis. The single left–right reflection across a vertical external axis may also suggest some difficulty in representing polarity correspondences when relating one external frame to another. This suggestion is buttressed by the results from the previously discussed arrows task (see Fig. 15–4). The left–right and up–down reflections observed for tilted arrows cannot be attributed to polarity-correspondence errors in relating object to external reference frames. However, these errors could have resulted from misrepresentation of polarity correspondences when relating external frames to one another.

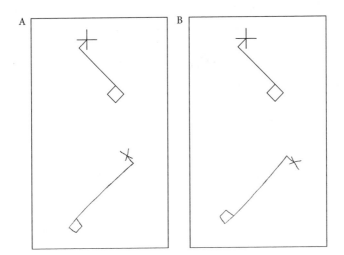

Figure 15–9. (A) AH's direct copy of a tilted asymmetric figure, illustrating reflection across an external vertical axis. (B) Hypothetical error resulting from misrepresentation of tilt direction. (AH made no such errors.) Adapted from McCloskey, M., Valtonen, J., & Sherman, J. (2006). Representing orientation: A coordinate-system hypothesis, and evidence from developmental deficits. *Cognitive Neuropsychology, 23*, 680–713. Copyright 2006 Taylor & Francis. Used with permission.

Within-Object Misorientations

In addition to errors involving reflection of the entire stimulus object, AH made a number of errors in which she reflected individual object parts within the object as a whole. Figure 15–10 presents an example in which AH reflected the half-filled square relative to the object's principal axis. I will not discuss the within-object errors in detail. However, I note that these errors are consistent with the assumption made by some theorists (e.g., Marr, 1982) that object-based representations are hierarchically structured. In the present example, representing the stimulus figure may involve (among other things) generating an object-based representation of the half-filled square and then specifying the position of the square within the object by relating the square's reference frame to a frame for the object as a whole. Errors in specifying relationships among reference frames within an object-based representation could lead to misplacement or misorientation of object parts relative to one another. For example, the error shown in the figure might have occurred when AH misrepresented the polarity correspondence between an axis of the square's reference frame (more specifically, an axis perpendicular to the division between light and dark halves) and the principal axis of the whole-object frame.

A Note on the Mirror Engram Hypothesis

I have interpreted AH's orientation-reflection errors by reference to specific assumptions about the form of orientation representations, arguing that

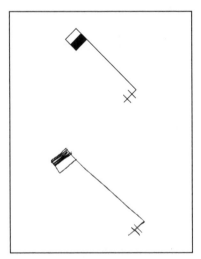

Figure 15–10. Within-object orientation error in AH's direct copy of a tilted asymmetric figure. Adapted from McCloskey, M., Valtonen, J., & Sherman, J. (2006). Representing orientation: A coordinate-system hypothesis, and evidence from developmental deficits. *Cognitive Neuropsychology, 23,* 680–713. Copyright 2006 Taylor & Francis. Used with permission.

her errors arose from mis-specification of particular representational components. This approach to interpreting orientation reflections may be contrasted with a very different approach that does not address the format of orientation representations. In particular, some researchers have interpreted errors involving confusion between left–right mirror images by invoking a mirror engram hypothesis (e.g., Heilman, Howell, Valenstein, & Rothi, 1980; Noble, 1968; Orton, 1937; Lambon-Ralph et al., 1997). The mirror engram hypothesis assumes that when a visual form is presented a representation of the form's actual orientation is generated in one cerebral hemisphere and a representation of the left–right mirror image—a *mirror engram*—is created in the other hemisphere. This assumption is often motivated by reference to homotopic connections between hemispheres, the notion being that when a representation is generated in one cerebral hemisphere the interhemispheric connections will lead to creation of a mirror-image representation in the opposite hemisphere (e.g., Noble, 1968).

As one might expect, the mirror engram hypothesis attributes left–right mirror image errors to the mirror engrams. For example, some theorists (e.g., Orton, 1937) assume that mirror engrams are usually inhibited in normal adults, allowing left–right mirror images to be distinguished. According to this view, mirror-image confusions occur when the mirror engrams are not successfully inhibited. In one form or another the mirror engram hypothesis has been applied to a variety of normal and pathological phenomena involving the confusion of left–right mirror images, including reading and writing errors in normal and dyslexic children (e.g., Orton, 1937), mirror reading and writing in brain-damaged adults (e.g., Heilman et al., 1980; Lambon-Ralph et al., 1997), and left–right reversals in spontaneous-drawing and delayed-copying tasks (e.g., Lambon-Ralph et al., 1997). Corballis and Beale (1976) have also proposed that mirror engrams play a role in normal symmetry perception.

The mirror engram hypothesis can be questioned on both logical and empirical grounds. Interhemispheric transfer of information, even if via homotopic connections, would not necessarily produce a mirror-reflected neural representation. Also, even if the neural representation in one hemisphere were a mirror reflection of that in the other hemisphere, it would not necessarily follow that the two representations specified mirror-image stimulus orientations. For example, given a neural representation specifying the correct orientation for the letter *b*, the mirror image of that representation would not necessarily specify the mirror-image orientation *d*. Furthermore, the neurophysiological evidence adduced in support of the mirror engram hypothesis (e.g., Noble, 1968; Rollenhagen & Olson, 2000) is subject to alternative explanations (see, e.g., Corballis & Beale, 1976).

However, the primary point to be made here is that the mirror engram hypothesis is not adequate for interpreting AH's orientation errors. In the first place, the hypothesis posits only left–right mirror engrams, but AH made up–down as well as left–right orientation reflections. One might consider extending the hypothesis to posit both up–down and left–right mirror engrams. However, the motivation for such an extension is far from obvious. The (somewhat dubious) rationale for positing left–right mirror engrams comes from assumptions about the brain's left and right hemispheres and the connections between them. This rationale does not extend to up–down mirror engrams, and no alternative rationale is immediately apparent.

A second issue for the mirror engram hypothesis is that AH's orientation errors included reflections across object axes (see, e.g., Fig. 15–7) as well as reflections across external axes (e.g., Fig. 15–9). To account for these results one would presumably have to posit both (up–down and left–right) object-axis and (up–down and left–right) external-axis mirror engrams, thereby further enlarging—again on ad hoc basis—the inventory of mirror engram types. Hence, AH's results place the mirror engram hypothesis in the unappealing position of needing to postulate, without obvious motivation, a separate type of mirror engram for each of the several observed forms of orientation reflection. In contrast, the COR hypothesis provides a well-motivated interpretation for all of AH's orientation errors, explaining these errors in terms of the same representational assumptions put forth to account for accurate representation of orientation. Further, the COR hypothesis can be applied to orientation errors other than reflections (e.g., tilt errors), whereas the mirror engram hypothesis speaks only to orientation reflections.

Three Additional Studies

My colleagues and I have recently carried out three additional studies in which we observed systematic patterns of orientation-reflection errors. Two of these studies involved individuals with developmental spatial deficits (McCloskey et al., 2006; Valtonen et al., 2008), and the third probed orientation representations in normal adults (Gregory & McCloskey, 2007). In the following sections I describe the studies briefly, arguing that the COR hypothesis provides a basis for interpreting the results.

TM

TM is a right-handed girl who presented with developmental reading and visuospatial deficits. Janet Cohen Sherman and I studied TM over a 3-year period during which she was 13–15 years old. Neurological examination at age 14 revealed no sensory deficits or other disturbance of neurological function. For a more detailed case history and results of neuropsychological testing, see McCloskey et al. (2006).

In direct-copying tasks TM made orientation-reflection errors very similar to those observed for AH. When presented with complex nonsense figures, she frequently left–right or up–down reflected the entire figure. Figure 15–11 presents three examples of her errors. With simpler stimuli

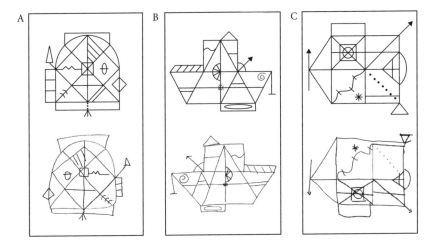

Figure 15–11. TM's direct copies of three complex figures (Savage et al., 2001). From McCloskey, M., Valtonen, J., & Sherman, J. (2006). Representing orientation: A coordinate-system hypothesis, and evidence from developmental deficits. *Cognitive Neuropsychology, 23*, 680–713. Copyright 2006 Taylor & Francis. Reproduced with permission.

TM's performance was somewhat better, but she still made occasional reflection errors (see Fig. 15–12).

One striking feature of TM's performance suggested that her orientation reflections arose in constructing perceptual representations of the visual stimuli, rather than in producing the response drawing: She was entirely unaware of her copying errors, even when asked to make a careful comparison between the stimulus figure and her drawing. For example, asked to compare the stimulus and copy shown in Figure 15–11B, TM made a lengthy examination and then pointed to the spiral in her copy, stating that "the circle things are a little bit different." When asked what she meant, she said that the shapes were different. She failed to notice any further differences when asked to examine the figures again. TM also failed to detect orientation errors when asked to inspect copies made by the examiner.

TM's orientation-reflection errors, like those observed for AH, are readily interpreted by the COR hypothesis. The reflections for nontilted stimuli may be attributed to polarity-correspondence errors in relating an object-based frame to a stimulus external frame or in mapping one external frame onto another. The reflections of tilted stimuli may be explained as tilt-direction errors or polarity-correspondence errors in relating one external frame to another.

Interestingly, TM did not show impairment similar to that of AH in visual localization tasks. She made no errors in reaching for a wooden block on a table in front of her, and she also reached accurately for a specified object

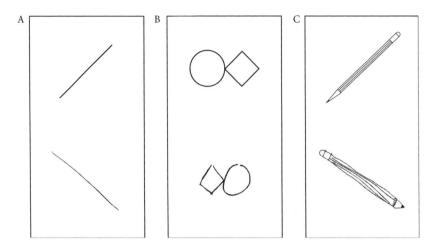

Figure 15–12. TM's direct copies of three simple stimuli. (A, B) Stimuli from the Visual-Motor Integration test (Beery & Buktenica, 1997). Reproduced with permission. (C) Stimulus from the Boston Naming Test (Goodglass & Kaplan, 1983). From McCloskey, M., Valtonen, J., & Sherman, J. (2006). Representing orientation: A coordinate-system hypothesis, and evidence from developmental deficits. *Cognitive Neuropsychology, 23,* 680–713. Copyright 2006 Taylor & Francis. Reproduced with permission. The Boston Naming Test is a subtest of the Boston Diagnostic Aphasia Examination (3rd ed.), by H. Goodglass, E. Kaplan, and B. Barresi, Copyright 2000 by Pro-Ed, Inc. Used with permission.

within a complex array of objects. I will return to this point in a later section when I discuss the relationship between AH's location and orientation errors.

BC

BC is a left-handed girl with severe visual–spatial impairment resulting from a presumed herpes encephalitis infection at age 3; for more information, see Valtonen et al. (2008). BC was tested at age 15–16 on orientation tasks with simple line stimuli. Jussi Valtonen was the primary investigator in the study, with Daniel Dilks and myself serving as collaborators.

Reproducing Line Orientation

A target line was displayed in the upper half of a computer screen, and a response line was presented on the lower half of the screen (see Fig. 15–13A). BC's task was to adjust the orientation of the response line until it matched that of the target line, by turning a dial that caused the response line to rotate about its center.

BC's performance was highly inaccurate: Her absolute orientation errors ranged from 1° to 88°, with a mean of 29°. Considering that the largest possible

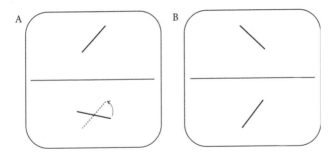

Figure 15–13. (A) The line orientation reproduction task presented to BC. A target line was presented on the upper half of a computer monitor, and BC turned a dial to adjust the orientation of a response line displayed on the lower half of the monitor. (B) One of BC's reflection errors. From McCloskey, M., Valtonen, J., & Sherman, J. (2006). Representing orientation: A coordinate-system hypothesis, and evidence from developmental deficits. *Cognitive Neuropsychology, 23*, 680–713. Copyright 2006 Taylor & Francis. Reproduced with permission.

error in the task was 90°, BC's errors were remarkably large. Examination of the data suggested that many of the errors took the form of mirror reflections; an example is presented in Figure 15–13B. The scatterplot in Figure 15–14 confirms this impression. For each trial the response orientation (*y* axis) is plotted against the target orientation (*x* axis); 0° corresponds to vertical, and tilts clockwise and counterclockwise from vertical are designated positive and negative, respectively. The diagonal with positive slope indicates correct responses (e.g., target 45°, response 45°), whereas the negative diagonal corresponds to mirror-reflection responses (e.g., target 45°, response –45°). BC's responses are distributed along the two diagonals, with a substantial proportion (27/72) falling closer to the mirror-reflected orientation than to the correct orientation. This pattern indicates a systematic tendency to mirror-reflect the target orientation.

Also apparent from the scatterplot is that most of the points do not lie exactly on the diagonals. This finding indicates that BC's responses—both reflections and nonreflections—show substantial imprecision. Nonreflection responses differed from the target orientation by an average of 13.4°, and reflection responses differed from the reflection orientation by an average of 15.7°.

BC's performance pattern suggests that two distinct forms of error play a role in her responses: imprecision and a tendency to mirror-reflect the target orientation. Some responses show imprecision alone, whereas others show mirror reflection plus imprecision. Results from control participants reveal, not surprisingly, that BC's performance is strikingly impaired. Dilks et al. (2004) tested twelve normal adults in the task and found highly accurate performance (mean absolute error = 1.6°). Results from ten normal children ages 3–4 years showed greater imprecision (mean absolute error = 13.9°)

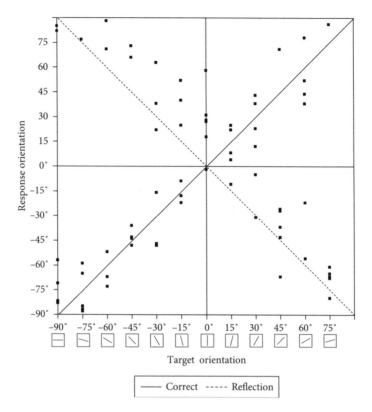

Figure 15–14. Scatterplot of results from the line orientation reproduction task. The response orientation (*y axis*) is plotted against the stimulus orientation (*x axis*) for each trial. The diagonal with positive slope (from *lower left* to *upper right*) corresponds to correct responses, and the negative diagonal corresponds to mirror reflections. From Valtonen, J., Dilks, D. D., & McCloskey, M. (2008). Cognitive representation of orientation: A case study. *Cortex, 44,* 1171–1187. With permission of Elsevier.

and only occasional reflection errors. Hence, BC's imprecision was comparable to that of children aged 3–4 years, and her rate of reflection errors was higher.

Lines with Differentiated Ends

A second task was identical to the first, except that each target and response line had a red tip at one end (see Fig. 15–15A). BC was instructed to adjust the response line so that it matched the target line in orientation and in placement of the tip. The aim in introducing the red tip was to learn more about the nature of BC's reflection errors. The simpler stimuli in the first task were insufficient to distinguish reflections across a vertical axis (left–right

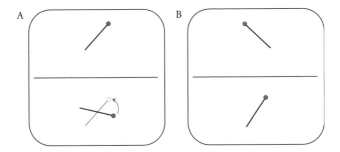

Figure 15–15. The line orientation reproduction task in which stimulus lines had a red tip at one end (indicated by *gray dots*). (A) Target and response lines displayed on a computer monitor. (B) Example of a left–right reflection error made by BC. From McCloskey, M., Valtonen, J., & Sherman, J. (2006). Representing orientation: A coordinate-system hypothesis, and evidence from developmental deficits. *Cognitive Neuropsychology, 23*, 680–713. Copyright 2006 Taylor & Francis. Reproduced with permission.

reflections) from reflections across a horizontal axis (up–down reflections). For example, the error shown in Figure 15–13B could have resulted from either a left–right or up–down reflection of the stimulus line. Given lines with differentiated ends, however, left–right and up–down reflections can be distinguished (see Fig. 15–15B).

The scatterplot shown in Figure 15–16 presents the results. This scatterplot is more complex than that from the preceding task. Because the ends of the lines were differentiated, target and response orientations ranged from –180° through 165°, rather than –90° to 75°. For example, whereas the first task included only a single horizontal target orientation (–90°), the modified task included two: –90° (horizontal with red tip on the left) and 90° (horizontal with red tip on the right). In the present scatterplot correct responses once again fall along the positive diagonal. Left–right reflections (e.g., target 45°, response –45°) lie along the negative diagonal, and up–down reflections (e.g., target 45°, response 135°) lie along the negative diagonals through the lower left and upper right quadrants of the plot.

Several points are apparent from the scatterplot. First, BC's responses again show considerable imprecision. For nonreflection responses (i.e., those falling closer to the target orientation than to either the left–right or up–down reflection orientation) BC's mean absolute error was 12.7°. Second, BC made many left–right reflection errors: Approximately one-fourth of her 192 responses were closer to the left–right reflection orientation than to the correct orientation (mean distance from reflected orientation = 11.1°). Third, BC made far fewer up–down than left–right reflection errors. In fact, it is unclear whether any of her responses were true up–down reflections. Only thirteen of the responses (7%) were closer to the up–down reflection orientation than to the correct orientation. Further, ten of these thirteen responses

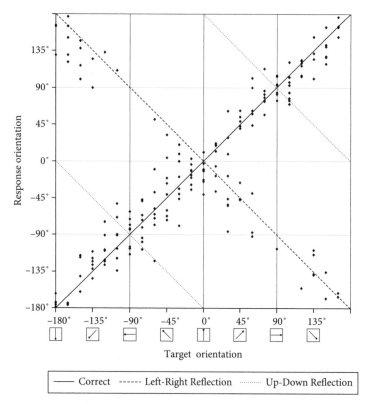

Figure 15–16. Scatterplot of results from the orientation reproduction task involving lines with differentiated ends. The response orientation (*y axis*) is plotted against the stimulus orientation (*x axis*) for each trial. The diagonal with positive slope (from *lower left* to *upper right*) corresponds to correct responses. The major negative diagonal (*upper left* to *lower right*) corresponds to left–right reflections. The minor diagonals in the lower left and upper right quadrants correspond to up–down reflections. From Valtonen, J., Dilks, D. D., & McCloskey, M. (2008). Cognitive representation of orientation: A case study. *Cortex, 44,* 1171–1187. With permission of Elsevier.

involved target orientations only 15° away from horizontal (e.g., –75°, 105°), and the remaining three involved targets 30° from horizontal. For nearly horizontal targets, random imprecision alone could produce responses closer to the up–down reflection orientation than to the correct orientation. For example, given a target orientation of 75°, a random error of more than 15° in the clockwise direction would yield a response orientation closer to the up–down reflection orientation of 105° than to the correct orientation. Given that BC's nonreflection errors averaged nearly 13° (and some were as large as 50°), it seems likely that at least some of the apparent up–down reflections resulted simply from random imprecision. However, it is also possible that some of these errors were true up–down reflections.

Note that in contrast to the apparent up–down reflections, the left–right reflections clearly cannot be attributed to random imprecision. Many of the left–right reflection responses—in particular, those occurring for target orientations that are not close to vertical—are very distant from the corresponding correct responses and are clearly separated in the scatterplot from the responses clustering around the correct orientation.

Tactile Stimuli

A third task was carried out to determine whether BC's deficit affected only visual stimuli or extended to other modalities. The task was similar to the visual line orientation tasks, except that the stimuli were tactile. BC was blindfolded and felt the orientation of a wooden target bar placed on the table in front of her; the two ends of the stimulus bar were not differentiated. BC's task was to rotate a response bar to match the orientation of the target.

The results were very similar to those obtained with visual stimuli: BC frequently mirror-reflected the target line and also showed imprecision comparable to that observed in the visual tasks. These findings suggest that BC's orientation errors may arise not in the visual system but rather at a more central supramodal level of representation. Another possibility, however, is that BC drew upon impaired visual-system mechanisms in performing the tactile orientation task (e.g., by generating visual orientation representations from the tactile input).

Interpreting BC's Performance

Like the orientation errors made by AH and TM, BC's errors may be interpreted within the framework of the COR hypothesis. The gross imprecision in BC's responses—a phenomenon not observed in AH or TM—may be explained by assuming that BC's representations of tilt magnitude are much cruder or noisier than those of normal individuals. For example, given a target stimulus with a tilt of 30°, BC might have represented the tilt magnitude crudely as *roughly 45°* or more specifically but inaccurately as, say, *42°*.

BC's reflection errors admit of two interpretations within the COR framework because all of the line stimuli were bilaterally symmetric. First, the errors could have resulted from misrepresentation of tilt direction (e.g., representing a +45° tilt as –45°). On this interpretation the fact that BC made many left–right reflections but few, if any, up–down reflections implies that she represented the tilt of the principal object axis (i.e., the line's axis) relative to a vertical external axis. For example, Figure 15–15B illustrates one of BC's errors, in which she set the response line to an orientation of 32° in response to a target orientation of –45°. For this target orientation, the tilt direction should have been represented as negative (assuming that clockwise is the positive direction) and the tilt magnitude should have been represented as 45°. BC's response may be explained by assuming that she represented the tilt direction as positive and also represented the magnitude inaccurately.[3]

BC's reflection errors could also have resulted from misrepresentation of polarity correspondence in relating one external frame to another. For example, the error in Figure 15–15B could have occurred when BC misrepresented the polarity correspondence between the horizontal axes of stimulus and response external frames as negative rather than positive. On this interpretation the predominance of left–right reflections suggests that BC erred in representing polarity correspondence more often for horizontal than for vertical axes.

Reflection Errors in Normal Adults

A fundamental assumption of the COR hypothesis is that representations of object orientation implicate object-based representations. According to COR, orientation is represented by specifying the relationship between an object-based frame of reference and an external reference frame (which may then be related to other external frames). Orientation errors involving reflection across an object axis (see Fig. 15–7) constitute the clearest evidence for a role of object-based frames in orientation representation. However, errors can be identified unambiguously as reflections across object axes only for stimuli that are both tilted and asymmetric. As I pointed out in Chapter 14, previous studies have virtually never used such stimuli; and as discussed in the present chapter, almost all of the stimuli presented to AH, TM, and BC were either nontilted or symmetric. To my knowledge, the only unambiguous instances of errors involving reflection across object axes are the eight object-axis reflections made by AH in the direct-copy task with tilted asymmetric nonsense figures (Task 15–1).

In part to obtain more evidence on the role of object-based frames of reference in orientation representation, Emma Gregory and I recently carried out a series of studies with normal adult participants (Gregory & McCloskey, 2007). Stimuli were photographs of everyday objects that are typically encountered at a variety of orientations. All objects were asymmetric across both principal and secondary object axes; Figure 15–17 presents three examples. Stimulus objects were presented in one of sixteen orientations, which are illustrated in Figure 15–18.

On each trial two or more objects were presented in succession and participants responded by drawing each object at the depicted orientation or selecting the target orientation from an array showing the sixteen possible orientations. Across experiments we varied the number of stimuli presented on each trial, the exposure duration, and other aspects of the procedure. In all experiments the pattern of results was very clear: Errors involving reflection across object axes were far more frequent than any other form of orientation

Figure 15–17. Examples of stimuli from the Gregory and McCloskey (2007) orientation study with normal adults. (*See also* COLOR FIG. 15–17 in separate insert.)

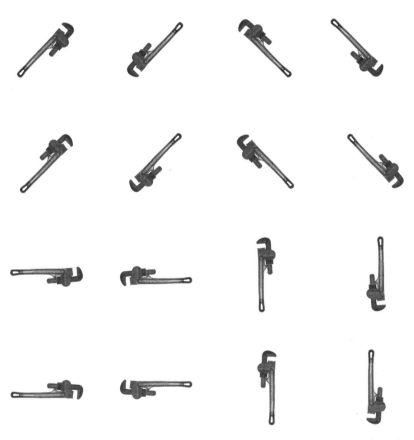

Figure 15–18. The sixteen orientations at which stimuli were presented. (*See also* COLOR FIG. 15–18 in separate insert.)

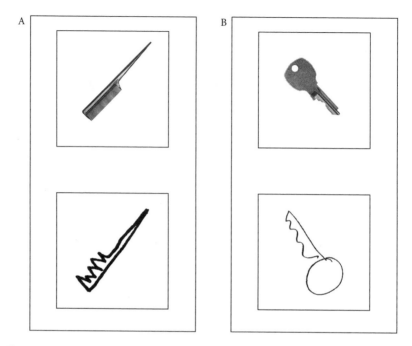

Figure 15–19. Two examples of object-axis reflection errors made by normal adult participants. (*See also* COLOR FIG. 15–19 in separate insert.)

error. Figure 15–19 presents two examples from an experiment with drawing responses.

According to the COR hypothesis, reflections across object axes result from misrepresentation of polarity correspondence in relating an object-based frame of reference to an external frame. If object-based representations are not posited, object-axis reflection errors have no straightforward explanation. Accordingly, the systematic pattern of object-axis reflections strongly supports the assumption that object-based frames of reference play a central role in orientation representations.

Interpreting Other Phenomena

In addition to the results from AH, TM, BC, and normal adults, the COR hypothesis can contribute to interpreting other orientation-error phenomena. The left–right orientation reflections made by the Swiss patient PR (Pflugshaupt et al., 2007) can be attributed to systematic misrepresentation of the polarity correspondence between the horizontal axis of an external reference frame and the corresponding axis of either an object-centered frame or another external frame. (Because all of the orientation reflections reported for PR involved stimuli in which object axes were aligned with external vertical and horizontal axes, it is not possible to determine whether the errors arose in relating an object-centered frame to an external frame or in relating one external frame to another.)

Impaired representation of polarity correspondence may also be implicated in the case of patient RJ (Turnbull & McCarthy, 1996a). As discussed in Chapter 11, RJ was able to discriminate between normally oriented and upside-down pictures but was severely impaired in distinguishing left–right mirror images. Indeed, RJ's verbal reports suggested that he was often unable to see any difference between a shape and its left–right reflection. These results suggest that RJ may often have failed to represent the polarity correspondence between the horizontal axis of an external reference frame and the corresponding axis of another frame. As an illustration, Figure 15–20 depicts a representation in which an object-centered reference frame is mapped onto an external frame. The representation specifies a positive polarity correspondence between the object's principal axis and the external vertical axis. However, the polarity correspondence between the object's secondary axis and the external horizontal axis is not specified. As a consequence, the representation simply fails to indicate whether the object is facing left or right. This sort of defective representation would suffice for distinguishing normally oriented and upside-down stimuli but would not allow left–right mirror images to be discriminated. Similar deficits in representing polarity correspondence may be implicated in other reported cases of impaired orientation discrimination (e.g., Davidoff & Warrington, 2001).[4]

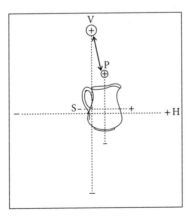

Figure 15–20. Illustration of orientation representation that fails to specify the polarity correspondence between the object secondary axis and the external horizontal axis. This representation fails to indicate whether the object is facing left or right. Pitcher drawing from Snodgrass & Vanderwart (1980). Used with permission of the publisher, Life Science Associates.

As a final example of the potential applications of the COR hypothesis, consider the remarkable phenomenon of inverted vision, in which the entire visual world appears temporarily to be upside down. This phenomenon may appear to suggest misrepresentation of vertical-axis polarity correspondence, at some visual-system level that represents the entire visual scene. However, several observations suggest that rather than mis-specification of polarity correspondence, inverted vision stems from misrepresentation of tilt magnitude—that is, from failures in representing the angle of tilt between the axes of one reference frame and those of another. In the first place, many of the inverted-vision patients described seeing the visual scene rotate from upright to intermediate orientations to an inverted state (Solms et al., 1988), suggesting a progressive change from an accurate representation of tilt to a representation that is wrong by approximately 180°. Also, the reported results from at least one patient imply that the perceived orientation of the visual world was not an up–down reflection of the correct orientation (as would be expected from a polarity-correspondence error) but rather a 180° rotation: An object actually in the upper right quadrant of the visual field was perceived to be in the lower left quadrant (River et al., 1998). Finally, in addition to patients who perceive the world as fully upside-down, patients who experience lesser tilts have been reported (e.g., Girkin et al., 1999; Ropper, 1983; River et al., 1998; Solms et al., 1988). Taken together, these results point to misrepresentation of the visual world's tilt relative to the observer.

Conclusions

I conclude this chapter by highlighting the implications of the reported results for foundational assumptions of the COR hypothesis and then exploring two sets of unresolved issues.

Fundamental COR Assumptions

The results from AH, BC, TM, and normal adults support two fundamental assumptions about the internal representation of object orientation. I have already discussed one of these assumptions in describing the study of normal adults (Gregory & McCloskey, 2007). In particular, I argued that the unambiguous reflections across object axes observed for AH and normal participants (see Figs. 15–7 and 15–19 for examples) strongly support the assumption that object-based frames of reference play a central role in representing the orientation of objects. (See Gregory & McCloskey, 2007, for more detailed discussion and additional evidence.)

Even more fundamental to the COR hypothesis is the assumption that internal representations of object orientation have a coordinate-system format. This assumption is supported by the systematic patterns of orientation-reflection errors observed for AH, TM, BC, and normal adults. Several features of the errors motivate the assumption of coordinate-system representations. First, the errors involve reflection of the target object across an (object or external) axis, suggesting that axes are implicated in representation of orientation. Second, in most of the errors the stimulus object was reflected across a single axis (e.g., external vertical axis, object principal axis), while orientation with respect to other axes was correct. This phenomenon suggests that in the underlying representations information about each axis is represented separately; only given such representations would we expect one axis, but not others, to be affected in an error. Third, the observed reflection errors were selective not merely in the sense of affecting only a single axis but also in another sense: Object parts were reflected from one side of an axis to the other but were not otherwise disarranged. For example, relative distances of parts from reference axes were preserved. This observation suggests that the underlying representations specify direction relative to an axis separately from other parameters such as distance. Finally, the COR hypothesis proved capable of interpreting the various specific types of reflection error observed in the studies I have described, and assumptions about coordinate-system representations played an essential role in the COR interpretations. For example, the reflections across object axes observed for AH and normal adults were interpreted as misrepresentations of polarity correspondences between the reference axes of object-based and external coordinate systems. This interpretation, and the other COR interpretations for errors, could not have been formulated in the absence of assumptions about coordinate-system representations.

Taken together, these points make a strong case for the claim that the observed orientation-reflection errors point to coordinate-system representations of orientation. In Chapter 13 I argued on similar grounds that AH's location-reflection errors implied coordinate-system representations for location. Accordingly, I suggest that reflection errors in location or orientation tasks should be viewed as a signature of coordinate-system representations.

Unresolved Issues

In discussing the results from AH, BC, TM, and normal adults I have focused almost exclusively on how the observed errors could have arisen within coordinate-system orientation representations. As a consequence, I have left several significant issues largely unexplored.

Levels of Representation and Reference Frames

One such issue concerns where in the stream of processing the observed orientation errors arose. Results discussed in earlier chapters (see especially Chapters 4 and 7) demonstrate that AH's errors originate within the visual system—for example, she showed normal performance in location and orientation tasks with nonvisual stimuli. However, BC made orientation-reflection errors with tactile as well as visual stimuli, raising the possibility that her deficit implicates a more central amodal level of representation (although as I noted in discussing BC's results, a visual-system locus of impairment is also possible). TM made reflection errors in describing as well as copying visual stimuli, suggesting that her deficit affects a level of representation not tied to a specific response modality. However, we cannot determine from the evidence we collected whether the affected representations lie within the visual system or instead at some more central level.

In the experiments with normal adults, errors probably did not result from misperception of the visual stimuli (given that exposure duration was 500 milliseconds or longer). Rather, the errors probably resulted from failures in short-term retention of initially accurate representations. This conclusion, however, does little to narrow down the level(s) of representation at which the errors originated; the representations giving rise to the errors may have been perceptual representations within the visual system or amodal spatial representations at a more central level.

Identifying the level at which errors arise is crucial for tying conclusions about the form of a representation to a particular perceptual-, cognitive-, or motor-system locus. I have argued that reflection errors are a signature of coordinate-system orientation representations. Hence, the systematic patterns of reflection errors observed for AH, BC, TM, and normal adults constitute evidence for coordinate-system representations of orientation. However, I can draw only limited conclusions about the functional loci at which orientation is represented in coordinate-system form. AH's results imply that some level(s) of the visual system implements coordinate-system orientation representations. TM's results are consistent with this conclusion, although a more central locus for her errors is possible. BC's performance pattern is perhaps most plausibly interpreted as evidence for coordinate-system orientation representations at some central amodal level, although her errors could conceivably have arisen within the visual system. Most other studies of orientation errors (including my studies with Emma Gregory on normal adults' errors) are subject to similar uncertainties. Hence, an important goal in future research should be to pin down more precisely the functional locus at which the observed orientation errors arise so that conclusions can be drawn about the form of orientation representations at particular levels of representation.

A related issue concerns the reference frames implicated in orientation errors. The COR hypothesis assumes that orientation representations, and hence orientation errors, involve not only object-based but also external frames of reference. However, I have no firm evidence about what specific external frames were implicated in the errors made by AH, TM, BC, or the normal adults. Consider, for example, AH's errors involving reflection across an external horizontal or vertical axis (e.g., Fig. 15–9A). These errors might have originated in representations relating an external frame defined by the stimulus page to a frame based on head or body axes or in representations relating a head- or body-based frame to a frame defined by the response page. Alternatively, the errors might have occurred in relating the stimulus external frame directly to the response frame, without the intervention of frames defined by body axes.[5] Hence, another goal in future research should be to identify the external reference frames implicated in representations of orientation.

The importance of these goals is underlined by the observation that orientation information is almost certainly processed at multiple loci within the brain. For example, the brain mechanisms that mediate visually guided action need orientation information for such purposes as positioning a reaching hand to grasp an object, and visual orientation information is also required for such perceptual functions as identifying visual symbols (e.g., *b* vs. *d*, ← vs. →), interpreting visual scenes, and mediating conscious awareness of object orientations. Orientation may also be processed within the somatosensory system, within systems that manipulate multimodal or amodal spatial representations, and so forth. Furthermore, within each of these brain systems, orientation information may be represented in multiple frames of reference. A central issue for subsequent research is whether orientation representations take the same basic form at all of these representational levels or whether instead the form of orientation representations varies across brain systems and/or across frames of reference within systems.

Location vs. Orientation Errors

Another unresolved issue concerns the interpretations I have offered for AH's location and orientation errors. I have suggested that AH's visual localization errors occur when direction of displacement along a reference axis is misrepresented and that her orientation errors probably stem from misrepresentations of the polarity correspondence between axes of different reference frames. These interpretations seem to imply that the location and orientation errors arise from different visual-system malfunctions.

In earlier chapters, however, I concluded that AH's orientation errors originate from the same underlying deficit as her location errors. This conclusion was motivated by two sets of results. First, AH presented with the same systematic and highly unusual error pattern—high rates of left–right and up–down reflection errors—in both location and orientation tasks (see Chapters 2 and 3); and second, the same visual variables affected her performance in both task types (see Chapter 7).

The obvious question, then, is how the seemingly divergent interpretations for AH's location and orientation errors can be reconciled with the hypothesis of a single underlying deficit. One possibility is that AH's location errors, like her orientation errors, have their genesis in misrepresentations of polarity correspondence. That is, the misrepresentations of displacement direction I have posited to explain the location errors may originate from misrepresentations of polarity correspondence.

This hypothesis may be explained with the aid of Figure 15–21. Panel A illustrates the generation of an accurate attention-centered location

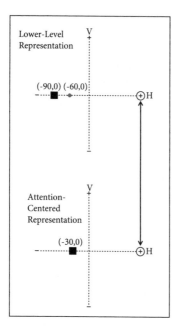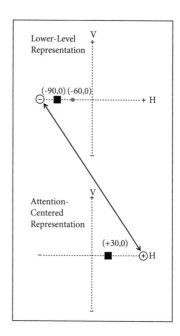

Figure 15–21. Conversion of a lower-level location representation to an attention-centered representation. (A) Accurate attention-centered coordinates generated on the basis of a correct representation of the polarity correspondence between the lower-level and attention-centered horizontal axes. (B) Inaccurate attention-centered coordinates computed on the basis of an incorrect polarity-correspondence representation. Note that the horizontal direction of displacement is misrepresented in the attention-centered coordinates.

representation from a lower-level representation. At the lower level the target stimulus has location coordinates (–90,0) and the focus of attention is at (–60,0). In transforming the target's lower-level coordinates into attention-centered coordinates a positive polarity correspondence is established between the horizontal axes of the two coordinate systems. Given this correspondence and taking into account the shift in origin, the target's attention-based coordinates are computed correctly as (–30,0).

Panel B illustrates the consequences of a polarity-correspondence error. The polarity correspondence between the horizontal axes of the lower-level and attention-centered frames is mistakenly specified as negative, and as a result the location of the target is misrepresented as (+30,0) in the attention-centered coordinate system. In other words, the target's direction of displacement along the horizontal axis of the attention-centered frame is represented as positive rather than negative. In this way, a polarity-correspondence error in mapping one coordinate system onto another could lead to a misrepresentation of displacement direction and, hence, to a location error. Accordingly, misrepresentations of polarity correspondence could provide a unitary account of AH's location and orientation errors. The interpretation could also be applied to the location and orientation reflections exhibited by patient PR (Pflugshaupt et al., 2007).

An important feature of AH's visual localization performance is that she often mislocalized one object in a scene while localizing other objects correctly (see, e.g., Tasks 6–1 and 6–2). Hence, a polarity-correspondence interpretation for her localization errors would presumably need to assume that attention-centered representations are generated separately for different objects in a scene such that polarity correspondence could be represented accurately in computing attention-centered coordinates for some objects and misrepresented for other objects.

Another observation relevant to the polarity-correspondence hypothesis is that orientation errors apparently resulting from misrepresentation of polarity correspondence may occur in the absence of location errors, as in the case of TM and possibly BC. Given this observation, the hypothesis would need somehow to accommodate the possibility that polarity-correspondence errors could occur in the construction of orientation representations without also occurring in the generation of location representations. Conceivably, specific assumptions about the level(s) of representation at which polarity-correspondence errors arose in different cases could plausibly account for the co-occurrence of location and orientation errors in some cases and the occurrence of orientation errors alone in other cases.

Further theoretical and empirical work will be required to elaborate and test the polarity-correspondence hypothesis. However, the present discussion should suffice to demonstrate that a unitary account of the location and orientation reflections observed for AH and PR is potentially feasible.

16

Visual Subsystems

One of the most prominent developments in vision research over the past quarter-century has been the emergence of large-scale theoretical frameworks concerning the functional organization of the cortical visual system. In 1982 Ungerleider and Mishkin (see also Mishkin, Ungerleider, & Macko, 1983; Ungerleider & Haxby, 1994) proposed that, subsequent to the early cortical visual areas, the visual system bifurcates into substantially independent object and spatial vision subsystems, localized to ventral and dorsal cortical processing streams, respectively. More recently, Milner, Goodale, and colleagues put forth an alternative hypothesis positing separate vision-for-perception (ventral) and vision-for-action (dorsal) subsystems (e.g., Goodale, 2000; Goodale & Milner, 1992; Goodale et al., 1991; Milner & Goodale, 1993, 1995). These multiple-subsystem hypotheses have had a major impact on theory and research concerning visual perception, spatial cognition, visually guided action, and even consciousness. For example, in studies of patients with visuospatial deficits researchers have increasingly designed tasks and interpreted data with reference to one or both hypotheses (e.g., Carey, Harvey, & Milner, 1996; Castiello, Paine, & Wales, 2002; Farah, Wallace, & Vecera, 1993; Jeannerod, Decety, & Michel, 1994; Lê et al., 2002; Milner, 1998; Robertson et al., 1997; Wilson, Clare, Young, & Hodges, 1997).

In Chapter 7 I reported results showing that AH's performance in visual location and orientation tasks is dramatically affected by several visual variables (e.g., exposure duration, contrast). On the basis of these results I sketched a multiple-subsystems hypothesis positing distinct transient and sustained subsystems in high-level vision. In the present chapter I develop this hypothesis more fully and relate it to knowledge about independent pathways in early vision. I then contrast my transient–sustained hypothesis with the Ungerleider-Mishkin what–where hypothesis and the Milner-Goodale perception–action hypothesis, arguing that AH's results are readily accommodated by my proposal but pose challenges for both the Ungerleider-Mishkin and Milner-Goodale positions. Finally, I show that the basic findings adduced in support of the what–where and perception–action hypotheses are entirely consistent with my assumptions about the functional architecture of the higher-level visual system. I begin the discussion with a brief summary of the relevant results from AH.

AH's Performance

Table 16–1 summarizes the effects of visual variables reported in Chapter 7. As the table indicates, AH showed good performance in visual location and orientation tasks with brief, moving, or flickering stimuli but poor performance (i.e., high rates of left–right and up–down reflection errors) with long-duration, stationary, steady stimuli. Further, AH was more accurate for low-contrast than high-contrast stimuli, and her performance improved with increasing stimulus eccentricity.

Also relevant in the present context are the results implying that AH's deficit affects high-level vision. As discussed in Chapter 6, her errors consistently respected the boundaries of objects. Although she frequently made errors that involved some, but not all, elements of a visual display, her errors never violated the integrity of objects. That is, she never made errors in which a part or feature of an object became separated from that object or errors in which parts or features of two objects were amalgamated into a single object. This observation strongly suggests that AH's errors arise not in low-level vision, where lines, edges, or other visual features are processed, but rather at a higher level or levels, subsequent to that at which the visual scene is parsed into objects. Results from Task 15–1, in which AH made object-based

Table 16–1. Summary of results reported in Chapter 7 concerning effects of visual variables on AH's performance in visual location and orientation tasks.

Visual variable	AH's Performance	
	Good	Poor
Exposure duration	brief	long
Motion	moving	stationary
Flicker	flickering	steady
Contrast	low	high
Eccentricity	high	low

orientation errors (i.e., reflections across an object axis) provide further support for this conclusion. Also pointing to a high-level locus of impairment are results from Chapter 13 demonstrating that AH's localization errors arise within an attention-based frame of reference. This finding implies that AH's deficit affects a level or levels of the visual system beyond the early retina-based (i.e., "retinocentric") levels.

Transient and Sustained Visual Subsystems

These results, and especially the effects of the visual variables, suggest a hypothesis about the functional architecture of the normal visual system. This hypothesis encompasses three major assumptions, the first concerning the partitioning of the visual system into subsystems, the second regarding the nature of the computations performed by each subsystem, and the third having to do with how representations generated by the subsystems can be used in subsequent processing and response production.

Assumption 1: Transient and Sustained Subsystems in High-Level Vision

My first major assumption is that the normal cortical visual system includes two subsystems—*transient* and *sustained*—that are specialized for processing different kinds of stimuli. More specifically, I assume (*a*) that the transient subsystem is most sensitive to rapidly changing visual stimuli (such as those that are brief, moving, or flickering), whereas the sustained subsystem is most strongly activated by static stimuli of relatively long duration; (*b*) that the transient subsystem is sensitive to low-contrast stimuli, whereas the sustained subsystem requires higher levels of contrast; and (*c*) that the transient subsystem is more responsive to peripheral than central stimuli, whereas the opposite is true of the sustained subsystem. These claims about the properties of the transient and sustained subsystems are summarized in Table 16–2.

I propose that the transient–sustained distinction applies to the level(s) of the cortical visual system giving rise to AH's location and orientation errors (and perhaps to other levels as well). In particular, having argued that AH's errors arise somewhere beyond the early cortical visual areas, I hypothesize that the transient–sustained distinction applies to a higher level (or levels) of the visual system.

These assumptions are motivated not only by AH's performance but also by evidence concerning lower levels of the visual system. Neuroanatomical and neurophysiological studies have identified two separate visual pathways—M (or magnocellular) and P (or parvocellular)—that originate in the retinal ganglion cells and remain distinct through the level of the lateral geniculate nucleus and (at least according to some theorists) into the early cortical visual areas V1–V3 (see, e.g., Livingstone & Hubel, 1988). The M

Table 16–2. Some hypothesized properties of the proposed transient and sustained visual subsystems.

Transient Subsystem	Sustained Subsystem
Highly sensitive to rapidly changing stimuli: • brief • moving • flickering	Most sensitive to sustained stimuli: • long-duration • stationary • constant
Sensitive to low contrast	Requires higher contrast
Most sensitive to peripheral stimuli	Most sensitive to central stimuli

and P pathways appear to differ functionally along a number of dimensions, three of which are germane to the present discussion. First, rapidly changing stimuli activate the M pathway much more strongly than the P pathway; second, the M pathway is more sensitive than the P pathway to low-contrast stimuli; and third, whereas the receptive fields of P-pathway cells are concentrated in the central region of the visual field, M-pathway receptive fields are concentrated in the periphery (e.g., Livingstone, 1990; Livingstone & Hubel, 1987, 1988).

Further evidence for independent pathways in early vision comes from psychophysical research. Results concerning detection thresholds and reaction times for spatial frequency gratings (e.g., Harwerth, Boltz, & Smith, 1980; Kulikowski & Tolhurst, 1973; Mitov & Totev, 2005; Tolhurst, 1975a, 1975b) have led psychophysicists to postulate separate transient and sustained visual processing channels. In addition, a variety of metacontrast masking phenomena have been interpreted in terms of inhibitory interactions between transient and sustained channels (Breitmeyer & Ganz, 1976; Breitmeyer & Ogmen, 2000; Ogmen, Breitmeyer, & Melvin, 2003). The properties ascribed to the transient and sustained channels on the basis of the psychophysical evidence are very similar to those attributed by neurophysiologists to the M and P pathways, respectively. Consequently, it seems reasonable to assume that the transient and sustained channels correspond to the M and P pathways, and some theorists have made this assumption explicitly (e.g., Breitmeyer & Ogmen, 2000).

The M–P distinction and the corresponding distinction between transient and sustained channels apply to low-level vision—that is, precortical and early cortical visual processing. In contrast, I have posited a distinction between transient and sustained subsystems in higher-level vision. How, then, does my transient–sustained distinction relate to the prior M–P and transient–sustained distinctions? And how can the evidence supporting the prior distinctions be said to motivate the distinction I am proposing?[1]

The answers are straightforward. Although the M and P processing streams do not remain completely separate beyond the early cortical visual areas, many theorists have assumed that some higher visual areas receive input predominantly from the M pathway, whereas other areas receive predominantly P-pathway input (e.g., Livingstone & Hubel, 1987, 1988; Livingstone, 1990). I adopt this assumption, proposing in particular that the transient and sustained subsystems in higher-level vision receive their inputs largely from the earlier M and P pathways, respectively, as illustrated in Figure 16–1. Given these proposed relationships, one would expect the transient and sustained subsystems to share many of the stimulus sensitivities and insensitivities exhibited by the M and P pathways, respectively (e.g., sensitivity or insensitivity to low-contrast stimuli). In this way, the ascription of particular characteristics to high-level subsystems can be motivated independently of AH's performance.

I do not assume that inputs to the transient subsystem come solely from the M pathway or that the sustained subsystem receives input solely from the P pathway (see Fig. 16–1). Consequently, the transient and sustained subsystems may not have all of the sensitivities and insensitivities attributed to the M and P pathways, respectively. For instance, whereas the M pathway is thought to be largely insensitive to color, the same may not be true of the higher-level transient subsystem (which may receive some non-M input).

Livingstone and Hubel (1987, 1988; Livingstone, 1990) suggest that the M and P pathways project primarily to the dorsal and ventral cortical processing streams, respectively. Therefore, one might speculate that the transient and

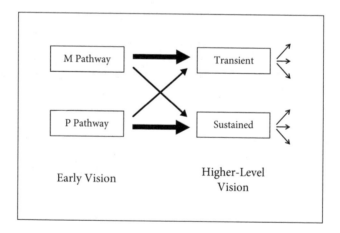

Figure 16–1. Schematic representation of the assumption that the transient subsystem in higher-level vision receives input primarily (although not entirely) from the M pathway in lower-level vision, whereas the sustained subsystem receives input predominantly (but not entirely) from the P pathway. *Arrows* leading from the transient and sustained subsystems indicate that the location and orientation representations generated by these assumptions are subsequently used by other processing mechanisms (see Fig. 16–2).

sustained cortical subsystems are localized to the dorsal and ventral streams, respectively. However, I make no strong claims on this point; in my view, the available evidence is not sufficient to warrant such claims (among other reasons because Livingstone and Hubel's position about the projections of the M and P pathways is by no means universally accepted; see, e.g., Jeannerod, 1997; Merigan & Maunsell, 1993; Milner & Goodale, 1995).

Assumption 2: Spatial Processing in Both Visual Subsystems

My second major assumption is that both transient and sustained subsystems process visual location and orientation information—for example, both subsystems could compute the location of an object on a table or the orientation of a letter on a page (given appropriate stimulus conditions). In this respect, the present proposal differs from the Ungerleider and Mishkin what–where hypothesis, which assumes that only one of the two posited subsystems (the spatial subsystem localized to the dorsal stream) is concerned with spatial processing (Ungerleider & Mishkin, 1982; Mishkin et al., 1983; see also Livingstone, 1990; Livingstone & Hubel, 1987, 1988).

Assumption 3: Availability of Subsystem Outputs

My third assumption is that the location and orientation representations computed by both the transient subsystem and the sustained subsystem are available—directly or indirectly—to a broad spectrum of processes (e.g., visually guided action processes, higher-level spatial processes, object-recognition processes, language processes) and, hence, can contribute to the production of many forms of response. This assumption is illustrated in Figure 16–2.

In assuming that the outputs of the transient and sustained subsystems are available to a broad range of subsequent processes, the present hypothesis contrasts with the perception–action hypothesis proposed by Milner, Goodale, and colleagues (e.g., Goodale, 2000; Goodale & Milner, 1992; Goodale et al., 1991; Milner & Goodale, 1995). These theorists assume that the vision-for-perception and vision-for-action subsystems both process spatial information, but they also assume that the outputs of each subsystem are restricted in their availability for use by subsequent processes. For example, representations computed by the vision-for-action subsystem are assumed to be available only to processes that control natural visually guided actions (such as reaching for a visible object) and not to processes that perform perceptual judgments or mediate awareness of the visual world.

Interpreting AH's Performance

Given my assumptions about transient and sustained subsystems in the normal high-level visual system, the effects of visual variables on AH's performance

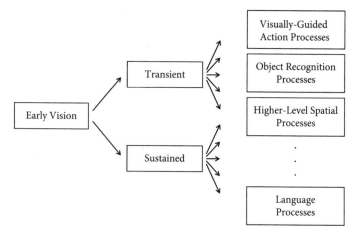

Figure 16–2. Schematic illustration of the assumption that the outputs of the transient and sustained subsystems are available to a broad range of subsequent visual and nonvisual processing mechanisms. For the sake of simplicity, the M and P pathways in early vision are not distinguished.

may be explained by assuming that her transient subsystem is intact but her sustained subsystem is impaired, such that it often produces incorrect representations of stimulus location and/or orientation. When a stimulus activates the transient subsystem more strongly than the sustained subsystem—as for brief, moving, flickering, low-contrast, or eccentric stimuli—AH's response will usually be accurate. When, however, the sustained system is more strongly activated—as for static, long-duration, high-contrast, central stimuli—a location or orientation error will be likely to occur. (I assume that when both subsystems are activated and generate incompatible representations of location or orientation, the conflict is resolved in favor of one or the other subsystem, with the more strongly activated subsystem usually prevailing.)

Note that all three of my assumptions about the normal visual system are required to account for the observed effects of visual variables. The first assumption, concerning the distinction between transient and sustained subsystems, is obviously crucial. The second, that both subsystems compute the location and orientation of visual stimuli, is required to explain why AH showed both very good performance under some stimulus conditions and very poor performance (with systematic errors) under other conditions. To explain high accuracy in conditions with brief, moving, flickering, low-contrast, or eccentric stimuli, we need to assume that (accurate) representations of location and orientation were computed by the transient subsystem; and to explain low (sometimes below-chance) accuracy accompanied by left–right and up–down reflection errors in conditions with static, long-duration, high-contrast, central stimuli, we need to assume that the sustained subsystem also computed location and orientation representations (which were frequently inaccurate in highly systematic ways). The third assumption—that representations computed by either subsystem are available to a broad spectrum of processes and, hence, can contribute to many forms of response—has a very similar motivation. To explain the observed effects of the visual variables in any given task, we need to assume that location and orientation representations from both subsystems are available to the processes that perform the task. For example, AH's impaired reading performance with long-duration, continuous presentations of letters, words, and word sequences implies that reading processes receive location and orientation information from the (impaired) sustained subsystem, whereas her dramatically better performance with brief or flickering displays indicates that the reading processes also receive input from the (intact) transient subsystem.

Implications for the Ungerleider-Mishkin What–Where Hypothesis

The Ungerleider and Mishkin (1982) hypothesis assumes that, following early visual processing, the cortical visual system bifurcates into a dorsal-stream subsystem specialized for spatial processing ("where") and a ventral-stream subsystem specialized for object recognition ("what"). In its original form the hypothesis makes no assumptions about how variables such as exposure duration, motion, and contrast should affect either of the posited subsystems and, thus, has nothing to say about the effects of these variables on AH's performance.

The hypothesis might be modified by assuming that the dorsal ("where") processing stream is subdivided into separate *transient–where* and *sustained–where* subsystems that receive their input primarily from the earlier M and P pathways, respectively. (Note that this assumption is different from Livingstone and Hubel's proposal that the M and P pathways project predominantly to the "where" and "what" cortical subsystems, respectively; see, e.g., Livingstone & Hubel, 1988.) The effects of the visual variables on AH's performance could be explained by positing a deficit affecting the sustained–where subsystem.

Even with this modification, however, the what-vs.-where hypothesis probably does not merit strong endorsement. Among other reasons, Ungerleider and Mishkin's assumptions about the relationship between object recognition and spatial processing are questionable at best. The "what" and "where" subsystems are assumed to be independent in the sense that neither needs information from the other in order to perform its computations. This point can be appreciated by noting that the principal support for the Ungerleider-Mishkin hypothesis (see Ungerleider & Mishkin, 1982) came from animal lesion studies purportedly showing that ventral-stream lesions impair object recognition but not spatial processing, whereas dorsal-stream lesions affect spatial processing but not object recognition. (I say "purportedly" because this characterization of the evidence has been called into question; see, e.g., Milner & Goodale, 1995).

The assumption that object recognition proceeds independently of spatial processing is questionable on conceptual grounds because object recognition requires spatial information—in particular, information about the spatial relations among the parts of an object. For an object to be a cup or a tree or the letter *b* not only must it have certain component parts but in addition these parts must be arranged in a particular spatial configuration. Thus, object-recognition processes presumably must have access to certain forms of spatial information. The hypothesis I have proposed acknowledges this point by assuming that the spatial representations computed by the transient and sustained subsystems are available to object-recognition processes (see Fig. 16–2).

Some empirical basis for questioning the independence of object recognition from spatial processing may be found in AH's impaired performance on letter-recognition tests (at least insofar as letter recognition is considered a form of object recognition). When recognition of a letter required accurate information about the relative locations of its parts—as in distinguishing *b* from *p*, *d*, and *q*—AH showed clear impairment. Further, her letter-recognition performance showed the same effects of exposure duration and flicker as were observed in other visual location and orientation tasks, indicating that the letter-recognition errors reflected the same underlying deficit as her location and orientation errors in other tasks. These results argue that letter recognition, like other cognitive functions that are more obviously spatial, draws upon the spatial representations computed by the transient and sustained visual subsystems.

Implications for the Milner-Goodale Perception–Action Hypothesis

Milner, Goodale, and colleagues propose a functional distinction between vision-for-action and vision-for-perception subsystems and identify these subsystems with the dorsal and ventral cortical processing streams, respectively (e.g., Milner & Goodale, 1995). Milner and Goodale assume that the vision-for-action subsystem evolved to subserve natural visually guided actions that were important for survival, such as reaching for and grasping visible objects. The vision-for-perception subsystem, they assume, is evolutionarily more recent and underlies such cognitive functions as conscious visual perception, perceptual judgments, object recognition, and actions not within the scope of the vision-for-action subsystem. This last category includes actions not directed toward the visual stimulus—such as copying a drawing or pressing a button to indicate the location of a stimulus—and any actions performed more than a few seconds after the target object is no longer visible. Milner and Goodale assume that both subsystems process spatial information (although for different purposes and within different frames of reference).

According to the Milner-Goodale hypothesis, a deficit affecting the vision-for-action subsystem should impair the ability to carry out at least some natural visually guided actions, while sparing the ability to perform perceptual judgments, nonnatural actions, and other functions of the vision-for-perception subsystem. In contrast, a vision-for-perception deficit should lead to impairment on at least some tasks mediated by this subsystem but should not affect natural visually guided actions.

The results of the present study challenge Milner and Goodale's hypothesis because AH presented with the same specific pattern of impairment in both vision-for-action and vision-for-perception tasks. The visually guided reaching task in which AH reached for wooden blocks (Task 3–1) falls clearly within the domain of the posited vision-for-action subsystem, as does the task in which she reached to touch a stationary or moving stimulus on a computer screen (Task 7–1). In both cases AH's task was to reach directly to a visual stimulus while that stimulus remained in view. Tasks in which she reached to the location of a target stimulus immediately upon stimulus offset (e.g., Tasks 3–2 and 13–1) would, according to the Milner-Goodale hypothesis, probably also have been performed via the vision-for-action subsystem. The remaining visual location and orientation tasks—for example, saying "left" or "right," moving a mouse, or pressing a button to indicate the location or orientation of stimuli—should have recruited the vision-for-perception subsystem.

In both vision-for-action and vision-for-perception tasks AH showed the same pattern of impairment: high rates of errors in the form of left–right or up–down reflections. Furthermore, the one visual variable manipulated in both action and perception tasks—motion—had the same effect in both types of task: AH's performance was dramatically better for moving than for stationary stimuli.

These results are difficult to accommodate within the framework of the Milner-Goodale hypothesis. One might suggest that AH has two separate deficits, one affecting the vision-for-action subsystem (leading to impairment in the visually guided reaching tasks) and the other affecting the vision-for-perception subsystem (causing impaired performance in the other tasks). However, one would have to assume that both of the deficits happened to cause the same highly specific and highly unusual types of errors. This assumption would amount to positing a coincidence of cosmic proportions, especially given that the vision-for-action and vision-for-perception subsystems are assumed to process spatial information within different frames of reference for different purposes.

Alternatively, one might suggest that AH has a single deficit affecting the visual system at a point prior to the bifurcation into dorsal (vision-for-action) and ventral (vision-for-perception) streams. However, this interpretation runs afoul of the results indicating that AH's deficit affects high-level vision—specifically, the findings showing that her errors arise in an attention-based frame of reference, consistently respect the integrity of objects, and (in the case of orientation errors) sometimes involve reflection across object axes. These findings strongly suggest that AH's deficit affects a level (or levels) of the visual system subsequent to the bifurcation into dorsal and ventral streams. I conclude that the results from AH argue against the Milner-Goodale hypothesis.[2]

A Potential Counterargument

In drawing conclusions about normal visual-system organization from AH's performance, I have assumed that her visual system has the same organization as the normal system and is defective only in that specific parameters of coordinate-system representations (e.g., polarity correspondence) are frequently miscomputed within the sustained subsystem. However, AH's impairment is not an acquired deficit in which an initially normal visual system sustained damage in adulthood but, rather, a developmental deficit in which the visual system failed to develop normally. Hence, it might be suggested that abnormal neurological development gave rise in AH to a visual system that not only has a specific defect in computing certain parameters of coordinate-system representations but also differs in its basic functional organization from visual systems that developed normally. If this were the case, my conclusions about visual subsystems might be correct as applied to AH but not generalizable to normal individuals.

This possibility cannot be ruled out entirely; however, the claim that AH's visual-system organization is abnormal proves rather difficult to motivate. Nothing in AH's performance suggests that her visual system is aberrant in any way other than in computing specific parameters of coordinate-system representations within a sustained subsystem. Hence, to argue that AH has an aberrant visual-system architecture, one would have to suppose that despite her visual system being profoundly different from the normal system, her performance differs from normal only in ways attributable to the miscomputation of particular coordinate-system parameters. Thus, the assumption that AH's visual-system organization is abnormal would be unmotivated and would do no explanatory work, serving only to insulate the Ungerleider-Mishkin and Milner-Goodale hypotheses from the implications of AH's performance. I will have more to say about inferences from developmental deficits in Chapter 19.

Can the Transient–Sustained Hypothesis Explain What–Where and Perception–Action Dissociations?

If the hypothesis I have proposed is to be considered a viable alternative to the Mishkin-Ungerleider and Milner-Goodale hypotheses, it must be able to accommodate not only the results from AH but also the evidence cited in support of the earlier hypotheses. The evidence supporting the Milner-Goodale hypothesis (see Goodale, 2000, for an overview) for the most part takes the form of so-called perception–action dissociations, which are perhaps more accurately characterized as dissociations between tasks involving natural, direct, immediate visually guided actions and tasks with other forms of response. The most influential evidence comes from patient DF, who shows a selective sparing of natural visually guided action in the face of otherwise severely impaired performance on visual tasks (Milner & Goodale, 1995; Goodale et al., 1991, 1994; Goodale, 2000; Milner et al., 1991; Carey et al., 1996; Murphy, Racicot, & Goodale, 1995). For example, DF was largely unable to report the orientation of a slot verbally or by rotating her hand without reaching toward the slot. However, when she reached to post a card through the slot, she oriented her hand correctly, rotating it toward the correct orientation as soon as she began the reaching movement. Milner, Goodale, and colleagues assume that the vision-for-perception subsystem is required for the verbal responses and the "nonnatural" hand-rotation response, whereas the vision-for-action subsystem can perform the natural action of orienting the hand while reaching. Accordingly, they interpret DF's performance by assuming that her vision-for-perception subsystem is damaged, whereas her vision-for-action subsystem is intact. A variety of other perception–action dissociations have also been reported, involving both brain-damaged patients and normal individuals.

As far as I can see, the reported perception–action dissociations are entirely consistent with my hypothesis. These dissociations make a strong case for the claim that the brain includes special-purpose mechanisms for performing natural, direct, on-line visually guided actions such as reaching for and grasping visible objects. However, nothing in the evidence forces the assumption that these special-purpose mechanisms are separate from other visual processes as early in the visual system as the point of bifurcation into dorsal and ventral streams. Nor need we assume that the distinction between the special-purpose mechanisms and other visual-system mechanisms is the most fundamental distinction around which the visual system is organized. The labels *vision-for-perception* and *vision-for-action* may suggest a division of the visual system into two subsystems of approximately equal scope; however, the labels are not entirely apt. The distinction proposed by Milner and Goodale is more accurately characterized as a distinction between vision for natural, direct, immediate visually guided action and vision for everything else (including nonnatural actions, object recognition, perceptual judgments, conscious awareness, and so forth).

Accordingly, my hypothesis retains the Milner-Goodale special-purpose mechanisms but relegates these mechanisms to a less prominent position in the architecture of the brain. As illustrated in Figure 16–3, I assume that the brain includes, subsequent to the transient and sustained subsystems, special-purpose mechanisms for natural visually guided actions as well as the general-purpose visually guided action mechanisms that (according to both the Milner-Goodale hypothesis and the present proposal) are required for performing "nonnatural" actions. Therefore, just as in the Milner and Goodale hypothesis, perception–action dissociations may be interpreted in terms of selective damage to, or sparing of, the special-purpose mechanisms. On this interpretation AH fails to show perception–action dissociations because her deficit arises earlier in the processing stream in a visual subsystem that provides input to both the special- and general-purpose visually guided action processes.

Milner and colleagues have reported interesting results concerning effects of delay on the performance of DF and the optic ataxic patient AT. DF performed normally in pointing to a visible stimulus; however, her performance deteriorated drastically when she was forced to wait for 10 seconds following stimulus offset before pointing (Milner, Dijkerman, & Carey, 1999). In contrast, the pointing performance of the optic ataxic patient AT was improved by a 5-second delay (Milner, Paulignan, Dijkerman, Michel, & Jeannerod, 1999; see also Milner et al., 2001, for related results from another

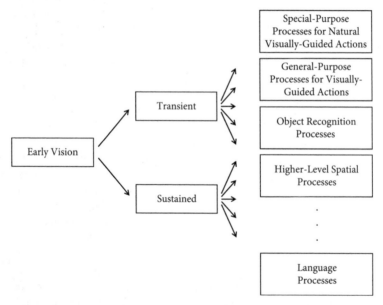

Figure 16–3. Schematic showing proposed special- and general-purpose visually guided action processes and their place in the proposed visual-system functional architecture. The distinction between general visually guided action mechanisms and special-purpose mechanisms for natural, direct, immediate visually guided action provides a basis for explaining perception–action dissociations within the framework of the transient–sustained subsystems hypothesis. Adapted from McCloskey, M. (2004). Spatial representations and multiple visual systems hypotheses: Evidence from a developmental deficit in visual location and orientation processing. *Cortex, 40,* 677–694. With permission of Elsevier.

patient). Milner and colleagues interpret these findings as follows: The vision-for-action system, which evolved for on-line control of natural visually guided actions, cannot retain information about visual targets for more than a few seconds. Hence, in the delayed pointing conditions, the vision-for-action system could not function and the responses had to be generated instead by the vision-for-perception system (which can retain stimulus information for longer periods). Because DF's vision-for-action system is intact but her vision-for-perception system is impaired, she performed better in reaching for visible targets than in reaching after a 10-second delay. In contrast, the optic ataxic AT, who has an impaired vision-for-action system but an intact vision-for-perception system, performed better in the delay condition because the impaired vision-for-action system could not be brought into play. The same interpretation may be offered within the framework of my hypothesis, by assuming that the special-purpose mechanisms for natural visually guided actions retain stimulus information only briefly, whereas the general-purpose visually guided action mechanisms exhibit longer retention. Note that this assumption in no way conflicts with the position that both the special- and general-purpose action mechanisms have access to information from both the transient and sustained visual subsystems. Although memory for stimuli that are no longer present may be transient in the special-purpose mechanisms and sustained in the general-purpose mechanisms, this does not imply that the special-purpose mechanisms receive only transient-subsystem input or that the general-purpose mechanisms receive only sustained-subsystem input.

Turning now more briefly to the evidence supporting the Ungerleider-Mishkin hypothesis, most of this evidence takes the form of dissociations between object-recognition tasks and spatial tasks requiring participants to respond to locations of, or spatial relations among, visual stimuli (e.g., Pohl, 1973; Haxby et al., 1991; see Ungerleider & Haxby, 1994, for an overview). Such dissociations can readily be interpreted within the framework of the proposed functional architecture, by assuming selective damage to object-recognition or spatial-processing mechanisms subsequent to the transient and sustained subsystems. Also, some processing within the transient and sustained subsystems may be more important for object recognition than for spatial tasks and vice versa; hence, lesions affecting the transient and sustained subsystems themselves could conceivably lead to what–where dissociations.

Differences between object-recognition and spatial tasks in patterns of brain activation (e.g., Haxby et al., 1991) can be interpreted analogously. For example, a finding of stronger ventral-stream activation for an object-recognition task than for a spatial task could be accommodated by assuming that the object task drew more heavily than the spatial task on object-recognition processes localized to the ventral stream.

I conclude that the types of result adduced in support of the Milner-Goodale and Ungerleider-Mishkin hypotheses can also be accommodated by the hypothesis I have put forth and, hence, that my hypothesis represents a viable alternative to the prior proposals. However, much more empirical and theoretical work will be required before anything approaching firm conclusions can be drawn. At present, our knowledge of the visual system is limited, especially with respect to levels beyond the early cortical areas. As a consequence, inferences about high-level visual-system organization are fraught with uncertainty. Hypotheses proposing simple dichotomies (what–where, perception–action, transient–sustained) are appealing precisely because of their simplicity, but the reality may turn out to be considerably more complex (e.g., Van Essen, Anderson, & Felleman, 1992).

17

Mental Imagery and the Visual System

Research on visual mental imagery has centered around two related yet distinct issues. The first, which concerns the form(s) of representation underlying visual imagery, is typically posed in terms of a contrast between depictive (i.e., picture-like) representations and nondepictive (e.g., propositional) representations (e.g., Kosslyn, 1980, 1994; Pylyshyn, 1973, 2003). This issue remains unresolved after a debate extending over more than 30 years, at least in part because of a failure to clarify what is meant by a depictive representation (e.g., McCloskey, 2000; Pylyshyn, 1973, 2003). The second issue, and the one on which I will focus, concerns the neural substrates of visual imagery and, specifically, whether imagery relies upon (at least some of) the brain mechanisms responsible for visual perception. Evidence that the visual system may be implicated in imagery comes from studies showing parallels between visual imagery and visual perception with respect to behavioral phenomena (e.g., Finke, 1980; Kosslyn, Ball, & Reiser, 1978) and from studies of brain-damaged patients with imagery deficits apparently resulting from visual-system damage (e.g., Farah, Soso, & Dasheiff, 1992; for reviews, see Farah, 1984; Ganis, Thompson, Mast, & Kosslyn, 2003). However, the interpretation of these findings has been controversial (e.g., Moscovitch, Behrmann, & Winocur, 1994; Pylyshyn, 2003). Furthermore, other studies have shown divergences between imagery and perception (e.g., Chambers & Reisberg, 1985) as well as intact visual imagery in the presence of visual-system damage sufficient to impair visual perception (e.g., Bartolomeo et al., 1998; Behrmann, Moscovitch, & Winocur, 1994; Chatterjee & Southwood, 1995; Moscovitch et al., 1994).

Kosslyn and colleagues (1999) have reported that occipital repetitive transcranial magnetic stimulation (rTMS) slowed response times on both a visual perception and a visual imagery task. However, this result does not necessarily imply that occipital cortex (or other visual-system regions) are required for visual imagery because Kosslyn et al. did not convincingly demonstrate that the effects of rTMS were restricted to the visual system. For example, the study lacked a control condition involving neither visual perception nor visual imagery and, thus, failed to rule out the possibility that the rTMS caused a general slowing of reaction time unrelated to visual processing.

The neural substrates of visual imagery have also been probed with functional neuroimaging methods. A number of studies have found that visual imagery tasks activate visual areas of the brain, including regions as early in the visual system as V1 (e.g., Chen et al., 1998; Kosslyn et al., 1993; Klein et al., 2004; Kosslyn, Thompson, Kim, & Alpert, 1995; Kosslyn & Thompson, 2003; Slotnick, Thompson, & Kosslyn, 2005) and even the lateral geniculate nucleus in the thalamus (Chen et al., 1998). Although some studies have failed to find imagery-induced activation in early visual-system regions (see Kosslyn & Thompson, 2003, for a review), the available evidence suggests that imagery does activate at least some parts of the visual system. However, this conclusion does not necessarily imply that the activated visual-system areas play a functional role in visual imagery (e.g., Moscovitch et al., 1994). Visual imagery tasks activate not only brain areas dedicated solely to vision but also high-level multimodal or amodal areas (e.g., Ganis et al., 2004). Conceivably, imagery-induced activity originating in brain areas that are not purely visual could lead via feedback connections to activation within the visual system, without the visual areas playing any functional role in the creation or processing of visual images. Indeed, Chen et al. (1998) suggest a feedback interpretation for their finding of lateral geniculate nucleus activation in imagery tasks (although for some reason they fail to consider the same interpretation for activation of other visual-system structures).

My intent is not to argue strongly that visual-system activation is epiphenomenal in visual imagery tasks (especially given the results I report below); my point is simply that results showing activation of a brain area during a task do not constitute definitive evidence that the area plays a functional role in performing the task. Perhaps the most reasonable conclusion to be drawn from the available behavioral and neuroimaging results is that visual imagery does not require all of the brain's visual machinery—given, for example, that imagery may be preserved in the face of visual-system damage—but may well draw upon some parts of the visual system.

The two issues I have discussed—the form(s) of representation underlying visual imagery and the brain mechanisms required for visual imagery—are often conflated in discussions of visual imagery but are nevertheless distinct. In particular, evidence for a visual-system role in visual mental imagery would not necessarily mean that imagery is mediated by picture-like representations. Especially at the higher levels of the visual system, representations are not necessarily depictive. Indeed, even at early levels of the visual system, representations may not be depictive in any interesting sense. (For further discussion of this point, see McCloskey, 2000; Pylyshyn, 2003.)

In the present chapter I offer a modest contribution to the body of evidence bearing on the role of the visual system in visual imagery. I report AH's performance on two imagery tasks, both of which had the same rationale: If visual imagery requires the level(s) of the visual system at which AH's perceptual errors arise, then her visual images, like her perceptions, should misrepresent locations and orientations. Furthermore, the misrepresentations in imagery should take the same form as AH's errors in perception: left–right and up–down reflections.

Task 17–1: Dot Localization

In this task a location (e.g., "down right") was dictated and, after a 5-second delay, AH pointed to the corresponding dot in a circular array (see Fig. 17–1). In the imagery condition she was instructed that during the 5-second interval between stimulus and response she should make a vivid visual image of the dot array with a small object, such as a penny, resting on the dot at the dictated location. In the no-imagery condition AH was instructed not to make a visual image. To assist her in complying with this instruction, she was asked to view, during the 5-second delay between stimulus and response, a computer display of rapidly changing geometric figures. (Conceivably, the display could also have interfered with AH's ability to remember the dictated location across the 5-second delay. However, the results discussed below demonstrate that this potential problem did not arise.)

Because the stimuli were nonvisual, I expected AH to show normal performance in the no-imagery condition. The predictions of principal interest concerned the imagery condition. If visual imagery requires the level(s) of the visual system giving rise to AH's perceptual errors, then her images

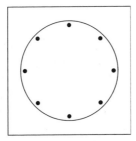

Figure 17–1. The circular array of dots used by AH for responding to dictated locations (e.g., "down left") in Task 17–1.

should sometimes misrepresent the stimulus location, leading to erroneous pointing responses. For example, given the dictated stimulus "down left," AH's image might represent an object resting on the down right location in the dot array, leading her to err by pointing to the down right dot. On the other hand, if visual imagery does not recruit the visual-system mechanisms that are impaired in AH, her performance should be normal in the imagery condition as well as in the no-imagery condition.

One potential complication was that AH's perceptual deficit might come into play in both the imagery and no-imagery conditions when she looked at the dot array in the course of making her pointing responses. The arrows experiment reported in Chapter 4 (Task 4–7) showed that when drawing arrows in response to nonvisual stimuli (e.g., "down left" dictated), AH made reflection errors if she looked at the response sheet while drawing. This result strongly suggested that in the present task she might misperceive locations on the dot array and make pointing errors for that reason. To avoid this complication, the dot array was illuminated with a flickering strobe light in both the imagery and no-imagery conditions. Given the prior results showing that AH's location perception was largely, if not entirely, normal for flickering stimuli (see Chapters 7 and 9), I expected AH to perceive the dot array accurately under the strobe lighting.

Method

Eight stimulus locations were tested: up, up right, right, down right, down, down left, left, and up left. In each block of trials the eight locations were presented once each, in random order. Across several testing sessions seven blocks of trials were presented in the no-imagery condition and nine blocks were tested in the imagery condition. On each trial the dot array was covered during dictation of the stimulus location and during the 5-second stimulus–response interval. At the end of this interval the array was uncovered and AH made her pointing response. Throughout the testing in both conditions the only illumination in the testing room came from a strobe light flashing at 25 Hz.

Results

In the no-imagery condition AH was 100% correct: She pointed to the correct location on all fifty-six trials. In the imagery condition, however, she was only 79% correct (57/72), $\chi^2(1, n = 128) = 13.2, p < 0.001$. Furthermore, her errors were of the same types as those she made in visual localization tasks: thirteen of the fifteen errors involved left–right and/or up–down reflection of the target location (e.g., pointing to the left location for the stimulus "right," pointing to the down left location for the stimulus "up right"). Additional examples of AH's errors in the imagery condition are presented in Figure 17–2.

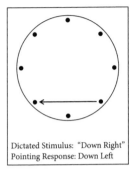 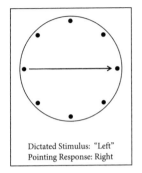 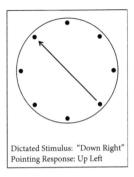

| Dictated Stimulus: "Down Right" | Dictated Stimulus: "Left" | Dictated Stimulus: "Down Right" |
| Pointing Response: Down Left | Pointing Response: Right | Pointing Response: Up Left |

Figure 17–2. Examples of AH's errors in Task 17–1. *Arrows* point from the target location to AH's erroneous response location.

AH's perfect performance in the no-imagery condition demonstrates that she could comprehend the dictated stimuli and further that with flickering illumination of the dot array she had no difficulty identifying and pointing to the target location. Accordingly, her impaired performance in the imagery condition can be attributed to the visual images she generated in this condition. Presumably, her image sometimes misrepresented the stimulus location, leading her to point to the wrong location on the dot array. For example, given the stimulus "right," her image may have represented an object resting on the dot at the left location in the array, leading her to point erroneously to that location.

This pattern of results strongly suggests that in generating visual images AH recruited the visual-system mechanisms that lead her to err in perceiving visual stimuli: She made errors only in the imagery condition, and the errors took the characteristic form of her perceptual errors (i.e., left–right and up–down reflections). Accordingly, the results support the hypothesis that visual imagery relies upon the visual system.

Task 17–2: Letter Orientation

In this tactile orientation task AH felt an embossed lowercase letter (*b*, *d*, *p*, or *q*) with her eyes closed and, after a 5-second delay, said the name of the letter. In the imagery condition AH made a visual image of the stimulus letter during the 5-second stimulus–response interval. In the no-imagery condition she was instructed not to make an image; as in the preceding task, she viewed a display of rapidly changing geometric figures to help her comply with the no-image instructions.

Predictions were the same as for Task 17–1. In the no-imagery condition AH's performance should be normal because the stimuli were nonvisual. In the imagery condition, however, she should show impaired performance if visual imagery implicates the level(s) of the visual system giving rise to her orientation errors in visual perception.

Method

Stimuli were the four lowercase letters *b*, *d*, *p*, and *q*. The letters were embossed on a hard plastic sheet, with a height of 10 mm and a width of 5 mm. The letters were identical except for orientation.

Four blocks of eight trials from each condition (imagery and no-imagery) were presented in counterbalanced order. In each block the four stimulus letters were presented twice each, in random order. On each trial AH closed her eyes and felt the stimulus letter with the index finger of her right hand, making a single left-to-right pass across the letter.

Results

AH was 100% correct (32/32) in the no-imagery condition but only 56% correct (18/32) in the imagery condition, $\chi^2(1, n = 64) = 15.45, p < 0.001$. Her errors in the imagery condition included both left–right and up–down reflections (e.g., $b \rightarrow d, p \rightarrow b$). Like the results of Task 17–1, these findings imply that in generating visual images AH recruited the visual-system mechanisms that give rise to her errors in perceiving visual stimuli. Hence, the task provides further support for the hypothesis that visual imagery relies upon the visual system.

Summary and Conclusions

When instructed not to form visual images, AH performed without error in reporting the location (Task 17–1) and orientation (Task 17–2) of nonvisual stimuli. However, when told to generate visual images of the stimuli, she made many errors in subsequently reporting locations and orientations. Furthermore, her errors took the same forms—left–right and up–down reflections—as the errors she characteristically committed in tasks with visual stimuli. These results imply that the level(s) of the visual system giving rise to AH's perceptual errors plays a functional role in visual imagery. Accordingly, the findings support the hypothesis that visual imagery draws upon (at least some of) the brain mechanisms for visual perception.

The results of the present tasks do not allow conclusions about the specific level(s) of the visual system implicated in visual imagery. However, given the evidence that AH's perceptual deficit affects high-level vision, the present findings indicate that some high-level visual mechanisms play a functional role in visual imagery.

A final point concerns a different topic, the cognitive processes mediating tactile letter identification. One might suppose that identifying a letter by touch involves first creating a visual representation of the letter—that is, a visual image—and then applying visual letter recognition processes to that representation. According to this hypothesis, AH should have made errors in the no-imagery condition of Task 17–2, either because she was unable to make images of the letters while viewing the visual display or because she made images that (as in the imagery condition) frequently misrepresented the orientation of the stimulus letter. Her perfect performance in the no-imagery condition accordingly suggests that she was able to identify the letters without generating visual images.

18

Visual Updating and Visual Awareness

In this chapter I present results concerning AH's head and eye movements and the consequences of these movements for her visual location perception. I first show that AH often moved her head and eyes in the wrong direction when attempting to orient toward a visual stimulus. I then report a far more surprising result: AH's misperceptions of object location often remained stable across head and eye movements. For this latter result I offer a speculative interpretation concerning the processes that generate high-level visual location representations. Finally, I discuss the implications of AH's performance for issues concerning the levels of the visual system implicated in conscious visual experience.

Head and Eye Movements

Like visually guided reaching movements, head and eye movements directed toward a visual target require information about the location of the target. This observation raises the question of whether AH's visual localization deficit comes into play when she moves her head and eyes. In the visually guided reaching task (Task 3-1) AH was instructed to look straight ahead at the middle of the table when first opening her eyes on each trial but was then free to shift her head and eyes. Although head and eye movements were not explicitly scored, informal observation made clear that these movements were entirely consistent with AH's reaching responses: On trials in which she reached to the wrong location, she also directed her head and eyes to that erroneous location. For example, when she reached to the far right for a target presented at a far left position, AH oriented her head and eyes to the far right location before or while she reached to that location. This phenomenon and its implications were explored in several subsequent tasks.

Tasks 18–1 and 18–2: Saccades to Visual Targets

Two saccadic eye-movement tasks were administered during a clinical neuro-ophthalmological exam. In Task 18–1 AH was seated with her head stabilized by a chin and forehead rest, fixating a central point. On each trial a red light-emitting diode (LED) was illuminated at a location 10°, 20°, or 30° to the left or right of fixation and AH was instructed to shift her eyes to the target. The target light stayed on until after AH had completed her eye movement. Surface electrodes recorded extraocular muscle activity, providing measures of direction and amplitude of eye movements.

AH shifted her eyes in the wrong direction (e.g., left for a target on the right) on sixteen of sixty-four trials (25%). Further, although amplitude measures obtained from extraocular muscle activity are not very precise, the data suggested that AH's wrong-direction saccades were directed toward the left–right reflection of the target location: Mean amplitude for wrong-way saccades was 11° for targets at an eccentricity of 10°, 25° for targets of eccentricity 20°, and 27° for targets of eccentricity 30°. As noted in Chapter 11, wrong-direction saccades were also observed in patient PR (Pflugshaupt et al., 2007), the recently described patient with a perceptual deficit very similar to that of AH.

Task 18–2 demonstrated that flicker increased the accuracy of AH's saccades. Three blocks of trials were administered. In blocks 1 and 3 the target LED was illuminated steadily, whereas in block 2 the target flickered. AH made wrong-direction saccades on 40% of the steady-target trials (78/195) but only 8% of the flicker trials (7/86), χ^2 (1, $n = 281$) = 27.2, $p < 0.001$. The results from these tasks imply that AH's saccadic eye movements, like her other responses to visual location information, are affected by her visual localization deficit. The performance difference between steady and flickering targets also implies that both transient and sustained visual subsystems can provide input to processes that compute target locations for saccadic eye movements.[1]

Persisting Visual Mislocalizations

Additional tasks provided further evidence of erroneous head and eye movements. More importantly, these tasks revealed that AH's misperceptions of location often remained unaltered when she moved her head and eyes.

Task 18–3: Localizing Before and After Gaze Shifts

In this task AH reported the locations of target objects on a table in front of her. Targets were the wooden cube and cylinder from the visually guided reaching task (Task 3–1), and the four stimulus locations (near left, near right, far left, far right) were a subset of those used in the reaching task (see Fig. 18–1). Horizontal eccentricity was approximately 8° of visual angle for the near locations and 14° for the far locations.

On each trial AH's head and eyes were initially directed straight ahead, toward a central fixation point. She closed her eyes while the cube or cylinder was placed at one of the four stimulus locations and then opened her eyes without shifting them from the straight-ahead direction. While looking straight ahead, she identified the target as a cube or cylinder and raised her left or right hand to indicate the side on which she saw the object. Next, she was instructed to look at the target. After shifting her eyes and head to the perceived target location, she again reported what she saw. Across thirty-two trials the cube and cylinder were each presented four times at each of the four locations, in a random order.

Figure 18–2 illustrates the sequence of events for a trial in which AH responded correctly to a cylinder presented at the near right location. Initially looking straight ahead, AH said, "I see a cylinder here," and raised her right hand. Instructed to look at the cylinder, she shifted her head and eyes to the near right location and said, "I see a cylinder here," again raising her right hand.

On all thirty-two trials AH correctly identified the target as a cube or cylinder. On twenty-one of the trials (66%) she accurately indicated the

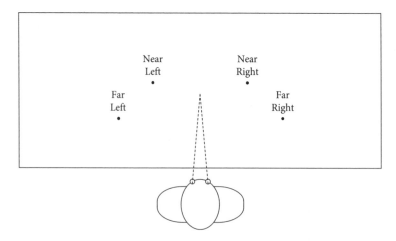

Figure 18–1. The four stimulus locations in Tasks 18–3 and 18–4. AH's head and eyes were initially pointed straight ahead, with her eyes directed at a central point on the table (as indicated by the *dashed lines*).

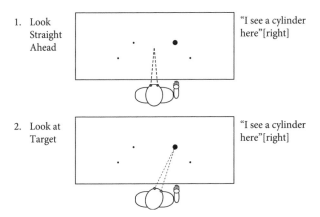

Figure 18–2. Sequence of events on a trial in Task 18–3 in which AH responded correctly.

target's location throughout the trial: She raised the correct hand while looking straight ahead, then looked at the correct location and again raised the correct hand while stating that she saw the target. However, on eleven trials (34%) AH mislocalized the target while looking straight ahead, by raising her right hand for a target on her left or vice versa. On one of these trials she realized her error when asked to look at the target. Remarkably, however, on the remaining ten trials she maintained her initial erroneous target localization even after looking in the wrong direction: She shifted her gaze to the left–right reflection of the target location and then reported seeing the target at that location. Figure 18–3 shows AH's responses for a trial in which a cube was presented at the near left location. While looking straight ahead, AH raised her right hand, saying "I see a cube here." Instructed to look at the cube, she shifted her gaze to the near right location. She then again raised her right hand and said, "I see a cube here," notwithstanding the fact that the cube was actually on the other side of the table.

The pattern was the same for all ten trials in which AH was consistently incorrect: She not only mislocalized the target while looking straight ahead and then turned her head and eyes to the erroneous location; she also continued to perceive the target at the same erroneous location even after shifting her gaze to look at that location. As a consequence, she believed herself to be looking directly at the target object when in fact she was looking at an empty region of the table and the target was elsewhere in her visual field. For ease of reference, I will refer to the errors in which AH maintained an initial mislocalization even after shifting her gaze as "persisting visual mislocalization" (PVM) errors.

Informal follow-up testing revealed that AH made PVM errors only if the target remained within her visual field after an erroneous shift of gaze. The near and far locations in Task 18–3 were sufficiently central that the target

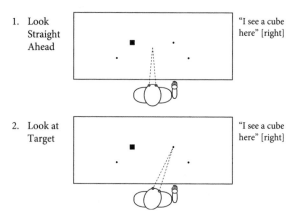

1. Look
   Straight
   Ahead

"I see a cube
here" [right]

2. Look at
   Target

"I see a cube
here" [right]

Figure 18–3. Sequence of events on a trial in Task 18–3 in which AH mislocalized the visual target and persisted in the error even after looking at the erroneous location.

object remained visible to AH even when she looked in the wrong direction. In the follow-up testing target objects were presented more peripherally (at approximately 50° eccentricity) so that they were visible when AH was looking straight ahead but no longer in her visual field when she shifted her gaze in the wrong direction. Under these conditions, AH made localization errors while looking straight ahead but always realized and corrected her error immediately after looking in the wrong direction. This finding indicates that the PVM errors cannot be explained by assuming that AH simply failed to process incoming visual information after shifting her gaze and somehow continued to represent the visual scene entirely on the basis of information obtained while she was initially looking straight ahead.

Task 18–4: Target Size and Eccentricity

One of the many questions raised by the PVM errors concerns the lower acuity of peripheral than central vision. When an observer shifts her gaze to look at a visual stimulus, the stimulus can be perceived more clearly because it has moved into the high-acuity foveal region of the visual field. In contrast, when AH shifted her gaze in the wrong direction when attempting to fixate a visual stimulus, the stimulus moved not into central vision but instead farther into the periphery. The result should have been reduced, rather than enhanced, clarity. Why, then, didn't the low clarity cause AH to realize that she had shifted her eyes in the wrong direction and was not looking at the target?

Brenda Rapp and I explored this question in a task involving large and small visual stimuli presented at low- and high-eccentricity locations. Our hypothesis was as follows: Under some circumstances, AH may be able to perceive a target stimulus with sufficient clarity to perform the task at hand even after she shifts her gaze in the wrong direction. For example, in Task 18–3 the cube and cylinder were sufficiently large to be distinguished even when AH was looking in the wrong direction. Under such conditions, the reduced clarity of the target might not call itself to AH's attention. Due to many years of shifting her gaze sometimes toward and sometimes away from a visual target when attempting to look at it, AH probably accepts without question that objects sometimes look more clear and sometimes less clear when she looks at them. However, under circumstances in which a wrong-direction gaze shift prevents the target stimulus from being seen with clarity adequate to a task she is attempting to perform, AH should realize that something is amiss.

Stimuli in the task were a large circle, a large diamond, a small circle, and a small diamond. The large shapes were 3.5 cm in diameter, corresponding to a visual angle of approximately 3.6°; the small shapes were 1 cm in diameter (1°). Each shape was printed on a 10 × 10 cm slip of paper. In the first block of trials—the low-eccentricity block—the stimuli were presented at near left and near right locations 10° of visual angle from the central fixation point. In the second, high-eccentricity, block, stimuli were presented at far left and far right locations with eccentricities of 30°. For both low- and high-eccentricity locations, the target stimulus remained within AH's visual field when she shifted her gaze to the corresponding location on the wrong side.

On each trial AH sat with head and eyes oriented toward the central fixation point. She then opened her eyes and, while looking at the fixation point, raised her left or right hand to indicate the location of the target. She was then instructed to look at the target and name it as a circle or diamond.

When presented at the low-eccentricity locations, both the small and large target shapes could be identified whether AH was looking straight ahead, at the target, or at the corresponding position on the wrong side. At the high-eccentricity locations, the large shapes could still be identified at all three gaze locations (straight ahead, correct location, incorrect location). However, when the small shapes were presented at the high-eccentricity locations, they were difficult to distinguish when looking straight ahead and could not be distinguished after a gaze shift to the wrong side.

Forty trials were administered in the low-eccentricity condition. On eleven of the trials (28%) AH raised the wrong hand while looking straight ahead. On four of these trials she realized her error after shifting her gaze in the wrong direction and looked to the correct side before naming the target shape. On the remaining seven trials she persisted in the initial error, continuing to look at the incorrect location while naming the target. AH correctly identified the target as a circle or diamond on all twenty large-shape trials and on 19/20 small-shape trials. The single error—identifying a small circle as a diamond—occurred on a trial in which she looked in the wrong direction and did not subsequently correct the localization error.

In the high-eccentricity condition testing was aborted after sixteen trials because AH became too distressed to continue after two small-target trials in which she indicated and then looked to the wrong side. On the first of these trials a small diamond was presented at the far left location. AH raised her right hand to indicate that the stimulus was on the right and then looked at the far right location. She immediately appeared confused, leaning forward and squinting as if trying to see more clearly. After staring for several seconds, she shook her head and spoke with me about what she had experienced:

> AH: I don't...I don't...It's not there....I don't know what it is....It's over here [indicating the correct—left—side].
> MM: What happened when you looked over there [right]?
> AH: I couldn't...I couldn't tell what...I couldn't tell what...I couldn't tell what it was on the paper.
> MM: You were looking at the paper as far as you knew, but you couldn't make out the object?
> AH: Right.
> MM: Then what happened?
> AH: Then I saw it over here [left].

A few trials later a small circle was presented at the far right location. AH indicated the left side with her hand and looked to the far left location. Once again, she seemed bewildered and distressed, stating, "Well, I don't think it's there....I see a purple dot [marking the far left location], so I guess it would be over there [right]." Tears welled up in her eyes and she said, "I look at it and I can't see it." At this point the testing was terminated.

These results demonstrate that AH behaves as expected given the difference in acuity between peripheral and central vision. When a wrong-direction gaze shift results in target clarity inadequate for the task at hand—or perhaps when target clarity is grossly discrepant from that expected from fixating the target—AH recognizes that something has gone awry. If, however, target clarity remains adequate for performing the current task (or perhaps if the discrepancy is not too great between actual clarity and that expected at fixation), AH may fail to realize that she has shifted her gaze in the wrong direction and is not looking at the target. Under everyday conditions, AH may automatically shift her gaze to the other side when target clarity is unexpectedly poor and, thus, may not become aware of the problem. In the present task, however, she was not allowed to move her eyes freely; and as a result, her inability to discriminate a small target after a wrong-direction shift of gaze was brought forcefully to her attention.

The next two tasks speak to the robustness of the PVM phenomenon, showing that PVM errors can persist over multiple gaze shifts and may occur when more than one target stimulus is presented on each trial.

Task 18–5: Multiple Gaze Shifts

Task 18–5 was the same as Task 18–3, except that two additional gaze shifts occurred on each trial. As in the earlier task, AH first identified and localized a target cube or cylinder while looking straight ahead, then looked at the perceived target location and reported what she saw. However, following this report, she was asked to shift her gaze to the corresponding position on the other side and report what she saw there. Finally, she was asked to shift back to the first side she had viewed and once again report what she saw. Figure 18–4 illustrates the sequence of events for a trial in which AH's responses were all correct. Across sixteen trials the cube and cylinder were each presented twice at each of the four locations.

AH correctly identified the target as a cube or cylinder on all sixteen trials. On ten of the trials her head and eye movements, hand-raising responses, and verbal reports were correct throughout the trial (as in Fig. 18–4). However, on six trials (38%) she localized the target to the wrong side while initially looking straight ahead. On two of these trials she realized her error after looking at the erroneous location and then responded correctly for the remainder of the trial. On the other four trials she made PVM errors,

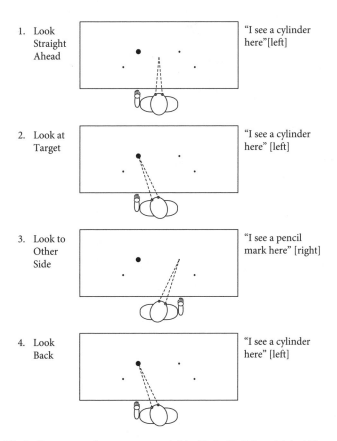

Figure 18–4. Sequence of events on a trial in Task 18–5 in which AH responded correctly throughout the trial.

continuing to report the target at the erroneous location after shifting her gaze to that location. After then shifting her gaze to the corresponding position on the other side (where the target actually was), she realized her mistake on one of the four trials and thereafter responded correctly. However, for the remaining three trials she reported, while looking at the target, that she was looking at a pencil mark. (The four stimulus locations were labeled with small pencil marks so that I could position targets accurately.) Finally, after looking back to the side she had initially viewed, AH realized her error on two of the three trials, but on the remaining trial she continued localizing the target to the erroneous location.

Figure 18–5 illustrates a trial in which AH realized her error on the final gaze shift. The target was a cube at the near left location. While looking straight ahead, AH erroneously raised her right hand. She then looked to

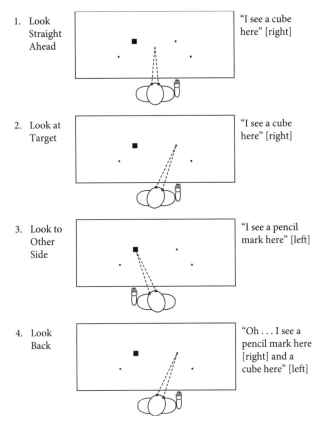

Figure 18–5. Sequence of events on a trial in Task 18–5 in which AH mislocalized the visual target and persisted in the error even after looking at the erroneous location and back at the target location. AH realized the error only after looking a second time at the incorrect location.

the near right location and reported seeing the cube at that location. Next, she shifted her gaze to the near left location and reported seeing a pencil mark, even though she was looking directly at the cube. Finally, after shifting back to the near right, she realized her mistake, reporting that she now saw a pencil mark on the right and a cube on the left. Questioned after the trial, AH said that while she was looking to the left and perceiving a pencil mark (see diagram 3 in Fig. 18–5), she had continued to perceive the cube at the near right location; only when she shifted her gaze back to the near right did she realize that the cube was not there. Hence, the initial mislocalization persisted over two gaze shifts. According to AH, the same was true for the other trial in which she realized her error after the final gaze shift. For the single trial in which AH was incorrect throughout the trial, her initial mislocalization remained stable over three shifts of gaze: looking at the perceived target location, looking to the other side, and finally looking back to the first side. Hence, the results from Task 18–5 demonstrate that although gaze shifts often led AH to correct her localization errors, the errors sometimes persisted across multiple shifts.

Task 18–6: Two Target Stimuli

Targets in this task were colored plastic shapes 2.5 cm in diameter: a red square, a red circle, a green square, and a green circle. On each trial AH closed her eyes while two targets were placed on the table at corresponding left and right locations (near left and near right, far left and far right). She then opened her eyes while looking straight ahead. A few seconds later she was instructed to look at one of the targets (e.g., "Look at the red circle"). After shifting her gaze, she raised her left or right hand to indicate the side where she saw the specified target. Next, she looked at the corresponding location on the other side and described what she saw. Finally, she looked back to the first side and again reported what she saw. Sixteen trials were administered.

On ten of the sixteen trials AH's responses were correct throughout the trial. On the remaining six trials her initial localization response was incorrect: She looked to the wrong side and raised the wrong hand. On two of these trials she realized the error when asked to look at the other side (where the specified target was actually located). However, on the remaining four trials she maintained the initial target mislocalization after shifting her gaze, and on two of these trials the mislocalization persisted throughout the trial. Figure 18–6 illustrates a trial in which a green square and a red square were presented at the near left and near right locations, respectively. Asked to look at the green square, AH directed her head and eyes to the near right position, where the red square was located. She then raised her right hand to indicate that the green square was on the right. Instructed to look toward the other side, AH shifted her gaze to the near left so that she was now looking directly at the green square. However, she stated that the red square was on that side.

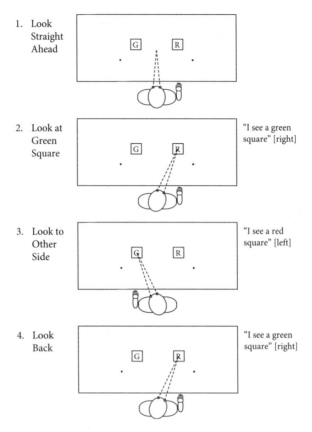

Figure 18–6. Sequence of events on a trial in Task 18–6 in which AH mislocalized the target stimuli throughout the trial.

Finally, she was asked to look back to the first side, and after doing so she reported seeing the green square. Hence, AH apparently mislocalized both target stimuli, and her mislocalizations remained stable across several gaze shifts.

Interpreting the Persisting Visual Mislocalizations

Even in the context of AH's highly unusual deficit, the PVMs seem bizarre: AH claimed to be looking at targets that were actually elsewhere in her visual field and claimed not to be looking at targets that she was in fact fixating. These errors are surprising not only on an intuitive level but also in light of previous results and conclusions concerning AH's impairment. I argued in Chapter 13 that AH's localization errors arise in an attention-centered frame of reference and take the form of reflections across the focus of attention.

However, the PVM errors observed in Tasks 18–3 through 18–6 do not appear to be reflections across the attended location. Consider, for example, the trial in Figure 18–3. After AH's initial mislocalization and corresponding erroneous gaze shift, she was looking at (and presumably attending to) the near right location. Nevertheless, she persisted in localizing the target to that location. This error was clearly not a reflection across the attended location but rather a mislocalization of the target *to* the attended location. How, then, can the PVMs be understood?

I propose that these errors may be explained by assuming that AH, after shifting her gaze, did not always use the visual information obtained from the new point of view to construct a new attention-centered representation. Rather, I suggest, she sometimes generated a new attention-centered representation from the original attention-centered representation, thereby perpetuating errors in the original representation. This interpretation may be clarified with an example. Figure 18–7 illustrates the sequence of events on the trial previously shown in Figure 18–3 as well as hypothesized low-level (retinocentric) and higher-level (attention-centered) location representations.[2] In accord with conclusions from prior chapters, I assume that the

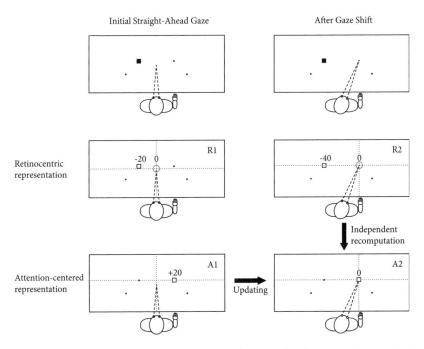

Figure 18–7. Sequence of events on the trial originally shown in Figure 18–3, with hypothesized retinocentric and attention-centered location representations. *Horizontal arrow* illustrates the process of constructing a new attention-centered representation by updating the existing attention-centered representation.

low-level representations are accurate and that AH's errors arise at the attention-centered level. In the diagrams showing the retinocentric and attention-centered representations, the unfilled squares depict the *represented* position of the target (which, at the attention-centered level, does not correspond to the actual target position). The numbers in the figure are hypothesized horizontal coordinates for the target object and the focus of attention (unfilled circle). Vertical coordinates are not relevant to the interpretation and are omitted.

The top left diagram in the figure shows the situation at the beginning of the trial, with AH looking straight ahead. The middle diagram on the left shows the corresponding retinocentric representation, which I will refer to as "R1." The target has a horizontal location coordinate of –20, indicating a position 20 units in the negative direction (i.e., left) from the point of fixation. (Distance units are arbitrary.) The retinocentric representation also specifies that the focus of attention has a horizontal coordinate of 0 and, thus, coincides with the point of fixation.

The bottom left diagram shows the attention-centered representation (A1) constructed from the R1 representation. At this level the target's location is misrepresented. The horizontal coordinate should be –20, indicating a displacement of 20 units in the negative direction (left) from the attentional focus.[3] However, in accord with the prior conclusion that AH is impaired in representing displacement direction at the attention-centered level, I assume that the horizontal direction was misrepresented as positive rather than negative, yielding the erroneous coordinate +20. AH's initial mislocalization on the trial is thereby interpreted as a left–right reflection across the focus of attention.

When asked to look at the target, AH shifted her gaze to the near right location, as shown in the top diagram on the right side of the figure. The middle right diagram shows the accurate retinocentric representation (R2) generated from the new view of the stimulus display. The target's new horizontal coordinate is –40 because AH's gaze—and hence the origin of the retinocentric coordinate system—has shifted 20 units to the right. The horizontal coordinate of the attentional focus is, however, once again 0, in accord with the assumption that AH's attention moved with her eyes.

Finally, the bottom right diagram presents the hypothesized A2 representation—that is, the attention-centered representation constructed after the gaze shift. As shown in the figure, I assume that the A2 representation erroneously specified a target location coinciding with the focus of attention. This assumption provides a basis for interpreting AH's persisting mislocalization of the target to the near right location (where she was looking and attending). How, though, could the hypothesized A2 representation have been generated?

The most obvious possibility is that the A2 representation was generated from the R2 representation, just as A1 was generated from R1. On this account, which I will refer to as "independent recomputation," the process that generates the new attention-centered representation makes no reference to the prior attention-centered representation or to any other visual representations constructed prior to the gaze shift; instead, the process starts from scratch, relying only on visual information obtained from the postshift view of the stimulus display.

The independent recomputation assumption appears plausible. However, independent recomputation would not have produced the A2 representation in Figure 18–7 and, thus, cannot account for AH's persisting mislocalization of the target to the near right location. A process that computed A2 from R2 might have misrepresented the horizontal direction of displacement, yielding an erroneous horizontal coordinate of +40 (instead of the correct coordinate of −40). However, the result would then have been an error in which AH mislocalized the target to a position substantially to the right of the near right location, instead of the actual error in which AH reported the target to be at the near right location. More generally, adopting the independent recomputation assumption would lead us to expect that AH's errors following gaze shifts would be reflections across the new focus of attention; however, none of the PVM errors took this form.

Fortunately, independent recomputation is not the only way a new attention-centered representation could be generated; a new representation could also be created by updating the existing attention-centered representation. For example, the A2 representation in Figure 18–7 could have been generated by updating the A1 representation to account for the shift in attentional focus. Given information about the direction and distance of the attentional shift, the A2 representation could be computed straightforwardly: The target's horizontal coordinate was +20 in the A1 representation, and the focus of attention then shifted 20 units in the positive direction; the target's A2 horizontal coordinate would therefore be 0, indicating a location directly at the attentional focus. In this way, the updating interpretation can explain how the hypothesized A2 representation came about and, hence, can interpret the observed PVM error. In fact, all of the PVM errors observed in Tasks 18–3 through 18–6 can be interpreted in terms of updating.

The updating hypothesis accounts for the puzzling features of the PVM errors. First, the hypothesis straightforwardly explains why AH's initial mislocalizations often persisted over one or more gaze shifts: When new attention-centered representations were generated by updating preexisting attention-centered representations, errors in the earlier representations were perpetuated in the later representations. Second, the updating hypothesis offers an explanation for the bizarre form of the PVM errors, in which AH claimed to be looking at targets that were in fact elsewhere and vice versa. The hypothesis holds that after AH shifted her gaze her visual system sometimes generated new attention-centered representations without reference to visual information obtained from the new view of the stimulus display, leading in some instances to errors that would never have occurred had the new visual information been taken into account. Implicit in this account is an assumption I will discuss more fully later (see "Visual Awareness"): AH's visual awareness of an object's location is mediated by high-level attention-centered representations (or perhaps by still higher-level representations computed from the attention-centered representations); although her visual system generates accurate lower-level representations, these representations are not accessible to awareness. Hence, in the case of the PVM error shown on the right side of Figure 18–7, the updating account holds that the accurate R2 representation neither played a role in generating the A2 representation nor itself gave rise to awareness.

The updating interpretation raises the interesting possibility that—for normal individuals as well as for AH—attention-centered location representations are not continuously and automatically recomputed from lower-level representations. Instead, the attention-centered coordinates for an object may simply be updated as necessary to reflect shifts of attention, as long as the object remains stationary. Recomputation may be carried out only when the object moves.

Information about whether an object has moved could be obtained from low-level representations. For example, in the trial shown in Figure 18–7 the target's retinocentric location representation changed when AH shifted her gaze but the change was entirely attributable to the gaze shift. In other words, the difference between the R1 and R2 representations of the target was exactly that expected from the eye movement, implying that the target had not moved. As a consequence, the target's coordinates in the new attention-centered location representation (A2) could be generated simply by updating the A1 coordinates, without reference to the R2 representation.

In contrast, when changes in an object's retinocentric representation are not entirely attributable to eye movements, the visual system can conclude that the object itself has moved. In this case, the object's new retinocentric representation must be considered in computing its new attention-centered representation. Accordingly, I assume that when movement is detected, new attention-centered representations are created by recomputation from the new retinocentric information (at least for the objects that have moved and perhaps for other objects as well). Consistent with this assumption, informal testing revealed that when AH shifted her gaze in the wrong direction and then claimed to be looking at the target, she realized her error if the target was moved or if another object was moved into a position near the target. Apparently, the movements triggered recomputation of the target's attention-centered location from lower-level representations and blocked the application of updating processes. (The recomputed representations may have been accurate at least in part because the transient visual subsystem was activated when the target was moved or an additional object was inserted.)

The assumption that recomputation is triggered by detection of movement also bears on the interpretation offered in Chapter 8 for results from the nonballistic reaching task (Task 8–1). In this task AH often began reaching in the wrong direction but then corrected the movement and eventually reached the target. I suggested that the sight of her moving hand may have helped AH localize not only the hand but also the target stimulus. In light of the movement–triggers–recomputation assumption, this account may be elaborated to propose more specifically that detection of the hand's motion triggered recomputation of attention-centered location representations for the hand and for the target.

The preceding discussion highlights an important point: The updating interpretation I have offered for the PVM errors does not assume that AH fails to process the new information her visual system receives after a gaze shift. According to the interpretation, low-level representations are generated from the new incoming information and used in determining whether updating or recomputation is appropriate. Also, the updating hypothesis is entirely compatible with the possibility that even when attention-centered location representations do not undergo recomputation, other forms of high-level visual representation may be recomputed from new low-level representations. For example, shifting the eyes to fixate an object provides more detailed visual information about the object's shape. As a consequence, high-level shape representations might well be recomputed after the eye movement, even if the object's attention-centered location representation underwent updating rather than recomputation. For example, in the task with large and small diamonds, AH probably computed new target shape representations from visual information received after she shifted her gaze to look at the target (and became distressed when the computation unexpectedly failed). Also, when a wrong-direction gaze shift moved the target out of AH's visual field, she may have recognized her error because processes for computing high-level shape representations unexpectedly failed to find information about the target in the new low-level representations.

In discussing the updating interpretation, I have thus far assumed that new attention-centered representations are generated by updating whenever possible, with recomputation occurring only when triggered by detection of movement. Another possibility is that both updating and independent recomputation are carried out in parallel for objects that have not moved. In a normal visual system the two processes would generate the same result. For AH, however, conflicts could arise when the original attention-centered representation was inaccurate. Updating this representation would perpetuate the original error, whereas independent recomputation from new low-level representations could produce an accurate attention-centered representation. If the conflict were resolved in favor of the updated representation, the result would be a PVM error. On the other hand, resolution in favor of the recomputed representation would result in accurate postshift perception of the target's location. In this way, parallel updating and recomputation could explain not only the PVM errors but also the instances in which AH corrected an error after a gaze shift.

Whichever version of the updating hypothesis we choose to adopt, the hypothesis raises a number of issues. One of these concerns the information available to visual processes. The updating hypothesis assumes that the visual system can use information about eye movements (in assessing whether objects have moved) and also information about shifts in the focus of attention (in updating attention-centered location representations after attentional shifts). The assumption about eye-movement information is clearly well-motivated: The visual system obviously has access to information about eye movements and uses this information in assessing whether objects in the visual scene have moved. For example, when the eyes are shifted to the left, the retinal image changes in a way that is consistent with a rightward movement of the entire visual scene. Nevertheless, the scene is not perceived as moving because the visual system takes account of the eye movement.[4] The assumption that visual processes have access to information about attentional shifts is more speculative; nevertheless, the assumption appears plausible, especially in light of the visual system's ability to use eye-movement information.

Another issue concerns why, after a shift of gaze and attention, the visual system would generate new attention-centered representations by updating the preshift attention-based coordinates, instead of relying solely on recomputation from lower-level visual information. A possible answer is suggested by the observation (e.g., Crick & Koch, 2003) that the visual system probably evolved under selection pressures that favored speed of processing. If updating were at least sometimes faster than recomputation, then processing speed could be enhanced by updating (instead of, or in addition to, recomputing) whenever possible.

Finally, the updating hypothesis raises questions about the circumstances under which high-level visual representations—not only attention-centered location representations but also other forms of high-level visual representation—are created and changed. For example, are high-level shape, color, or size representations continuously computed and recomputed from low-level representations, or might such representations instead be generated and modified only under certain conditions? The latter possibility would be compatible with the claim that visual scene representations are less detailed and complete than intuition suggests (e.g., Ballard, Hayhoe, Pook, & Rao, 1997; Blackmore, Brelstaff, Nelson, & Troscianko, 1995; Dennett, 1991; O'Regan, Rensink, & Clark, 1999; but see, e.g., Noë, Pessoa, & Thompson, 2000, and Simons & Rensink, 2005, for arguments against the strongest forms of this claim).

Visual Awareness

The results reported in this chapter highlight an important point about AH's conscious visual experience: Her localization errors do not result from uncertainty or confusion about the locations of objects in her visual field. As her performance in Tasks 18–3 through 18–6 suggests and as she confirmed in discussions, AH literally sees objects at erroneous locations. Given this observation, AH's perceptual deficit may have implications for our understanding of visual awareness and, more specifically, for questions concerning the level(s) of the visual system that contributes to awareness. Some theorists have suggested that low-level visual areas, including V1, play a role in visual awareness (e.g., Tong, 2003); others, in contrast, have argued that awareness is mediated by higher levels of the visual system (e.g., Crick & Koch, 2003; Koch & Braun, 1996; Koch & Crick, 1995). The available evidence is sparse at best, and the issue remains entirely open.

Results from AH strongly suggest that high-level visual representations contribute to awareness. This claim follows straightforwardly from the conclusion that her deficit is restricted to high-level vision. I have argued that AH's location representations are accurate at lower levels of the cortical visual system, with errors arising only at higher visual-system levels. This conclusion was motivated by several aspects of AH's performance. For example, her errors consistently respected the boundaries of objects (see Chapter 6), indicating that the errors arose at a level of the visual system beyond that at which the visual scene is parsed into objects; and her left–right and up–down reflections across the focus of attention (see Chapter 13) could be explained only by assuming that erroneous high-level (i.e., attention-centered) representations were computed from accurate lower-level (e.g., retinocentric) representations.

The conclusion that AH's deficit selectively affects high-level vision implies that her low-level location representations are accurate even on occasions in which higher-level representations are erroneous. Therefore, if visual awareness were mediated only by low-level representations, we would not expect AH to make visual localization errors in tasks that presumably draw upon her conscious visual experience—for example, tasks in which she verbally reports the locations of target stimuli. In fact, however, AH did make localization errors in such tasks, clearly suggesting that erroneous high-level location representations played a role in her conscious visual experience. More specifically, the localization errors suggest that visual awareness is mediated at least in part by visual representations at or beyond the level at which AH's errors arise.

The claim that high-level visual representations are implicated in visual awareness is certainly consistent with the nature of our subjective visual experience. That is, the contents of awareness appear to reflect the properties of high-level visual representations: We experience a three-dimensional visual world populated by objects and not, say, a two-dimensional array of pixels or edges.

What, though, of lower-level visual representations, which appear to be normal in AH? Do these representations make any contribution to visual awareness? If so, one would presumably expect AH to experience some form of confusion or uncertainty when high-level representations were inaccurate, due to the inconsistency between erroneous high-level representations and accurate low-level representations.

However, numerous discussions with AH yielded no indication of confusion or uncertainty. Even when questioned immediately after making a localization error, she adamantly denied that she was guessing, or even unsure, about the target's location. She said that she saw the target at a particular location, and responded accordingly. According to AH, her conscious experience was just as compelling on trials in which her response turned out to be incorrect as on trials in which she had responded correctly.

In Tasks 18–3 through 18–6 AH sometimes corrected an initial localization error when asked to shift her gaze. However, these corrections were apparently not triggered by uncertainty about her initial perception of the target's location. On several occasions I asked AH, immediately after she had corrected an error, to describe what had happened. She consistently stated that the change in perceived target location had not been intentional and denied noticing anything amiss in her initial perceptual experience. AH further said that she had not seen two targets, one at the correct location and one at the incorrect location; and she also reported that the target did not appear to move or jump from one location to the other. In describing the experience she was able to say only that she had seen the object first at one place and then later somewhere else.

In Task 18–4 AH became confused and distressed when she looked in the wrong direction in an effort to fixate a small, high-eccentricity target. However, the confusion stemmed from her unexpected difficulty in identifying the target and apparently not from any ambiguity in her perception of the target's location. Although she perceived the target first at an incorrect location and then at the correct location, both the erroneous and veridical perceptual experiences were, according to AH, unambiguous.

These observations may be summarized succinctly: Nothing in AH's performance suggests that low-level visual representations contribute to her awareness. On trials in which she mislocalized visual stimuli, her conscious visual experience was apparently determined solely by erroneous high-level representations, with accurate low-level representations playing no role. More generally, the results suggest that conscious visual experience may be mediated entirely by high-level visual representations and that low-level representations are inaccessible to awareness.

Two caveats are in order here. First, the results from AH obviously do not provide a basis for identifying the specific high-level visual areas implicated in awareness. The argument I have developed implies only that awareness involves one or more areas at or beyond the level at which AH's errors arise. As discussed above (see also Chapters 6 and 13), I assume that AH's errors originate at a level beyond that at which the visual scene is parsed into objects and further that this level represents location in an attention-centered frame of reference. These properties point to a locus of impairment higher than, and perhaps considerably higher than, the V1/V2/V3 complex; however, firmer conclusions cannot be drawn given current knowledge of visual-system architecture. Hence, the strongest conclusion to be drawn is that some visual area(s) beyond V1–V3 are implicated in visual awareness. Similar considerations apply to the conclusion that low-level visual areas are not implicated in awareness. Given the assumption that AH's errors arise at some level beyond V1–V3, the conclusion about low-level visual areas implies at least that V1–V3 are not implicated in awareness. This point is interesting in light of recent arguments that areas as early as V1 may contribute to conscious visual experience (e.g., Tong, 2003).

The second caveat is more significant: My conclusions about visual awareness depend crucially on the assumption that AH's impairment affects high-, but not low-, level visual representations. This assumption, although reasonably well-motivated, is not beyond question. For example, in accord with theories of awareness that emphasize recurrent processing across multiple visual-system levels (e.g., Lamme, 2006), one might suggest that feedback from higher to lower levels of AH's visual system introduces error into low-level representations. On this account, low-level representations initially generated from incoming visual information may well be accurate; however, when erroneous high-level representations are constructed from the low-level representations, feedback from these high-level representations alters the initial low-level representations, creating inaccurate low-level representations consistent with the inaccurate high-level representations. If high-level misrepresentations were thereby fed back to lower levels, AH's performance could be explained without assuming that low-level visual representations are entirely inaccessible to awareness.

The feedback argument cannot be dismissed entirely. However, at least in the context of early cortical visual areas—especially V1—the argument does not appear highly plausible. In many tasks the target stimulus remained in view until AH made her localization response. In these tasks the early visual areas presumably continued to receive bottom–up visual input throughout the trial. Therefore, to maintain that feedback created early visual representations consistent with erroneous higher-level representations, one would have to assume that the continuing bottom–up input had no influence on the early representations once feedback came into play.

A combination of bottom–up input and feedback from erroneous high-level representations might plausibly create early visual representations that to some degree specified both correct and incorrect target locations. However, if such representations contributed to awareness, one would presumably expect AH to experience confusion or uncertainty about the target's location. As discussed at length above, no such confusion or uncertainty was observed. Regardless of the feedback interpretation's strengths and weaknesses, however, the general point remains: The assumption that AH's low-level visual representations are normal could be incorrect, and conclusions about the role of low-level representations in visual awareness must therefore be drawn with caution.

Concluding Remarks

In discussing visual awareness, I have focused on questions concerning the levels of the visual system that contribute to awareness. However, the results from AH also bring home with considerable force a more basic point about visual awareness. Our conscious visual experience is so immediate, so compelling, so seemingly direct that we have difficulty even imagining that what we are seeing could be different from what is actually out there in the world. Despite the phenomenological immediacy, however, vision does not place us in direct contact with external reality: The objects of our awareness are not objects in the world but representations of objects constructed by our visual systems. If these representations are inaccurate, as they often are for AH, we quite literally see a world different from the one that is actually before us.

19

Conclusion

In the preceding chapters I have presented an extensive single-case study of a young woman, AH, who has a remarkable deficit in visual perception. In this concluding chapter I first summarize the principal results and conclusions from the study and mention several unanswered questions; next, I return briefly to points made in the introductory chapter about the value of cognitive neuropsychological research and discuss the role of developmental deficits in cognitive neuropsychology; finally, I provide an update on AH's status since the completion of the study.

Principal Results and Conclusions

Part I of the book presented the basic empirical evidence concerning AH's deficit. From this evidence I drew a number of conclusions. First, AH's deficit is selective to vision: She is impaired on a broad range of location and orientation tasks with visual stimuli but performs normally in tasks with auditory, tactile, and kinesthetic stimuli. Second, her location and orientation errors are highly systematic, taking the form of left–right and up–down reflections. Third, AH's deficit is developmental—the deficit has been present at least since her elementary school years and arose in the absence of any known neural insult. Fourth, the deficit affects high- and not low-level vision. Fifth, AH's visual location and orientation perception are dramatically affected by several visual variables, including motion, exposure duration, flicker, and contrast. Sixth, AH's deficit causes significant problems in her daily life; nevertheless, she is able to function successfully in most circumstances because the deficit is selective and she has developed sophisticated compensatory strategies. In reading, for example, AH is remarkably skilled at compensating for the visual location and orientation errors introduced by her deficit.

Part I concluded with a review of prior research on deficits in processing visual location and orientation information. In this review I highlighted the recent report of a brain-damaged patient, PR, who presented with a pattern of impairment very similar to that of AH (Pflugshaupt et al., 2007). I also described several other forms of visual–spatial impairment, arguing that these impairments show some similarities to, but do not closely resemble, the deficit exhibited by AH.

Part II of the book explored the theoretical implications of AH's deficit and presented additional data bearing on these implications. AH's performance, I argued, suggests hypotheses about the architecture of the visual system and about visual location and orientation representations. With respect to visual-system architecture, I proposed a distinction between transient and sustained subsystems in high-level vision. In contrast to other multiple-visual subsystems hypotheses (e.g., Milner & Goodale, 1995; Mishkin et al., 1983), the transient–sustained hypothesis assumes that both visual subsystems compute the locations and orientations of visual stimuli and that the outputs of both subsystems are available to a broad range of perceptual, cognitive, and motor processes. With respect to representations, I argued from AH's systematic reflection errors that at some level(s) of the visual system location and orientation are represented in coordinate-system form, such that locations are specified in terms of distance and direction of displacement from an origin along reference axes and orientations are represented in terms of relationships among coordinate systems. I also presented evidence suggesting that at the level of the visual system giving rise to AH's errors, location is represented in an attention-centered frame of reference—that is, a frame of reference in which the origin is defined by the focus of attention. In discussing these representational claims I attempted to clarify two concepts that have been the subject of some confusion in cognitive and neurophysiological research on visual–spatial representation: the concept of a reference frame, and the concept of a coordinate-system representation. Finally, I suggested that results from AH shed light on issues concerning mental imagery, visual awareness, and the processes that create and modify high-level visual representations.

In proposing hypotheses about the normal visual system I drew not only upon AH's performance but also on other empirical and theoretical work. Nevertheless, for most of the proposed hypothesis, the body of relevant data is not large and more evidence is certainly needed. Relevant evidence could potentially be obtained from a broad spectrum of methods, including not only cognitive neuropsychological research on acquired and developmental deficits but also behavioral studies of normal individuals, functional neuroimaging studies, and neurophysiological research.

Although I have focused primarily on issues concerning normal visual representations and processes, AH's performance also has implications for understanding cognitive deficits. For example, the results from the reading tasks clearly demonstrated that developmental reading impairment can be caused by impaired visual location and orientation perception. These and other results also offered insights into the difficulties that may arise in identifying and diagnosing developmental cognitive deficits.

Unanswered Questions

Despite the substantial number of issues I have discussed in light of AH's performance, several important questions remain largely unexplored. Perhaps the most obvious concerns where in the brain AH's perceptual errors arise. An answer to this question would, of course, shed light on where in the normal brain the proposed representations and processing mechanisms are to be found. I have argued that the behavioral data from AH place some constraints on the neurological locus of impairment; however, the precise brain area(s) implicated in her deficit remains unidentified. Functional neuroimaging studies using functional magnetic resonance imaging and/or magnetoencephalography might well shed light on the matter. At the time the study was conducted, from 1991 through 1995, these methods were not available at Johns Hopkins; nor has AH subsequently been available for testing. Conceivably, however, functional neuroimaging studies with AH could be carried out in the future. Functional imaging might also prove informative in the case of PR (Pflugshaupt et al., 2007), the Swiss patient with a deficit closely resembling that of AH. Unfortunately, however, PR has moved away from Switzerland, and the researchers who studied her deficit are no longer in contact with her (Pflugshaupt, personal communication, April 11, 2007).

A second unanswered question concerns the neural implementation of the hypothesized coordinate-system location and orientation representations: How could such representations be instantiated in neural tissue? Conceivably, each component of a coordinate-system representation—for example, horizontal direction, horizontal distance, and so forth, for a location representation—could be represented by a distinct population of neurons. As discussed in Chapter 13, some neurophysiological evidence consistent with this suggestion has been reported (Lacquaniti et al., 1995). However, much more evidence will be needed before any firm conclusions can be drawn.

A third, and closely related, question concerns the nature of the neural dysfunction in AH (and PR): How might an aberration in brain development, or an acquired brain lesion, disrupt location or orientation representations in such a way that specific components are systematically misrepresented? For example, what type of neural dysfunction could cause polarity correspondence to be specified as negative rather than positive? Obviously, resolution of this issue must await more knowledge about the neural implementation of the representations.

A final unanswered question concerns the etiology of AH's deficit: Did the deficit originate from a genetic defect or from some other cause (e.g., an undetected abnormality in the prenatal environment)? Family history data could potentially shed light on this issue. According to AH, her family history includes learning disabilities on both sides of the family, but no family members are known to have deficits similar to hers. Given, however, that the nature of AH's deficit became clear only after considerable testing, conclusions about the nature and extent of cognitive dysfunction in AH's family would require systematic testing of the individual family members. Such testing has not yet been carried out.

Advantages of Cognitive Neuropsychological Research

I suggested in Chapter 1 that cognitive neuropsychological research, despite some inherent disadvantages, has two significant strengths. First, cognitive deficits often provide especially clear windows onto normal mental representations and processes. Second, cognitive neuropsychology provides greater opportunity than most other methods for serendipitous discovery— that is, for turning up unanticipated phenomena that yield novel theoretical insights. Rather than beginning with a predefined question and designing experiments to address that question, the cognitive neuropsychologist begins with an experiment of nature—a largely uncharacterized deficit—and asks what this natural experiment might reveal about normal mental representations and processes. When preliminary testing uncovers phenomena that may shed light on normal cognition, these phenomena are then subjected to extensive experimental investigation. Cognitive neuropsychological research is therefore opportunistic, looking to nature for clues about normal cognition and following these clues wherever they may lead.

The study of AH serves, I hope, to illustrate both of these strengths. With respect to the first, AH's impaired performance shed strong and direct light on multiple aspects of the normal visual system. For example, AH's highly systematic pattern of left–right and up–down reflections offered clear and compelling evidence concerning the form of high-level location and orientation representations; her reflections across the focus of attention made a convincing case for attention-centered location representations; the dramatic effects of visual variables—exposure duration, motion, flicker, contrast, eccentricity—pointed clearly to a distinction between transient and sustained subsystems in high-level vision; and AH's persisting visual mislocalization (PVM) errors led straightforwardly (albeit tentatively) to claims about processes that update high-level location representations. An important point made by these examples is that cognitive neuropsychology can offer insights not only into the general functional architecture of a cognitive system but also into the fine-grained structure and functioning of the system.

With respect to the second strength of cognitive neuropsychological research, the AH study provides a striking illustration of the potential for serendipitous discovery in cognitive neuropsychology. I certainly did not begin the study with the aim of exploring visual location and orientation representations or visual subsystems. In fact, I did not intend to investigate visual perception at all; the initial topic of the study was AH's spelling. As the study progressed, however, clues began to accumulate suggesting a deficit extending beyond the domain of spelling, and these clues eventually led to an unanticipated but fruitful shift in focus. Even once the study was firmly focused on visual perception, many of the significant phenomena, including the effects of visual variables, were discovered serendipitously.

Cognitive Neuropsychology and Developmental Deficits

One important issue concerning cognitive neuropsychological research remains to be discussed: the potential of developmental deficits for shedding light on normal cognition. In most cognitive neuropsychological research, inferences about normal cognition are drawn from adult acquired deficits, in which an initially normal and fully developed system suffers damage. Inferences from an adult acquired deficit to normal cognitive representations and processes are founded on the assumption that the damaged brain has not substantially reorganized and, hence, that the observed performance reflects a largely normal brain with one or more specific malfunctions (e.g., Caramazza, 1986).

AH's deficit, however, is developmental, and controversy has attached to the use of developmental deficits as a basis for inferences about normal cognition (see, e.g., the target article and commentaries in Thomas & Karmiloff-Smith, 2002). The principal concern is as follows: In a developmental deficit, neural development could conceivably have followed a far from normal course, producing not a basically normal brain with specific malfunctions but instead a brain that differs in its fundamental structure and functioning from the normal brain. Conclusions about normal cognition drawn on the basis of a brain with fundamentally abnormal organization would probably be erroneous, especially if the possibility of abnormal organization were not recognized. Given that one usually has no way of knowing whether brain organization is fundamentally normal or abnormal in cases of developmental impairment, developmental deficits do not provide a sound basis for inferences about normal cognition.

In my view, this argument is too strong. I agree that inferences from developmental deficits to normal cognition must be drawn with some caution and are subject to some uncertainty. However, a blanket rejection of all such inferences does not appear to be warranted. I suggest that the issue should be considered on an inference-by-inference basis: Given a potential inference about normal cognition from a pattern of performance observed in a case of developmental impairment, one should ask whether the performance could be explained in terms of abnormal brain organization without making claims about normal cognition. To the extent that plausible abnormal-organization accounts can be formulated, the inference about normal cognition is weakened. However, to the extent that abnormal-organization interpretations appear implausible, the inference can be drawn (albeit with caution).

For example, I have inferred from the reflection errors observed for AH that normal brains implement coordinate-system representations of location and orientation. The implicit chain of reasoning was as follows: (1) The reflection errors imply that AH's brain implements coordinate-system representations; (2) AH's brain has the same forms of location and orientation representation as normal brains (although malfunctions occur in the generation or use of these representations); and (3) therefore, normal brains implement coordinate-system representations of location and orientation.

An alternative interpretation positing abnormal brain organization would not question step 1 of the argument: What is at issue with respect to developmental deficits is not whether one can draw valid conclusions about the representations and processes of a developmentally impaired individual but whether the conclusions can be generalized to normal individuals. The point of attack for an abnormal-organization account would be step 2. The interpretation would assert that AH's brain does not have the same forms of representation as normal brains and, therefore, that conclusions about location and orientation representations cannot be generalized from AH to normal individuals.

This interpretation is committed to a very strong claim—namely, that abnormal brain development in AH somehow produced new forms of location and orientation representation not present in the normal brain. AH clearly made use of location and orientation information—she often responded correctly in location and orientation perception tasks, and her errors were definitely not random. Therefore, one must assume that AH's brain represents location and orientation, even if one does not agree with the suggestion that the representations were in coordinate-system form. Hence, an abnormal-organization account must assume that AH's brain implements some specific forms of location and orientation representation that are not present in the normal brain.

This claim cannot be dismissed entirely but does not appear highly plausible and is not supported by any empirical evidence. Furthermore, the results from patient PR (Pflugshaupt et al., 2007) argue against an abnormal-organization account of AH's performance. The striking similarity in performance between AH and PR—a case of adult acquired impairment—strongly suggests that AH's performance reflects a basically normal brain with a selective malfunction, rather than a fundamentally abnormal brain.

If AH's brain had followed a grossly abnormal course of development, we would not expect to find a close resemblance between her deficit and that of an individual whose brain was presumably normal before suffering damage in adulthood. Also, as I have noted throughout the book, many of the conclusions drawn on the basis of evidence from AH converge with claims emerging from other neuropsychological studies, from behavioral research with normal participants, and from neurophysiological research with nonhuman animals. Hence, I suggest that inferences from AH's performance to normal visual representations and processes are justified. More generally, I suggest that formulaic rejection of inferences from developmental deficits to normal cognition is unwarranted.

Ultimately, the value of developmental deficits as a basis for conclusions about normal cognition can be determined only by accumulating experience with the approach. If we find, over time, that inferences from developmental deficits tend to converge with those from other methods (e.g., studies of normal children and adults, studies of adult acquired deficits), then we will have more confidence that developmental deficits can inform us about normal cognition. If, however, we find that conclusions from developmental deficits do not fit well with those emerging from other types of research, we will have to consider the possibility that developmental deficits are not a sound basis for conclusions about normal cognition (or at least that inferences need to be more complex, taking into account abnormal development more explicitly).

AH: Life After the Study

I conclude with a brief update on AH's life in the years following the study. Despite her deficit, AH has enjoyed considerable success. She graduated with honors from Johns Hopkins University in 1995, entered law school, and completed her legal training in the customary 3 years. Thereafter she has worked as an attorney in both the United States and the United Kingdom. She is married and has two children.

In a recent conversation AH reported that, as far as she can tell, her perceptual difficulties have remained unchanged. She continues to have problems whenever she encounters numbers (e.g., in reading addresses, phone numbers, or prices); she continues to make reaching errors, as when she takes the wrong item down from a shelf; and she continues to have difficulty in other everyday tasks that require visual location and orientation perception (e.g., reading an analogue clock, interpreting a map, using a diagram to assemble a toy for her son). Nevertheless, she is able to cope with these problems at home and at work and does not consider herself significantly disadvantaged.

Notes

Chapter 1

1. Throughout the book I use the terms "perception" and "perceptual" in a broad and neutral sense, consistent with usage in cognitive psychology. In particular, my use of the terms does not imply that the representations or processes so described necessarily fall within the domain of vision-for-perception (as opposed to vision-for-action) in the conceptual framework proposed by Milner and Goodale (1995). Nor do I intend to imply by "perception" or "perceptual" that the designated representations or processes necessarily give rise to conscious visual experiences. Hence, by a "deficit in visual location and orientation perception" I mean a deficit in generating visual location and orientation representations for use in subsequent perceptual, cognitive, or motor functions, regardless of whether these functions fall within the perception or action domains defined by Milner and Goodale (1995) and regardless of whether the functions give rise to awareness.

Chapter 2

1. Throughout this book I use italics (e.g., *bell*) to indicate visual stimulus words and written word responses; it should be understood that neither the stimulus words presented to AH nor her written responses were in italics. I use quotation marks for spoken responses (e.g., "bell") and a horizontal arrow for the relationship between stimulus and response. For example, in the context of the direct-copy task, *bell* → *dell* indicates that the visual stimulus word *bell* was copied as *dell* and in a word-reading task *bell* → "dell" would indicate that the stimulus *bell* was read aloud as "dell."

Chapter 3

1. Six of the twelve stimulus pictures showed objects that have a canonical up-down orientation (e.g., truck); the objects depicted in the remaining six pictures did

not have an obvious canonical orientation (e.g., hairbrush). Tabulation of results for these two subsets of stimuli revealed no obvious effect of canonical orientation on AH's processing of up–down orientation information. The frequency of up–down errors was approximately the same for objects with and without a canonical orientation (seven and five errors, respectively). Further, for objects with a canonical orientation, the frequency of errors was approximately the same for pictures presented at canonical and noncanonical up–down orientations (three and four errors, respectively). In other words, AH did not appear more likely to perceive a picture presented upside down as right side up than vice versa.

2. The assumption that errors for *P* resulted from confusion of uppercase *P* with lowercase *b, d,* or *q* seems plausible in the context of the present task, given that each block of trials included both upper- and lowercase letters. However, if upper- and lowercase letters were presented in separate trial blocks, so that *b, d,* and *q* were not possible stimuli in blocks containing uppercase *P,* we might expect AH to name *P* correctly even if it were perceived at an incorrect orientation. This prediction was confirmed in two blocked-presentation tasks involving a total of sixteen uppercase and sixteen lowercase trial blocks. For lowercase letters and uppercase *M* and *W,* blocked presentation had no apparent effect on the rate of orientation confusions. However, whereas AH erred on six of twenty-one presentations of uppercase *P* under mixed-presentation conditions, she made no errors on *P* over sixteen presentations in pure uppercase blocks.

Chapter 6

1. One might wonder why AH did not adapt to her visual deficit in such a way as to avoid significant errors in visual location and orientation tasks. After all, normal individuals who wear distorting goggles—even goggles that invert the visual world—quickly adapt and thereafter do not exhibit gross errors in reaching or other visually guided behaviors (e.g., Ewert, 1930; Harris, 1965; Kohler, 1964; Stratton, 1896, 1897a, 1897b; Werner & Wapner, 1955). This question may be answered in part by noting that AH's condition is probably not entirely analogous to that of a person wearing distorting goggles because her visual system apparently does not always err in computing locations and orientations. Rather, the location and orientation representations generated by her visual system are probably sometimes accurate and sometimes inaccurate (as indicated by the finding that in any given visual location or orientation task some of her responses were correct and some were incorrect). In this respect, her experience may resemble that of a hypothetical normal individual wearing sophisticated goggles that unpredictably distort some, but not all, visual inputs. Under such conditions, fully successful adaptation would probably not be possible. A second point to be made regarding AH's adaptation to her deficit is that she has developed a variety of compensatory strategies that ameliorate the effects of the deficit. See Chapters 8–10 for further discussion.

Chapter 8

1. One can gain a sense of AH's blink rate by looking at a watch or clock with a sweep second hand and blinking once per second.

Chapter 9

1. Many of AH's word-reading errors were neither letter-orientation confusions nor letter-sequence confusions. I offer a possible interpretation for these additional errors in Chapter 10.

2. In Chapter 5 I suggested that AH's poor spelling may reflect weaknesses in lexical–orthographic representations caused by her perceptual deficit. An unresolved question in the study of lexical processing is whether a single set of stored orthographic representations underlies performance in both reading and spelling or whether instead the orthographic representations implicated in spelling are distinct from those involved in reading. Accordingly, data suggesting deficiencies in the lexical–orthographic representations involved in spelling do not necessarily imply that the orthographic representations required for reading are also deficient. Nevertheless, if AH's perceptual deficit impaired her ability to learn the lexical–orthographic representations implicated in spelling, it seems reasonable to suppose that the deficit would also have affected learning of the orthographic representations required for reading; even if the reading and spelling representations are distinct, experience with visually presented words presumably underlies learning of both.

3. We could have explored whether the stored lexical–orthographic representations required for reading are deficient in AH by studying her word-reading performance more thoroughly under conditions that allowed her to perceive the stimuli accurately—for example, by determining whether variables such as regularity and word frequency affect her accuracy in reading flickering or briefly presented words. However, this course of action did not occur to us during the study.

Chapter 10

1. Conceivably, other factors could also contribute to AH's word-reading errors. For example, as mentioned in Chapter 9, her stored lexical–orthographic representations may not be entirely normal. Also, her visual system might sometimes introduce errors other than letter-orientation and letter-sequence errors—for example, errors involving misrepresentation of the relative locations of features within a letter could conceivably lead to errors other than orientation errors.

2. It should be evident from this discussion that even though AH was correct only about half of the time for nonword stimuli, her performance is by no means at chance. Chance performance on the task would mean that she was entirely unable to distinguish between word and nonword stimuli, classifying both types of stimuli equally often as words. For example, given that AH classified 48% of the nonwords as words, her performance would have been at chance only if she had also classified about 48% of the word stimuli as words. In fact, she classified 99% of the word stimuli as words, clearly showing an above-chance ability to distinguish words from nonwords. To make the point another way, AH's performance would have been at chance only had she been about 50% correct overall (i.e., collapsing over word and nonword stimuli). However, she was actually 75% correct overall (362/480), a level well above chance.

Chapter 11

1. Septic shock is a life-threatening condition in which inflammatory responses to massive infection cause reduced perfusion, and therefore reduced oxygenation, of body tissues, including the brain.

2. The mirror writing may have been a deliberate strategy adopted by PR, as opposed to an impairment resulting from her brain damage. The authors state, "The patient was fully aware of her mirror writing and stated that it was mandatory so that she can read what she writes" (Pflugshaupt et al., 2007, p. 2080).

3. The term optic ataxia is sometimes used to refer not just to the symptom of impaired visually guided reaching but instead to a pattern of performance in which

impaired reaching occurs largely in the absence of other deficits. However, I use the term to refer to the symptom of impaired visually guided reaching not attributable to visual-field defects or motor impairments, regardless of whether this symptom occurs alone or in the presence of other deficits.

Chapter 12

1. In discussing the definition question I use terms such as *retina-based* and *head-based* rather than the more common *retinocentric* and *head-centered* because *centric* and *centered* seem to imply a claim that the reference point for defining locations (e.g., the head) is at the center of the represented space. However, locations can be defined by their relation to a reference point without that point in any sense being represented as the center of a space (and without locations near the reference point being represented as near the center of the space and so forth); see the discussion of noncompositional representations in the following section. For example, locations in a retina-based frame of reference need not be represented in a form that specifies their distance from the fovea (or from the point of fixation). Furthermore, evidence bearing on the basis for defining locations may not—and usually does not—have anything to say about whether the locations are represented in a form that specifies their spatial relationship to a central location. I therefore adopt the neutral term *based* to avoid blurring the boundary between definitional and format claims about reference frames.

Chapter 13

1. The formulation of the coordinate-system hypothesis in terms of two-dimensional representations is purely a matter of expository convenience; the hypothesis generalizes straightforwardly to three-dimensional representations. For example, the left–right and up–down errors illustrated in Figure 13–1 could be interpreted in terms of a three-dimensional coordinate system with horizontal, vertical, and depth axes. Also a matter of convenience is the characterization of the coordinate system as a Cartesian system, in which magnitude of displacement from the origin is specified as distance along each axis. Coordinate systems involving angular displacements from reference axes—for example, a spherical coordinate system specifying azimuth (horizontal angular displacement), elevation (vertical angular displacement), and radial distance—could also provide a basis for interpreting AH's errors. The important assumption is that the location representations are compositional, with components specifying direction and magnitude of displacement relative to a reference point and reference axes.

2. The retinal midline, like the head and body midlines, could serve to define the horizontal position of the origin, with the vertical position being defined on some other basis. However, for my purposes, there is little substantive difference between an origin defined by the point the eyes are fixating and an origin defined in part by the retinal midline. Accordingly, I will not consider the latter as a separate case.

3. I refer to the posited spatial representations as "attention-centered," rather than "attention-based," because my proposal concerning these representations incorporates not only a claim about the definitional reference-frame question (i.e., that locations are defined by their relation to the focus of attention) but also a claim about the format question (i.e., that the focus of attention defines the origin of a spatial coordinate system and, hence, constitutes the center of the represented space). More generally, I use the term "x-centered" (e.g., attention-centered, fixation-centered) when referring to representations in a spatial coordinate system with an origin defined on

the basis of x. When discussing representations that are not necessarily in coordinate-system form, I use the more neutral term "x-based."

4. In this task (and in the other tasks I report) no attempt was made to dissociate or otherwise manipulate potential bases for defining the orientation of reference axes. As in the task discussed in the previous section, AH's retinal, head, and body midlines, the side borders of the display screen, and the gravitational vector all had the same (vertical) orientation. Accordingly, I expected that in the present task one of the reference axes in the coordinate system giving rise to localization errors would have a vertical orientation and that AH's errors would take the form of reflections across this vertical axis.

5. The error counts reported above include not only the trials on which AH was correct in counting the dots presented at the attended location but also the trials on which she gave an incorrect counting response. However, the pattern of localization errors remains the same if we consider only the trials with correct dot-counting responses. For these trials AH made twenty-three errors involving reflection across the attended intermediate location (versus twenty-eight for the full data set), and twelve of the attention-related reflections—the same number as in the full data set—occurred on no-dot trials.

6. As in Task 13–2, the pattern of localization errors remains the same if analysis is restricted to trials on which AH correctly reported the number of dots presented at the attended location. Excluding trials with incorrect dot-counting responses reduces the number of attention-related reflections from nineteen to seventeen, but all other error counts—including the count of attention-related reflections occurring on no-dot trials—are unchanged.

7. The pattern of localization errors is unchanged if analyses are restricted to trials on which AH correctly reported the number of dots. Excluding trials with incorrect dot-counting responses reduces the number of attention-related reflections from forty-seven to forty-six, but all other error counts—including the count of attention-related reflections occurring on no-dot trials—remain the same.

8. Two points of clarification are worth mentioning. First, I do not assume that an attention-based coordinate system is necessarily created whenever attention is directed to a location; for example, attention-based representations may perhaps be generated only when needed for some ongoing cognitive processing. Second, if the focus of attention corresponded to a region rather than a point in the parent representation, the origin of the attention-based coordinate system would presumably be defined to coincide with a point in that region (e.g., the centroid).

9. Given a parent representation in the form of a coordinate system, the computation of attention-based coordinates would amount to a coordinate transformation as defined in analytic geometry (e.g., Wentworth, 1886). As I noted earlier, however, the parent representation need not be in coordinate-system form. For example, neural network simulations developed by Zipser and Andersen (1988) demonstrate that coordinate-system representations can be computed from parent representations not in coordinate-system form. These researchers developed neural networks simulating the transformation of retinal to head-based location representations. The retinal input representations consisted of patterns of activation across retinal units with roughly circular receptive fields; these representations in no sense included an origin, reference axes, or coordinates specifying displacements from an origin along axes. In some of the networks, however, the head-based output representation was in the form of coordinates: One set of output units represented the horizontal coordinate of a

head-based location, and another set represented the vertical coordinate. These networks therefore transformed a location representation not in coordinate-system form into a coordinate-system representation.

Chapter 14

1. Note that an orientation-invariant representation is not necessarily viewpoint-independent. A representation of a three-dimensional object that described only the aspects of the object visible from the observer's viewpoint would be viewpoint-dependent but could still be invariant with respect to orientation in the picture plane. Hence, in positing orientation-invariant representations I do not intend to take a stance on the issue of viewpoint-dependent vs. -independent representations of three-dimensional objects.

2. In a two-dimensional representation, once a mapping has been established between an object axis and an external axis, the other mapping is fixed; there are no other degrees of freedom. For this reason, I posit a single axis correspondence component with two values, rather than assuming two separate representations, one for each object–external axis pair (e.g., P–V and S–H). For three-dimensional representations the situation is more complex: Establishing a mapping between one object axis and one external axis does not fully determine the other mappings. Therefore, positing a separate representation for each of the three object–external axis pairings may be most plausible. Given this point, one might want to assume individual object–external axis representations even in the two-dimensional case, to maintain consistency with the three-dimensional representations. However, as far as I can see, the choice between a single representation (e.g., PVSH) and separate representations (PV, SH) in the two-dimensional case has no implications for any of the issues I will discuss. Hence, for convenience, I adopt the single-representation alternative.

3. Once again, the situation is more complex for three-dimensional representations, and considerations of consistency with these representations might lead one to posit separate tilt representations for each object–external axis pair even in the two-dimensional case.

Chapter 15

1. In the figure the origin of the object-based frame is offset slightly from the origin of the external frame so that both sets of axes can readily be seen. The interpretations I offer for orientation errors do not depend on the relative locations of the origins in the reference frames in question; only the relative orientations of the reference axes are relevant. For example, orientation-reflection errors are ambiguous whenever object and external axes are parallel; object axes need not overlay external axes as they would if the origins of object and external frames coincided.

2. Although AH's errors for both tilted and nontilted stimuli are each subject to two potential interpretations, one of the interpretations is shared by the two types of error: Both error types could have resulted from misrepresentation of polarity correspondence in relating one external reference frame to another. However, I do not consider this point a sufficient basis for ruling out the other possible interpretation for each error type.

3. For convenience, I have stated the interpretation in terms of representing the target line. However, errors could also have originated in BC's representations of response lines.

4. Researchers reporting impaired discrimination of left–right mirror images in brain-damaged patients have often attributed the impairment not to selective

defects in representations of orientation but, rather, to the patient's use of alternative representations that, while intact, do not fully specify orientation (e.g., Davidoff & Warrington, 2001; Turnbull & McCarthy, 1996a; Warrington & Davidoff, 2000). More specifically, the discrimination deficits have often been attributed to patients' use in orientation tasks of representations that normally mediate object recognition, on the assumption that these representations do not specify left–right orientation. When stated explicitly (e.g., Davidoff & Warrington, 2001), this interpretation turns out to be rather complex; and at least in my view, the supporting evidence is not compelling. In any event, however, the issue is not especially germane to the present discussion. Regardless of whether the underlying representations are assumed to be defective orientation representations or normal object-recognition representations, impaired discrimination of left–right mirror images can be explained by assuming that the representations fail to specify horizontal-axis polarity correspondence.

5. In Chapter 13 I reported evidence that at least some of AH's localization errors arise within an attention-based frame of reference, in which the origin of the coordinate system is defined by the focus of attention. However, AH's orientation errors were not addressed in the attention study.

Chapter 16

1. To avoid potential confusion resulting from application of the terms transient and sustained to both low-level and higher-level visual mechanisms, I will henceforth refer to low-level visual pathways or channels only as M and P, reserving transient and sustained for the higher-level subsystems I am positing.

2. A similar—although not identical—argument has been made by Robertson et al. (1997) and Riddoch et al. (2004). On the basis of results showing impaired performance on both vision-for-perception and vision-for-action tasks in brain-damaged patients with parietal lesions, these researchers have argued that, contrary to the Milner- Goodale hypothesis, the dorsal stream plays a role in vision-for-perception as well as vision-for-action.

Chapter 18

1. One might wonder whether AH's wrong-direction eye movements could conceivably be the cause, rather than an effect, of her visual localization deficit. If for some reason AH's eyes often moved in a direction opposite to the intended direction, could the erroneous eye movements perhaps cause the location and even the orientation of visual stimuli to be misperceived? Although this interpretation is worth considering, it proves untenable for several reasons, most notably because AH made location and orientation errors not only in tasks where she was free to move her eyes but also in tasks that required her to maintain fixation (e.g., Tasks 3–2 and 13–1 through 13–4).

2. I characterize the low-level representations as retinocentric coordinate-system representations merely for convenience. The interpretation I will develop for the PVM errors requires only that some form of low-level location representation be computed from incoming visual information; these low-level representations need not be in the form of coordinates and need not even be retina-based.

3. I assume for convenience that the distance units are the same at retinocentric and attention-centered levels. Given this assumption, the attention-centered coordinates for the target should be the same as the retinocentric coordinates because the origin of the attention-centered reference frame (the focus of attention) coincides with the origin of the retinocentric frame (the point of fixation).

4. The visual system's ability to take account of eye movements is made especially clear by cases in which the process fails. When the visual system lacks information about an eye movement, changes in the retinal image resulting from that movement are falsely attributed to movement of the external world. For example, close one eye and press lightly on the open eye by touching the eyelid. The entire visual scene appears to jump, indicating that the visual system failed to account for the eye movement and instead attributed the shift in the retinal image to motion of the world. Evidently, the visual system does not have access to eye-movement information unless the movements are produced in the ordinary way, via motor commands to the extraocular muscles.

References

Allison, R. S., Hurwitz, L. J., White, G., & Wilmot, T. J. (1969). A follow-up study of a patient with Balint's syndrome. *Neuropsychologia, 7*, 319–333.

Andersen, R. A. (1989). Visual and eye movement functions of the posterior parietal cortex. *Annual Review of Neuroscience, 12*, 377–403.

Andersen, R. A., & Mountcastle, V. B. (1983). The influence of the angle of gaze upon the excitability of the light-sensitive neurons of the posterior parietal cortex. *Journal of Neuroscience, 3*, 532–548.

Andersen, R. A., Snyder, L. H., Bradley, D. C., & Xing, J. (1997). Multimodal representation of space in the posterior parietal cortex and its use in planning movements. *Annual Review of Neuroscience, 20*, 303–330.

Appelle, S. (1972). Perception and discrimination as a function of stimulus orientation: The "oblique effect" in man and animals. *Psychological Bulletin, 78*, 266–278.

Ardila, A., Botero, M., & Gomez, J. (1987). Palinopsia and visual allesthesia. *International Journal of Neuroscience, 32*, 775–782.

Arguin, M., & Bub, D. N. (1993). Evidence for an independent stimulus-centered spatial reference frame from a case of visual hemineglect. *Cortex, 29*, 349–357.

Bálint, R. (1909). Seelenlähmung des "Schauens", optische Ataxie, räumliche Störung der Aufmerksamkeit. *Monatschrift fur Psychiatrie und Neurologie, 25*, 5–81.

Bálint, R. (1909/1995). Psychic paralysis of gaze, optic ataxia, and spatial disorder of attention. *Cognitive Neuropsychology, 12*, 265–281. (Original work published 1909; translation published 1995.)

Ballard, D. H., Hayhoe, M. H., Pook, P. K., & Rao, R. P. N. (1997). Deictic codes for the embodiment of cognition. *Behavioral and Brain Sciences, 20*, 723–767.

Bartolomeo, P., Bachoud-Lévi, A.-C., de Gelder, B., Denes, G., Dalla Barba, G., Brugières, P., & Degos, J.-D. (1998). Multiple-domain dissociation between impaired visual perception and preserved mental imagery in a patient with bilateral extrastriate lesions. *Neuropsychologia, 36,* 239–249.

Battaglia-Mayer, A., & Caminiti, R. (2002). Optic ataxia as a result of the breakdown of the global tuning fields of parietal neurones. *Brain, 125,* 225–237.

Baxter, D. M., & Warrington, E. K. (1987). Transcoding sound to spelling: Single or multiple sound unit correspondence? *Cortex, 23,* 11–28.

Baylis, G. C., & Baylis, L. L. (2001). Visually misguided reaching in Balint's syndrome. *Neuropsychologia, 39,* 865–875.

Beauvois, M. F., & Dérouesné, J. (1981). Lexical or orthographic agraphia. *Brain, 104,* 21–49.

Beery, K. E., & Buktenica, N. A. (1997). *VMI (The Beery-Buktenica Developmental Test of Visual-Motor Integration)* (4th ed., Rev.). Parsippany, NJ: Modern Curriculum Press.

Behrmann, M. & Moscovitch, M. (1994). Object-centered neglect in patients with unilateral neglect: Effects of left-right coordinates of objects. *Journal of Cognitive Neuroscience, 6,* 1–16.

Behrmann, M., Moscovitch, M., & Winocur, G. (1994). Intact visual imagery and impaired visual perception in a patient with visual agnosia. *Journal of Experimental Psychology: Human Perception and Performance, 20,* 1068–1087.

Bender, L. (1938). *Bender motor gestalt test.* New York: American Orthopsychiatric Association.

Bender, M. B., Wortis, S. B., & Cramer, J. (1948). Organic mental syndrome with phenomena of extinction and allesthesia. *Archives of Neurology and Psychiatry, 59,* 273–291.

Benton, A. L. (1983). *Judgment of Line Orientation.* Lutz, FL: PAR, Inc.

Benton, A. L., Sivan, A. B., Hamsher, K. d. S., & Spreen, O. (1994). *Contributions to neuropsychological assessment: A clinical manual* (2nd ed.). New York: Oxford University Press.

Berti, A., Papagno, C., & Vallar, G. (1986). Balint syndrome: A case of simultanagnosia. *Italian Journal of Neurological Science, 7,* 261–264.

Best, F. (1917). Hemianopsie und Seelenblindheit bei Hirnverletzungen. *Albrecht von Graefe's Archiv für Ophthalmologie, 93,* 49–150.

Beyer, E. (1895). Ueber Verlagerungen im Gesichtsfeld bei Flimmerskotom. *Neurologisches Centralblatt, 14,* 10–15.

Bigsby, P. (1985). The nature of reversible letter confusions in dyslexic and normal readers: Misperception or mislabeling? *British Journal of Educational Psychology, 55,* 264–272.

Blackmore, S. J., Brelstaff, G., Nelson, K., & Troscianko, T. (1995). Is the richness of our visual world an illusion? Transsaccadic memory for complex scenes. *Perception, 24,* 1075–1081.

Bornstein, M. H. (1982). Perceptual anisotropies in infancy: Ontogenetic origins and implications for inequalities in spatial vision. *Advances in Child Development, 16,* 77–123.

Bradley, L., & Bryant, P. E. (1978). Difficulties in auditory organization as a possible cause of reading backwardness. *Nature, 271,* 746–747.

Bradley, L., & Bryant, P. E. (1983). Categorizing sounds and learning to read—A causal connection. *Nature, 301,* 419–421.

Bradley, L., & Bryant, P. E. (1985). *Rhyme and reason in reading and spelling.* Ann Arbor, MI: University of Michigan Press.

Brain, W. R. (1941). Visual disorientation with special reference to lesions of the right hemisphere. *Brain, 64,* 244–272.

Breitmeyer, B. G., & Ganz, L. (1976). Implications of sustained and transient channels for theories of visual pattern masking, saccadic suppression, and information processing. *Psychological Review, 83,* 1–36.

Breitmeyer, B. G., & Ogmen, H. (2000). Recent models and findings in visual backward masking: A comparison, review, and update. *Perception and Psychophysics, 62,* 1572–1595.

Brewer, B., & Pears, J. (1993). Introduction: Frames of reference. In N. Eilan, R. McCarthy, & B. Brewer (Eds.), *Spatial representation: Problems in philosophy and psychology* (pp. 25–30). Oxford: Blackwell.

Broom, Y. M., & Doctor, E.A. (1995). Developmental surface dyslexia: A case study of the efficacy of a remediation programme. *Cognitive Neuropsychology, 12,* 69–100.

Buxbaum, L. J., & Coslett, H. B. (1997). Subtypes of optic ataxia: Reframing the disconnection account. *Neurocase, 3,* 159–166.

Caramazza, A. (1986). On drawing inferences about the structure of normal cognitive systems from the analysis of patterns of impaired performance: The case for single-patient studies. *Brain and Cognition, 5,* 41–66.

Caramazza, A., & Miceli, G. (1990). The structure of graphemic representations. *Cognition, 37,* 243–297.

Caramazza, A., Miceli, G., Villa, G., & Romani, C. (1987). The role of the graphemic buffer in spelling: Evidence from a case of acquired dysgraphia. *Cognition, 26,* 59–85.

Carey, D. P., Harvey, M., & Milner, A. D. (1996). Visuomotor sensitivity for shape and orientation in a patient with visual form agnosia. *Neuropsychologia, 34,* 329–337.

Castiello, U., Paine, M., & Wales, R. (2002). Perceiving an entire object and grasping only half of it. *Neuropsychologia, 40,* 145–151.

Castles, A., & Coltheart, M. (1993). Varieties of developmental dyslexia. *Cognition, 47,* 149–180.

Caterini, F., Della Salla, S., Spinnler, H., Stangalino, C., & Turnbull, O. H. (2002). Object recognition and object orientation in Alzheimer's disease. *Neuropsychology, 16,* 146–155.

Cave, K. R., Pinker, S., Giorgi, L., Thomas, C. E., Heller, L. M., Wolfe, J. M., & Lin, H. (1994). The representation of location in visual images. *Cognitive Psychology, 26,* 1–32.

Chambers, D., & Reisberg, D. (1985). Can mental images be ambiguous? *Journal of Experimental Psychology: Human Perception and Performance, 2,* 317–328.

Chapman, L. J., & Wedell, K. (1972). Perceptual-motor abilities and reversal errors in children's handwriting. *Journal of Learning Disabilities, 5,* 5–325.

Charles, N., Froment, C., Rode, G., Vighetto, A., Turjman, F., Trillet, M., & Aimard, G. (1992). Vertigo and upside down vision due to an infarct in the territory of the medial branch of the posterior inferior cerebellar artery caused by dissection of a vertebral artery. *Journal of Neurology, Neurosurgery, and Psychiatry, 55,* 188–189.

Chatterjee, A. (1994). Picturing unilateral spatial neglect: viewer versus object centred reference frames. *Journal of Neurology, Neurosurgery, and Psychiatry, 57,* 1236–1240.

Chatterjee, A., & Southwood, M. H. (1995). Cortical blindness and visual imagery. *Neurology, 45,* 2189–2195.

Chen, W., Kato, T., Zhu, X.-H., Ogawa, S., Tank, D. W., & Ugurbil, K. (1998). Human primary visual cortex and lateral geniculate nucleus activation during visual imagery. *NeuroReport, 9*, 3669–3674.

Cohn, M., & Stricker, G. (1976). Inadequate perception vs. reversals. *The Reading Teacher, 30*, 162–167.

Colby, C. L. & Goldberg, M. E. (1999). Space and attention in parietal cortex. *Annual Review of Neuroscience, 22*, 319–349.

Cole, M., Schutta, H. S., & Warrington, E. K. (1962). Visual disorientation in homonymous half-fields. *Neurology, 12*, 257–263.

Collette, M. A. (1979). Dyslexia and classic pathognomic signs. *Perceptual and Motor Skills, 48*, 1055–1062.

Connor, C. E., Gallant, J. L., Preddie, D. C., & Van Essen, D. C. (1996). Responses in area V4 depend on the spatial relationship between stimulus and attention. *Journal of Neurophysiology, 75*, 1306–1308.

Connor, C. E., Preddie, D. C., Gallant, J. L., & Van Essen, D. C. (1997). Spatial attention effects in macaque area V4. *Journal of Neuroscience, 19*, 3201–3214.

Cooper, A. C. G., & Humphreys, G. W. (2000). Task-specific effects of orientation information: Neuropsychological evidence. *Neuropsychologia, 38*, 1607–1615.

Corballis, M. C., & Beale, I. L. (1976). *The psychology of left and right*. Hillsdale, NJ: Erlbaum.

Corballis, M. C., & Beale, I. L. (1984). *The ambivalent mind: The neuropsychology of left and right*. Chicago: Nelson-Hall.

Craft, J. L., & Simon, J. R. (1970). Processing symbolic information from a visual display: Interference from an irrelevant directional cue. *Journal of Experimental Psychology, 83*, 415–420.

Crick, F., & Koch, C. (2003). A framework for consciousness. *Nature Neuroscience, 6*, 119–126.

Critchley, M. (1949). Metamorphopsia of central origin. *Transactions of the Ophthalmological Societies of the UK, 69*, 111–121.

Critchley, M. (1951). Types of visual perseveration: "Paliopsia" and "illusory visual spread." *Brain, 74*, 267–299.

Damasio, A. R., & Benton, A. L. (1979). Impairments of hand movements under visual guidance. *Neurology, 29*, 170–178.

Davidoff, J., & Warrington, E. K. (1999). The bare bones of object recognition: Implications from a case of object recognition impairment. *Neuropsychologia, 37*, 279–292.

Davidoff, J., & Warrington, E. K. (2001). A particular difficulty in discriminating between mirror images. *Neuropsychologia, 39*, 1022–1036.

Dennett, D. C. (1991). *Consciousness explained*. Boston: Little, Brown, & Co.

Deregowski, J. B., McGeorge, P., & Wynn, V. (2000). The role of left–right symmetry in the encodement of spatial orientations. *British Journal of Psychology, 91*, 241–257.

De Renzi, E. (1996). Balint-Holmes' syndrome. In C. Code, C.-W. Wallesch, Y. Joanette, & A.-R. Lecours (Eds.), *Classic cases in neuropsychology* (pp. 123–143). Hove, UK: Psychology Press.

Dilks, D. D., Reiss, J. E., Landau, B., & Hoffman, J. E. (2004). *Representation of orientation in Williams syndrome*. Paper presented at the meeting of the Psychonomic Society, Minneapolis, MN.

Doughty, M. J. (2001). Consideration of three types of eyeblink activity in normal humans: During reading and video display terminal use, in primary gaze, and while in conversation. *Optometry and Vision Science, 78*, 712–725.

Driver, J., & Halligan, P. (1991). Can visual neglect operate in object-centered co-ordinates? An affirmative single-case study. *Cognitive Neuropsychology, 8*, 475–496.

Duhamel, J.-R., Bremmer, F., BenHamed, S., & Graf, W. (1997). Spatial invariance of visual receptive fields in parietal cortex neurons. *Nature, 389*, 845–848.

Eretto, P. A., Schoen, F. S., Krohel, G. B., & Pechette, D. (1982). Palinoptic visual allesthesia. *American Journal of Ophthalmology, 93*, 801–803.

Ellis, A. (1985). The cognitive neuropsychology of developmental (and acquired) dyslexia: A critical survey. *Cognitive Neuropsychology, 2*, 169–205.

Ewert, P. H. (1930). A study of the effect of inverted retinal stimulation upon spatially coordinated behavior. *Genetic Psychology Monographs, 7*, 177–363.

Farah, M. J. (1984). The neurological basis of mental imagery: A componential analysis. *Cognition, 18*, 245–272.

Farah, M. J., Brunn, J. L., Wong, A. B., Wallace, M. A., & Carpenter, P. A. (1990). Frames of reference for allocating attention to space: Evidence from the neglect syndrome. *Neuropsychologia, 28*, 335–347.

Farah, M. J., Soso, M. J., & Dasheiff, R. M. (1992). Visual angle of the mind's eye before and after unilateral occipital lobectomy. *Journal of Experimental Psychology: Human Perception and Performance, 18*, 241–246.

Farah, M. J., Wallace, M. A., & Vecera, S. P. (1993). "What" and "where" in visual attention: Evidence from the neglect syndrome. In I. H. Robertson & J. C. Marshall (Eds.), *Unilateral neglect: Clinical and experimental studies* (pp. 123–137). Hillsdale, NJ: Erlbaum.

Finke, R. A. (1980). Levels of equivalence in imagery and perception. *Psychological Review, 87*, 113–132.

Finucci, J. M. (1985). Approaches to subtype validation using family data. In D. B. Gray & J. F. Kavanagh (Eds.), *Biobehavioral measures of dyslexia* (pp. 137–153). Parkton, MD: York Press.

Fischer, F. W., Liberman, I. Y., & Shankweiler, D. (1978). Reading reversals and developmental dyslexia: A further study. *Cortex, 14*, 496–510.

Flanders, M., Helms Tillery, S. H., & Soechting, J. F. (1992). Early stages in a sensorimotor transformation. *Behavioral and Brain Sciences, 15*, 309–362.

Foss, D. J. (1982). A discourse on semantic priming. *Cognitive Psychology, 14*, 590–607.

Friedman-Hill, S. R., Robertson, L. C., & Treisman, A. (1995). Parietal contributions to visual feature binding: Evidence from a patient with bilateral lesions. *Science, 269*, 853–855.

Frith, U. (1980). Unexpected spelling problems. In U. Frith (Ed.), *Cognitive processes in spelling* (pp. 496–515). London: Academic Press.

Galaburda, A. M., & Livingstone, M. (1993). Evidence for a magnocellular deficit in developmental dyslexia. In P. Tallal, A. M. Galaburda, R. R. Llinás, & C. Von Euler (Eds.), *Annals of the New York Academy of Sciences: Vol. 682. Temporal processing in the nervous system: Special reference to dyslexia and dysphasia* (pp. 70–82). New York: New York Academy of Sciences.

Gallistel, C. R. (1990). *The organization of learning*. Cambridge, MA: MIT Press.

Ganis, G., Thompson, W. L., & Kosslyn, S. M. (2004). Brain areas underlying visual mental imagery and visual perception: An fMRI study. *Cognitive Brain Research, 20*, 226–241.

Ganis, G., Thompson, W. L., Mast, F. W., & Kosslyn, S. M. (2003). Visual imagery in cerebral visual dysfunction. *Neurologic Clinics of North America, 21*, 631–646.

Girkin, C. A., Perry, J. D., & Miller, N. R. (1999). Visual environmental rotation: A novel disorder of visuospatial integration. *Journal of Neuro-Ophthalmology, 38*, 13–16.

Godwin-Austen, R. B. (1965). A case of visual disorientation. *Journal of Neurology, Neurosurgery, and Psychiatry, 28*, 453–458.

Goodale, M. A. (2000). Perception and action in the human visual system. In M. S. Gazzaniga (Ed.), *The new cognitive neurosciences* (pp. 365–377). Cambridge, MA: MIT Press.

Goodale, M. A., & Haffenden, A. (1998). Frames of reference for perception and action in the human visual system. *Neuroscience and Biobehavioral Reviews, 22*, 161–172.

Goodale, M. A., Meenan, J. P., Bülthoff, H. H., Nicolle, D. A., Murphy, K. J., & Racicot, C. I. (1994). Separate neural pathways for the visual analysis of object shape in perception and prehension. *Current Biology, 4*, 604–610.

Goodale, M. A., & Milner, A. D. (1992). Separate visual pathways for perception and action. *Trends in Neurosciences, 15*, 20–25.

Goodale, M. A., Milner, A. D., Jakobson, L. S., & Carey, D. P. (1991). A neurological dissociation between perceiving objects and grasping them. *Nature, 349*, 154–156.

Goodglass, H., & Kaplan, E. (1983). *Boston naming test.* Philadelphia: Lea & Febiger.

Goodglass, H., Kaplan, E., & Barresi, B. (2000). *Boston Diagnostic Aphasia Examination.* (3rd Ed.) Dallas, TX: Pro-Ed, Inc.

Goodman, R. A., & Caramazza, A. (1985). *The Johns Hopkins University Dysgraphia Battery.* Baltimore, MD: Johns Hopkins University.

Goodman, R. A., & Caramazza, A. (1986a). Aspects of the spelling process: Evidence from a case of acquired dysgraphia. *Language and Cognitive Processes, 1*, 263–296.

Goodman, R. A., & Caramazza, A. (1986b). Phonologically plausible errors: Implications for a model of the phoneme–grapheme conversion mechanism in the spelling process. In G. Augst (Ed.), *New trends in graphemics and orthography* (pp. 300–325). Berlin: Walter de Gruyter.

Graziano, M. S. A., Yap, G. S., & Gross, C. G. (1994). Coding of visual space by premotor neurons. *Science, 266*, 1054–1057.

Gregory, E., & McCloskey, M. (2007). *Representing the orientation of objects: Evidence from adults' error patterns.* Poster presented at the meeting of the Vision Sciences Society, Sarasota, FL.

Grossi, D., Imperati, F., Carbone, G., Maiorino, A., Angelillo, V., & Trojano, L. (2005). Visual and spatial positive phenomena in the neglected hemifield: A case report. *Journal of Neurology, 252*, 725–726.

Halligan, P., Marshall, J. C., & Wade, D. T. (1992). Left on the right: Allochiria in a case of left visuo-spatial neglect. *Journal of Neurology, Neurosurgery, and Psychiatry, 55*, 717–719.

Harris, I. M., Harris, J. A., & Caine, D. (2001). Object orientation agnosia: A failure to find the axis? *Journal of Cognitive Neuroscience, 13*, 800–812.

Harris, S. H. (1965). Perceptual adaptation to inverted, reversed, and displaced vision. *Psychological Review, 72*, 419–444.

Harvey, M., & Milner, A. D. (1995). Bálint's patient. *Cognitive Neuropsychology, 12*, 261–264.

Harwerth, R. S., Boltz, R. L., & Smith, E. L. I. (1980). Psychophysical evidence for sustained and transient channels in the monkey visual system. *Vision Research, 20*, 15–22.

Hatfield, F. M., & Patterson, K. (1983). Phonological spelling. *Quarterly Journal of Experimental Psychology, 35A*, 451–468.

Haxby, J. V., Grady, C. L., Horwitz, B., Ungerleider, L. G., Mishkin, M., Carson, R. E., et al. (1991). Dissociation of object and spatial visual processing pathways in human extrastriate cortex. *Proceedings of the National Academy of Sciences USA, 88*, 1621–1625.

Hedge, A., & Marsh, N. W. A. (1975). The effect of irrelevant spatial correspondences on two-choice response time. *Acta Psychologica, 39*, 427–439.

Heilman, K. M., Howell, G., Valenstein, E., & Rothi, L. (1980). Mirror-reading and writing in association with right-left spatial disorientation. *Journal of Neurology, Neurosurgery, and Psychiatry, 43*, 774–780.

Heilman, K. M., & Nadeau, S. E. (1998). What's up? *Archives of Neurology, 55*, 1285–1286.

Herrmann, G., & Pötzl, O. (1928). Die Optische Allaesthesie: Studien zur Psychopathologie der Raumbildung. Berlin: S. Karger.

Holmes, G. (1918). Disturbances of visual orientation. *British Journal of Ophthalmology, 2*, 449–468, 506–516.

Holmes, G. (1919). Disturbances of visual space perception. *British Medical Journal, 2*, 230–233.

Holmes, G., & Horrax, G. (1919). Disturbances of spatial orientation and visual attention with loss of stereoscopic vision. *Archives of Neurology and Psychiatry, 1*, 385–407.

Hommel, B. (1993). The role of attention for the Simon effect. *Psychological Research, 55*, 208–222.

Howard, I. P. (1982). *Human visual orientation.* Chichester, UK: Wiley.

Howard, I. P., & Templeton, W. B. (1966). *Human spatial orientation.* London: Wiley.

Hubel, D. H., & Wiesel, T. (1968). Receptive fields and functional architecture of monkey striate cortex. *Journal of Physiology, 160*, 106–154.

Ittelson, W. H., Mowafy, L., & Magid, D. (1991). The perception of mirror-reflected objects. *Perception, 20*, 567–584.

Jacobs, L. (1980). Visual allesthesia. *Neurology, 30*, 1059–1063.

Jamison, K. R. (1995). *An unquiet mind.* New York: Alfred A. Knopf.

Jeannerod, M. (1997). *The cognitive neuroscience of action.* Oxford: Blackwell.

Jeannerod, M., Decety, J., & Michel, F. (1994). Impairment of grasping movements following a bilateral posterior parietal lesion. *Neuropsychologia, 32*, 369–380.

Joanette, Y., & Brouchon, M. (1984). Visual allesthesia in manual pointing: Some evidence for a sensorimotor cerebral organization. *Brain and Cognition, 3*, 152–165.

Karnath, H. O., & Ferber, S. (2003). Friedrich Best's case Z with misidentification of object orientation. In C. Code, C.-W. Wallesch, Y. Joanette, & A.-R. Lecours (Eds.), *Classic cases in neuropsychology* (Vol. 2) (pp. 191–198). Hove, UK: Psychology Press.

Karnath, H. O., Ferber, S., & Bülthoff, H. H. (2000). Neuronal representation of object orientation. *Neuropsychologia, 38*, 1235–1241.

Karnath, H. O., Schenkel, P., & Fischer, B. (1991). Trunk orientation as the determining factor of the 'contralateral' deficit in the neglect syndrome and as the physical anchor of the internal representation of body orientation in space. *Brain, 114*, 1997–2014.

Kase, C. S., Troncoso, J. F., Court, J. E., Tapia, J. F., & Mohr, J. P. (1977). Global spatial disorientation. *Journal of the Neurological Sciences, 34*, 267–278.

Kasten, E., & Poggel, D. A. (2006). A mirror in the mind: A case of visual allaesthesia in homonymous hemianopia. *Neurocase, 12*, 98–106.

Kastner, S., Pinsk, M. A., De Weerd, P., Desimone, R., & Ungerleider, L. G. (1999). Increased activity in human visual cortex during directed attention in the absence of visual stimulation. *Neuron, 22,* 751–761.

Kim, M.-S., & Robertson, L. C. (2001). Implicit representations of space after bilateral parietal lobe damage. *Journal of Cognitive Neuroscience, 13,* 1080–1087.

Klein, I., Dubois, J., Mangin, J.-F., Kherif, F., Flandin, G., Poline, J.-B., et al. (2004). Retinotopic organization of visual mental images as revealed by functional magnetic resonance imaging. *Cognitive Brain Research, 22,* 26–31.

Koch, C., & Braun, J. (1996). Towards the neuronal correlate of visual awareness. *Current Opinion in Neurobiology, 6,* 158–164.

Koch, C., & Crick, F. (1995). Are we aware of neural activity in primary visual cortex? *Nature, 375,* 121–123.

Kohler, I. (1964). The formation and transformation of the perceptual world. *Psychological Issues, 3,* 19–171.

Kosslyn, S. M. (1980). *Image and mind.* Cambridge, MA: Harvard University Press.

Kosslyn, S. M. (1994). *Image and brain.* Cambridge, MA: MIT Press.

Kosslyn, S. M., Alpert, N. M., Thompson, W. L., Maljkovic, V., Weise, S. B., Chabris, C. F., et al. (1993). Visual mental imagery activates topographically organized visual cortex. *Journal of Cognitive Neuroscience, 5,* 263–287.

Kosslyn, S. M., Ball, T. M., & Reiser, B. J. (1978). Visual images preserve metric spatial information: Evidence from studies of image scanning. *Journal of Experimental Psychology: Human Perception and Performance, 4,* 47–60.

Kosslyn, S. M., Pascual-Leone, A., Felician, O., Camposano, S., Keenan, J. P., Thompson, W. L., et al. (1999). The role of area 17 in visual imagery: Convergent evidence from PET and rTMS. *Science, 284,* 167–170.

Kosslyn, S. M., & Thompson, W. L. (2003). When is early visual cortex activated during mental imagery? *Psychological Bulletin, 129,* 723–746.

Kosslyn, S. M., Thompson, W. L., Kim, I. J., & Alpert, N. M. (1995). Topographical representations of mental images in primary visual cortex. *Science, 378,* 496–498.

Kulikowski, J. J., & Tolhurst, D. J. (1973). Psychophysical evidence for sustained and transient detectors in human vision. *Journal of Physiology, 232,* 149–162.

Lacquaniti, F., Guigon, E., Bianchi, L., Ferraina, S., & Caminiti, R. (1995). Representing spatial information for limb movement: Role of area 5 in the monkey. *Cerebral Cortex, 5,* 391–409.

Làdavas, E. (1987). Is the hemispatial deficit produced by right parietal damage associated with retinal or gravitational coordinates? *Brain, 110,* 167–180.

Lambon-Ralph, M. A., Jarvis, C., & Ellis, N. (1997). Life in a mirrored world: Report of a case showing mirror reversal in reading and writing and for non-verbal materials. *Neurocase, 3,* 249–258.

Lamme, V. A. F. (2006). Towards a true neural stance on consciousness. *Trends in Cognitive Sciences, 10,* 494–501.

Lê, S., Cardebat, D., Boulanouar, K., Hénaff, M.-A., Michel, F., Milner, D., et al. (2002). Seeing, since childhood, without ventral stream: A behavioural study. *Brain, 125,* 58–74.

Lennie, P. (1980). Parallel visual pathways: A review. *Vision Research, 20,* 561–594.

Levelt, W. J. M. (1996). Perspective taking and ellipsis in spatial descriptions. In P. Bloom, M. Peterson, L. Nadel, & M. F. Garrett (Eds.), *Language and space* (pp. 77–107). Cambridge, MA: MIT Press.

Levine, D. N., Kaufman, K. J., & Mohr, J. P. (1978). Inaccurate reaching associated with a superior parietal lobe tumor. *Neurology, 28,* 556–561.

Levinson, S. C. (1996). Frames of reference and Molyneux's question: Crosslinguistic evidence. In P. Bloom, M. Peterson, L. Nadel, & M. F. Garrett (Eds.), *Language and space* (pp. 109–169). Cambridge, MA: MIT Press.

Liberman, I. Y. (1982). A language-oriented view of reading and its disabilities. In H. R. Myklebust (Ed.), *Progress in learning disabilities, Vol. 5* (pp. 81–101). New York: Grune & Stratton.

Livingstone, M. S. (1990). Segregation of form, color, movement, and depth processing in the visual system: Anatomy, physiology, art, and illusion. In B. Cohen & I. Bodis-Wollner (Eds.), *Vision and the brain: The organization of the central visual system* (pp. 119–138). New York: Raven Press.

Livingstone, M. S., & Hubel, D. H. (1987). Psychophysical evidence for separate channels for the perception of form, color, movement, and depth. *Journal of Neuroscience, 7*, 3416–3468.

Livingstone, M. S., & Hubel, D. H. (1988). Segregation of form, color, movement, and depth: Anatomy, physiology, and perception. *Science, 240*, 740–749.

Logan, G. D. (1995). Linguistic and conceptual control of visual spatial attention. *Cognitive Psychology, 28*, 103–174.

Lovegrove, W. (1993). Weakness in the transient visual system: A causal factor in dyslexia?. In P. Tallal, A. M. Galaburda, R. R. Llinás, & C. Von Euler (Eds.), *Annals of the New York Academy of Sciences: Vol. 682. Temporal processing in the nervous system: Special reference to dyslexia and dysphasia* (pp. 57–59). New York: New York Academy of Sciences.

Lu, C.-H., & Proctor, R. W. (1995). The influence of irrelevant location information on performance: A review of the Simon and spatial Stroop effects. *Psychonomic Bulletin & Review, 2*, 174–207.

Luck, S. J., Chelazzi, L., Hillyard, S. A., & Desimone, R. (1997). Neural mechanisms of spatial selective attention in areas V1, V2, and V4 of macaque visual cortex. *Journal of Neurophysiology, 77*, 24–42.

Marr, D. (1982). *Vision.* New York: W. H. Freeman.

Martin, R. (1995). Heterogeneity of deficits in developmental dyslexia and implications for methodology. *Psychonomic Bulletin & Review, 2*, 494–500.

Mayer, A. B., Ferraina, S., Marconi, B., Bullis, J. B., Lacquaniti, F., Burnod, Y., et al. (1998). Early motor influences on visuomotor transformations for reaching: A positive image of optic ataxia. *Experimental Brain Research, 123*, 172–189.

McCloskey, M. (2000). Spatial representation in mind and brain. In B. Rapp (Ed.), *The handbook of cognitive neuropsychology: What deficits reveal about the human mind* (pp. 101–132). Philadelphia: Psychology Press.

McCloskey, M. (2004). Spatial representations and multiple visual systems hypotheses: Evidence from a developmental deficit in visual location and orientation processing. *Cortex, 40*, 677–694.

McCloskey, M., Badecker, W., Goodman-Schulman, R., & Aliminosa, D. (1994). The structure of graphemic representations in spelling: Evidence from a case of acquired dysgraphia. *Cognitive Neuropsychology, 11*, 341–392.

McCloskey, M., & Rapp, B. (2000a). A visually based developmental reading deficit. *Journal of Memory and Language, 43*, 157–181.

McCloskey, M., & Rapp, B. (2000b). Attention-referenced visual representations: Evidence from impaired visual localization. *Journal of Experimental Psychology: Human Perception and Performance, 26*, 917–933.

McCloskey, M., Rapp, B., Yantis, S., Rubin, G., Bacon, W. F., Dagnelie, G., et al. (1995). A developmental deficit in localizing objects from vision. *Psychological Science, 6*, 112–117.

McCloskey, M., Valtonen, J., & Sherman, J. (2006). Representing orientation: A coordinate-system hypothesis, and evidence from developmental deficits. *Cognitive Neuropsychology, 23*, 680–713.

Merigan, W. H., & Maunsell, J. H. R. (1993). How parallel are the primate visual pathways? *Annual Review of Neuroscience, 16*, 369–402.

Miceli, G., Silveri, M. C., & Caramazza, A. (1985). Cognitive analysis of a case of pure agraphia. *Brain and Language, 25*, 187–212.

Michel, F., Jeannerod, M., & Devic, M. (1965). Trouble de l'orientation visuelle dans les trois dimensions de l'espace. *Cortex, 1*, 441–466.

Milner, A. D. (1998). Neuropsychological studies of perception and visuomotor control. *Philosophical Transactions of the Royal Society of London B, 353*, 1375–1384.

Milner, A. D., Dijkerman, H. C., & Carey, D. P. (1999). Visuospatial processing in a pure case of visual-form agnosia. In N. Burgess, K. J. Jeffery, & J. O'Keefe (Eds.), *The hippocampal and parietal foundations of spatial cognition* (pp. 443–466). Oxford: Oxford University Press.

Milner, A. D., Dijkerman, H. C., Pisella, L., McIntosh, R. D., Tilikete, C., Vighetto, A., & Rossetti, Y. (2001). Grasping the past: Delay can improve visuomotor performance. *Current Biology, 11*, 1896–1901.

Milner, A. D., & Goodale, M. A. (1993). Visual pathways to perception and action. In T. P. Hicks, S. Molotchnikoff, & T. Ono (Eds.), *Progress in brain research* (Vol. 95, pp. 317–337). Amsterdam: Elsevier.

Milner, A. D., & Goodale, M. A. (1995). *The visual brain in action*. Oxford: Oxford University Press.

Milner, A. D., Paulignan, Y., Dijkerman, H. C., Michel, F., & Jeannerod, M. (1999). A paradoxical improvement of misreaching in optic ataxia: New evidence for two separate visual systems for visual localization. *Proceedings of the Royal Society of London B, 266*, 2225–2229.

Milner, A. D., Perrett, D. I., Johnston, R. S., Benson, P. J., Jordon, T. R., Heeley, D. W., et al. (1991). Perception and action in "visual form agnosia." *Brain, 114*, 405–428.

Mishkin, M., Ungerleider, L. G., & Macko, K. A. (1983). Object vision and spatial vision: Two cortical pathways. *Trends in Neurosciences, 6*, 414–417.

Mitov, D., & Totev, T. (2005). How many pathways determine the speed of grating detection. *Vision Research, 45*, 821–825.

Morris, R. K. (1994). Lexical and message-level sentence context effects on fixation times in reading. *Journal of Experimental Psychology: Learning, Memory, and Cognition, 20*, 92–103.

Morris, R. K., & Folk, J. (1998). Focus as a contextual priming mechanism in reading. *Memory & Cognition, 26*, 1313–1322.

Moscovitch, M., Behrmann, M., & Winocur, G. (1994). Do PETs have long or short ears? Mental imagery and neuroimaging. *Trends in Neurosciences, 17*, 292–294.

Motter, B. C. (1993). Focal attention produces spatially selective processing in visual cortical areas V1, V2, and V4 in the presence of competing stimuli. *Journal of Neurophysiology, 70*, 909–919.

Murphy, K. J., Racicot, C. I., & Goodale, M. A. (1995). The use of visuomotor cues as a strategy for making perceptual judgments in a patient with visual form agnosia. *Neuropsychology, 10*, 396–401.

Nakajima, M., Yasue, M., Kaito, N., Kamikubo, T., & Sakai, H. (1991). A case of visual allesthesia. *No To Shinkei [Brain and Nerve], 43*, 1081–1085.

Nicoletti, R., & Umiltà, C. (1989). Splitting visual space with attention. *Journal of Experimental Psychology: Human Perception and Performance, 15,* 164–169.

Nicoletti, R., & Umiltà, C. (1994). Attention shifts produce spatial stimulus codes. *Psychological Research, 56,* 144–150.

Noble, J. (1968). Paradoxical interocular transfer of mirror-image discriminations in the optic chiasm sectioned monkey. *Brain Research, 10,* 127–151.

Noë, A., Pessoa, L., & Thompson, E. (2000). Beyond the grand illusion: What change blindness really teaches us about vision. *Visual Cognition, 7,* 93–106.

Ogmen, H., Breitmeyer, B. G., & Melvin, R. (2003). The what and where of visual masking. *Vision Research, 43,* 1337–1350.

O'Keefe, J. (1993). Kant and the sea-horse: An essay in the neurophilosophy of space. In N. Eilan, R. McCarthy, & B. Brewer (Eds.), *Spatial representation: Problems in philosophy and psychology* (pp. 43–64). Oxford: Blackwell.

O'Keefe, J., & Nadel, L. (1978). *The hippocampus as a cognitive map.* Oxford: Oxford University Press.

Olson, D. R. (1970). Cognitive development: The child's acquisition of diagonality. New York: Academic Press.

O'Regan, J. K., Rensink, R. A., & Clark, J. J. (1999). Change-blindness as a result of "mudsplashes." *Nature, 398,* 34.

Orton, S. T. (1937). Reading, writing, and speech problems in children: A presentation of certain types of disorders in the development of the language faculty. New York: Norton.

O'Seagdha, P. D. (1989). The dependence of lexical relatedness effects on syntactic connectedness. *Journal of Experimental Psychology: Learning, Memory, and Cognition, 15,* 73–87.

O'Seagdha, P. D. (1997). Conjoint and dissociable effects of syntactic and semantic context. *Journal of Experimental Psychology: Learning, Memory, and Cognition, 23,* 807–828.

Osterrieth, P. A. (1944). Le test de copie d'une figure complex: Contribution a l'étude de la perception et de la mémoire. *Archives de Psychologie, 30,* 286–356.

Perenin, M.-T., & Vighetto, A. (1983). Optic ataxia: A specific disorder in visuomotor coordination. In A. Hein & M. Jeannerod (Eds.), *Spatially oriented behavior* (pp. 305–326). New York: Springer-Verlag.

Perenin, M.-T., & Vighetto, A. (1988). Optic ataxia: A specific disruption in visuomotor mechanisms. *Brain, 111,* 643–674.

Pflugshaupt, T., Nyffeler, T., von Wartburg, R., Wurtz, P., Lüthi, M., Hubl, D., et al. (2007). When left becomes right and vice versa: Mirrored vision after cerebral hypoxia. *Neuropsychologia, 45,* 2078–2091.

Phan, M. L., Schendel, K. L., Recanzone, G. H., & Robertson, L. C. (2000). Auditory and visual spatial localization deficits following bilateral parietal lobe lesions in a patient with Balint's syndrome. *Journal of Cognitive Neuroscience, 12,* 583–600.

Piccirilli, M., Piccinin, G. L., Ricci, S., Taramelli, M., Piccolini, C., Floridi, P., & Agostini, L. (1983). Pure optic ataxia. *Acta Neurologica, 5,* 38–42.

Pisella, L., Gréa, H., Tilikete, C., Vighetto, A., Desmurget, J., Rode, G., et al. (2000). An "automatic pilot" for the hand in human posterior parietal cortex: Toward reinterpreting optic ataxia. *Nature Neuroscience, 3,* 729–735.

Pohl, W. (1973). Dissociation in spatial discrimination deficits following frontal and parietal lesions in monkeys. *Journal of Comparative and Physiological Psychology, 82,* 227–239.

Posner, M. I. (1980). Orienting of attention. *Quarterly Journal of Experimental Psychology, 32,* 3–25.

Posner, M. I., & Cohen, Y. (1984). Components of visual orienting. In H. Bouma & D. G. Bouwhuis (Eds.), *Attention and performance X* (pp. 531–556). Hillsdale, NJ: Erlbaum.

Potter, M. C., Moryadas, A., Abrams, I., & Noel, A. (1993). Word perception and misperception in context. *Journal of Experimental Psychology: Learning, Memory, and Cognition, 19,* 3–22.

Potter, M. C., Stiefbold, D., & Moryadas, A. (1998). Word selection in reading sentences: Preceding versus following contexts. *Journal of Experimental Psychology: Learning, Memory, and Cognition, 24,* 68–100.

Pouget, A., Fisher, S. A., & Sejnowski, T. J. (1993). Egocentric spatial representation in early vision. *Journal of Cognitive Neuroscience, 5,* 150–161.

Priftis, K., Rusconi, E., Umiltà, C., & Zorzi, M. (2003). Pure agnosia for mirror stimuli after right inferior parietal lesion. *Brain, 126,* 908–919.

Pylyshyn, Z. (2003). Return of the mental image: Are there really pictures in the brain? *Trends in Cognitive Sciences, 7,* 113–118.

Pylyshyn, Z. W. (1973). What the mind's eye tells the mind's brain: A critique of mental imagery. *Psychological Bulletin, 80,* 1–24.

Rapp, B., Epstein, C., & Tainturier, M.-J. (2002). The integration of information across lexical and sublexical processes in spelling. *Cognitive Neuropsychology, 19,* 1–29.

Ratcliff, G., & Davies-Jones, G. A. B. (1972). Defective visual localization in focal brain wounds. *Brain, 95,* 49–60.

Rayner, K., Murphy, L. A., Henderson, J. M., & Pollatsek, A. (1989). Selective attentional dyslexia. *Cognitive Neuropsychology, 6,* 357–378.

Rayner, K., Pacht, J. M., & Duffy, S. (1994). Effects of prior encounter and global discourse bias on the processing of lexically ambiguous words: Evidence from eye fixations. *Journal of Memory and Language, 33,* 527–544.

Rey, A. (1941). *L'examen clinique en psychologie.* Paris: Press Universaire de France.

Riddoch, G. (1935). Visual disorientation in homonymous half-fields. *Brain, 58,* 376–382.

Riddoch, M. J., & Humphreys, G. W. (1988). Description of a left/right coding deficit in a case of constructional apraxia. *Cognitive Neuropsychology, 5,* 289–315.

Riddoch, M. J., Humphreys, G. W., Jacobson, S., Pluck, G., Bateman, A., & Edwards, M. (2004). Impaired orientation discrimination and localisation following parietal damage: On the interplay between dorsal and ventral processes in visual perception. *Cognitive Neuropsychology, 21,* 597–623.

River, Y., Ben Hur, T., & Steiner, I. (1998). Reversal of vision metamorphopsia: Clinical and anatomical characteristics. *Archives of Neurology, 55,* 1362–1368.

Rizzo, M., & Vecera, S. P. (2002). Psychoanatomical substrates of Bálint's syndrome. *Journal of Neurology, Neurosurgery, and Psychiatry, 72,* 162–178.

Robertson, L. C., Treisman, A., Friedman-Hill, S. R., & Grabowecky, M. (1997). The interaction of object and spatial pathways: Evidence from Balint's syndrome. *Journal of Cognitive Neuroscience, 9,* 295–317.

Roeltgen, D. P., Sevush, S., & Heilman, K. M. (1983). Phonological agraphia: Writing by the lexical–semantic route. *Neurology, 33,* 755–765.

Rollenhagen, J. E., & Olson, C. R. (2000). Mirror-image confusion in single neurons of the macaque inferotemporal cortex. *Science, 287,* 1506–1508.

Romani, C., Ward, J., & Olson, A. (1999). Developmental surface dysgraphia: What is the underlying cognitive impairment? *Quarterly Journal of Experimental Psychology, 52A*, 97–128.

Rondot, P., De Recondo, J., & Dumas, J. L. R. (1977). Visuomotor ataxia. *Brain, 100*, 355–376.

Ropper, A. H. (1983). Illusion of tilting of the visual environment. *Journal of Clinical Neuro-Ophthalmology, 3*, 147–151.

Ross Russell, R. W. R., & Bharucha, N. (1984). Visual localisation in patients with occipital infarction. *Journal of Neurology, Neurosurgery, and Psychiatry, 47*, 153–158.

Rossetti, Y., Pisella, L., & Vighetto, A. (2003). Optic ataxia revisited: Visually guided action versus immediate visuomotor control. *Experimental Brain Research, 153*, 171–179.

Rudel, R. G. (1982). The oblique mystique: A slant on the development of spatial coordinates. In M. Potegal (Ed.), *Spatial abilities: Development and physiological foundations* (pp. 129–146). New York: Academic Press.

Savage, C. R., Bohne, A., Deckersback, T., Bitran, S., Chugani, H., & Rauch, S. L. (2001). Validation of 3 alternate figures for the Rey-Osterrieth Complex Figure Test. *Journal of the International Neuropsychological Society, 7*, 134.

Sereno, M. I., Dale, A. M., Reppas, J. B., Kwong, K. K., Belliveau, J. W., Brady, T. J., et al. (1995). Borders of multiple visual areas in humans revealed by functional magnetic resonance imaging. *Science, 268*, 889–892.

Shankweiler, D., & Liberman, I. Y. (1972). Misreading: A search for causes. In J. F. Kavanagh & I. G. Mattingly (Eds.), *Language by ear and by eye: The relationships between speech and reading* (pp. 293–317). Cambridge, MA: MIT Press

Sharkey, A. J. C., & Sharkey, N. E. (1992). Weak contextual constraints in text and word priming. *Journal of Memory and Language, 31*, 543–572.

Simons, D. J., & Rensink, R. A. (2005). Change blindness: Past, present, and future. *Trends in Cognitive Sciences, 9*, 16–20.

Sivan, A. B. (1992). *Benton Visual Retention Test* (5th ed.). San Antonio, TX: Psychological Corporation.

Slotnick, S. D., Thompson, W. L., & Kosslyn, S. M. (2005). Visual mental imagery induces retinotopically organized activation of early visual areas. *Cerebral Cortex, 15*, 1570–1583.

Smith, S., & Holmes, G. (1916, March). A case of bilateral motor apraxia with disturbance of visual orientation. *British Medical Journal, 1*(2882), 437–441.

Snodgrass, J. G., & Vanderwart, M. (1980). A standardized set of 260 pictures: Norms for name agreement, image agreement, familiarity, and visual complexity. *Journal of Experimental Psychology: Human Learning and Memory, 6*, 174–215.

Snowling, M., & Hume, C. (1989). A longitudinal case study of developmental phonological dyslexia. *Cognitive Neuropsychology, 6*, 379–401.

Soechting, J. F., & Flanders, M. (1989). Errors in pointing are due to approximations in sensorimotor transformations. *Journal of Neurophysiology, 62*, 595–608.

Soechting, J. F., & Flanders, M. (1992). Moving in three-dimensional space: Frames of reference, vectors, and coordinate systems. *Annual Review of Neuroscience, 15*, 167–191.

Solms, M., Kaplan-Solms, K., Saling, M., & Miller, P. (1988). Inverted vision after frontal lobe disease. *Cortex, 24*, 499–509.

Solms, M., Turnbull, O. H., Kaplan-Solms, K., & Miller, P. (1998). Rotated drawing: The range of performance and anatomical correlates in a series of 16 patients. *Brain and Cognition, 38,* 358–368.

Steiner, I., Shahin, R., & Melamed, E. (1987). Acute "upside down" reversal of vision in transient vertebrobasilar ischemia. *Neurology, 37,* 1685–1686.

Stoffer, T. H. (1991). Attentional focussing and stimulus–response compatibility. *Psychological Research, 53,* 127–135.

Stoffer, T. H., & Yakin, A. R. (1994). The functional role of attention for spatial coding in the Simon effect. *Psychological Research, 56,* 151–162.

Stratton, G. M. (1896). Some preliminary experiments on vision without inversion of the retinal image. *Psychological Review, 3,* 611–617.

Stratton, G. M. (1897a). Vision without inversion of the retinal image. *Psychological Review, 4,* 341–360.

Stratton, G. M. (1897b). Vision without inversion of the retinal image [concluded]. *Psychological Review, 4,* 463–481.

Tabossi, P. (1988). Accessing lexical ambiguity in different types of sentential contexts. *Journal of Memory and Language, 27,* 324–340.

Tada, W. L., & Stiles, J. (1996). Developmental change in children's analysis of spatial patterns. *Developmental Psychology, 32,* 951–970.

Tainturier, M.-J., & Rapp, B. (2001). The spelling process. In B. Rapp (Ed.), *The handbook of cognitive neuropsychology: What deficits reveal about the human mind* (pp. 263–289). Philadelphia: Psychology Press.

Taube, J. S., Muller, R. U., & Ranck, J. B., Jr. (1990). Head-direction cells recorded from the postsubiculum in freely moving rats. II. Effects of environmental manipulations. *Journal of Neuroscience, 10,* 436–447.

Temple, C., & Marshall, J. (1983). A case study of developmental phonological dyslexia. *British Journal of Psychology, 74,* 517–533.

Thomas, M., & Karmiloff-Smith, A. (2002). Are developmental disorders like cases of adult brain damage? Implications from connectionist modeling. *Behavioral and Brain Sciences, 25,* 727–788.

Tipper, S. P., & Behrmann, M. (1996). Object-centered not scene-based neglect. *Journal of Experimental Psychology: Human Perception and Performance, 22,* 1261–1278.

Tipper, S. P., Weaver, B., Jerreat, L. M., & Burak, A. L. (1994). Object-based and environment-based inhibition of return of visual attention. *Journal of Experimental Psychology: Human Perception and Performance, 20,* 478–499.

Tolhurst, D. J. (1975a). Reaction times in the detection of gratings by human observers: A probabilistic mechanism. *Vision Research, 15,* 1143–1149.

Tolhurst, D. J. (1975b). Sustained and transient channels in human vision. *Vision Research, 15,* 1151–1155.

Tong, F. (2003). Primary visual cortex and visual awareness. *Nature Reviews Neuroscience, 4,* 219–229.

Tootell, R. B. H., Reppas, J. B., Kwong, K. K., Malach, R., Born, R. T., Brady, T. J., et al. (1995). Functional analysis of human MT and related visual cortical areas using magnetic resonance imaging. *Journal of Neuroscience, 15,* 3215–3230.

Treisman, A., & Gelade, G. (1980). A feature-integration theory of attention. *Cognitive Psychology, 12,* 97–136.

Turnbull, O. H. (1997). A double dissociation between knowledge of object identity and object orientation. *Neuropsychologia, 35,* 567–570.

Turnbull, O. H., Beschin, N., & Della Salla, S. (1997). Agnosia for object orientation: Implications for theories of object recognition. *Neuropsychologia, 35*, 153–163.

Turnbull, O. H., Della Salla, S., & Beschin, N. (2002). Agnosia for object orientation: Naming and mental rotation evidence. *Neurocase, 8*, 296–305.

Turnbull, O. H., Laws, K. R., & McCarthy, R. (1995). Object recognition without knowledge of object orientation. *Cortex, 31*, 387–395.

Turnbull, O. H., & McCarthy, R. (1996a). Failure to discriminate between mirror-image objects: A case of viewpoint-independent object recognition? *Neurocase, 2*, 63–72.

Turnbull, O. H., & McCarthy, R. (1996b). When is a view unusual? A single case study of orientation-dependent visual agnosia. *Brain Research Bulletin, 40*, 497–503.

Tversky, B. (1981). Distortions in memory for maps. *Cognitive Psychology, 13*, 407–433.

Tversky, B. (1996). Spatial perspective in descriptions. In P. Bloom, M. Peterson, L. Nadel, & M. F. Garrett (Eds.), *Language and Space* (pp. 463–491). Cambridge, MA: MIT Press.

Umiltà, C., Castiello, U., Fontana, M., & Vestri, A. (1995). Object-centred orienting of attention. *Visual Cognition, 2*, 165–181.

Umiltà, C., & Liotti, M. (1987). Egocentric and relative spatial codes in S-R compatibility. *Psychological Research, 49*, 81–90.

Umiltà, C., & Nicoletti, R. (1992). An integrated model of the Simon effect. In J. Alegria, D. Holender, J. J. Morais, & M. Radeau (Eds.), *Analytic approaches to human cognition* (pp. 331–350). Amsterdam: North-Holland.

Unfug, H. V. (1978). Visual disorientation in allesthesia and palinopsia. *Journal of the American Medical Association, 239*, 56.

Ungerleider, L. G., & Haxby, J. V. (1994). "What" and "where" in the human brain. *Current Opinion in Neurobiology, 4*, 157–165.

Ungerleider, L. G., & Mishkin, M. (1982). Two cortical visual systems. In D. J. Ingle, M. A. Goodale, & R. J. W. Mansfield (Eds.), *Analysis of visual behavior* (pp. 549–586). Cambridge, MA: MIT Press.

Valtonen, J., Dilks, D. D., & McCloskey, M. (2008). Cognitive representation of orientation: A case study. *Cortex, 44*, 1171–1187.

van der Heijden, A. H. C. (1992). *Selective attention in vision*. London: Routledge.

Van Essen, D. C., Anderson, C., & Felleman, D. J. (1992). Information processing in the primate visual system: An integrated systems perspective. *Science, 255*, 419–423.

Warrington, E. K. (1986). Visual deficits associated with occipital lobe lesions in man. *Experimental Brain Research Supplementum, 11*, 247–261.

Warrington, E. K., & Davidoff, J. (2000). Failure at object identification improves mirror image matching. *Neuropsychologia, 38*, 1229–1234.

Wehner, R., Michel, B., & Antonsen, P. (1996). Visual navigation in insects: Coupling of egocentric and geocentric information. *Journal of Experimental Biology, 199*, 129–140.

Wentworth, G. A. (1886). *Elements of analytic geometry*. Boston: Ginn and Company.

Werner, H., & Wapner, S. (1955). The Innsbruck studies on distorted visual fields in relation to an organismic theory of perception. *Psychological Review, 62*, 130–138.

West, R. F., & Stanovich, K. E. (1986). Robust effects of syntactic structure on visual word processing. *Memory & Cognition, 14*, 104–112.

Williams, J. N. (1988). Constraints upon semantic activation during sentence comprehension. *Language and Cognitive Processes, 3,* 165–206.

Wilson, B. A., Clare, L., Young, A. W., & Hodges, J. R. (1997). Knowing where and knowing what: A double dissociation. *Cortex, 33,* 529–541.

Wright, B., & Garrett, M. F. (1984). Lexical decision in sentences: Effects of syntactic structure. *Memory & Cognition, 12,* 31–45.

Yealland, L. R. (1916). Case of gunshot wound involving visual centre, with visual disorientation. *Proceedings of the Royal Society of Medicine, 9,* 97–100.

Zeki, S. (1993). *A vision of the brain.* Oxford: Blackwell.

Zipser, D., & Andersen, R. A. (1988). A back-propagation programmed network that simulates response properties of a subset of posterior parietal neurons. *Nature, 331,* 679–684.

Author Index

Subject Index

Note: *Italics* denotes figures, whereas **bold** denotes tables.